A. Arbre de la Laque. B. Ouvrages de Laque. C. Sceaux, ou Cachets. D...
F. Faiseurs d'encre. G. Usage de l'encre. H. Pigeon porteur de lettre...

A. Lakboom. B. Lakwerken. C. Seegels. D. Papier. F₁. Riet bla...
H. briefdragende duif. I. Tee drinken.

LAKWERKEN etc

Ouvrages de circ etc dans la Chine.

re vander Aa.

COFFEE FLOATS
TEA SINKS

Filter coffee, short black and cappuccino.

COFFEE FLOATS
TEA SINKS

Through History and Technology
to a Complete Understanding

IAN BERSTEN B.Com.(Ecs)

HELIAN BOOKS SYDNEY

A COMPLETELY AUSTRALIAN PUBLICATION

First published in Australia 1993 by Helian Books
105 Roseville Avenue, Roseville, 2069, Australia
Phone: 61 2 417 4469, Fax: 61 2 417 6738

National Library of Australia Cataloguing-in-Publication Data

Bersten, Ian, 1939-
Coffee floats, tea sinks.

Bibliography
Includes index
ISBN 0 646 09180 8

1. Coffee. 2. Coffee - History. 3. Tea. 4. Tea trade. I. Title

641.3373

Acknowledgements

Edited by Anne Kern, North Epping, N.S.W., Australia
Designed by Karen Jeffery, Fox Badger Ferret, Balmain, N.S.W., Australia
Typeset by Fox Badger Ferret Balmain, N.S.W., Australia
Film by Locographics, Harris Park, N.S.W., Australia
Printed by Griffin Press, Adelaide, S.A., Australia

Text photographs by Michelle Goldman, Andrew Newlyn, Ian Bersten
Jacket photographs by Jack Mandelberg

Drawings by Kristin Hardiman and Helen Bersten
Computer images by Ian Bersten
Other credits at back of book

Contents

SOME IMPORTANT MILESTONES IN THE
EVOLUTION OF COFFEE EQUIPMENT AND KNOWLEDGE

1400s   Drinking of coffee made from the flesh of the coffee cherry begins in the Yemen.

1520s   Roasted coffee is brewed for the first time, probably in Syria.

1550s   Coffee shops open for the first time in Istanbul probably using roasted coffee.

1573   Venetian ambassador makes the first report about roasted coffee to Europe.

1600s   Coffee drinking spreads slowly through Europe via Venice, Marseilles, London and Vienna.

1700s   Filtering coffee becomes known using cloth, paper and metal filters.

1751   First report of reversible filter coffee makers in Italy

1819   Jones pumping percolator appears in England

1827   Nörrenberg makes first drawing of vacuum coffee maker.

1838   Lebrun invents first working espresso.

1844   Gabet invents balance coffee maker.

1852   Mayer & Delforge invent first press/plunger coffee maker.

1864   Jabez Burns makes his first patent for coffee roasters.

1868   Welter publishes book.

1869   Reiss invents the first Vienna coffee machine.

1878   Kessel invents the first espresso coffee machine with water and steam control.

1883   First electric coffee grinder is used in New York.

1885   Boehnke-Reich prints informed book on coffee.

1885   Moriondo patents first commercial bulk brewing espresso machine in Turin.

1890   Sigmund Kraut invents greaseproof paper lined bags in Berlin.

1891   Salomon of Braunschweig invents new style of quick roaster.

1898   Edwin Norton vacuum packs coffee for the first time.

1900   First gear-driven electric coffee grinder by the Enterprise Company.

1901-1906   Bezzera and Pavoni produce the first commercial quick filter espresso machine.

1904-1908   Alonzo Warner and Landers Frary Clark patent the ideas for the recirculating percolator.

1906   Decaffeinated coffee process discovered.

1906   Gebrüder Schürmann make filter coffee machine for commercial use.

1908   Melitta Bentz makes domestic model paper filter.

1916   Le Page cutting rolls for grinding coffee.

1922   William Ukers book published.

1926   Introduction of high pressure gas in roasters increases capacity.

1927   August Carton produces the first coffee maker with a built-in timer and separate filter.

1927   Caasen patents the first fluid bed roaster.

1931   Paul Ciupka writes his first book about the technology of coffee.

1932   Aluminiumwerk Göttingen invents the first quickfilter.

1934   Melitta introduces a similar filter with great success.

1935   Jabez Burns makes the Thermalo roaster.

1944   Willy Brandl invents the first electric drip coffee maker.

1947   Sortex produces the first sorting machine to raise the quality of the coffee beans.

1947   Gaggia invents the first real espresso machine.

1957   The Lurgi Company makes a fluid bed coffee roaster for commercial use.

1958   Wigomat makes the first popular electric drip coffee maker after a Brandl patent.

1961   Valente makes the first espresso machine with an electric pump.

1963   Sivetz and Foote book published.

1968   Goglio valve bag introduced.

1969   Smit perfects the electric drip machine.

1979   Neotec begins development of the rotation fluid bed roaster.

1985   Bernhard Rothfos book on coffee.

Introduction

*T*his is a book for the coffee trade, for foodies, coffeeholics, tea fanatics, food writers and restaurant reviewers - for anyone who would really like to understand coffee and tea. It has also been written so that in a few decades museum curators, antique collectors and those interested in social history will have a reasonably complete record of how coffee and tea were being made throughout the last part of the twentieth century.

This book traces the development and evolution of the ideas and equipment associated with coffee and tea from their earliest introduction into Europe in the early 1600s. There has been such a rapid evolution of coffee equipment over the past three hundred years that the materials and brewing equipment of today would be totally unrecognisable to a person living at the beginning of the twentieth century, let alone the nineteenth. Teapots, on the other hand, have had hardly any evolution and would be easily recognised by a person living in the eighteenth century. For this reason, my book is weighted heavily towards the story of coffee and less to tea and minimally to chocolate, where there has been virtually no development in equipment.

Myths and ideas have become facts over the centuries. I have tried to sift the myths from the ideas in order to weave a logical story showing how the ideas evolved and were combined with the technology of the times, to produce ever-improving coffee makers.

Coffee is accepted as the second most valuable commodity in the world after oil and yet no serious analytical work has been written about its development over the centuries. In 1922, William Ukers of the United States, who had spent many years editing coffee and tea trade journals, published *All About Coffee*, a second edition of which was published in 1935. These books were accepted at the time as being the last word on the subject. While they were monumental works and covered the topic in depth, I have found that they lack accuracy on the subject of evolution. This is not surprising as Ukers had to rely on fourteen overseas correspondents to supply him with information. By going back to the original records, I have been able to establish what really happened.

The First World War certainly interrupted the information-gathering process for his book and the result is flawed as a consequence. In addition, the general negative perception of Germany during and after this war may have distorted the historical recording process. Certainly Germany, as a major contributor to the history of coffee, did not receive due mention.

Ukers' books have been the basis for many others written in the last fifty years about coffee, two of which have actually plagiarised his work without even mentioning him in the bibliography. Where Ukers got it wrong, they and others got it wrong. So many books about coffee are nothing more than a few chapters derived from Ukers and many pages of colourful recipes. Ukers wrote many things as facts without references. Wherever possible I have tried to go back to more original sources and have examined the original equipment. This has enabled me to evaluate the information and place it in perspective.

I believe my book is the first major book in the last fifty years to cover the evolution of coffee and tea drinking and all coffee roasting, grinding and brewing equipment. It corrects many mistakes of the past and presents a critical interpretation of most of the important developments.

It has been an enormous task to identify the major themes which form the history of coffee and to present them in a coherent way. The individual themes of country, time, inventor and type of maker crisscross at random and do not allow for a simple logical story.

While the book has as its major theme the history of coffee equipment, it also includes the logical relationships between all the factors that make a cup of coffee - such as roasting, grinding and brewing - so that readers are given, for the first time, a complete explanation of the process plus a discussion of the qualities of the bean. The story of the coffee bean can be traced from the plantation to the roaster, through the grinder, the packaging machine, into the brewer then into the cup. Each of these areas is examined in detail to provide a real understanding of the subject to the hordes of coffee lovers who cannot find the information readily. The range of this book is basically limited to the domestic and retail spheres.

Many of the existing books are very similar and full of absolute answers, where none exist. A full understanding of coffee will show that there are no absolutes when it comes to answering the question of what is the best coffee, until the desired cup has been defined. There is a logical progression through all the processes with multiple choices at every step to satisfy individual taste. The consequences of each decision will be apparent in the final cup and this makes a nonsense of any simple statement about any coffee.

There is a strong connection in many different countries between the standard of living and the amount of money and time spent on coffee. The methods for brewing coffee to make a better cup are becoming more and more sophisticated and - perhaps because better brewed coffee is more widely available - consumption of instant coffee, which lacks flavour and satisfaction, seems to have levelled. At the same time there seems to be a consumer reaction to the standards of the supermarket which have dictated the quality available. There has been a change in emphasis from making a better cup of coffee to making a good cup of coffee with convenience. If you want to take the trouble to brew your coffee and tea, the future looks good for a better cup of both.

Tea and teapots, which have been in the West for the same time as coffee and coffee pots, and which have shown far less evolution, have been the subject of several excellent books. The reasons for this are connected with the high values of porcelain teapots and other tea objects such as caddy spoons and some beautiful wooden tea caddies. There is precious little written about the evolution of tea equipment except for the different types of porcelain and the different shapes of the pots. Even the most specific books do not show that many different teapots were invented over the centuries. I have tried not to go over the same material but have concentrated instead on showing some of the developments and the reasons for some of the changes. There is no point at all in writing about the Chinese and Japanese tea cultures - this has been so well done by others.

William Ukers wrote several books about tea, but his book, *All About Tea*, published in 1935, is practically unavailable in any but the best libraries. While his book has several very detailed chapters about the evolution of equipment, the line of evolution is not spelled out.

Tea, in the last few decades, has become a pale imitation of itself in the form of the tea bag. The tea bag market continues to rise which shows that the consumer prefers convenience to flavour.

A small part of the book is about cocoa and drinking chocolate. All the evolution has been in the product itself and practically none in the chocolate pot. Cocoa has been very much the minority product and seems likely to remain that way.

SOURCES

A book such as this, which traces the evolution of practices, must be based upon facts and theories passed on from former times. These facts and theories can come from various sources and these are set out below, along with the limitations and biases associated with each.

PATENTS

In the case of coffee and tea brewing it would be easy to place complete trust in patent sources. But I believe, in many cases, that early patent documents do not indicate the actual situation. What the earliest patent documents really reflect is the existence or non-existence of patent systems. France, Germany and the United States scarcely had patent systems in the eighteenth century. The United States patent system started in 1790, France in 1791 and Switzerland in 1888. The first English patent was to John Kempe, a Flemish weaver, in 1331.[1] Modern English patent law dates from the Statute of Monopolies in 1624.

The patent information available also reflects the inaccessibility of existing patent systems. Somewhere in Italy and Germany are archives which contain what passed for patents in the states of Italy and unified Italy pre-1901 and the states of Germany pre-1877. The first patent law in Venice was enacted in 1474, so there must be volumes of Italian patents prior to 1900. Nothing less than a full-scale assault will unearth these hidden documents and even then I suspect they will not change the basic story substantially.

A patent applies to a particular country, but does not tell you whether the item existed in an unpatented form prior to the patent. It is important to remember that not all inventions were patented and not all patents were put into production.

I have read American and English patents, as well as French, Italian and German patents in the original languages. The patents have to be read in detail to reveal their secrets and sometimes I have had to rely on the comments of contemporary writers to identify patents which showed significant advances.[2]

Ukers, in particular, based his book on a cursory examination of early French patent documents and there are glaring errors involving names, dates and what was actually invented. Items which appear to be of French origin are actually, as often admitted to in the patents themselves, German imports. Appendix I of this book redresses such errors in Ukers' book through a reappraisal of these sources.

ANTIQUES

Antiques are found in antique markets and shops all over the world. Like collections in museums, where you see a reflection of the values of curators and the fashionable impulses of collectors, they are not an accurate reflection of the past. Antiques of brass and copper, as valued metals, are collected, but tin-plate is not. Art Deco, as a distinctive style, is valuable. Things without style are uninteresting and so worth nothing. The everyday items of life are generally not featured as much as the luxurious.

Coffee pots and teapots are lost between two worlds - good enough to be seen in the bric-a-brac markets, but often not good enough to be seen in antique shops. Because of their lack of real value most dealers do not see them as being items worth trading. When the profit motive is absent, as it is when there is no real market, the objects are downgraded to weekend markets and flea markets and in many cases melted down or doomed to end up on the scrap heap.

In addition, the fragility of glass and porcelain leaves machines made from these materials under-represented. An imaginary line is drawn between household curios and valuable household collectables. Metals were melted down for wars and so the items remaining are not representative.

The lack of a comprehensive reference book which categorises all the items, including coffee pots and teapots, has further hampered the growth of this neglected area of antiques. Dealers and buyers alike must have an authoritative guide to what they are buying.

BOOKS AND ADVERTISEMENTS

Many foreign language books from my large collection which I have used as sources have not been used before by English writers.

Books come in two types - general books on coffee and tea and books which are manufacturer-sponsored and have only a veneer of history. The general books reflect their authors' knowledge and particular interests, while others relate only to a particular country. Mostly the general books are not very accurate and pass on inaccuracies from one book to the next. Many written sources present a distorted view of life in past centuries because so little was written about the poorer classes. The upper classes could afford fads and new things. The poor used simple pots, but these were not mentioned even though they were the most common utensil.

The books and trade pamphlets written by manufacturers must be treated even more carefully because they can actively rewrite history in their own favour. Self-promotion is hardly surprising but these versions have sometimes become accepted fact. In an era when writers get a lot of information from companies who may be anxious to exaggerate their own role, it is important to know that other companies and people had an historical role which has been consigned to non-existence through the vagaries of war and time, and through their own demise. History truly belongs to the victors - if they write.

In this book very little reliance has been placed on advertising sources, because advertisements are very selective by nature, generally being used by the large firms. Written advertisements are the only ones which are easily accessed by historians. Radio and television advertisements are less readily available, and have been totally ignored.

PERSONAL SOURCES

I have spoken to many people who have had connections with the coffee industry, in some cases from before the Second World War, but memories are tricky things and I have found it really difficult to assess what happened. Most of these people can only remember the broad outlines and not the details.

Germany and Italy are two countries which present problems with respect to history. The damage of war in Germany has resulted in the destruction of many companies and their records, and the deaths of many people who cannot state their cases in the annals of history. In Italy the social turmoil of war and a weak economy have caused the collapse of companies which have been taken over by others who have no interest at all in the past. In Germany and Italy a detailed history of the events relating to coffee machinery in this century may already be impossible - only the broad picture is left. In many cases people give dates for when things happened or when something was first invented. I have found that many dates are the result of guesses or poor research. A further problem is that while it is easy to say approximately when an item was invented or introduced to the market, it is difficult to be precise about its duration in the market.

I have also spoken to most of the important collectors of coffee and tea paraphernalia and the contact with them has been helpful.

ACKNOWLEDGMENTS

The Johann Jacobs Museum in Zurich, Switzerland, has been a major source of information and this book would have been very different without access to the Museum's resources.

I would also like to acknowledge the help of the following people who generously shared their knowledge with me:
Daniela Ball, curator, Johann Jacobs Museum, Zurich, Switzerland

Ursula Becker, collector and researcher of coffee ephemera, Cologne, Germany

Martin Beutelspacher, coffee history specialist, formerly of Minden Museum, Germany

Joan and Edward Bramah, collectors and authors, England

Cees Brouwers, Douwe Egbert, Utrecht, Netherlands - for information on current equipment

M. Le Cardinal, French Archives, Compiègne, France

Bernard Finn, National Museum of American History, Smithsonian Institution, Washington, USA

Ambrogio Fumagalli, collector of espresso machines, Milan, Italy

François Herpin, collector of grinders, Paris, France

Philippe Jobin, an expert on green coffee, Le Havre, France

George Kepper, my first mentor - 50 years in the coffee trade, Sydney, Australia

Alf Kramer, coffee expert, formerly of Nordic Coffee Center, Oslo, Norway

Albert W. Kuhlfeld, curator, The Bakken Library and Museum of Electricity in Life, Minneapolis, Minnesota, USA

Christopher Middleton, coffee enthusiast and researcher, Sydney, Australia

Francesco Rossini, curator and collector, Lavazza Coffee Museum, Torino, Italy

Terje Tranberg, coffee expert, formerly of Nordic Coffee Center, Oslo, Norway

John Woods, many years' experience in the tea and coffee trades, Guildford, England

Gordon Wrigley, author, England

Katerina Vatsella,(now of Germany) former curator, Jacobs Suchard Museum, Zurich, Switzerland.

Many thanks also to the many other collectors and experts who have imparted their knowledge about various aspects of the subject of this book.

This book is necessarily the balanced assessment of all the foreging sources. It will be obvious where I have had doubts. With new evidence which has not yet come to light, it will be possible for future reseachers to arrive at different conclusions.

The evolution of coffee and equipment is a combination of invention and commercialisation. One of the problems in writing this book has been to find a way to give credit to the inventor as well as the company or person responsible for commercialisation of the invention. The idea and will to bring an idea to fruition have been equally important in making coffee history.

I started my own coffee roasting business in 1968 and over the years have developed a passion for the whole topic of coffee. There are thousands of coffee experts who know a great deal about special areas but very few who have had retail, wholesale and machinery experience, as I have. This range of experience and personal contact with people at the retail level has given me an understanding of what consumers want from their coffee. It has been a great pleasure for me to acquire one of the largest collections in the world of tea and coffee antiques and books. From these I have developed the ideas in this book.

SPECIAL THANKS

I am grateful to Michelle Goldman for the time she spent helping with photography and graphics.

This book owes its literary character and precision to my wife, Helen, who is a librarian and archivist, and to the editor Anne Kern. Helen displayed immense patience while our lives revolved around producing this book and our home was turned over to housing my collection of seven hundred antiques. In addition, her skills and patience in proofreading the many changing versions of the text over a period of six years can only be marvelled at. After cataloguing the more than three hundred books about coffee and tea in my private collection, she compiled a complete bibliography from which she has produced the selected bibliography in the book.

Anne Kern immersed herself in the facts and with great understanding has helped to create a tight, logical book. Her comments as an outsider with no prior knowledge of the subject have been of inestimable value.

The accuracy of the endnotes are a testament to the many hours which Helen and Anne devoted to checking and rechecking.

To Helen and Anne, my heartfelt thanks.

Ian Bersten

CHAPTER 1

Coffee Floats - Tea Sinks

W *HY COFFEE POTS ARE TALL AND TEAPOTS ARE SQUAT*

'Coffee Floats, Tea Sinks' might seem like an unusual title for a book about coffee and tea but this difference, which has escaped the notice of most people in the trade, is highly significant. I believe that this fact has determined the basic shape of coffee pots and teapots and is the intrinsic reason for the different evolution of coffee pots and teapots. It is also the reason for the problems in designing a first class coffee maker.

When boiling water is poured over freshly ground, freshly roasted coffee, much of the coffee forms a mass of bubbles and floats while the balance sinks, whereas freshly brewed tea leaves sink to the bottom of the pot. Coffee, if left to float, does not brew properly so it needs to be held in such a way that the water passes through it. Aside from espresso coffee, the basic approach has been to suspend the coffee grounds above the liquid coffee storage point and to allow the brewed coffee to pass, either by gravity or by pressure, positive or negative, through the grounds. Tea leaves require the opposite approach - the tea, after brewing, should be removed to stop the brewing process.

Inventions were being worked on in isolation and early coffee writers and inventors do not seem to have based their work on existing information. The lack of communication would not have been assisted by the language barrier between the various countries. It is not surprising therefore that so few pots were of a universal form, for both tea and coffee.

Count Rumford, an American author of the early 1800s, understood the brewing process very well, but he was ignored.[1] Henry Sandon, an English author and authority, in his book about teapots and coffee pots, states: 'With regard to the positioning of the spouts, there is really no reason why those of coffee pots should come from the bottom, while those of teapots emerge from half way up the vessel.'[2] Many of the pots shown in his own book do not conform to his own description of them - their spouts come from top and bottom. Teapots are generally squat and round and coffee pots are tall, but Sandon did not try to explain this. A German author in 1987 stated: 'That teapots possess a squat apple-like form and coffee pots are more elongated and pear-shaped has nothing to do with the properties of the two drinks but is accounted for by their origins.'[3]

There is indeed an explanation for the positioning of the spout even though it does not appear in the same place in all pots. Many designers over the centuries have designed pots for tea and coffee without understanding the fundamentals of tea and coffee and the floating-sinking phenomenon. Amazingly, most got it right. The tea spout needs to be in such a position that the liquid tea pours into the cup without tea leaves. In most teapots the spout is in the middle of the bulge. Originally, the coffee pot was designed with the spout above the bulge or in such a position that the grounds were trapped in the base below the bulge, so that a clearer cup of coffee could be poured.

TALL COFFEE POTS

The geometry of not having straight sides or of having a bulge, determined that the pot had to be tall. There was no single reason why a coffee pot had to be tall, but there were certainly several factors which were important. A tall coffee pot meant a greater distance between the floating grounds and the grounds on the bottom, with a clearer brew in between. This meant fewer grounds in the cup. As the grounds became

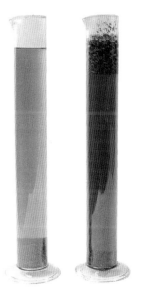

When boiling water is poured over freshly ground coffee, the grounds float in a mass of bubbles. When boiling water is poured over tea leaves, the leaves settle at the bottom.

saturated and were stirred and sank, it was important to have the spout as far from the grounds as possible.

In the eighteenth and nineteenth centuries it was likely that a simple coffee pot, into which boiling water was poured over grounds was the most common coffee maker of all. A tall coffee pot has an angle of repose from the handle of about 45 degrees when in the pouring position. This means that the grounds which have sunk to the bottom fall to the lowest point, which is below the spout, thereby minimising the grounds in the cup. When there was a bulge below the spout, the grounds were caught there too.

A tall coffee pot also made it possible for a filter bag to be suspended from the rim and when the filtering had finished, the bag would not be in the brewed coffee. In addition coffee was sometimes boiled with milk. A tall pot would minimise the chance of liquid boiling over.

These considerations would have influenced the early designs and once the forms were established, there was really no good reason to change them. After all, the differing designs for tea and coffee pots gave factories good reason to produce and sell two pots where one might have done.

The Turkish Influence on European Pots

Up to 1730, there was an export trade of *faïence* coffee pots from Marseille to the Barbary Coast and to the Ottoman Empire. The models for export, in the same shape as the tall traditional Turkish coffee pot must have influenced the design for the French home market and would have been an influence for a taller coffee pot.[4] The traditional Turkish coffee pot, or *ibriq*, may well have been tall to minimise boil-overs because the coffee had to rise higher, and needed a broad base to prevent tipping over in an open fire. The *cezve* or triangular open-mouthed boiler was probably designed to catch the grounds and at the same time allow the desirable froth to pour into the cups. Control in pouring both the coffee and the froth into small cups may well have been easier because each degree of tilt pours less from a narrow pot than from a broad one. These facts, combined with the catching of the grounds in the bulge, may have determined the basic Turkish shape and the Western makers adopted the same basic shape. The word *ibriq* was still being used for a coffee pot as late as 1755.[5] There must have been the feeling that the tall style of the Turkish pot was the 'legitimate' style.

A tall classical bulbous coffee pot.

A classic pot for Turkish coffee.

A Meissen pot from around 1740 showing similar shape.

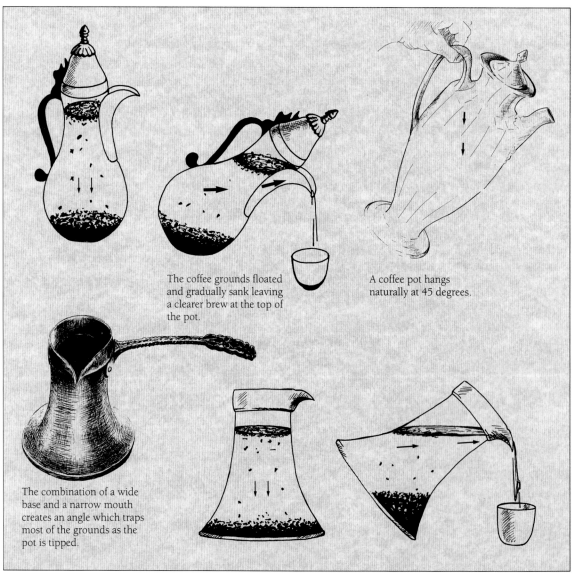

The coffee grounds floated and gradually sank leaving a clearer brew at the top of the pot.

A coffee pot hangs naturally at 45 degrees.

The combination of a wide base and a narrow mouth creates an angle which traps most of the grounds as the pot is tipped.

KH

SQUAT TEAPOTS

A squat teapot allows the tea leaves a larger area on the bottom to infuse and make a stronger, better cup of tea. If you make tea in a glass pot, when you stir the leaves, you can see the dark essence, which has settled between the leaves, swirling into the brew from the tea leaves which have settled on the bottom. The larger the surface area of the base, the more easily this essence will come into solution and make better first cups, because the larger the surface area, the closer the essence is to the surface. A very narrow, tall pot would leave the tea leaves and the essence largely undisturbed at the bottom. Of course the ideal is to stir the leaves and let them settle just before pouring, to get maximum flavour.

Teapots have a bulbous shape so that when the tea is poured, the tea leaves will fall towards the spout which becomes a funnel with a filter, and the liquid will pass though the leaves again. In fact the teapot balances vertically off its handle but it cannot go immediately to this position for pouring because the tea would pour out the lid opening.

For this reason, there have been many teapots with designs for lids that would not fall out and very few for coffee. The design objective was to put the tea leaves in the flow as much as possible.

The possibility of making an excellent cup of tea from a simple pot removed the need to make complicated pots and brewing systems as with coffee. There were undoubtedly successful teapot inventions but not one has withstood the test of time, except for the suspended tea filter bag and the more permanent versions of the same idea, the plastic and metal filter suspended in the mouth of the pot.

The consideration of tea sinking and coffee floating and sinking may well have been paramount in determining the design and shape of early tea and coffee pots. Once the tall coffee pots and squat teapots were established, later designers copied the basic form and varied it for aesthetic reasons. As they did not actually understand the function, they often produced pots which did not work. A coffee pot with the spout coming from the bottom will pour a lot of grounds with the liquid into the cup.

For some strange reason, there are large numbers of teapots with the most exotic designs - elephants, human beings, cars. Virtually any combination of a spout and a handle with anything between them has been produced as a teapot. There are books devoted to eccentric teapots, while hardly an eccentric coffee pot exists.

The emphasis on whimsical design far outweighed the desire to make a practical, bulbous teapot. The desire to improve teapots and coffee pots manifested itself in two very different ways. Teapots showed relatively few innovations but many strange designs, while coffee pots showed a never-ending stream of inventions, all trying to make a better cup of coffee.

A classical squat teapot.

A teapot hangs naturally in a vertical position and the leaves fall into the strainer.

KH

Planting

Plucking

Withering

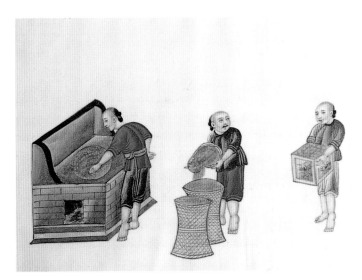

Firing

Tasting and selling

Packing

Chinese paintings on rice paper illustrating the green tea industry in China, mid nineteenth century.

C H A P T E R   2

Tea

T ea comes from the newest leaves of a bush that has seemingly grown in China forever. The first mention in Chinese literature dates from the twenty-eighth century BC. Tea seems to have arrived in Japan around the eighth century AD from China. Both countries treat tea with great reverence.

BLACK, GREEN AND OOLONG TEA

Tea is sold in three different groups which are called black, green and oolong but they are merely the same leaves processed differently. They can come from the same bush but usually regions and estates specialise in only one type. It was believed that green tea and black tea came from completely different plants. When Robert Fortune visited China in 1843 it was found that they were from the same bush, with only the method of manufacture differing.[1]

Green tea is made by steaming green tea leaves to stop oxidation and then drying them in a heated pan.

Black tea is made by taking the green leaves, drying them and then applying hot air to stop the oxidation process.

Oolong teas are prepared like black teas except that they are given a shorter drying period. They share some of the taste characteristics of both black and green tea.

The whole leaf may be prepared for processing in either the orthodox manner or the CTC method - crush, tear, curl. Tea leaves prepared in the orthodox manner, which is labour intensive, can be recognised by their longer, thinner appearance. In the 1930s the CTC method was introduced to give a more economical method of production. CTC teas are generally very small leaf and quick brewing.

The larger the leaf, the longer the brewing time. The smaller the leaf, the shorter the brewing time.

CHINESE TEAS

There are many hundreds of different teas from China and they fall broadly into a few categories - green unfermented, oolong semi fermented, red fully fermented, which is called black in the West, and rare PU-ERH teas which may be white. The best grades are harvested in March to April before the Clear Light Festival, the next best before the spring rains and the poorest after the spring rains. The time of harvesting is most important in determining quality and yet it is almost impossible to find out when the teas have been harvested.

The names of many Chinese teas seem very closely associated with mysticism and the prices for the most exotic are equally beyond

Above: Soden teapot with lift up basket. France - 1900.

Below: Note the shape of the teapot and the large size of the cup in the illustration from Dufour's book on coffee, tea and chocolate (in Latin) Paris, 1685.

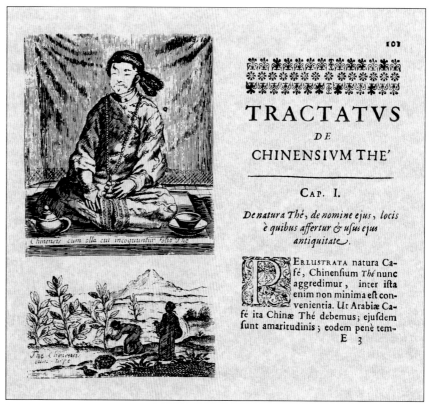

comprehension. Not surprisingly, the qualities valued by experts in Chinese tea are different to those valued by experts brought up in a western black tea tradition because they are applying different criteria from their own traditional fields.

JAPANESE TEA AND THE JAPANESE TEA CEREMONY

Japanese tea and the Japanese tea ceremony are perceived as one and the same thing in the western mind, but the tea does have its own identity and characteristics. The main difference between the Japanese and Chinese tea practices seems to be the Japanese insistence on boiling the water and then cooling it and a preoccupation with the quality of the water itself. The tea ceremony is the expression of a set of rules known as the Hundred Articles of the Sen Rik Yu some of which do not seem to have anything to do with brewing tea at all, for example: 'And in a picture scroll the string should be on the side of the signature', 'Sticking to rules in arranging charcoal is no good if the kettle does not boil', 'When tea is whisked this too should be done from the elbow and not from the wrist'.[2]

Japanese green teas have several grades, of which SENCHA is the most popular. The leaves are steamed, rolled and dried until they become like green needles. GYOKURO means 'gem of dewdrop' and is the best tea. The leaves are both a darker green or blackish colour than Sencha and more carefully prepared. The boiled water is allowed to cool and a short brewing time produces a stronger flavour with less bitterness than Sencha. BANCHA is the lowest grade of Sencha. HOUJICHA is roasted Bancha. GENMAICHA is a mixture of Bancha and popped Genmai or hulled rice kernels. MATCHA is made by grinding the finest dried tea leaves to a fine powder and is the type of tea used in the tea ceremony. There is a great emphasis in Japan on the healthy aspects of green tea.

TEAS FROM INDIA, SRI LANKA, KENYA AND INDONESIA

The best teas from India and Sri Lanka generally have some geographic or estate name. While there are dozens of tea-growing areas, just a few are famous. Three are Indian and three are Sri Lankan.

The most famous of all is DARJEELING in the Himalayas in India. The leaves are generally very large and the liquor very aromatic with hints of muscatel in the flavour. The liquor is very light in colour but the tea is exceptional in its flavour level and, although called the champagne of teas, has more similarity to a very fruity Lexia wine. It is rather difficult to find very good Darjeeling tea as its price is so high.

Just south of the Himalayas is a large region which produces ASSAM teas which have in some grades a malty flavour. Assams are noted for their heavy body. In Southern India the NILGIRI teas are found. Some of both the estate teas and blended teas from these areas are superb.

Sri Lanka has three famous teas: UVAS, NUWARA ELIYAS and DIMBULAS. At various times you can find excellent teas from all three areas. Kenya and Indonesia also grow good teas but usually these are only available to large packers and are not known by their areas.

Generally, it is very difficult to buy estate teas because they are thought to be inconsistent - something the market does not want. In markets that do not want to pay a lot of money, fine teas are more difficult to sell.

FAMILY TEA.

BLACK TEA is now become an article of general consumption in this colony, and in the course of time, will no doubt be as freely drank as it is in Great Britain. It is an innocent, exhilirating and pleasant beverage, producing none of those nervous wakeful symptoms experienced after a strong infusion of Green Tea. The undersigned, therefore, recommend Families either to use Black Tea exclusively, or a mixture composed of Half Black and Half Green. The Green Tea adds a mellowness to the strong rough flavour of the Black, which cannot be produced by either separately, and forms, perhaps, the most agreable narcotic yet discovered.

Orders from Dealers and others requiring a supply of Teas, &c., will receive the usual attention, but punctuality in remittances is indispensable.

S. PEEK & CO.

George-street, Sydney.

The Australian, Sydney, June 11, 1839

FROM LARGE LEAF GREEN TEA TO SMALL LEAF BLACK TEA

While Chinese and Japanese green teas remained popular in some countries, England at the end of the nineteenth century developed a preference for black tea. This came about partly because of preferential purchase from India and Ceylon and partly because English tea packers owned both the plantations and the means of distribution. There was some prejudice against green tea but precisely why is not clear. An 1834 journal stated: 'The most exquisite tea is not perhaps the wholesomest. The more green tea there is in it, certainly the less wholesome it is: though green adds to the palatableness.'[3] At the time it was believed that green tea and black tea came from completely different bushes. It was not until Robert Fortune visited China in 1843 that they were found to be from the same bush, with only the method of manufacture differing.

China's exports dropped dramatically at the turn of the century because of Japanese and Russian intrusions, which resulted in reduced production, and also because of the confrontationist relationship between the Chinese Empress and Western countries.[4] Another factor, affecting China's standing as the tea giant, was price. The black teas from Ceylon and India were cheaper than the Chinese teas and had the advantage that more cups could be brewed per pound. In 1840 the price of labour was lower in India, being two to three pence per day while in

China it was five pence for women and seven pence for men.[5]

The Irish, who consume more tea per capita than anyone else in the world, based their consumption on the small leaf, stronger Indian teas which in 1855 almost completely replaced the large leaf Chinese green teas.

In 1875 Francis Thurber on a trip to China found that 'of 1,818,000 piculs [133 pounds or 60 kilograms] 1,438,000 were black, 210,000 were green and 167,000 brick, which was tea leaves specially treated and compressed into a brick-like mould, all of which went to Russia. England took only 70,000 piculs of green tea.' Chinese black tea was mostly the large leaf tea and not like the broken leaf from India and Ceylon.[6]

The end result was a lowering of the quality of Chinese teas through adulteration. In 1885 a book on tea blending stated:

The demand for green tea in England is not nearly as large now as it was before the last Adulteration Act. All green tea is coloured to some extent, and Canton Gunpowders are heavily faced. On the passing of that Act the public became afraid to drink green teas, and grocers nervous of trading in them, consequently the demand for them rapidly decreased. Since the said Act, Canton green teas have nearly gone out of consumption, and the public are well rid of them, as they must have been detrimental to health, being highly faced with gypsum, Prussian blue, magnesia, and other colouring matters.[7]

Nothing really succeeds, in scaring people off a product like a good medical controversy and in 1886, the following appeared:

The exciting effects of fresh tea are such that ... where indulged in, it produces great disturbance of the mind, almost resembling inebriation, like the action of the Erythrovylon Coca among Peruvians, and inducing a tremulous motion of the limbs. This property is reduced by repeated roastings, but as green tea is less exposed to heat than black it retains more of this power...It is certain that all green tea is exceedingly pernicious. having a strong tendency to injure the stomach and the bowels and whole nervous industry...Dr. John Burdell, a distinguished young dentist of New York, informs us he boiled down a pound of young hyson tea (green), from a quart to half a pint, and ten drops killed a rabbit three months old; and when boiled down to one gill, eight drops killed a cat of the same age in a few minutes...if boiled down to a gill, it contains enough poison to kill 10,860 cats in a day.[8]

The evidence was conclusive. Green tea was bad. At least for rabbits and cats if not for humans.

Until the Second World War there was a developed market for China tea in England and small amounts of green tea around the world, but there has been little interest in the post-war years in western households.

The English love of sweets and sugar must also have been a factor in the decline of green tea.

---

preferred by him to every breathing mortal. What was the grief and mortification of Anne at the close of her toilsome journey, to find not merely that he was wooing but that he was actually married to another. Shocked and disgusted at his falsehood, indignation enabled her to act with becoming resolution. She immediately withdrew from the ingrate, and returned to France.

(*To be continued.*)

CULTIVATION OF THE TEA-PLANT BY THE ENGLISH.

It is well for the celestial empire that the trade carried on with England is of such trifling importance to China as not to weigh in the estimation of the emperor and his sage advisers " the down of a feather," as we deem it more than probable that ere long we shall be able to treat the people of the flowery empire with as good a cup of tea as they can grow for themselves. This will no doubt surprise the mandarins of all sorts of *buttons*, though in the matter of war they have no longer to learn that English barbarians can " give them as good as they can send."

Dr. Royle has recently laid before the Royal Asiatic Society an important exposition of what may be expected from an attempt to raise tea in England. He has shown that " in ascending from the forest-clad bases of the Himalaya, to their summits covered with eternal snows, we meet with almost every variety of climate that is encountered in proceeding from the equator to the poles, so there would appear to be no difficulty in finding congenial climates for the tea-plant, especially as in these mountains are found genera such as camellia, eurya, and cleyera, allied to the teas, as well as other Chinese genera, such as Deutzia, Houttuynia, Stauntonia, Kadsura, Hovenia."

On these grounds Dr. Royle in 1827, and again in 1831, recommended to the East India Company the cultivation of the tea plant; and in the latter year, " the India Government, with the sanction of the Court of Directors, determined upon attempting the cultivation of tea in India. A committee was formed, and reports called for. Dr. Falconer, in reply, recommended the same tract of country as Dr. Royle had done, in a report which is remarkable for coincidence in argument and opinion with that at the same time published by Dr. Royle, though the two must have crossed each other in their passage to and from India. Mr. Gordon was sent with Mr. Gutzlaff to obtain seeds, and as much information as possible from the tea districts of China, together with some tea manufacturers. They visited the Ankoy Tea Hills,

obtained a considerable quantity of seeds, and made an unsuccessful attempt to reach the Bohea Tea Hills, when they were recalled in consequence of the discovery of the tea-plant of Assam.

" The seeds obtained by Mr. Gordon having been sent to Calcutta, and sown in the Botanic Garden, numbers vegetated, though many failed. Nurseries having been established both in Assam and in Kemaon and Sirmore, at elevations of from 2000 to 7500 feet, seedlings were sent, but of 12,000 sent to Assam, only 500 arrived alive, and of 10,000 sent to N. W. India, only 1326 reached the hills in the beginning of the year 1836. In December, 1838, Dr. Falconer wrote to Dr. R. that the tea-plant was thriving vigorously in two, and had flowered in three, of the above nurseries. On the 21st April, 1841, Dr. Falconer reported that from the 500 plants originally introduced into the Kemaon nurseries, 5000 had been produced from layers, and from the seeds ripened. Many of them had grown to the size of bushy shrubs, about five feet high.

" In 1842, nine Chinese tea-manufacturers who had been in Assam, were sent to the tea-nurseries of Kemaon and Gurhwal. They united in declaring that the tea-plants of the Kemaon plantations were the genuine cultivated Chinese plant, and far superior to that grown in Assam, but that they required cutting down before they would be in the best state for yielding good tea-leaves. On the 12th Oct., Dr. Jameson, who succeeded to the charge on Dr. Falconer having been obliged to leave from ill health, wrote, ' The tea-plantations in the Deyrah Doon and in Kemaon are thriving admirably.'

" In the early part of last year some tea was prepared from the above plants by the Chinamen. On 20th Jan., a portion was sent to Calcutta, and a small canister to Dr. Royle at the India House. The former was reported on, on the 11th of May, by members of the Chamber of Commerce, and stated to be a very good marketable article, and valued in London at about 2s. 6d. per lb.; and the specimen sent to London, was, on the 23rd May, 1843, reported on by Messrs. Thompson, and pronounced to be of the Oolong Souchong kind, fine flavoured and strong, equal to the superior black teas generally sent as presents, and better, for the most part, than the China teas imported for mercantile purposes.

" Dr. Falconer having brought a specimen of tea from Kemaon, submitted it to Messrs. Ewart, Maccaughey, and Co., of Copthall-court, who report, 8th Sept., 1843, that it resembles most nearly the description occasionally imported from China under the name of Oolong; it is not so high flavoured as the fine Oolong tea; it has been

too highly burnt in the preparation, but it is of a delicate, fine flavour, and would command a ready sale here. Dr. Royle considers that nothing could be more satisfactory than these reports by experienced tea-brokers, as the first attempts to make tea in the Himalayan nurseries, called attention to the curious fact, that all the brokers coincided in comparing this tea with the Oolong and Tetsong teas of China, which, he was informed by Mr. Ball, were obtained from the Ankoy tea-district, that is, the very locality where Mr. Gordon obtained the tea-seeds.

" The latest letters from Dr Jameson continue to give the most favourable accounts of the tea-nurseries, while others from Captain Cautley speak in the same style of the tea-nurseries in the Deyrah Doon, where, he

says, the plants are looking splendidly, and are growing vigorously. Dr. Jameson states, that though he will be able to send only a few hundred pounds of teas this year, several thousand pounds will be sent next season. There are about 100,000 plants in all the above nurseries, and they may be rapidly increased. The Court of Directors have ordered that the experiment be continued."

The above important facts, for which we are indebted to the *Gardeners' Chronicle*, it will be seen fully justify the opinion we have expressed that England will shortly derive a large portion of her supplies of tea from India. When we see how the culture of sugar has progressed, what may we not expect when like attention is paid to growing and preparing for use the tea-plant ?

The introduction of small leaf Indian tea changed the market.
The Mirror of Literature, Amusement and Instruction, London, June 8, 1844

Family Herald,
London,
Nov.13, 1852

Another recipe for brick-tea. *The Penny Magazine,*
London, Oct.19, 1839.

Many centuries ago it was the normal thing to present tea in the form of brick-tea. The tea was grated off the brick and boiled. Most brick-teas were divided into rectangles on the back so that they could be used as money for trading. The fronts had fancy patterns.

Brick-tea presented to the Czar of Russia in 1868.
China - 1868.

Green Chinese teas, and the more delicate blacks, were not the sort of teas with which to take milk and sugar. The annual consumption of sugar, in the period 1801 to 1814, in England, was 6.67 kilograms per head and this figure had risen to 13.75 kilograms by 1855. In 1810 annual tea consumption was 0.62 kilograms per head and this figure had risen to 1.02 kilograms by 1856 [9] There is even a case that the use of teas was just the excuse for having milk and sugar. Much of the tea bag tea drunk today has only colour and little flavour but is still stirred carefully with milk and sugar.

BLACK TEAS AND THEIR SIZE GRADINGS

The black teas are the most commonly used types in the western world and are graded by size. Whole leaf grades are rarely seen since whole leaf teas are unpopular, but they do include Pekoe and Orange Pekoe - the orange referring to the colour of some of the leaves and not to the taste. Normally the leaves are broken during processing into differing sizes. The most popular grade is Broken Orange Pekoe which is a smallish leaf giving a good, quick extraction while still large enough to be caught in the strainer.

Fannings are just a little smaller and give an even quicker, stronger extraction. Fannings brew almost too quickly and become bitter unless taken from the pot very quickly. Dust grades and fannings are used in tea bags for really fast extractions.

BRICK-TEA

This is one variation of black tea which is still available in very limited quantities today, doubtless in a purer version than that formerly made.

Tea is prepared in a peculiar form, for the use of the Tartars; before the leaves are quite dry, they are moistened with a slightly glutinous liquid, said to be the serum of the blood of sheep, and then pressed into moulds, from which they take the form of a large brick, whence this tea is denominated brick-tea. All Tartars, from the borders of Russia to the Eastern Ocean, use this tea: they prepare their drink by scraping off a portion of the brick and boiling it in a saucepan with butter, flour and milk - a mixture which would scarcely seem palatable to our palates, but which Europeans who have partaken of it assure us is palatable, and after a very little use, equally pleasant with tea prepared in our way.[10]

BREWING AND FLAVOUR

It is just as impossible to tell the flavour of tea by the size of the leaf as it is to tell the flavour of an orange by its size. In theory, the different parts and sizes of the leaves should have approximately the same flavour provided the brewing time is adjusted. The brewing of the tea depends very much on leaf size. Smaller leaves require a shorter brewing time than larger leaves to produce the same strength liquor. However, because different flavour components brew at different rates, this is not quite true. Large leaf grades such as Darjeeling may need up to seven minutes to release all their flavour while small leaf fannings and CTCs may need only a minute or two. The only way to stop the brewing process is to remove the tea leaves from the pot or to compress them at the bottom of a plunger.

SELECTING THE BEST TEAS

Originally the prime aim of blending was to get improved flavours by balancing the attributes of the teas and there were many different grades and qualities sold in specialised shops. With mass marketing, the aim has changed to providing the same-flavoured tea year round at very reasonable prices. The quality of blends varies tremendously, as with all foods, but good teas can be found among them with careful selection.

It is no use expecting to buy good quality teas judging them by name, grade or leaf size. The only way is to taste the tea and after a time, you will recognise the qualities that give the tea its reputation. The best teas will cost a lot of money. What makes a tea good is that special character distinguishing it from other types of tea and other teas of the same type. At one time a Nuwara Eliya may be better than an Uva because their peak seasons are different, but at the same time one Nuwara Eliya may be better than another. If you keep trying teas you will, after some time, be able to distinguish fine, delicate flavour attributes and find an excellent tea. There is really no best tea except the tea with the finest flavour preferred by you.

The qualities that differentiate a fine tea from a poor one are its flavour and smoothness. Other criteria are that it must be aromatic and must have a good colour when served in a porcelain tea cup. A rough tea becomes more palatable with the addition of sugar and milk, whereas a tea with a good, clean, smooth flavour stands on its own.

RETAIL TEA MARKETS

English tea has an excellent reputation but even the expensive grades in some well known brands are cheaper and of lower quality than the best teas on the German market. The best teas at retail are found in Germany and other northern European countries, but at prices that leave you wondering if there has been a ticketing mistake. They are sold in an enormous range of qualities from small canisters in the old fashioned way. The German public's interest in good quality tea is incredible and sustains tea shops in numbers that are surprising. I cannot think of one English tea shop of the same calibre as the German shops and yet the Germans still go to England to buy tea, thinking that it is in some way superior to that available in their own shops. Hannover and Hamburg have specialty tea shops with excellent ranges of teas and tea equipment. The quality of tea available in Germany, the Netherlands, and Scandinavia can be high if you are prepared to pay the price.

HOW TO MAKE THE BEST TEA

The first requirements are freshly boiled water, a clean pot and the correct quantity of tea for the number of cups. Freshly boiled water means water that has just come to the boil and is used before all the oxygen and life have been boiled away.

Because tea sinks, it requires a less complicated brewing technique than coffee. The method involves obtaining a flavourful brew from the tea leaves and then removing the leaves. The ability to make a first class brew in a simple pot without any devices explains why more sophisticated methods have not been developed.

The water should be poured over the tea leaves in a round or squat teapot, a shape which allows for a larger infusion area. Because the essence of the tea rests between the tea leaves and the strength of the tea is greater towards the bottom, the tea should be stirred before serving. This method is excellent provided the tea leaves are removed once the correct brewing time is finished. The old saying about the five-minute brew is fine for large leaf teas, but should be reduced when a

Tea drinking on the Neva. *The Penny Magazine,* London, Apr.22, 1843.

British growth meant tea grown in the Empire and that meant India and Ceylon. This packet dates from the turn of the century.

smaller tea leaf is used. Often, too much tea is made and the tea leaves are left in the pot, so the last cups overbrew, becoming tanniny or bitter through over-extraction.

From the earliest days a removable, biggin-type filter was used to hold the tea in the top of the pot. These filters now come in a variety of forms - permanent and disposable. The quality of the permanent filters, which is usually excellent, depends on the filtering material's fineness and its lack of flavour. Japanese filters of nylon are excellent. There are many European biggin-type filters which incorporate a disposable filter-paper bag. Whilst there are sound theoretical reasons why these should not be good, they are practical and do work. Every drop of flavour might not be surrendered but they are much better than the other methods and make an excellent cup of tea.

Since the last years of the nineteenth century teaspoons with incorporated filter holders have been made, as have tea-eggs. This type of tea maker is rarely satisfactory. The boiling water is unable to swirl around the tea leaves and as the tea leaves swell in the container, water flow is further restricted. If the tea swells and completely fills the space, the tea essence is actually prevented from leaving. The result, unless there is vigorous shaking, is a weak brew.

Tea bags have the same drawback but nevertheless have grown immensely in popularity, to the point that many people actually believe they are synonymous with tea. They are but a pale imitation.

DRINKING TEA, ENGLISH-STYLE

Under the influence of the Temperance Movement, the English began to drink tea religiously in the 1830s. In a poster to the inhabitants of Clerkenwell, England, in 1831, giving advice on preventing Indian cholera, Sir Gilbert Blane recommended persons to guard against its approach by moderate and temperate living. Temperate living at the time certainly meant tea and not alcohol.[11] At the same time the price of tea fell as coffee lost its popularity. The price of coffee in England in 1807 was 52 to 66 pence per pound; in 1817 it was 22 to 40 pence; in 1827, 13 to 33 pence.[12]

Brightly painted tins with Chinese figures, numbers and descriptions filled the shelves of the best tea merchants in England. The ordinary grocer used counter dispensers with three compartments for the loose tea. The words Premium Tea were always used even though the tea might be of any quality. England - late 19th century.

England was the largest consumer of tea and set the fashion for most of the world. The English reputation for tea was well established in the last century and many books gave specific examples of just how to make tea 'English style'. After a detailed description of finely worked mahogany tables on four legs, black, yellow or blue Wedgwood teapots or even the new Lustre ceramics and all the attendant trimmings, a German book of 1836 gave the following instructions for making English tea:

> Boil the water as fast as possible so that it does not get a smoky flavour and affect the tea. Pour the water in the pot, not once but several times so that the tea does not get too strong. From the first pour, you get the quintessence, and then you must pour the second brewing into the cup. The colour of the tea must always be golden yellow, never red or brown. The tea can be served with cream and sugar and for the men, arak and rum.[13]

The little leaves of black tea, which increasingly came from India and Ceylon in the second half of the nineteenth century, presented new problems. The small tea leaves brewed very quickly and the brewing process had to be controlled if bitterness was to be avoided. In addition, large leaf tea could be strained easily through large holes in porcelain teapots, but very small leaf tea required small holes. These were difficult to manufacture in porcelain and metal was more suitable. This led to an increasing use of secondary strainers, which sit over the cup.

The Cadogan pot was produced by many different manufacturers in England during the period 1830 to 1880.

An unusual Chinese cup. The little man in the hole floats up as the cup is filled.

A picnic teapot with a wooden handle. The two cream bowls could fit into the teapot. The one with the removable handle was for hot cream and the other for cold cream. England - c.1800.

Hot Cream and Cold Cream in Tea

'Why sure, Betty, you are bewitched, the cream is burnt too', cried Lady Answerall when Lady Smart had commented on the tea being hot, in Swift's satirical *Genteel and Ingenious Conversation,* published in 1738. The illustration shows a rare teapot from around 1800 which demonstrates that tea was still being drunk with hot and cold cream. The very idea of hot cream in tea sounds fantastic but the proof is in the picture.

THE NON-EVOLVING TEAPOT

The teapots illustrated in Nicholas de Blegny's book, *Le Bon Usage de Thé, du Café et du Chocolat* in 1687 show strong Chinese influence.

The evolution of the teapot is a misnomer because there is no final, higher form of the teapot today. You will find nothing that is substantially different from all the basic teapots used in China and Japan for centuries. Most Chinese and Japanese teapots have a round, squat shape. There are only a few which have the design characteristics of a tall coffee pot. The size of Chinese pots ranges from very small to large, corresponding to the styles of tea making.

Teapot collectors in both the east and the west have been mainly interested in the different design styles and the quality of manufacture. These are the dominant themes in all the books about teapots and only in passing does the odd invention rate a mention. Possibly, this is a reflection of the lack of patented teapot collections. There are many collectors of teaspoons, tea caddy spoons, teapots, teapots with strange shapes, tea caddies, tea tins, and tea paraphernalia, but very few, if any, of patented teapots.

One of the earliest inventions was by Sarah Guppy in England in 1814 who had one of the earliest innovative teapots, one which cooked an egg in the pot. The same idea appeared some years later in France where another woman, Mme Eriberta Predari, tried to do the same in a coffee pot, perhaps with more grounds for success.

Chinese Innovation

The most common innovation is the teapot with no lid but a hole in the base. This now comes in many forms, especially from Taiwan. It originally had the shape of a peach, a shape in which it was manufactured in England where it was called a Cadogan teapot.

In the last century a teapot with two compartments was invented in Hsi Shing province, China - there was a filter between the two compartments. The west does not seem to have copied the idea and they are no longer available except as antiques. The only idea that has been copied is the placement of a strainer in the spout, but it would be difficult to ascribe a precise origin of this to any one time or place or individual teapot.

Western Innovation

In the early days the European use of large leaf green tea meant that there was little need for innovation as the big leaves of green tea are easily strained by the coarse holes of a teapot. Mostly the tea leaves sink to the bottom and stay there.

The first European trading of tea was by the Dutch in the first decade of the seventeenth century. It was to be another fifty years before tea became well known and then for the next two hundred years, if we are to believe all the books about teapots and tea, it was only brewed in quality pots of luxurious silver and porcelain.

The English factories were producing enormous quantities of pottery teapots. With porcelain it was very difficult to make a fine strainer in the spout - necessary to stop the smaller leaf tea leaves, lying in the bottom of the pot, from going into the cup. Porcelain pots had spouts which were prone to breakage and needed replacement, but porcelain was pleasing to the eye and could be decorated in the most delightful ways. For sheer elegance nothing could surpass a decorated tea service. The poorest tea immediately tasted better.

One of the earliest strainers was the mote spoon which was used to pick up the motes or dust floating on the surface of the tea.

Metals could be made into fine strainers very easily and they were incorporated into metal pots as an intrinsic part. In the 1800s a toughened form of pewter, Britannia metal, was being widely used. Sheffield plate, the combination of three layers of metal - copper sandwiched between two layers of silver - became very popular for teapots and coffee pots. In 1840, the firm of Elkington discovered the technique of electroplating silver onto copper or nickel. This is commonly called EPNS - electroplated nickel silver. Nickel gets its name from causing a lot of problems in bronze castings in the Middle Ages. The blame was laid at the door of the devil, Old Nick - hence nickel. Metal brought with it new possibilities and problems. One problem related to the fact that some metals tainted the tea. In addition, the metal handles became too hot to hold and the pots too hot to stand on a wooden table. A hollow metal handle with air vents was developed to cool the handle, while to protect the tabletops, teapots were supported on a stand from which they could be tilted to pour the tea.

The original lidless teapot was probably a Chinese wine pot designed in the shape of a peach. It can be filled with brewed tea in the following way: remembering that the water level remains horizontal, the pot is filled and then revolved 180 degrees handle down, spout up. In this way, only a little tea is lost. The pot on the right shows the bottom hole.

Three compartment teapots from Yixing, a city famous for its porcelain in the nineteenth century. There is a filter between the two compartments.
China - 1860s.

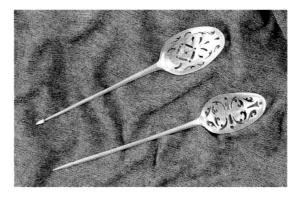

Silver mote spoons were developed very early to scoop the 'motes' (flecks floating on the surface) of the tea. The pointed tips were for spearing pieces of fruit at the bottom of a punch bowl or clearing the strainer in the spout.
England - 1770s.

Castleford teapot with a sliding brass lid.
England - 1810.

A patent was granted to W.J.Houlgate for 'rubber bands provided with suitable nozzles'. England -1900.

A metal teapot with a wooden handle. The style seems similar to a 'Grainger' - a style of porcelain teapot popular 1825-30.
England - c.1840

An English tea caddy by Pearce, 77 Cornhill, London. Tea was very valuable and kept in the locked caddy. Later examples included a glass bowl for mixing the teas together or holding sugar. Even though tea cost more on the Continent than in England, European caddies are much rarer than English ones. England - early 1800s.

The metal teapot on a stand was the height of elegance for decades. England.

The problem of the handle being too hot was partially solved by making the metal handle hollow with aeration holes. Patent by J.E. Bingham. England - 1878.

An example from a later period of a copper teapot with porcelain lining and some type of artificial material as handle and base. England - 1900s.

Metal teapots had a problem in the unequal expansion of the walls and base which could cause separation and splitting. The rings on this patented 'expansion bottom' teapot were an attempt to solve the problem. Patented by P.H. Ashberry England - 1889.

Royle's self-pouring or pumping teapot was patented with a sieve at the bottom. The lid had a small hole at the top which was covered by your finger as you pressed and pumped down, forcing the tea up the spout. England -1886.

5598. Crookes, H. April 22.

Tea &c. making apparatus. —The handles of tea urns and similar vessels are coated with a special heat-indicating paint to show whether they are too hot to be taken hold of. The double iodide of mercury and potassium is first prepared by adding mercuric chloride to a solution of potassium iodide as long as the precipitate of mercuric iodide redissolves in the excess of potassium iodide. The solution is then heated with a solution of copper sulphate and boiled to expel the iodine which is liberated ; the iodide of mercury and copper is filtered off and dried and powdered, and then mixed with oil and turpentine to form a paint. The paint is red at ordinary temperatures, but when heated to 110° F. it darkens until at 140° F. it becomes dark brown.

The David Lindo teapot with the strainer on the bottom was a recognition that the tea leaves sank to the bottom. England - 1884.

In 1868, the first patent for a teapot with Britannia metal on the outside and an earthenware lining appeared. It was the first of many attempts to get the best of both worlds. In the 1870s a series of patents was registered which used cork or bone washers or disc inserts in the handles to act as insulators. In 1874 a perforated metal strainer with an outer cloth was introduced into the teapot and in 1877 a suspended tea strainer sat in the pot. This was new and yet old, as it closely resembled Soutens' invention for coffee in 1835. In fact it is just a biggin or strainer sitting in the pot for tea.

THE INVENTIONS

In 1884 a veritable flood of inventions commenced, most involving metal. The increasing use of Indian and Ceylonese fine leaf tea, which needed finer strainers, was the catalyst. In 1886 the Royle teapot was invented. Boiling water was poured over the tea leaves and pumped out by moving the lid up and down. This certainly solved the problem of burning your hand by holding the pot. Of all the early inventions, this is the most easily found in antique markets. It comes in several different forms made from both metal and earthenware and probably evolved from English inventor David Lindo's teapot with the strainer at the bottom.

The dominant threads of invention were based on three ideas - to remove the tea leaves from the brew in some type of strainer device, to reposition the tea leaves in the pot by some type of device, or simply to have a better strainer. The first is the only one to show any evolution - this was the idea of the biggin, a very early idea. There has been a wide range of removable strainers, starting with metal and porcelain eggs and spoon strainers and even plastic eggs. Mesh of various types was used and more recently filter paper bags held in place by plastic rings were introduced.

Electric teapots and automatic teapots have had only a small influence on the brewing of tea. They have mostly incorporated waking devices which boiled the water and brewed the tea. The first machine was the English Hawkins which dated from the 1930s and worked by the weight of the boiler being overbalanced when the water boiled out. In 1990 several German electric machines came onto the market.

Most of the post-war developments have gone into making more effective tea bags. Tea bags have several major problems. The first relates to the fact that the water brews the tea in the bag and unless the bag is jiggled to encourage a crossflow of water, the tea flavour will remain in the bag. The flavour release is rarely very good. Another problem relates to the packaging. If the tea bag is not packed in a separate envelope, the amount of oxygen in the pack will cause a relatively quick staling. The market share going to tea bags seems to be rising in most countries with a corresponding decline in interest in fine teas.

Customers will pay as much as they are asked for tea bags with separate envelope packaging, despite the quality of tea in the bag. Yet, they will not pay even an equivalent amount for better quality loose leaf tea. The quality of tea has been totally sacrificed for the convenience.

To put this in perspective it is necessary to examine the prices of other products. The cost for the best Darjeeling tea might be about $300 per kilogram. With a yield of 500 cups per kilogram this price equates to sixty cents per cup, or the equivalent of three dollars for a bottle of wine which is at the very bottom of the price range for low quality wines, or around the same price as a bottle of beer. It is apparent that in most of the sophisticated countries of the world the same value is not placed on tea as on wine. For some reason there is snobbishness attached to wine and this may be related to the fact that bottles of wine are almost the only food or beverage placed on the table with the label still on.

With increasing income levels in the United States, more attention is being paid to coffee than to fine teas. The old ex-British Empire countries are generally drinking more tea bags and poorer teas. The general lack of interest has meant very little evolution in tea equipment and the new devices have not been accepted in the major tea-drinking countries of the world. There have been major improvements in the quality of the filter paper used in tea bags in terms of strength and flow properties. These new filter papers have enabled the development of other forms of filters.

On the other hand there has been a world-wide surge of interest in flavoured teas, especially Earl Grey. This tea is made with Bergamot oil or lemon grass, allegedly to duplicate the flavour of teas which had become tainted from the long period of travel to England from China in the nineteenth century. In recent years, there has been much more interest in developing flavoured teas containing fruit pieces, flowers and essences. These teas are being drunk weak and black like much tea bag tea. The opportunity for drinking a first class tea brewed correctly is declining.

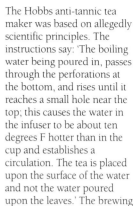

The Hobbs anti-tannic tea maker was based on allegedly scientific principles. The instructions say: 'The boiling water being poured in, passes through the perforations at the bottom, and rises until it reaches a small hole near the top; this causes the water in the infuser to be about ten degrees F hotter than in the cup and establishes a circulation. The tea is placed upon the surface of the water and not the water poured upon the leaves.' The brewing time was about three to four minutes. The simple fact was that the Hobbs' filter completely underbrewed the tea and was anti-flavour as well as anti-tannic. England - 1885.

A teapot cum water boiler from a picnic basket for train travel. The warning on the pot was sensibly given - not to boil the water with the spout cap still screwed on. England.

Fenton's patent teapot. After brewing, the basket with the tea leaves inside was levered up and kept up by the metal clasp near the handle. England - 1903.

A Royal Doulton tea caddy. Honesty is the best policy. England.

An electric tea kettle. USA - 1907.

In 1900, A.J. Hayward had the idea to rotate the pot ninety degrees, but did not seal off the partition completely. In 1901, the Earl of Dundonald almost got it right. His 1905 patent for the S.Y.P. worked. It was Simple Yet Perfect. The tea and water were put into the pot while it stood on its handle. The lid was placed on and the pot turned upright. England - 1905.

In this form and with the name Cunard underneath, the Cube was known as the Cunard teapot. It was believed to be very steady in rough weather because it could be stored next to another without slipping and sliding. England - 1916.

An Art Deco style, seven-sided teapot. The metal spout holes were finer than ceramic. England - 1922.

The ceramic Cosy teapots came in two designs - with a loose lid and with a lock-in lid. England - 1923.

An English teapot with non-drip spout. The drip either fell down or rolled back into the pot.

Teapot with an unusual spout to prevent drips. England.

Teabags, made in the USA in the 1920s, were originally of cotton gauze or cellophane. They were very popular and spread to the United Kingdom where they now command more than half the market. Teabags are now made of special paper which is heat sealable and they come in two versions - with tags, or tagless.

Cotton re-usable filter bags were widely used in Denmark after the Second World War.

A special pair of tongs for squeezing tea bags. Hong Kong - 1980s.

Three filter paper biggins. The red one by Filtropa of Holland used a stainless steel clip to hold the bag in place. The white one by Tebrygg of Denmark used a friction fit to hold the bag. In the brown one by Götz & Co. of Hannover the bag was held in place by the plastic springing open to keep the tension. 1980s.

The idea was first invented by the Swede Rolf Wallin in 1969. These types of tea brewers are better known in Northern Europe than in England or other major tea-drinking countries.

Left: A filter bag designed to be filled with tea and then hung in the pot. France - 1980s.

A German advertisement for teabags during World War 1. An opportune article as a gift for our brave fighters in the field. TEA-BOMBE. Unit price 10 pfennig made from ground tea and sugar. Produces 1/2 to 1 litre of ready-to-drink sweetened aromatic tea. [English translation]

Above: A European teapot with electric warmer. There was a little 5 Watt lamp underneath. Probably German. 1920s.

Left: The Abram Cosy metal teapot. The intention was to catch all the drips. England - 1923.

A two-spout teapot from J.Lyons & Co., designed for fast pouring in restaurants and cafeterias. England - 1930.

The internal strainer was the height of the pot. The idea was to let the tea liquor from all the levels pour into the spout.

A patented stackable teapot. England.

The metal spout was inserted to stop the spout breaking and also to provide smaller filter holes. It was not easy to make small holes in ceramic. England - 1930s.

The Woods pot had a spout with a small vertical hole at the end. The drip either fell into the cup or stayed up. It could not drip onto the tablecloth.

The Heatmaster Dubl-Deka stacking teapot. England.

The Hall had a lid which locked on. USA - 1970s.

The Japanese have been using biggin-type teapots for a long time.

The Master pot. A ceramic filter in a metal pot. England - 1933.

An aluminium Swan picnic teapot. The lid screwed on so that water could be carried without spilling. England.

The Paramount Brewmaster had a depression in the base to locate a filter which contained the tea. The lid was locked into the pot and the little spring-loaded knob pushed down to express all the flavour from the tea leaves.

The original Melitta tea filter had a rod to block the exit hole and control the brewing time. It was designed to use filter paper. Germany - late 1930s.

The Melitta tea filter was still produced after World War II. Germany.

A Robur metal biggin. Australia - 1927.

The Akechi biggin teapot has a filter made of plastic with very fine nylon mesh. Japan - 1985.

The lid was held in place by the two lugs. England.

An aluminium teapot using a similar lid to the Abram Cosy. Hong Kong - 1980s.

A teapot of pressed stainless steel with an unusual lid and handle - Hong Kong. 1980s.

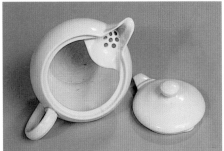

The Copeland teapot had a special spout designed so that if the tea leaves blocked the spout strainer, the liquid could run over two channels on the upper side of the open spout. England - 1944.

The Jena heat resistant glass biggin. East Germany - 1970s.

A Chinese teapot. The rising steam causes the dragon's tongue to pop out. China - 1980s.

Electric teapots are very unusual. This model is probably Hungarian. It uses the same rubber spout-stopper as the Perlusz electric coffee machine. The tea basket is on an heloidical screw and is lowered into the water after the whistle indicates that the water is boiling.

The Kissl has a coarse filter and a magnet attached to the lid to prevent it falling off. Japan - 1992.

A Gemco glass and plastic biggin. USA - 1980s.

A Hario teapot with removable basket. Japan - 1990.

In Australia, 'billy tea' was popular in the 'bush' (outback or back country). The billy-can was a tin pot of water which was suspended over an open fire to boil. A carefully-gauged handful of tea was dropped in for a good strong brew and then the 'billy' was swung in a big circle over the shoulder, probably to help the tea leaves settle. Australia.

The Quart pot served a similar purpose for the Australian drover. It could be attached to the saddle in its leather case. Pint pots also existed but were smaller, a quart being equivalent to two pints. Australia.

Melitta also produced a tea grinder so that large expensive tea leaves could be reduced in size and better, faster extraction achieved. Germany - 1970s.

A one cup tea brewer using a gold non-woven filter. The filter basket was lowered into the cup and lifted out when ready. Switzerland - 1989.

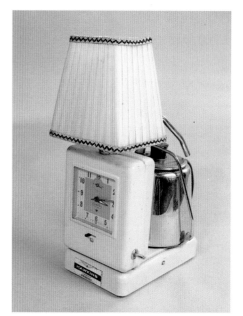

The Hawkins tea maker was the first of a series of electric alarm clock tea makers. The first patents for these started at the turn of the century using clockwork match-striking units which, if they lit, ignited the gas, and if they did not, gassed you. England 1940s or even 1930s.

A 1980s model Teasmade. England.

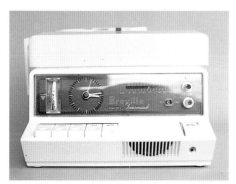

A Breville radio Teasmade with clock, radio and automatic teamaker. Australia - 1980s.

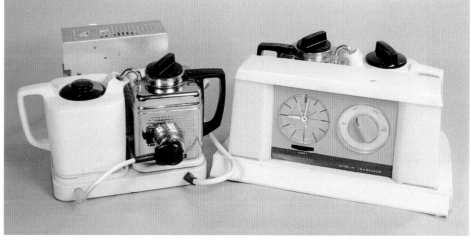

The Teasmade was the most famous name and had the pot intrinsic to the unit. The picture shows the cube water kettle and the cube teapot. England.

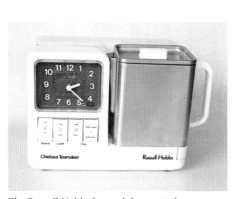

The Russell Hobbs brewed the tea in the same stainless steel pot in which the water was boiled. England - 1980s.

The first Teasmade was made of wood, later made of bakelite and then plastic. England - 1936.

TEAPOTS WITH UNUSUAL DESIGNS.

Teapots with unusual designs are common throughout the Orient and the Western world. Equivalent coffee pots are almost non-existent.

Chinese

English

English

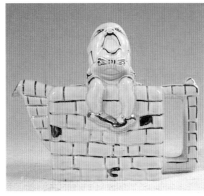

English

American

English

Japanese

Japanese

TEASTRAINERS

One of the earliest forms of strainer was made by weaving wire into the desired shape. These carry no names or countries of origin and they may well have come from China and Japan where such techniques are still common today using bamboo.

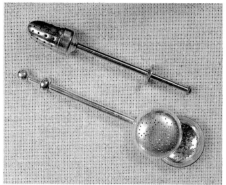

Spoons with tea containers were popular from early in the 1900s, but never made good tea because the water did not flow through properly. Lower - the top side of the compartment was controlled by a spring-loaded handle. Upper - a spoon of Russian origin. By pushing the rod in the handle, the tea could be compressed.

The Chinese silver strainer from the nineteenth century on the left had a drip catcher underneath. The strainer with the little spout and bone handle is the English Harris and Fredericks patent of 1906.

A simple but effective wire strainer was inserted into the spout of the teapot. First invented by D. Chambers. England - 1901.

Commercial or pot eggs had measures on the side. The aluminium egg could take six tablespoons of tea and the one on the right was adjustable in size.

A Kaho patented egg had a woven mesh filter underneath and room for the essence to pass through.

A spring-loaded tea strainer with drip catcher.

Two teafilter spoons. The model with the crossover arms was first patented by Gallus and Wolf and the spring-loop added in 1907 by K.J. Cooper. England. The spoon on the right is possibly of Continental origin.

A plastic tea filter with very fine nylon mesh moulded into the plastic. USA - 1990.

The Kwik-Cup. The filter rested on the cup and the boiling water was poured through. It worked. Australia - 1950s.

Tea eggs have been very popular for a long time even though they do not work very well. The tea swells, effectively stopping water flow and proper extraction. The egg (top left) is Britannia metal; the one in the middle is German plastic which has become discoloured and the one on the right is spring loaded. Chains indicate that these eggs were removed from the pot after brewing.

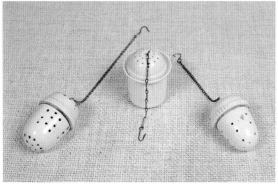

Ceramic tea eggs are mostly of Continental origin.

Below: Some other tea implements. From left, clockwise:
1. A Yerba Maté straw for sucking tea out of gourds which were passed around by gauchos in Uruguay and Argentina. Yerba Maté is a form of tea native to that area.
2. A woven filter mesh which could be fixed into a spout.
3. A French filter to put over a spout.
4. A strainer to hang at the end of the spout.
5. A German tea measure.
6. A spoon for measuring tea.

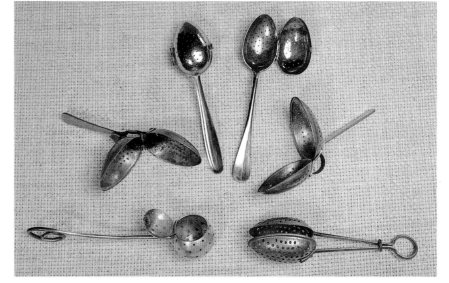

Five spoon brewers. (All strainers like this sacrificed flavour for convenience).
Two top - as in Cook and Banks patent. England - 1899. Middle right - Pearce. England - 1905. Lower right - Davis, Hall & Axten. England - 1906. Middle left - this had a coil spring inside. Lower left - spherical strainer from France.

Below: Four simple strainers which did not catch the drips.

CHAPTER 3

Drinking Chocolate

*I*n 1528 Hernando Cortez took the first drinking chocolate from Mexico to Spain. At first, the Spanish tried to keep it a secret, but eventually word got out and it reached France in 1615 and England by 1650. Sugar was added to drinking chocolate at the end of the sixteenth century in Spain which resulted in increased consumption. The story goes that an Englishman in 1730 added milk to drinking chocolate creating the drinking chocolate we know today. Chocolate for eating was yet to be discovered.

Most of the history of chocolate relates to how eating chocolate developed and there is little on drinking chocolate. This is because it is essentially a product that is prepared in a factory, as powdered cocoa, and then the ingredients are heated up in the kitchen. The preparation is very simple and has scarcely changed in centuries.

Cocoa powder was originally used as a base for other spices and flavours - these ingredients were heated up with water and stirred with a wooden stirrer with a round shape at the end. In the brewing process a scum appeared on the surface, which had to be removed. The powder was meant to be drunk with the liquid and there was no attempt to strain it or remove it. For this reason, there is always a stirrer in the chocolate pot to agitate the cocoa just prior to serving.

In terms of evolution, there has been very little, compared with coffee and tea. Drinking chocolate in its earliest form must have been similar to Phillipe Sylvestre Dufour's recipe in his book on Coffee Tea and Chocolate, French edition, 1688[1]. He quoted this recipe as derived in 1618 from Barthelemy Marradon, a doctor from Marchena, near Seville in Spain:

Seven hundred cocoa beans
One and a half pounds of sugar
Two ounces of cinnamon
Fourteen grains of Mexican pepper called chili or pimento
One half ounce of cloves
Three pods of vanilla or two ounces of aniseed
The large part of the Anchiote nut (from a Mexican tree like an orange tree)
Some put a little orange flower water, a grain of musk or ambergris or powder of Scolopendre (poisonous centipedes), almonds and the pod of the Tlixochitla tree (another Mexican tree).
[English translation.]

The ingredients have more resemblance to a

A *Limoges* chocolate pot showing the wooden stirrer for agitating the cocoa on the bottom of the pot before pouring. France.

prescription for Chinese medicine than a popular beverage. At first sight the recipe would appear to be the original recipe from Mexico but it contained spices, such as cinnamon and cloves, which were not native to Mexico. The almonds mentioned were possibly not real almonds but the fruit of some other tree from the West Indies or Peru - perhaps a palm. They were better than maize to mix with the cocoa because they gave more body. Dufour's book goes on to say that maize was the same as wheat. Obviously there were problems in describing all the new plants from the Americas.

The ingredients were reduced to powder and grilled to the right colour in the correct order. Then they were placed in a vessel and mixed with a spoon, heated and passed through a sieve and pressed into tablets. The Mexicans drank it mixed with soaked cornflour. Another way was to dissolve the tablet in hot water and pour in the hot cornflour porridge and mix the lot with the *moulinet* - the little stirrer, and then drink it, mouthful by mouthful.

Dufour refers to different ways of drinking chocolate in various countries. Thomas Gage, an Englishman, said that the tablet was to be dissolved in cold water, sugar added and the mixture boiled up and drunk hot. But the most common way was to heat the water, dissolve one or two tablets with sugar in a cup and stir. In Leghorn in Italy and other places where iced drinks were customary, people often drank iced chocolate, which was not at all disagreeable. In France, the powder was put into a pot with water and sugar, heated and stirred with the *moulinet*. It was poured into the goblets with the *mousse* on the top and served as hot as possible. It was the addition of sugar which was the catalyst for hot chocolate becoming popular.[2]

In 1853 Alexis Soyer in his book, *The Pantropheon* said that the Spanish roasted their cocoa beans lighter than the Italians.[3] After roasting, the beans were separated from the shells, 'which in England, Switzerland and Germany were used to make an infusion with boiling water, mixed with milk and drunk instead of the real thing' [cocoa]. Normally hot chocolate was made with ground cocoa paste, sugar and cinnamon. From Mexican times, vanilla had been added to chocolate and it is still a recommended additive to this day, as a sweetener.

Today, the quality of a cup of hot chocolate varies with the quantities and proportions used. The more sugar you mix with unsweetened cocoa powder, the sweeter the drink will be. The more milk, or milk and water, you mix with a given quantity of cocoa and sugar, the weaker it will be. The flavour of the chocolate varies with the brand, each of which has been developed with a particular market in mind.

Chocolate, and its health qualities, has been the subject of much discussion, both positive and negative. Chocolate certainly contains caffeine and yet it never attracted the amount of opprobrium with which coffee was inflicted. In fact, advertising and posters show children happily drinking hot chocolate. The answer may lie in its advent to Europe through the Spanish monks and as a food for the upper classes who would never condemn their own luxuries. Later factors could have been the relatively small number of large manufacturers who were able, via advertising pressure, to contain criticism. Abstinence is not much of an alternative for such a delicious substance. Certainly there is a growing use of carob as a substitute for chocolate, but I feel this is a spin-off from the caffeine controversy in coffee rather than a campaign against chocolate as such.

The evolutionary process of chocolate brewing equipment is not easily seen from books or antique markets. Most objects are either large, commercial and uninteresting or small chocolate pots with stirrers, having a high value deriving from their age or the materials used. Patents show that there were developments such as agitating the chocolate as it was being served, but I have never seen a pot with this innovation anywhere.

Note the Mexican with cocoa-making equipment in the illustration from Dufour's book on coffee, tea and chocolate (in Latin) Paris, 1685.

CHAPTER 4

Raw to Roasted - Yemen to Europe

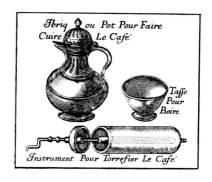

COFFEE, A NEW DRINK IN THE ARAB WORLD

It is interesting to speculate on what caused coffee, a product which had probably been known as a medicine for the best part of a millenium, to suddenly start on a path of diffusion through the Arab countries during the fifteenth century. Sometime in the early 1400s coffee ceased to be merely a drink with medicinal properties and became a recreational hot drink. The appropriate myths are associated with its discovery, but all of them leave out the important steps between finding the cherries on bushes and drinking a beverage made from roasted and ground coffee beans, from a cup. The theory that coffee drinking had begun spontaneously among the tribes of the Yemen area could be correct, *but is not supported by any facts.*

The Coffee Cherry and the Bean

The fruit of the coffee tree is known as a coffee cherry and the bean or *bunnu* is in the centre, surrounded by a fleshy outer covering, *qishr*, which contains sugar as sweet as ripe fruit, and one per cent caffeine.

The word coffee is often used as if it only has its current meaning. There is usually no hint that the word coffee was used in Arabic texts with two very distinct meanings - the husks or flesh around the beans and the beans themselves. The word *qishr* is an Arabic word which really means covering or flesh of a coffee bean, like the flesh around an olive. *Qishr* was always sweetish, either when chewed or brewed, and coffee beans were neutral or bitterish. There is a logical progression from making a drink using the husk of the coffee cherry to making Turkish coffee.

FROM CHEWING TO BREWING

Since ancient times in Aden it has been the social custom to chew the fresh leaves of *qat*, which have a mild narcotic effect. This custom may have been the basis for chewing coffee beans. The juice of *qat* is swallowed and new leaves are used every few minutes. Moseley in 1792 wrote about the use of *qat* as the base for an infusion, made like tea.[1]

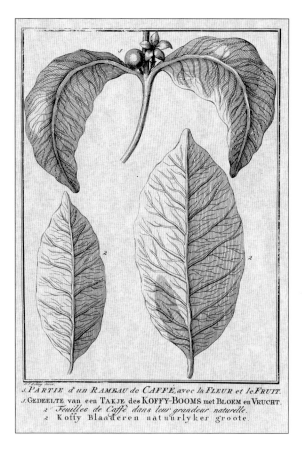

J.P ARTIE d'un RAMEAU de CAFFÉ, avec la FLEUR et le FRUIT.
J. GEDEELTE van een TAKJE des KOFFY-BOOMS met BLOEM en VRUCHT.
2 Feuilles de Caffé dans leur grandeur naturelle.
2 Koffy Blaaderen natuurlyker groote.

J.A RBRE DU CAFFÉ, Dessiné en Arabie.
J. DE KOFFY BOOM, in Arabie afgetekent.
2 Fruit sec. 3 Coupe du Fruit. 4 Noiau ou Feve du Caffé.
2 Drooge Vrucht. 3 Schaal van de Vrucht. 4 Koffy Boon.

There were many illustrations of the coffee tree, its leaves and fruit. Most of the illustrators copied from each other and had never seen the original tree in its country of origin. These two etchings by Schley were probably based on drawings done during Jean de la Roque's voyage to Arabia in 1708.

Map of Yemen. From Jean de la Roque's book, *Voyage de l'Arabie Heureuse*, Amsterdam 1716. Interestingly Willem Blaeu's Atlas 1630-1662 did not show Mocha while Guillaume Delisle's map in 1700 did show it.

It is certain that raw beans were chewed for centuries in Ethiopia and the Yemen. At some time in the 1400s, a drink called coffee, made from the *qishr* or flesh of the bean, began to be drunk in the Yemen. Prior to 1400, the Arab word *qahwa* could mean either wine or coffee and there is no certainty that coffee is being referred to when the word appears in Arab texts. Hattox, an American writer, considers that a potion made from the *qishr* seems to have gained popularity in the mid-1400s.[2] There are strong references to the *Sufis*, a mystical religious sect, using coffee in some form for devotional purposes and also references to the consumption of coffee by the general public.

The drink was made from the husks of the coffee cherry which had been lightly roasted in an earthenware dish. The sweetness of the *qishr* - concentrated by roasting in the same way that dried sultana grapes are sweeter than fresh grapes - would have produced a sweet drink. The sweetness of the pulp and the caffeine would have made it the early equivalent of a hot cola drink. Perhaps the beans were not used or roasted because the heat reached in earthenware roasting dishes would have been insufficient to achieve pyrolysis or the transformation into roasted coffee; however they could have been used in a semi-roasted form.

Possible Chinese Influences on Qishr Drinking

There may well have been a connection between the drinking of coffee and the long distance cruises of the Chinese Admiral, Cheng Ho, who led seven expeditions to the Red Sea entrance and the African coast between 1405 and 1433, when the Chinese withdrew from foreign trade.[3] Admiral Cheng Ho took tea with him on his voyages and on the Emperor's order gave tea as a gift to friendly countries.[4] The Yemeni ruler acknowledged receiving rich gifts from China and must surely have been impressed with the habits of a highly civilised culture which suddenly arrived in his territory. As a traditional drink of hospitality, it was probably offered by Cheng Ho to the local rulers who saw it as a sophisticated part of life. The real catalyst was most likely seeing the tea made as part of a ritual and being able to watch it made properly. There was little use in knowing that tea existed if you could not make it properly. There are stories that when tea was first introduced into England the leaves were stewed

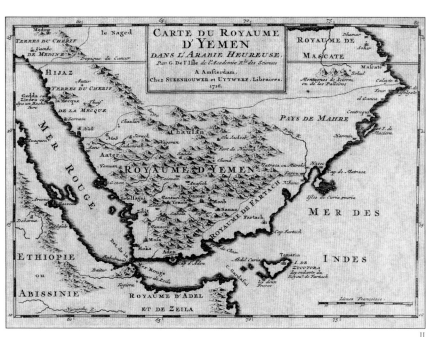

The Port of Mocha. (*The Mirror*, Saturday April 16, 1831).

and eaten like cabbage. It is possible that the tea that Cheng Ho brought was brick-tea, a moulded brick of compressed tea leaves. This was then grated and boiled, which was very similar to the method that the Arabs later developed for making coffee. The cessation of trade with China may have left a vacuum for a stimulant drink and coffee or *qishr* was used as the substitute.

The Chinese can be seen to have shown tea to the local inhabitants and the idea of a hot recreational drink would have been novel. Tea had been known to Arab traders since the ninth century.[5] However, for the Arabs to see the Chinese drinking tea, which contains the stimulant caffeine, for pleasure and not as a medicine, might have given legitimacy to the idea of drinking coffee, which they probably also knew to be a stimulant. The Arabs may have adopted the porcelain drinking cups that the Chinese used for tea. The coincidence of time and place in the arrival of the Chinese and the start of coffee drinking in similar cups by the Arabs, suggests that there was a direct connection. On the other hand, the large dishes more recently used by Persians and northern Muslims for drinking tea probably derived from the trade with China via the land route of the Silk Road. The same size cups were used by the Turks in the sixteenth century for drinking coffee. Certainly in the Yemen today *qishr* is drunk from large cups.

Qishr Spreads North to Mecca

Hattox continues that *qishr* for chewing was known in Rey in Mecca twenty years before *qahwa* for drinking, and that by 1511 coffee was well established in Mecca and was being consumed by Sufis in the Yemeni quarter of Cairo at approximately the same time.[6] Jaziri, who made the comments on the Mecca situation talks about the beans and the husks being boiled to make *qahwa*.[7] It can be assumed from this that roasted coffee was not being used at this time, or at least not in religious circles in the Yemen and Mecca. In 1511 in Mecca, coffee drinking was banned by religious leaders.

The fact that *qishr* has a limited life leads to the possibility that it was used only in cities close to the Yemen and that in more distant cities the beans in a lightly roasted form were used instead.

THE OTTOMAN TURKS EXPORT COFFEE FROM THE YEMEN

In 1517 the Ottoman Turks captured Cairo from the Mamelukes and also came to the Yemen but did not occupy it. This was part of the Turks' attempt to exclude the Portuguese and the spread of Christianity from Ottoman territories. In the same year they captured Damascus which became the departure point for the annual pilgrimage to Mecca, the *Haj*. The Ottoman Turks would not have been in the Yemen except for an event which took place over 100 years previously. In 1387, Philippa of Lancaster, the daughter of John of Gaunt, married John of Portugal. Their fifth son, Henry the Navigator, was very involved in this Portuguese opening up of the East and the subsequent spreading of Christianity to the East.[8]

In 1536 the Ottomans occupied the Yemen and very soon afterwards the export of coffee from the Yemen became important.[9] The presence of coffee in Cairo was mentioned in the early 1500s, later in 1532 to 1533 as a coffee drink and again in

Above: A Turkish coffee pot - *Cezve*. The broad base acts as a trap for the grounds when pouring. These are often called *ibriqs* in other countries. The Italian word for a coffee pot, *bricco*, derives from *ibriq*.

Left: A Turkish coffee pot - *Ibriq*. The bulbous base acts as a trap for the grounds when pouring.

1539 when coffee houses were banned temporarily.

In 1792 Carsten Niebuhr stated that the favourite drink of the Yemenite Arabs was prepared from the husks of coffee beans, slightly roasted and pounded. The drink was called *Kahwe* (coffee), or more commonly *Kisher* (which is obviously *qishr*).[10] Niebuhr described the *qishr* as being slightly roasted which is the same as today.[11] The method of producing *qishr* in the Yemen according to Ukers is for the cherries to be partly dried in the sun and then hulled between two small stones.[12] The beans and husks were then separated and sorted, but in the period prior to 1536 before the beans alone were needed for export, they may not have been separated. The toasted husks were boiled for thirty minutes and the drink was called *qishr* or Sultan or Sultana coffee. *Qishr* coffee is still available in the markets of the Yemen and is very widely used.

Coffee all over the Gulf region and around the Yemen to this day is a drink made from yellow half-roasted coffee beans mixed with cardamom, a strongly flavoured, sweetish spice seed imported from India. The description of the coffee being half-roasted and yellow indicates that the coffee is very mild, with a low coffee flavour. A current formulation from Jedda in Saudi Arabia, showing the drink to be sixty per cent cardamom and forty per cent coffee, is virtually unrecognisable as coffee. No sugar is used to make this Bedouin style coffee. It is possible that sugar was used but the only references are to the contrary. Ginger is sometimes used instead of cardamom. This is totally different to the style of coffee made far to the north in Syria and Turkey. It is reasonable to assume that roasted coffee, as we know it, was not and is not common around the Yemen.

Accidentally roasted coffee beans prepared in the same way would have had a very light, grassy flavour and would not have been bitter. If the beans were roasted more darkly, then the aroma would have been intensified as would the need for a sweetener, when the beans were boiled. Almost certainly it was the discovery of the heavenly smell of the roasted coffee which eventually encouraged people to find a way to use it. The lack of steel roasting dishes may have meant that it was impossible to actually roast coffee in the Yemen.

The Ottoman occupation of the Yemen from 1536 made a fundamental economic difference. Where products had been exported across borders by traders, there was now no border and the trade was between cities in the same country or between provinces. In these circumstances it is quite normal for the conquering country to harness the resources of the occupied territory for its own use. They apparently were interested in the by-product from the *qishr*, the beans, and traders must have known that the beans could be roasted and brewed and had a value which the Yemenis did not appreciate.

COFFEE ROASTING BEGINS TO SPREAD

While the theory that roasted coffee was discovered accidentally when coffee bushes were used to make fires in Ethiopia or the Yemen may be correct, the evidence points to roasted coffee being first used on a noticeable scale not where the trees grew and the branches burnt on fires, but far to the north in Syria, or perhaps Turkey or Egypt. Coffee roasting as a process was probably first practised in a place such as Damascus which had the relatively high level of technology necessary to make steel roasting dishes. Damascus steel was at one time famous and steel would transfer a higher roasting temperature to the beans than would be possible with earthenware dishes. The transition from drinking a *qishr* drink to a drink based on roasted coffee seems to have taken place without

Above: A wooden box with two compartments for coffee and sugar. Anatolia, Turkey - 19th century.

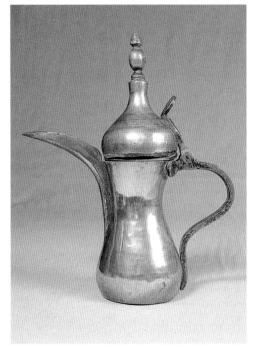

Right: The pot with a long thin spout from Syria is known as a *Dellel* or *Della*, or sometimes as a Baghdad boiler.

mention. The first roasting of beans was possibly an attempt to emulate the flavour of *qishr* and by roasting lightly a similar drink could be made. It was coincidental that the coffee grinder was developed in Syria in the first half of the sixteenth century.[13] This is consistent with roasted coffee being used in Syria because a coffee grinder needs crisp roasted coffee for grinding, not the soft texture of unroasted beans. It is not conclusive evidence, because it was most likely preceded by the use of mortar and pestle for grinding. There was probably a development from lightly roasted coffee beans, coarsely ground and boiled, to a darker roast coffee more finely ground and boiled, but there does not appear to be any mention of this in the literature nor any convincing physical evidence.

COFFEE REACHES ISTANBUL

Coffee appeared in Turkey in 1543 and became so popular that it was banned by religious leaders.[14] An edict against coffee during the *Haj* was issued by the Ottoman Sultan in Istanbul in 1544. It was possibly bean coffee but may have been *qishr* coffee. The first coffee house was set up in Damascus in 1530 and in Aleppo in 1532.[15] In 1554 Shems from Damascus and Hakkan from Aleppo opened a coffee shop in Istanbul. This reference to the opening of a coffee shop is very important because it probably indicates the transfer of the technology necessary to roast, grind and brew coffee. *Qishr* brewing should by now have been a fairly commonplace practice requiring no great skills, but brewing roasted coffee required a roasting dish and a grinder and a special pot to brew the coffee. The occasional mention of the special person, the *kahveci* in Turkish, to prepare the coffee, indicates that it was not something that could be simply prepared at home. Coffee must have been roasted in Turkey by 1570 because the

Turkish historian Pichiveli described the Dervishes in Istanbul in that year maintaining that roasted coffee was a sort of charcoal and forbidden by law.[16] The reference to charcoal indicates that the coffee must have been dark roasted and is the first clear unequivocal reference to coffee being roasted. There is no mention that it was Turkish coffee, the name given to the roasted coffee drink served in small cups with a lot of sugar. It was probably a brew of dilute coffee in a large cup.

Leonhard Rauwolf was in Aleppo in 1573 and ten years later, in 1583, he published his remarks on a drink he had observed there, that was almost as black as ink and called coffee.[17] In the same year 1573 Costantino Garzoni, the Venetian Ambassador in Constantinople, reported to Venice the drinking of a black water every morning.[18] This was the very first written report about coffee to appear in Europe. The first report of coffee from Cairo was in 1579 by Hans Jacob Breuning and in 1581 by Salomon Schweigger when he described a black/brown drink and again from Constantinople in 1585 by Gianfrancesco

A coffee set on a tray showing the *Ibriq*, the small cup called a *Finjan* and the metal holder, the *Zarf*.

'Illustration of a Cafe at Constantinople, 1831, with the customers Indulging in tiny cups of coffee, which is generally drunk by the poorer classes, not only without milk, but without sugar.'
The Penny Magazine,
London, June 16, 1838,
p.229.

Morosini to the Venetian Senate.[19] Coffee had been transformed from an alleged stimulant associated with a religious sect to a commercial product widespread among the people at large. From 1546 to 1549 Pierre Belon wrote about Egypt but did not mention coffee. He is considered to have been a very precise observer and the absence of any mention of coffee is sometimes given as an indication that it was not there at that time.[20] By the same token the fact that Marco Polo did not mention tea in China is no proof that it did not exist there. It did.

TURKISH COFFEE

There are three things which have their names connected with Turkey - Turkish baths, Turkish Delight and Turkish coffee. The last two have a very large sugar component as does *qishr* itself.

The cover illustration on Hattox's book of a Turkish coffee house in the mid sixteenth century is interesting because the cups used are much larger than expected, possibly coconut shells and certainly larger than a tiny cup as used for Turkish coffee today. It is possible that the large cup was used for making *qishr* coffee and bean coffee was initially used in the same cup. The size of the cup is basically the same size as illustrated in Dufour's book of 1685 where a Turk in a turban is holding a large cup with thumb on top and forefinger underneath.

In 1522 the Turks captured Rhodes, and in 1573 Cyprus, both countries where sugar was a major crop. While coffee in Turkey may be made without sugar, the coffee with sugar is the most famous. It would have been natural to add sugar to try and equate the light sweetness of *qishr* coffee. The excessive use of sugar and honey in the Middle East to make cakes indicates a passion for levels of sweetness not normally known in Western Europe. The same passion for an excessively sweet coffee drink led the Turks eventually to make a very sweet drink that could only be consumed in small quantities. As more and more sugar was added to the bitter coffee drink, so the size of the cup became smaller. This is in line with very sweet liqueur drinks being served in tiny glasses. Johann Vesling, a German botanist, mentioned that in Cairo in 1628 sugar was used with the coffee, but this can hardly be

the first time it was used.[21] It is therefore certain that coffee with sugar was being consumed before coffee was introduced to Marseilles in 1644, although there is no evidence to confirm whether sweetened or unsweetened coffee was the most popular.

There is some uncertainty about the size of the cup in Turkey. All the early paintings and drawings show a large cup while the words talk about a small cup. The idea of the large cup is confirmed by the Topkapi Palace Museum in Turkey which says that from visual documents, Turkish coffee after being boiled in large cauldrons, was drunk in big cups without sugar and that small European imported cups were used at home from the beginning of the eighteenth century. There is a collection of large cups in the Municipal Museum of Istanbul.[22] It may be that because of the high cost of sugar only the wealthy were able to use sugar and they used small cups at home with sugar, whereas the poor drank large cups of diluted coffee which they drank on the streets, without sugar. The situation may be similar to beer drinking - large glasses are served in taverns while smaller glasses are served at home. I feel that large cups predominated in the early years and that there was a slow change until the nineteenth century when sugar became cheaper and everybody could afford to drink sweetened Turkish coffee as we now know it, in small cups. In the south-east of Turkey, large cups are still being used.

THE REFINING OF TURKISH COFFEE

I have tried to grind coffee to powder in a mortar and pestle and it is not easy. The grounds are largely coarse, with a few fines. I have been told by a Greek friend that to make powder coffee, the grounds must be repeatedly sieved through a fine silk scarf. Very precise machining is required to produce a grinder with a close enough fit to grind coffee to powder. The fact that most European metal hand grinders were not capable of fine grinding and that Turkish technology was further behind suggests that a metal Turkish grinder was not generally introduced until late, perhaps well into the eighteenth century or even later. What little evidence there is suggests that coffee in Turkey started as a coffee made from coarse grounds, crushed in a mortar and pestle and served in large cups, with or without sugar.

Dufour in 1688 said that coffee from the Far East was coarser than the coffee in France. Stone mills could have ground the coffee to powder, but there is little if any mention of them. Reference is mostly made to mortars and pestles.

Techniques were eventually developed to crush the coffee to powder, and hand mills were introduced. Increasingly, sugar was added and the cup size was reduced, until Turkish coffee as we know it today appeared. A multitude of different practices throughout the Ottoman Empire at different times make it extremely difficult to know

Some early illustrations. Turkish coffee was originally drunk in large cups.

KH   KH

1. IBRIK (EWER); 2. LAYAN (BASIN); 3. ZARF AND FINJAN (COFFEE-CUP AND HOLDER); 4. JESBA (SAUCEPAN FOR BOILING COFFEE.)

Note that the ewer is called an *ibriq* and the *Jesba* or *Cezveh* [CW] is for boiling the coffee. Often an *ibriq* in this form is depicted as the coffee maker. Turkey - 1840s.

when Turkish coffee had its origin and when it supplanted coarsely crushed coffee served in large cups. In 1834 an English journal stated that, in the East, coffee was drunk without either sugar or milk and that it was unpalatable in that form.[23]

Charles White wrote a book on his experiences in Constantinople in 1844 and he included some rare first-hand information about how coffee was ground and brewed at that time in the Levant.

The mode of preparing coffee is simple. The bruised or ground beans are thrown into a brass or copper saucepan; sufficient water, scalding hot, is poured upon them, and, after being allowed to simmer for a few seconds, the liquid is poured into small cups without refining or straining. Those who have overcome the first introduction prefer it to that made after the French fashion, whereby the aroma is lost or deteriorated.[24]

He described the mills for pounding the beans:
...consist of three distinct horizontal wheels, each worked by two horses. Each wheel acts upon a set of levers, that turn a long cylinder, armed with semi-circular pegs, placed at regular intervals. These pegs, acting like the teeth of a barrel organ, rise in succession, and lift up an equal number of iron pestles, which are elevated about two feet, and then the pegs, revolving backward, allow the pestles to fall upon the beans strewed in a long stone trough. The powder, when sufficiently bruised, is swept out, and conveyed to an adjoining chamber to be weighed and sifted. The three mills pound an average of 2,750 lbs. per day.[25]

He concluded by saying that there were approximately 2,500 coffee shops in Constantinople.

COFFEE TRANSFERS FROM THE SUGAR COUNTRIES TO THE MILK COUNTRIES

The movement of coffee from Turkey and Arabia to Europe was very significant in the historical development of coffee, in that it passed from a group of people of Mediterranean and Near Eastern origin who were unable to digest milk, to Europeans, who could.[26] Lactose is milk sugar, and for digestion to take place the enzyme lactase needs to be present in the gut. Approximately seventy per cent of the world's population suffers from lactase deficiency, in particular Mediterranean peoples, Arabs, Greek Cypriots and Southern Italians. The Central Dairy in Milan offers special milk, Accadi, which has been partly hydrolysed to minimise the problem.[27] Attempts to digest milk by those with lactase deficiency would have resulted in digestive tract distress. This meant that the Turks were restricted to drinking coffee without milk, whereas Europeans could, and eventually did drink coffee with milk.

From the two ends of Europe, there eventually developed two totally different ways to brew this new commodity - either filtered in Northern Europe or espresso style in Southern Europe. The intolerance to milk may have even caused cappuccinos to be smaller in Italy so that milk intolerance problems could be minimised.

A tin pot with three legs. The bulbous shape is reminiscent of the Turkish *ibriq*. This style of pot can be seen from the early days of the eighteenth century. France.

A pewter pot. Germany - 1790.

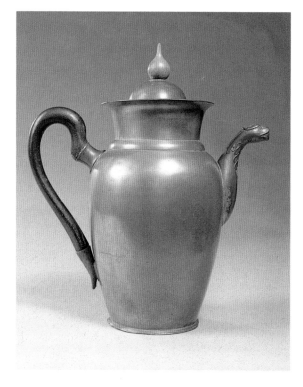

Right: An early pewter pot - Germany.

Far Right: An early tall pot for use without filters. Germany.

SUGAR

There is sound reason to believe that sugar was the catalyst which caused the explosion of the use of tea and coffee in Europe. Both are hot drinks which can dissolve sugar.

Sugar in tea and coffee has a direct and strong sweetening effect in comparison to the indirect and weak sweetening effect of sugar in a cake, where the sweetness is much less apparent. The effect is similar to the direct sensation of chutney on the side of a plate versus the same proportion dispersed through the cooked dish.

Sugarcane was native to Polynesia, and via India, China and Persia, it reached all the countries under Arab rule. The Arabs developed the technology to refine it and may have used it in small amounts with coffee. The limiting factor was probably the very high price - in the year 1100 sugar in England sold for its own weight in silver. In the Arab countries the Sultans drew large incomes and levied taxes on it.[28]

Coffee was introduced to Venice in 1615 and Holland in 1616. The first source showing that sugar was added to coffee in Cairo was printed in 1625.[29] The date is significant because it is well after 1512 when Spanish Santo Domingo started supplying sugar to Europe which may have caused prices to fall in the Ottoman Empire with consequently increased consumption.[30] By 1526 Brazil was shipping sugar to Europe and was to be the important exporter.[31] Coffee without sugar may not have been accepted by the west, but as a sweet drink, it was very successful. Even to this day Greeks order their coffee and indicate to the waiter the amount of sugar to be used. There is some evidence that coffee was drunk black in both England and Turkey in the early years and that adding sugar later became the habit. Bitter drinks

are not very popular today and there is little reason to imagine that they should have been relatively more popular in other centuries when sugar was becoming more readily available. It is difficult to establish to what extent sugar was used with both tea and coffee because there was very little written about it. Even today's recipe books discuss how to make tea and coffee but rarely mention the addition of sugar.

British sugar arrived from Barbados in 1655 and this was the beginning of the British sugar trade. English consumption of sugar rose quickly. From 1660 to 1753 it increased from 1000 to 104,000 hogsheads (each about 54 Imperial gallons).[32] The price of sugar fell by seventy per cent from 1645 to 1680.[33]

COFFEE REACHES
SEVENTEENTH CENTURY EUROPE

It was the roasted coffee drink of the Turks which was introduced into Europe, not the *qishr* coffee drink made from toasted husks as drunk by the *Sufis*.

After the battle of Lepanto in 1571, the myth about Turkish invincibility disappeared and it was possible to make closer observations about the Ottoman system. There was much more contact with Turks, and Levantine merchants began to frequent the streets of Venice. Venice concluded a peace treaty with the Turks and opened an embassy in Constantinople. Little by little, coffee became available in Venice in the same form as it appeared in Constantinople, through coffee shops. The traditional date for the arrival of coffee in Venice is 1615, the first major shipment was in 1624 and the first coffee shop opened in 1645.[34]

It was two years after the Lepanto battle that Leonhard Rauwolf made his voyage into the

Ottoman Empire.[35] The Venetian Ambassador's report to Venice, the first about coffee to reach Europe, preceded the publication of Rauwolf's book by ten years. By 1583 English merchants, closely followed by Dutch merchants, began trading in the Mediterranean for the first time and were able to purchase silks and spices direct instead of through the Venetians. Trade in coffee followed later. Charles de Lecluse saw coffee beans in Holland in 1596, the first time they had ever been seen north of the Alps.[36] It is almost certain that there were unrecorded importations into Europe prior to these dates.

The original images of Turks being menacing and war-like changed to insinuations that coffee was causing the men to be little interested in affairs of commerce or the opposite sex. Coffee was openly blamed for causing impotency and sterility. These ideas lasted into the seventeenth century. It seemed to Western observers that the Turkish men displayed growing effeminacy and that there were homosexual tendencies. They drank coffee exclusively in male company, and in public baths where there was a rigid separation of the sexes.[37] The fact that Murad the Third fathered one hundred and two children was conveniently ignored.

The panorama changed decisively towards the end of the seventeenth century with the Venetian victory in the battle of Candia or Heraklion in Crete, the apparent domestication of the Muslim world and the flowering of Turkish literature.[38] In 1683 another coffee shop opened in Venice and coffee seemed to lose its Turkish identity and to assume its own existence in Venetian life, becoming part of a vigorous intellectual scene in coffee houses which lasted for decades. The number of coffee houses in Venice increased from 108 in 1761 to 311 at the end of the century or one for every five hundred inhabitants. Venice was very much the coffee capital in Italy in the early years.[39]

Italy was very influential in French gastronomy, especially in the south. In 1644 Pierre de la Roque introduced coffee to Marseilles together with all the necessary equipment for roasting, grinding, brewing and serving in the little porcelain dishes. By 1660 coffee was available in shops and in 1671 a coffee house opened which was frequented by sailors, merchants and travellers to the Levant.[40] In 1669 the Turkish Ambassador in Paris offered coffee to guests and coffee became part of a new exotic and snobbish life.[41] Coffee spread through the hinterland around Marseilles and eventually through all the provinces. Books were very influential in spreading knowledge and ideas. Dufour's book about coffee was published in Lyons, a city much influenced by Italy. Coffee became the centre of medical controversy and the strangest ideas permeated society. A prime example is the citation in the book by F. Aignan in Paris in 1696 where he states that coffee from the

Levant, prepared with sugar in the same way that you would drink it by mouth, can be used as an enema. He continued that it worked wonders, sweetening and refreshing the lower bowel and making the complexion fresher. He concluded that it was a real delight for women.[42] Cadet-de-Vaux in 1806 recommended its use in the same way in the treatment of some cases of apoplexy and sleepiness.[43]

The growth in coffee consumption can be seen from the following French importation figures:
1700: 600,000 kilograms from Arabia via Egypt.
1730: The beginning of the competition from the French possessions in the West Indies which caused the price to halve.
1737: 1,000,000 kilograms from the Antilles.
1785: 7,000,000 kilograms from the Antilles.[44]

There were two things which transformed coffee into a highly acceptable beverage. One was the idea of coffee as a social drink and the second was the addition of sugar. When coffee was introduced into each European country, sugar was introduced with it.

Pasqua Rosée, who had the first coffee house in England in 1652, introduced the new drink with the advertisement, 'The Vertue of the Coffee Drink'. The claims were nothing like advertisements of today.

The quality of this Drink is cold & dry: and though it be a Dryer, yet it neither heats, nor inflames more than a hot Posset (a hot alcoholic milk drink) ... It is excellent to prevent and cure the Dropsy, Gout and Scurvy ... better than any other Drying Drink for ... running humors ... as the Kings evil & cet.[45]

In the same pamphlet the powder was described as being:
boiled up with Spring water, and about half a pint of it to be drunk...

The introduction of coffee to Germany seems to have been recorded in a letter from the firm of van Snuiten in Amsterdam, in May 1637. With the despatch of a sample of coffee to the firm of Hervannos in Merseburg near Leipzig came instructions to grind the coffee finely and then boil it. The next letter from van Snuiten, in September 1637, complained about hearing rudeness in exchange for goodwill and also about receiving an account for sixteen Groschen for a purgative for all the Hervannos staff who had become sick after drinking the coffee. The letter also recorded that the Burgers of Leipzig must have had better taste than the Burgers of Merseburg because they had enjoyed the five bales sent to them.[46]

In 1665 an Ottoman embassy opened in Vienna and there were increasing references in the Vienna Archives to the private consumption of coffee. This was many years before 1683 when legend tells of Kolschitzky who brought coffee to Vienna where Ukers says it was unknown at that time.[47]

It is not really clear from any source exactly

how coffee was prepared in different countries or what it tasted like. The size of the cup is sometimes large and sometimes small. It can only be assumed that the coffee in some way resembled that made in the Turkish manner, whatever that was at the time. There is no date given anywhere for the change from large cup size in Turkey to small cup size with sugar or Turkish coffee as we know it today. The European coffee trade would develop into three main branches: the German one based on filtered coffee, the Italian based on strong espresso and the French based on milk coffee.

COFFEE REPLACES ALCOHOLIC DRINKS

The only hot drinks in Europe until the arrival of coffee, tea and cocoa were soups and potions. Ale, mead and wine were the usual drinks and there is a good case for saying that Europe was in an alcoholic haze for decades until the new hot drinks stimulated everyday life. In the seventeenth century, wine was replaced by beer as Germany's national drink.[48]

Walter Rumsey in 1657 defended coffee on the grounds that,

whereas formerly apprentices and clerks used to take their morning's draught in ale, beer, or wine, which, by the dizziness they cause in the brain, made many unfit for business, they use now to play the goodfellows in this wakeful and civil drink.[49]

In northern Europe, ale and beer were the mainstays of the daily diet and the woman of the house made beer as naturally as she baked bread. The daily consumption of beer per head, including children, in the second half of the seventeenth century, was an unbelievable three litres. Around this time, beer soup, a forgotten dish today, was the normal breakfast. It was very nourishing.[50]

In 1650 Oxford had 350 ale houses.[51] Wallenstein's troops had a daily food ration of two pounds of bread, a pound of meat and two quarts of beer. Protestant reformers were very much against the high alcohol consumption and so coffee made a timely entrance, as an alcohol substitute, making their job much easier.

ARAB STYLE TO EUROPEAN STYLE COFFEE

Why do Turks and Arabs drink coffee with grounds in the cup while most Europeans prefer clear coffee? There is nothing written on the subject, but there are logical reasons for differing approaches. Throughout the Middle East and even in Africa today, it is quite common to cook on small braziers in the streets or in huts or tents. The small Turkish coffee pot was well adapted for this and for cooking on the heat of the ashes of a fire in a tent. The very first coffee pots were simple pots made of copper or brass and there was nothing novel about them - they were just pot boilers. Eventually a long spout was added for pouring coffee accurately into small cups. Brass was the most common material and being soft, it was

suitable for low heat but not for the high heat of the European stove.

In Europe, most cooking was done indoors in fireplaces when chimneys became common in the fourteenth century. The fireplaces provided cooking heat as well as warmth for a house in a cold climate. These fireplaces used large logs for heating the room and these would have been unsuitable for balancing small Turkish pots. It was common for food to be cooked in big pots suspended over the flames and for hot water to be available most of the time. This meant that water was normally boiled in these suspended pots and not directly on the fire, as in Arabia. A German illustrated vase from 1661 shows water being boiled in a kettle on a stove and the coffee being served in a separate pot at the table.[52] Early European pots and Turkish pots were similar.

The different methods of cooking eventually meant that two different ways of making coffee evolved. The use of copper and brass for cooking implements was much less common in Europe than in Arabia and Turkey. For Europe to have adopted the Turkish way of making coffee, the coffee importers would have had to import the Turkish coffee pots and instruct customers in their use. They probably did not, and Europeans adapted the preparation of a new product to local materials and local sources of heat. As a result the European coffee pots today have very little similarity to their Turkish and Arabian counterparts. The European pot which evolved had a broader spout which was ideal for pouring into the larger cups used for making long warming coffee drinks.

FILTERING

In Europe, cider, ale and wine were very common drinks in the Middle Ages and their production involved straining and filtering, which was easily adapted to coffee brewing. As alcoholic drinks were forbidden under Muslim law, these techniques were less well known and coffee was not filtered. Coffee arrived in Europe at a time when Europe was technologically much more advanced than Arabia.

The combination of the availability of boiling water, filtering devices and a desire for a large cup meant that European coffee brewing developed along a completely different path to that in the Levant. Coffee making was adapted to local conditions just as tea making had been - from the use of small Chinese pots and dishes to using large teapots and large cups.

There is no first date for filtering coffee although one reference gives the year 1670 and another 1662 in England for the introduction of the first filter coffee machines, either as biggins, which were pots with filter sacks, or as filters with filter paper.[53] What can be said for certain is that the process of adaptation was already under way. Europeans wanted to make coffee without buying a special pot and they made do with what they

KH

A metal filter. Filters have existed for over three thousand years. Egypt - 13th century, B.C.

had. It would be easy to imagine that the metal filter is something very new. There is a filter in the Egyptian tomb of Kha, dating from the thirteenth century BC which could pass for a coffee filter made three millenia later.[54]

THE EMERGENCE OF EARLY TECHNOLOGY

There are two early French books full of information about coffee and surprisingly they show that the seeds of later ideas already existed. M. de Blegny in 1687 has illustrations of coffee pots sitting on spirit warmers and discusses merchants who add a little new coffee to old grounds to make a terrible brew. The implication was that the coffee was made by pouring boiling water over the grounds. All the different ways to make coffee were basically very simple.

Dufour, in his book *A New and Curious Treatise About Coffee, Tea and Chocolate,* (in French) which was published in many editions and languages after 1671, discusses roasting with the intent of losing less aroma. The very idea of not only roasting coffee but enclosing the coffee so as to prevent aroma loss was at the heart of future developments. Aroma loss was to become the holy grail for hordes of inventors the world over, who would reap fame and fortune trying to make coffee taste as good as it smelled.

The illustration at the beginning of Dufour's 1688 edition shows a small, round coffee roaster,

heated over charcoal and made of tin-plate, which was also used to make coffee pots. Dufour describes the grinding in the Far East as being 'a little large and in France fine enough to go through a fine sieve'. The coffee was to be kept fresh in a sack of greased leather. The consequences to the flavour can only be imagined.

Dufour is careful to note that the coffee must not be boiled and even gives detailed instructions on how to drink a hot drink from a cup without burning yourself. The positions of the tongue and lips were all-important.[55]

You must not drink the coffee, but suck it in as hot as you can bear it: the hotter you drink it, the nicer it is. In order not to burn yourself, you must not put your tongue in the cup, but you keep the lip of the cup between your tongue and your lower and upper lips and then you suck in, drop by drop. [English translation.]

How much we take for granted. The fact that a book had to describe how to drink from a cup is an indication of just what a novelty coffee was. Up to that point, liquids had been drunk from dishes with spoons if they were hot, or, if they were cool, from mugs and glasses. Cups did not have handles - they were like bowls. Refrigeration was unknown and beer and ale must have been drunk warm as in England until recently. It is hard, if not impossible, to imagine just what a revolution in habits coffee, tea and chocolate must have wrought on seventeenth century Europe.

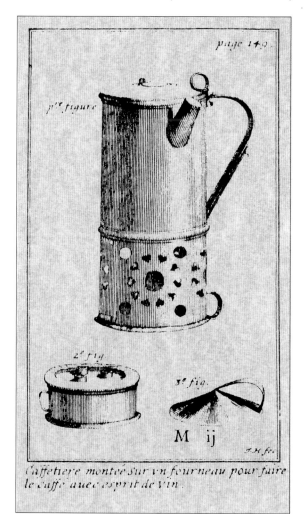

Far Left: A pot with spirit warmer. Illustrated in Blegny's book. France - 1687.

Left: Four pots. France - 1687.

Sugar was used to sweeten the potentially bitter brew and Dufour writes about the Parisians using so much that the coffee became a black-water syrup.

The English were not so interested in technology and played a limited role in the centuries ahead. Perhaps they just did not understand the problems. A tract published in London in 1682 states, 'as for the manner of preparing coffee, it is so easy and so commonly known, that we need not mention it'.[56] This lack of interest was reflected in world-wide condemnation of their coffee in the centuries ahead. Dufour had already written his detailed analysis of the subject in Lyons. The French interest was to continue for the next two centuries.

COFFEE CHANGES MEDICAL AND SOCIAL ATTITUDES

The arrival of coffee in Europe caused not only changes in what people drank, but also in practices and reasoning related to health and social attitudes.

The Curative Properties of Coffee

The subject of coffee and health must have been a non-stop source of confusion as coffee was reputed to have all sorts of powers. Arguments have raged over the centuries about every possible cure coffee could effect. Dufour mentions *café au lait* as an unbeatable cure for maladies of the chest, a cure which he says first came from a German doctor named Neuhosius: 'perhaps it was in imitation of the Chinese who gave tea with milk to Consumptives who take it as a feast'.[57] In general, Dufour is in favour of the medicinal powers of coffee with milk. Milk does in fact act as a lining on the stomach, slowing down the absorption of caffeine.

Dr. Lemery of Paris is quoted in Richard Bradley's book published in 1721 as stating that coffee 'comforts the brain, and dries up crudities in the stomach'[58] The book continues:

> Mr. Ray mentions it to be of singular use and efficacy to such as are afflicted with Pains in the head, Vertigo, Lethargy and Coughs: it has a good effect on cold and moist constitutions; but on the other hand, he disallows the use of it to such as are paralytic, and likewise such as are troubled with Melancholy vapours, or have hot brains. Other authors assert, it cures consumptions, Swooning fits, and the rickets; and that it helps the digestion, rarefies the blood, suppresses Vapours, gives life and gaiety to the spirits, prevents sleepiness after eating, provokes Urine and the Catamena. The Arabian women drink this liquor constantly in their periodical Visits and find a good effect from it. It contracts the bowels and confirms the tone of the Parts, being drank after Victuals, provided it is fresh made.

At the same time other books gave precisely the opposite advice. The problem was that medicine at that time was based on 'humours'

which had their origins in Greek and Turkish medicine. What to do with this new product which did not fit into the known categories of things? A healthy body is a wet body, with plenty of fluids. A sick body is a dry body. The problem was whether to consider coffee as a cold or hot thing, as a dry or moist thing.

Both tea and coffee were good for health because they used boiling water which improved the water drawn from wells and other sources. The quality of water in many crowded cities, especially London, was downright dangerous with open drains carrying sewage, polluting wells and spreading diseases such as cholera. The cholera epidemic, which arrived in England in 1831 and lasted for more than twenty years, must have been mitigated by the rapidly increasing use of tea and coffee from the 1830s. However, there seems to be no mention of the beneficial use of tea and coffee during this period.

Coffee Additives and Substitutes

Chicory is mentioned in Dufour's book as a substance which refreshes in its own right but not as an admixture to coffee. The use of chicory with coffee was to be a feature of French coffee drinking for the next three centuries as was *café au lait*. It is important to note that chicory had been known in Europe for two thousand years. It is attractive to imagine that ideas permeate through a whole society and change it - perhaps Dufour's book was the catalyst for *café au lait*. Hot milk is essentially sweet and the addition of chicory which is burnt and bitter makes for a more strongly flavoured drink. The chicory lowered the price of the coffee per kilogram and must have been irresistible to the legendary meanness of the French peasants. Dufour even gave detailed instructions on how to buy coffee. He notes that:

> Some people add by up to more than a third a mixture of burnt bread, toasted haricot beans and broad beans to the coffee and you have real trouble to detect it. A considerable and easy gain is a dangerous trap in a century like ours. Those lazy people who buy coffee which has not been roasted in front of them, or from people they don't know well, or buy at the lowest price expose themselves to the risk of being duped.[59]
> [English translation.]

...and this in 1688, so soon after the introduction of coffee to Europe.

The Social and Sexual Upheaval

The impact on life in England and the Continent from this new beverage is hard to imagine. It changed the whole way of life in the big cities. The next three centuries saw the establishment of coffee houses and cafes which became the centres of business, intellectual and musical life in all the major cities of Europe. Coffee, tea and sugar were imported commodities and stimulated commerce around the major ports.

The effect can be judged from three pamphlets

which were published soon after coffee arrived in England. From them it is obvious that the way of life both for tavern owners and women, who were not allowed into the new coffee shops, was undergoing large upheavals. The whole western world was changing from a society which had no hot drinks to one which now had hot coffee, tea and chocolate.

Three Old English Pamphlets

In many books about coffee you will see the front pages of these three pamphlets from the seventeenth century. The titles are intriguing, but I have never seen the contents printed anywhere, which makes me feel that all the comments about them have been based on a process of osmosis. The contents are titillating indeed and deserve to be read. They are evidence of the huge change in social behaviour brought about by the introduction of coffee to a beer-swilling society.[60]

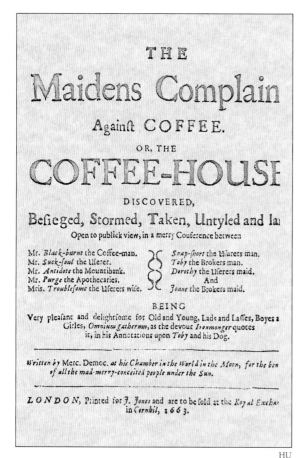

The first pamphlet is *THE MAIDENS COM-PLAINT AGAINST COFFEE, OR THE COFFEE-HOUSE DISCOVERED, BESIEGED, STORMED, TAKEN, UNTYLED AND LAID OPEN TO PUBLICK VIEW.* It was written in 1663 by 'Merc. Democ. at his Chamber in the World in the Moon, for the benefit of all the mad merry-conceited people under the Sun'. The World in the Moon does not appear as a coffee house in Bryant Lillywhite's excellent book of London Coffee Houses. Perhaps Merc. Democ. is alluding to the fact that he is a lunatic. The following passage is my abbreviated, modern English version of the pamphlet.

Following some banter between Mr. Blackburnt (the coffeeman), Mr. Suck-soul (the userer), Mr. Antidote (the Mountebank - a charlatan), Mr. Purge (the apothecary), Mrs. Troublesome (the userer's wife), Snapshort (the userer's man) and Toby (the Broker's man) - Dorothy (the userer's maid) and Joane (the Broker's maid) come into the coffee shop.

DOROTHY - Honest Joane, how fares it with you these hard times?

JOANE - Worse than ever I expected; for I believe I shall never enjoy any comfort from our man Snapshort since he went with my master to the coffee house, he is so dry as a kix [a dry, hollow stalk] that damned liquor will shorten his life and ability at least five in the fifteen.

DOROTHY - And truly our Toby is come to the same passe; for since he drank coffee, he is no more like the man he was than an apple's like an oyster. And now my master is at a coffee house, making a chimney of his noddle, where there is such an odious scent; fogh, fogh, fogh it makes my heart ake to think what a Jaques [peasant] he makes of his brains.

JOANE - I believe the Devil first invented this liquor, on purpose to plague our sex.

DOROTHY - I imagine so too, but rather than I'll dote upon a man who drinks coffee, I am resolved to lead apes in hell.

JOANE - And Devils too rather than I will think, Upon such sots as Hell-burn'd Liquors drink.

DOROTHY - I protest Joane there's a little comfort in Chocolate, but before I'll fling my self away upon such a dry horson [whore's son - mod. son of a bitch] as drinks coffee, I'll wrap my maidenhead in my smock, and fling it to the ocean to be bugger'd to death by young lobsters.

JOANE - And for my part, I'll hang my maidenhead on a windmill to be bated to death by the four winds, rather than be poisoned with the scent of old crusts, and threads of leather burned and beaten to powder of which I believe this cursed coffee is made.

TOBY - Heavens assist me! What's this, a vision! Sure it's honest Snapshort the userer's man! In faith it is he in his own likeness. How fares it with you ? I pray thee tell me what's the cause of thy sudden distemper.

SNAPSHORT - I went into a coffee house , took a dish of that hell burn'd liquor, thinking to settle my brains in their right Center. With the rattling noise of kettles, skimmers and ladles among the braziers, my brains run round as swift as a windmill, and all my joints are as numb as an old woman's troubled with the dead palsy. I went into Moorfields and took a turn in the Userers' Walk and drank a cup of good wholesome ale, with which I was revived, enlivened and restored to my memory so perfectly, that I had an account in my head of every penny due to my master since Creation.

TOBY - Since I drank coffee, twice I adventured to storm the fortress of our maid Joane, with as much eagerness as ever the Great Turk did attempt to gain Constantinople; yet all my hopes were frustrated, and I did but just fling away a night's lodging or two, to as little purpose as if I had run my head into a kitchen tub, But I'll leave coffee, for a cup of Bracket

Will fit a youngman for a Maiden's Pl——-

[Placket - an opening at the top of a skirt. The word must have had some vulgar meaning to have been censored in this context. Bracket is probably mead or ale sweetened with honey.]

SNAPSHORT - Aye - that's the liquor I fancy; for I've as great an ambition to try our maid Dorothy as ever I had to satisfy my hungry maw with a breakfast of poached eggs.

TOBY - Honest Snapshort, I'll help you to a cup of the best. Recently in Petit France I had a bottle or two and I grew so strong, that I called for a convenient room, went up the stairs, had a fresh bottle, flung her on the bed, and gave her as good a meal's meat as ever she ate since the prime of her understanding.

They proceed to have a fine meal where there is no coffee, but only good wholesome English Ale.

At one time in the late seventeenth century there were allegedly 3,000 (more likely 2,000) coffee houses in London for a population of 600,000, or one for every two to three hundred people. It is easy to imagine what this change to drinking coffee would have done to the taverns serving ales. In view of the fact that coffee is a stimulant and not like alcohol which puts you to sleep, it is unlikely that any maidens actually complained. At least the coffee was not to blame - more likely the activities in the coffee houses. It was probably a tavern owner who wrote *The Maidens Complaint Against Coffee,* because taverns were not receiving their normal patronage. The fact that women were not allowed in coffee houses was a factor in the origin of the pamphlet. This and Toby's comment about taking a woman on the premises makes me feel they may have been thinly disguised houses of ill repute. Their later decline and the growth of the English club in their stead suggests that there was a need for more respectable places.

In 1674 London saw THE WOMEN'S PETITION AGAINST COFFEE, presented to the Right Honorable the Keepers of the Liberty of Venus by a well-willer.

It was a Humble petition and address of several thousands of buxome Good-Women, languishing in extremity of Want that sheweth .. that in former times our men were justly esteemed as the ablest performers in Christendom: but to our unspeakable grief, we find of late a very great decay of that true old English vigour : our gallants being in every way so Frenchified, that they become mere Cock-sparrows, fluttering things that come on sa fa, with a world of fury but are not able to stand to it, and in the very first Charge fall down flat before us. Never did men wear greater breeches, or carry less in them of any mettle whatsoever. There was a glorious dispensation ('twas surely in the Golden Age) when lusty lads of seven or eight hundred years got sons and daughters; and we have read how a Prince of Spain was forced to make a law that Men should not repeat the Grand Kindness to their wives above NINE times in a night : but Alas! Alas! Those days are gone.

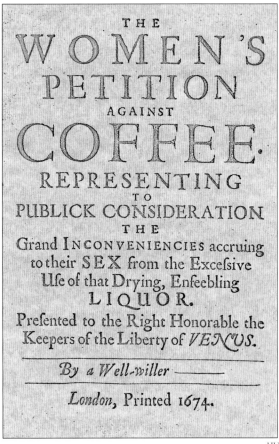

THE **WOMEN'S PETITION** AGAINST **COFFEE.** REPRESENTING TO PUBLICK CONSIDERATION THE Grand INCONVENIENCIES accruing to their SEX from the Excefsive Ufe of that Drying, Enfeebling LIQUOR. Prefented to the Right Honorable the Keepers of the Liberty of *VENUS.*

By a Well-willer ——

London, Printed 1674.

HU

For the continual sipping of this pitiful drink is enough to bewitch Men of two and twenty, and tie up the Codpiece point without a charm. It renders them that use it as lean as famine, as rivveled as Envy, or an old thin hagg over-ridden by an Incubus. They come from it with nothing moist but their snotty noses, nothing stiffe but their joints, nor standing but their ears. Nor can all the art we use revive them from this lethargy, so unfit are they for action, that like young Train-band-men when called upon for duty, their ammunition is found wanting; peradventure they present (arms), but cannot give fire, or at least do but flash in the pan, instead of doing execution.

Experience witnesses our damage, and necessity (which easily supersedes all the laws of decency) justifies our complaints : for can any woman of sense or spirit endure with patience, that when privileged by legal ceremonies, she approaches the nuptial bed, expecting a man that with sprightly embraces, should answer the vigour of her flames, she on the contrary should only meet a bedful of bones, and hug a meagre useless corpse rendered as sapless as a kix, and dryer than a pumice-stone and all this caused by tobacco and COFFEE.

Wherefore the premises being considered that our husbands may give us some other testimonies of their being men besides their beards and wearing of empty pantaloons and that they no more run the hazard of being cuckolded by dildos, we humbly pray that you our trusty patrons would improve your interest, that henceforth the Drinking of Coffee may on severe penalties be forbidden to all persons under the age of three score.

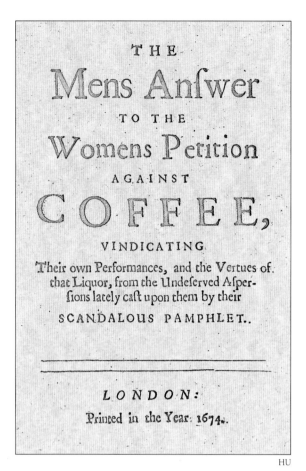

THE
Mens Anſwer
TO THE
Womens Petition
AGAINST
COFFEE,
VINDICATING

Their own Performances, and the Vertues of
that Liquor, from the Undeſerved Aſper-
ſions lately caſt upon them by their

SCANDALOUS PAMPHLET..

LONDON:
Printed in the Year. 1674.

HU

This was truly a cry from the heart and in the same year there was THE MEN'S ANSWER TO THE WOMEN'S PETITION AGAINST COFFEE:

Could it be imagined that ungrateful women should publickly complain. Certain we are that there was never age or nation more indulgent to your sex; have we not condescended to all methods of debauchery? Invented more postures than Aretine [an Italian satirist 1492-1556] ever dreamed of! Been pimps to our own wives, and courted gallants even with the hazard of our estates, to do us the civility of making us not only contented, but most obliged cuckolds: Is he thought worthy to be esteemed a gentleman, that has not seven times passed the torrid zone of a venereal distemper, or does not maintain at least a brace of mistresses; Talk not to us of those doting fumblers of seven or eight hundred years old, a lark is better than a kite; and cocksparrows, though not long lived, are undoubtedly preferable for the work of generation before dull ravens, though some think they live three hundred years: That our island is a paradise for women is verified by the brisk activity of our men, who with equal contempt scorn Italian padlocks, and defie French dildos, knowing that a small dose of nature's quintessence, satisfies better in a female limbock [symbolic - perhaps the supposed region on the border of hell or heaven], than the largest potion infused by art.

Certainly experienced Solomon was in the right when he told us that the grave and the womb were equally insatiable.

There is scarce a coffee hut but affords a tawdry woman, a wanton daughter, or a buxom maid, to accommodate customers; and can you think that any which frequent such discipline, can be wanting in their pastures, or defective in their arms. The news we chat of there, you will not think it impertinent, when you consider the fair opportunities you have thereby, of entertaining an obliging friend in our absence, and how many of us you have dubbed knights of the bullfeather, whilst we have sat innocently sipping the devil's holy water; we do not call it so for driving the Cace-daemon [evil spirit] of lechery out of us, for the truth is, it rather assists us for your nocturnal benevolences, by drying up those crude flatulent humours, which otherwise would make us only flash in the pan, without doing that thundering execution which your expectations exact. The physical qualities of this liquor are almost innumerable and when your kindness at the "close hugg" [sic] has bestowed on us a virulent gonorrhoea, this is our catholicon [universal cure]. It is base adulterate wine that makes a man as salacious as a goat and yet as impotent as Age, whereas coffee collects and settles the spirits, makes the erection more vigorous, the ejaculation more full, adds a spiritualescency to the sperme, and renders it more firm to the gusto of the womb, and proportionate to the ardours and expectation too of the female paramour. 'Till noon you lie abed hatching concupiscence, then having paid your adorations to the ugly idol in the glass, you descend to dinner and after that you are called out by a cozen [cheat] and hurried out in his honours coach (whose jogging serves as a preparative to your lechery) away to the playhouse, where a lascivious dance, a bawdy song, and the petulant gallants tickling of your hand, having made an insurrection in your blood, you go to allay it at the tavern, there you spend freely, yet being robbed of nothing we can miss, you come home in a railing humour, and at last give us nothing for supper but a buttered bun.

Cease then for the future your clamours against our civil follies.

Were coffee houses popular because they were houses of assignation? Perhaps the pamphlets represent a complaint by women at being left out of things in general - beer was probably accompanied by roisterous behaviour in which women could equally join.

Coffee was much more intellectually stimulating and because so much business was carried out in coffee houses, women would have found it more difficult to keep up-to-date and participate. How different it is in this century when men usually go to taverns and women to coffee shops. There is probably a case to be made for coffee causing Europe to come out of its drunken stupor and being the catalyst for the great developments of the next centuries.

These pamphlets were just three of many that appeared in England extolling and decrying the new beverage. There was a further pamphlet in

47

1675: *THE ALE WIVES COMPLAINT AGAINST THE COFFEEHOUSES*. This was another attack against the coffee houses attracting too much business. King Charles in 1675 finally assented to a Proclamation suppressing coffee houses but it caused such an uproar that eleven days later he rescinded it. It is hard for us to imagine just one product causing so much upheaval in such a short time.

France was apparently not much different. In 1782 Louis Sebastian Mercier wrote about Paris: 'It isn't decent to appear in cafés. It denotes absolute ignorance of good social habits'.[61]

There were others who proclaimed the opposite. Obviously there was a wide range of cafes to suit all tastes.

'The workshop of a tinsmith'. Etching from *'L'Encyclopédie de Diderot'*, Paris, 1762-1777.

CHAPTER 5

Tea in England - Coffee in Europe

E ngland and France were both originally coffee drinking countries although the amounts consumed were extremely small. During the course of the eighteenth century, tea became the dominant beverage in England and coffee predominated in France. The reasons usually given for this very significant development include the power of the English East India Company, the fact that the French possessions grew coffee, and that bitterness is more acceptable to the French taste, but this does not provide the complete picture.

The division of Europe into two areas - with England drinking tea and Europe drinking coffee - was of great significance to the future development of the major cash commodities of the European colonies and China. Imports of tea from British Commonwealth colonies certainly influenced the early development of India and Ceylon. Similarly, the development of Indonesia would have been different without tea manufacture and coffee growing for the Dutch. The spread of coffee production through South America and all the tropical colonies depended on European and North American acceptance of coffee as the major drink.

THE FIRST USE OF TEA AND COFFEE

From the beginning of the seventeenth century hot drinks were introduced all over Europe. They were sociable and, considering the climate and the lack of heating, a very welcome addition to the diet. It was a period when chairs were changing from vertical-backed, uncomfortable seating, to comfortable chairs much as we know them today. The design problems were in fact solved by Nicholas Andry de Boisregard in France in 1741.[1.] The discovery of the Argand lamp in 1783 in

Geneva extended day into night. The combination of comfortable seating and better lighting meant an increase in time available for socialising in comfort and drinking the new social drinks, tea and coffee. In the seventeenth century coffee and tea were both drunk in England and France. In France tea had a short fashionable period where it was possibly considered to be just another *tisane* or herbal tea among many already available in France. The popularity and penetration of both products was largely limited to the upper classes, from whose writings most of the information for the period has been gained. The arrival of the Turkish Ambassador in Paris in 1669 and his coffee drinking is mentioned as being very influential in popularising the drinking of coffee in France. In 1689 the Café Procope was opened in Paris. This was a most fashionable establishment and could well have influenced drinking habits. It was the forerunner of many other coffee shops.

Even though the year 1715 is often given as the time of firm establishment of tea in England, the change must have occurred over a period of time. Fairly certainly the changes had already begun by the first years of the eighteenth century and were cemented by the 1730s. In 1715, green tea was introduced to England. It was also one year after the date of accession to the English throne of George I from Hannover, one of the strongest tea-drinking areas of Germany even to this day.

Tea in England

A sense of proportion is required in considering tea consumption at this time. An annual consumption of 240,000 pounds (110,000 kilograms) of tea in 1717, the use of two grams per cup and a population of six million in England means a per capita consumption of around nine cups per person per annum. Put in another way, if one per cent of the population drank two and a half cups per day, there would have been no tea at all left for the other ninety-nine per cent. Even if these figures are multiplied several times to take account of substitutes and the multiple use of the tea, usage could hardly be considered widespread. Its impact on the bulk of the population was insignificant, because tea was not in general use until several decades later.

Coffee in England

Coffee was very popular in England but declined in popularity towards the end of the seventeenth century. It was sold in hundreds of coffee shops all over London which sold cups of tea as well. The upper classes left the coffee houses to form clubs where they could associate with other respectable people while the lower classes took over the coffee shops.

Tea in France

The French were buying tea mainly from the Dutch but France and Holland were at war from 1672 to 1678 and again from 1689 to 1697 when Louis XIV fought against an Anglo-Dutch coalition.[2] The only two sources of tea open to the French were at war with France. It is not just coincidence that in this period tea drinking was virtually abandoned in France as a result of all imports being banned from Holland. The war was probably the major cause even though in 1694 Pomet noted that tea consumption in Paris had dropped on account of the introduction of coffee and chocolate.[3]

Coffee in France

The French were in an excellent geographical position to dominate trade in the Mediterranean with short lines of communication to Alexandria, the port from which the coffee was shipped. In addition, French coffee importers in Lyons and Marseilles imported coffee direct from source in the Levant. It was a much shorter distance than tea had to travel from China to Amsterdam. Coffee drinking became general throughout the provinces, in Marseilles and Lyons as well as the capital. Under Louis XIV, France had the best road system in Europe and so coffee could be transported all over the country. Coffee was very much the dominant product in 1688 when Philippe Sylvestre Dufour devoted 216 pages to coffee, 138 to chocolate and 87 to tea in his book *Traitez Nouveau et Curieux du Café, du Thé et du Chocolat,* published not in Paris but in Lyons, a city subject to a lot of Italian influence and to that extent not representative of the whole of France.

PRICES FOR TEA AND COFFEE

It is hard to establish the prices for coffee and tea on a per cup basis because coffee was often used more than once and tea up to eight times, but tea was generally cheaper per cup in England than coffee and the opposite generally held true in continental Europe. There were two different markets in England for tea: high priced teas for the upper classes and cheaper teas for the non-discerning.

The price of coffee in France fell after 1710 when merchants from St. Malo began importing coffee from the Yemen via the Cape of Good Hope and avoided the taxes placed on coffee as it went overland from the Yemen.[4] From the 1730s the price for coffee fell in France again as supplies arrived from the French West Indies.

Singlo tea, which was just a little better than poor quality green dust, was most popular in England from 1702 and much cheaper than high grade teas. The price of tea fell when green tea began to be imported in 1715. From 1718 to 1725, the price of Mocha coffee rose at a time when Mocha coffee was considered to be very special. In 1723 almost two thirds of all the tea in England was smuggled to avoid the four shillings per pound tax. The price for smuggled tea is rarely mentioned because smugglers did not have published catalogues but their prices must have been lower.

Around the 1720s, it became popular to blend tea and merchants began to establish themselves as tea dealers, selling their products by brand names. It has always been the public perception that it is possible to make a superior tea from blending inferior teas. In some way the public thought that blending allowed ever better teas to be supplied at ever lower prices. In fact the delusion allowed the public to consume cheaper teas and think they were good. The price of tea in Europe ranged from five pence per pound up to twenty-four pence which meant that profits could be considerable for smugglers while still selling at lower prices.[5] As if the price of tea was not low enough, it was mixed with all sorts of substitutes. Exaggerated complaints were made that forests were disappearing to make sawdust to mix with tea. Used tea leaves and other substitutes, such as sawdust, were used to reduce the price or increase the profits.

DISTRIBUTION: CONCENTRATED FOR COFFEE; DISPERSED FOR TEA

In 1715 Paris had a population of a quarter of a million while the whole of France was around sixteen million. Toulouse, Marseilles and Rouen each had a population of more than fifty thousand inhabitants while Bordeaux, Nantes, Lille, Tournai and Strasbourg each had more than thirty thousand. In England with a population of six million, only London, Bristol and Norwich had more than thirty thousand.[6]

Coffee production requires a roasting machine and a skilled operator for it. In a small area such as Paris, or any of the larger cities of France, coffee could be sold fresh and the skills necessary to process it could be practised and the same equipment used many times a week. Coffee was less suitable in English country areas where the demand was lower and where there were fewer large cities to justify the expense of having a roasting machine. The smaller market also meant that the roasting machine was scarcely used, which in turn did not allow the development of the skills to roast it properly.

In France the aristocracy lived around the Court at Versailles and nearby Paris, and went to their country residences occasionally. The only French nobility who lived in the country were those who were in disgrace or who could not afford to live in Paris.[7] By contrast in England the aristocracy lived in their country homes and made only occasional visits to their London houses.

Tea was a much more suitable product for distribution to country areas, as it did not require skills for production or suffer from staling problems. It could be easily distributed from prestigious suppliers in London. The sedentary eighteenth century English enjoyed themselves in their country homes where they entertained each other and in the process turned tea drinking into a national ritual. The middle class imitated the habits of the upper class and spread the use of tea through society.[8]

INTERRUPTION OF COFFEE SUPPLIES TO ENGLAND AND HOLLAND

From 1689 to 1697 an Anglo-Dutch alliance was at war with France. The English and Dutch were practically driven out of the Mediterranean in 1693 and 1694 and would have been unable to get coffee. During the war around four thousand English and Dutch boats were destroyed or captured by French privateers who presumably supplied any captured coffee to the French market.[9] During the whole period France had continuity of supply and perhaps extra supplies from the privateers.

As well as a short period when the French controlled the English Channel, coffee supplies to England and Holland were severely disrupted in 1693, when the Smyrna convoy was lost at a cost of more than six hundred thousand pounds to the English and much more to the Dutch.[10] As a consequence, in 1696 the Dutch made their first attempt to grow coffee in Java and a second successful attempt in 1699.

In 1696 coffee was transported from Mecca to Jeddah, shipped to Suez and transported to Alexandria by camels where French and Venetian merchants bought it.[11] The War of the Spanish Succession from 1702 to 1713 which involved Spain and France against England and Holland must have caused disruption to supplies of coffee from the Levant making it even more likely that England turned to the substitute tea. English coastal ships en route to London were intercepted by French privateers based in Dunkirk.[12]

TRADE: DUTCH TEA VERSUS ENGLISH TEA

The Portuguese were the first to bring tea to Europe but the Dutch traded it all over Europe. In fact they supplied tea to England before the English East India Company was given the monopoly which meant that the Dutch East India Company could no longer supply - officially anyway. The monopoly which the English East India Company had over imports from the East and the introduction of a five shillings per pound tax in 1689 on leaf tea in England meant that smuggling became a very popular sport with large numbers of the population involved. The duty was reduced to one shilling in 1692 and varied from time to time. There was duty and smuggling until William Pitt, the English Prime Minister, reduced the duty substantially in 1784. India, Ceylon and Java did not produce tea until the nineteenth century. The situation was one in which the Dutch East India Company had a monopoly on tea and coffee imports into the Netherlands and the English East India Company had a monopoly over tea imports into England and the government had put an import duty onto tea. The Dutch were happy to supply tea to the smugglers.

The English East India Company wanted to maximise prices and profits but had to fight a price war with smugglers, and at the same time try to drive coffee off the market. In an era where there were no brand names, just products with descriptions, the Company was forced to lower prices and introduce cheaper grades and as a result the market for tea was expanded.

The English East India Company's monopoly of the tea trade within Britain meant that tea had better organised distribution than coffee. An organised marketer always has the advantage over disorganised competition. Tea was shipped once per year from China and steady prices were maintained throughout the year. The problems of distributing 240,000 pounds of tea in 1717 would have been considerable if not properly organised and especially in a period when it took up to two weeks to travel by coach between London and Edinburgh. At least tea did not become stale as fast as coffee. Good quality, freshly roasted coffee outside London must have been a rarity. For the dealers and shopkeepers, a product which stayed fresh, did not deteriorate and kept its value was a more profitable product than coffee, which deteriorated and was subject to competition.

The monopoly of the English East India Company meant that the policies of the company had a great influence on the market even if they were forced on it from outside. The possibility of buying cheap and selling dear existed and was exploited. Singlo tea was bought at one shilling per pound, offered at auction for ten shillings and sold at fifteen. Profits were not always so high but percentage returns were higher on cheap teas than on expensive teas. At the same time expensive teas were maintained in the marketplace to maximise profits. Reputable merchants established themselves in the early 1700s to sell quality tea. The smugglers would have found it very difficult to enter this market. In Göttingen, Germany, at the same time, tea was always several times more expensive than coffee.[13] The price for tea in the 1740s in Germany was from four to eight times the price for coffee.[14] This is probably what would have happened in England in the absence of competition from smugglers. The fact that cheap teas dominated the market in England is probably a direct result of the English East India Company's policies to compete with the cheaper smuggled teas. The company would also have perceived that cheap tea was a good competitor for expensive coffee and probably kept the price of some teas low for that reason.

THE FRENCH AND DUTCH COLONIES GROW THEIR OWN COFFEE

The French coffee plantations in the West Indies supplied the French markets in the 1720s. The English did not obtain coffee from their own plantations in Jamaica until much later in the 1730s and then only on a very small scale, but by then tea had taken hold of the market.

The Dutch market can be seen to have had two periods - the first when they imported both tea and coffee from non-colonies and the second when they imported coffee from their own colonies. Java was able to supply the Dutch market from 1711 with small quantities and with larger quantities from the 1720s.

Just as in England, tea became the drink of the Dutch upper classes. The growth in imports of coffee meant that coffee became the universal drink of the lower classes. The per capita coffee consumption in Holland was and is one of the highest in the world. France had a very large population and also developed a large market for coffee and took little interest in tea.

THE INGREDIENTS FOR A CUP OF TEA AND A CUP OF COFFEE

The necessary ingredients for a cup of tea or coffee were not just the tea and coffee alone. Tea can be served with a small amount of milk, sugar or a combination of both. Green teas seem less suitable for cream and sugar but were certainly combined with both in the early years. It seems likely that green tea with sugar was drunk for sweetness, rather than for the flavour of the tea. Black teas on account of their higher flavour levels and tendency to coarse and rough flavours are more suitable for both milk and sugar. Sugar is commonly used with both coffee and tea and probably much more than necessary to mask the bitterness or any unpleasant flavours. Coffee is prone to bitterness, and milk is a natural complement.

MILK COFFEE IN EUROPE

There are many mentions of both black coffee and milk coffee to the end of the eighteenth century and I suspect that the trend was to milk coffee. An English journal in 1834 reported that the favourite way of drinking coffee abroad was with a great superfluity of milk .... very properly called *café au lait*. The article adds that milk is for children not for adults, because their stomachs are weaker and upset by the milk.[15] *Café au lait* was first recommended for use as a medicine by Sieur Monin, a celebrated doctor in Grenoble, France in 1685.[16] Dufour specifically mentioned milk with tea and coffee in France in 1688.[17] After describing how two Capuchin monks drank coffee to repair their spirits, he continued in the next sentence to write that absolutely nothing was the equal of milk coffee in treating chest ailments.[18] Although there is no definite statement that the Capuchins drank milk coffee, the closeness of the statements perhaps assumes that they did, or it was later assumed that they did. This use by the Capuchins may be the origin of the word cappuccino. Doubtless it had been widely used for some time before that. Milk is an important addition to a cup of coffee because it contains lactose, or milk sugar, which is sweet and casein which softens any bitterness in the coffee. This is why coffee with milk is a much more pleasant drink than coffee alone. In a letter written in 1690 Mme de Sévigné highly commended milk coffee.[19] While black coffee became the mode, milk coffee grew very popular and was later considered the real French coffee. By the end of the eighteenth century it was in general usage in Paris, even among the workers, as well as Belgium, Switzerland and parts of Germany.[20]

Cornelius Bontekoe, a Dutch physician who opened the first coffee house in Hamburg, said that coffee was made worse by using sugar and honey because they increased the viscosity of the blood too much. He recommended half coffee, half milk to make an acceptable, nutritious drink.[21]

Any excess in milk supply, after allowing for cheese and butter requirements, could have been used for coffee. *Café au lait*, milk coffee, cappuccino and *café con leche* are all testaments to the popularity of milk coffee drinks all over the world. Indeed iced coffee is generally served with milk. Milk coffee does not necessarily need sugar.

Milk in England

The quality of milk in England would not have been conducive to drinking in any form, whether with coffee or alone. Smollett, an English writer, wrote in 1771 about the milk hawked in London and there is little reason to imagine that the situation was any better in the previous decades:

> But the milk itself should not pass unanalysed, the produce of faded cabbage-leaves and sour draff, lowered with hot water, frothed with bruised snails; carried through the streets in open pails,

exposed to foul rinsings discharged from doors and windows, spittle, snot, and tobacco quids, from foot-passengers; overflowings from mud carts, spatterings from coach-wheels, dirt and trash chucked into it by roguish boys for the joke's sake; the spewings of infants, who have slabbered in the tin-measure, which is thrown back in that condition among the milk, for the benefit of the next customer; and finally, the vermin that drops from the rags of the nasty drab that vends this precious mixture, under the respectable denomination of milkmaid.[22]

The quality of milk in England was so poor that it could not be used in tea but in its sour state was used in the traditional recipe for scones — sour milk, mixed with flour and baking soda and baked in a hot oven. Scones were not traditional in Europe which probably indicates that the quality of milk was superior there.

> " Coffee, as used on the Continent, serves the double purpose of an agreeable tonic, and an exhilarating beverage, without the unpleasant effects of wine. Coffee, as drank in England, debilitates the stomach, and produces a slight nausea. In France and Italy it is made strong from the best coffee, and is poured out hot and transparent. In England it is usually made from bad coffee, served out tepid and muddy, and drowned in a deluge of water. To make coffee fit for use, you must employ the German filter,—pay at least four shillings the pound for it, —and take at least an ounce for two breakfast cups. No coffee will bear drinking with what is called milk in London. London people should either take their coffee pure, or put a couple of tea-spoonsful of cream to each cup.

How to make Coffee: *The Penny Magazine*, August 24, 1833, p. 328.

The Weather and Milk Production

There were many hard winters in the 1690s and later problems with extreme heat, drought and the disease *rinderpest* which severely depleted cattle stocks, and hence milk supplies, up to 1719. In that year there was a hot dry summer in southern England and farmers had to buy water for their herds.[23] There was also a scarcity of fodder and large numbers of cattle were slaughtered. The same occurred in 1729. The net effect of all this was that milk was scarcer and more expensive than it would otherwise have been. Liquid milk had to be almost drunk on the spot or else made into butter or cheese.[24] In any event milk consumption was not very high - in 1771 in London it was estimated to be one and a half pints per person per week.[25] This compares with a consumption of nine and a half pints per week in 1985. London had a population of around half a million in 1715 and it must have been very difficult for those in the capital to get milk because the farms were so far from the consumers.

Just as it is difficult to estimate how much salt was sprinkled over meals because it was never mentioned, it is equally difficult to establish how much milk and sugar was used with tea. The rations supplied to convicts in 1826 in New South Wales, then a British colony and now a State of Australia, included a pound of sugar and two ounces of tea. While this does not define the way in which tea was consumed, it is an indication of what was considered to be acceptable rations by the authorities, who must have supplied the tea and sugar.[26] At the same time there was a great shortage of milk and milk products.

By contrast, most of France was warmer than England and probably had better pastures. Marseilles and Lyons, the major centres for coffee trading, were basically small cities in a warmer region of France, close to agriculture and a milk supply. The availability of milk and a ready supply of coffee to make *café au lait* must have helped to spread coffee drinking through France.

Sugar

In France restrictive trade policies reduced English sugar imports until 1740, which means that sugar must have been more expensive in France than England.[27] In 1785 the consumption of sugar was ten times greater in England than in France and was probably much the same in prior years.[28] The French needed milk to make the coffee palatable - the English did not have it. On the other hand the English had sugar which they consumed in ever greater quantities to sweeten tea and other drinks. Sugar could be used in cakes and puddings which dissipated the sweetness, whereas in tea and coffee, the sweetness was immediate and apparent. Tea is an excellent vehicle for sugar. The fact that tea had a lower price and was a hot drink which could dissolve sugar helped to satisfy the growing English demand for sweetness and was an important

From *The Mirror of Literature, Amusement, and Instruction,* June 11, 1836, p. 400.

The Gatherer.

Coffee and Sugar.—The following account of the quantity of coffee and sugar imported into Europe in 1835, appeared a short time since in a German journal:—

Coffee, 217,600,000 lbs. ; namely,—

Hamburg	41,000,000 *lbs.*
Amsterdam	36,000,000
Rotterdam	28,600,000
Great Britain	28,000,000
Antwerp	22,000,000
Trieste	19,900,000
Havre	15,400,000
Marseilles	9,600,000
Bremen	9,300,000
Bordeaux	4,100,000
Genoa	2,000,000
Leghorn	1,700,000

Sugar, 913,300,000 lbs.; namely,—

Great Britain	440,400,000 *lbs.*
Hamburg	79,500,000
Havre	73,000,000
Amsterdam	70,100,000
Trieste	56,800,000
Marseilles	55,300,000
Antwerp	41,700,000
Rotterdam	34,000,000
Genoa	21,500,000
Bordeaux	18,300,000
Bremen	13,000,000
Leghorn	9,700,000

W. G. C.

factor in the change to tea. A pot of tea was likely to be hotter than a pot of coffee, probably because of the reduced brewing time. The first French inventions of coffee pots in the 1800s mostly incorporated a *bain-marie* or warm water jacket to keep the coffee hot. There does not seem to be a reference to a *bain-marie* teapot anywhere.

REASONS FOR THE ENGLISH AND EUROPEAN PREFERENCES

The major factors involved in the English preference for tea and the European preference for coffee were:

- the interruption of supplies of coffee to England
- the price competition from smugglers which forced the price of tea down in England
- the Dutch tea monopoly in Europe which kept tea prices higher
- the lack of milk in England to make coffee palatable
- the easy supply of milk in France to make milk coffee
- the supply of sugar in England being relatively greater than in France
- the spread of population in France which was more suitable for coffee distribution
- the spread of consumers in England which was more suitable for tea distribution
- the supply of coffee to France and Holland from their own colonies

In many parts of France and Italy tea is classed by the excise in the list of drugs—is kept in bottles on the shelves of the apothecary, forms no part of the stock of the grocer, and is even anathematized by the lecturer on *hygiène* as unfited for ordinary consumption. It is therefore placed by common consent in the custody of the physician, to be dealt with as a remedial agent, *secundum artem*. Whether they manage these things best in France or in England remains to be seen. Mr. Cole thinks it probable that the great increase which has taken place in diseases of the heart in this country may be referred to the abuse of this beverage. He considers green tea to be productive of more uneasiness and excitement than black, and regards coffee as ranking next in this respect. With regard to *spurious* tea, Professor Burnett has proved that the practice is very common of adding the leaves of the sloe, the apple, the hawthorn, and the elm, to the Chinese leaf.

Tea and Drugs: *The Mirror of Literature, Amusement, and Instruction.* March 8, 1834, p.148.

Tea, Coffee and Health

Both tea and coffee arrived in Europe amidst claims and counter-claims by physicians who imagined detrimental and beneficial effects not only from tea and coffee, but many new products. For some reason, certain attitudes prevailed. Much of Europe today still treats tea as a drink with hints of medicinal qualities. The health reasons were translated into practical effect by the imposition of taxes and trade restrictions. Additional taxes imposed on an already highly-priced product would have further discouraged the European purchase of tea.

Tea for Protestants, Coffee for Catholics

In 1990 at an international conference on coffee, there was a serious discussion about tea being more appropriate for Protestants because of the high tea consumption in Friesland where the Protestants are indeed very strict. The example given for coffee was Vienna where mostly coffee is drunk. These ideas are almost certainly based on the facts of the early 1700s when coffee was still being imported through the Mediterranean and tea was coming from China through the two holders of the export monopoly, England and the Netherlands. It was surely geographical accident that Catholic countries, France and Italy, bordered the Mediterranean, while the Dutch and the English were Protestant. There is nothing in modern ideology to confirm these ideas and coffee and tea seem to be drunk indiscriminately by people of all religions.

It can only be a matter of conjecture about the influence of the English East India Company and the relative importance of the availability of complementary ingredients such as milk and sugar. The importance of the English East India Company in determining the tea habit in England must be considered, keeping all the other factors in the background. The argument is somewhat similar to considering the relative merits of heredity versus environment. There can be no clear-cut answer.

CHAPTER 6

Coffee - From Mystery to Mastery

KALDI AND HIS DANCING GOATS
THE LEGENDARY DISCOVERY OF THE COFFEE DRINK

No other product promises as much as coffee with its inviting aroma and no other product delivers so many different results. How coffee could have become so popular over the years, with results which often must have been disappointing, is an enigma. Part of the explanation is akin to the tenacity of prospectors who every so often find a few gold flecks in their pans and keep trying because of their belief that they will one day strike it rich. Early coffee drinkers must have persevered because they occasionally tasted a good cup of coffee and continued to try, hoping that the next cup would be a cup of the elusive aroma.

THE SMELL OF COFFEE
THE TASTE OF COFFEE

Inventors have dreamed and striven for three centuries to minimise this difference between the delightful aroma of the beans and the actuality in the cup. People are always saying that coffee never tastes as good as it smells, whereas they never say this about tea. It is this mystery - the apparent disappearance of the aroma - which gives coffee brewing the semblance of magic.

In their quest to make coffee taste as good as it smells, inventors devised ever more exotic equipment in an effort to unlock the secret.

Understanding about coffee was not widespread until the 1920s and 1930s and coffee developed its own mythology to explain the unknown. The acceptance for centuries that there was some connection between a seventh century goatherd and the roasting, grinding and brewing of coffee is stretching the imagination, to say the least. The story of Khaldi and his goats which became frisky after eating raw coffee cherries from a tree has been repeated countless times as if it were a serious introduction to the subject. Its

acceptance is an indication of the mystique which has surrounded coffee for centuries.

THE PROBLEM

The problem was overwhelmingly complex. If a bad cup of coffee was brewed it was impossible to know whether to blame the beans, the roasting, the freshness, the water quality or any other part of the whole process. There were literally dozens of variables involved and if hardly any were understood, how could goals be set to determine perfect coffee makers? The aim of all inventors was to make a better cup of coffee - whatever that was. Because of the lack of understanding, every failure produced another more complicated machine which did not solve the overall problem, as individual problems were approached and solved in isolation. Each new machine attempted to solve some part of the problem ignored by the old machine, but it often incorporated a new part of the problem or the same problem again, in a different guise.

UNDERSTANDING THE VARIABLES

The first inventors and writers about coffee knew very little if anything of the basic relationships between coffee roasting, the grinding, brewing time and water temperature. The following important relationships will provide an understanding of just what the variables are and how they interact in the brewing process:

Roasting and keeping. The green coffee must not have deteriorated in storage or been of variable quality. To get the same flavoured coffee, batch after batch, the coffee must be roasted consistently. This means that the time and final temperature of roasting must be the same and that all the resulting beans should be the same colour both inside and outside. The coffee should be fresh.

UNE CAFETIÈRE BREVETÉE

Je suis vraiment charmé de cette nouvelle invention : je n'ai pas mis plus de cinq minutes pour préparer mon café... il est vrai que j'ai mis cinq quart d'heures pour préparer ma cafetière !

More magic was needed. A patented coffee pot. 'I am truly charmed with this new invention. It only takes five minutes to make the coffee. It is true that it takes seventy-five minutes to prepare my coffeepot'. [English translation] From *La Caricature Journal* - France, 19th Century.

Stale coffee not only changes its flavour but it grinds differently as it becomes softer with age.

Grinding. The finer the coffee is ground, the faster and more completely it releases its flavour and the faster it goes stale. The higher the percentage of fine particles, the greater the resistance to the water passing through and thus the higher the pressure required to force the water through.

Brewing. All coffee swells when in contact with water. If coffee swells too much in an enclosed compartment such as in an espresso machine, it will require additional pressure to force the water through. To achieve a correct and complete extraction in any coffee brewer, it is necessary for the grounds to be completely immersed in and wetted by the water and to be prevented from floating. The correct brewing time is four to six minutes in a filter machine, fifteen to twenty-five seconds in a modern espresso machine with a pump, and an undefined time, but probably less than three minutes, in other types of espresso machines. If the brewing time is longer than recommended, bitterness is extracted and if the brewing time is too short the coffee is under-extracted and weak.

Water temperature. The flavour extraction varies with the temperature of the water. The correct temperature is 92 to 96 degrees Celsius for both filter and espresso coffee makers. If the temperature is closer to boiling point, the coffee will tend to be bitter. The lower the temperature, the lower the extraction and the weaker the coffee.

MASTERING THE BREW

The first coffee from the East was full of grounds and had to be clarified for western drinkers. The obvious answer was a filter of some sort. A cloth filter was the solution, but the cloth became dirty. In addition, the coffee floated and you did not get a proper extraction. If the coffee grounds remained in the liquid too long, it was overbrewed and became bitter. This was not satisfactory, so metal filters were tried. The holes were too big and let the coffee fall through. Blotting paper and other filters were tried but did not work very well.

In a way, early inventors forgot what they had set out to do. The means for making a good cup of coffee involved controlling the time and the temperature. The first inventors knew this had to be done and tried to find a simple way to do both at once. If they had simply used the filter to filter the coffee and incorporated a small hole to control the water flow, they would have solved the problem over a hundred years before they did. In fact the first filter to do this does not seem to have been widely used until introduced by August Carton around 1928. Technologically it could have been made in 1800, but de Belloy, Rumford and other inventors followed the wrong track.

The first filter machines attempted to control the brewing time and improve the brewing process by pressing the coffee to stop it floating, which introduced another problem: the swelling of the coffee in an enclosed compartment. This could prevent the water from passing through the coffee at all, so that in many cases, brewing times were extraordinarily long. The solution was to introduce pressure to force the water through the coffee. When positive pressure is applied to compressed coffee, espresso coffee is created; when negative pressure is used to draw the water through the coffee grounds, filtered coffee is created in a vacuum pot. If the grind was too fine in the espresso it could explode; if it was too fine in the vacuum pot, it could implode. The plunger system was invented to force the water through the coffee.

In 1812, the American author Count Rumford was in London, writing on the art of making coffee. His writings showed that he knew about some of the relationships involved in making good coffee, but he did not know precisely how they worked. At the same time in France, Cadet-de-

Vaux, a vigorous contributor to the coffee discussion, was writing about coffee, but he was not nearly as well-informed as Rumford .

In the early 1800s, France was the most active country for coffee patents and ideas and Cadet-de-Vaux's works written in the French language were more accessible to the French. This was unfortunate, because Rumford's ideas were on the right track and Cadet-de-Vaux was going in the wrong direction.

Rumford knew that coffee made in Cadet-de-Vaux's manner, with cold water and reheated, was bitter. He knew that boiling coffee was bad and that hot water was better than cold. He knew that fine coffee gave more flavour and that air particles attached to the coffee grounds caused them to float, reducing the flavour. He knew that a sufficiently thick layer of coffee compressed with sufficient pressure gave a better coffee than too thick or too thin with too much pressure. He understood coffee had to be levelled. He and another inventor, Hadrot, specified compression but not the grind.

The first grinders were crudely made with little attention to detail or fine engineering. For the whole of the nineteenth century there was no way to specify the precise grind required and no way to deliver it. The technology was simply not available to deliver what was most required - control over the grinding process.

A French book in 1868 stated that in most French pots filtration took place too fast, achieving only eleven to fifteen per cent extractibles instead of twenty to twenty-one per cent.[1] Fine grinding could have solved this problem

Ignoring the grinding created problem after problem and there was no solution until electric shop grinders and improved factory grinders were universally used. The American coffee trade in 1912 and Ukers' coffee book in 1922 were probably the first to broach the subject of grind particle size. In 1931 Paul Ciupka in Germany was the first to investigate the grinding process thoroughly. His later book in 1949 was even more explanatory about technicalities, but it was not translated into English and the information was more or less restricted to the German-speaking world. As far as most of the world was concerned, the secrets were still locked up. A few in the coffee trade read and understood the literature, but the general public all over the world was mostly unaware.

The timing problem was partially solved in the 1840s by self-extinguishing spirit burners which were a good idea if the boiling time coincided with the correct brewing time. Even in the 1990s the problem still has not been solved in most domestic electric filter machines which boil one cup of water per minute or ten cups in ten minutes. An egg boils in three minutes, and two eggs will boil in three minutes and ten eggs in three minutes. The timing does not vary with the number of eggs to be boiled. The logic for coffee brewing should be identical, but most machines do not follow it, which leads to overbrewing of the coffee. The excessive tannin or bitterness extracted from the grounds causes bitterness in the cup. All the Italian stove-top espresso machines have the same problem - the larger sizes take longer to brew than the smaller ones.

Even if all the correct logical relationships had been understood, and a good brewing process applied to the coffee, I suspect it would have been a waste of time because the coffee was so variable in quality, so badly packed and mixed with who knows what, that the flavour itself was not very attractive. The driving force that kept the attempts going was that almost any ground coffee smelled good and inventors and consumers were determined to find a way to make it taste as good.

New inventions became objects of prestige. Eventually a rising level of technology furnished the solutions with the introduction of filter paper and other sophisticated filters.

The introduction of electricity meant that coffee could finally be ground consistently and coffee makers were designed around that. In fact the use of electricity allowed the ultimate development of espresso coffee in 1961. The pressure from an electric pump allowed the complete and controlled extraction of the flavour from the bean as never before.

The combination of correctly ground coffee, filter paper and electric brewers meant a complete revolution in brewing practice. The early attempts to make a clear filtered coffee had at last succeeded. Bad results to a large extent were disappearing, even if the consumer still did not understand.

TYPES OF BREWERS

PERCOLATOR OR FILTER
Water percolates through the coffee grounds. When the grounds are supported by a filtering mechanism such as paper or fine metal mesh it is called a filter.

REVERSIBLE FILTER
The water is boiled in the base section, then the pot is tipped upside down allowing the water to percolate or filter through the grounds.

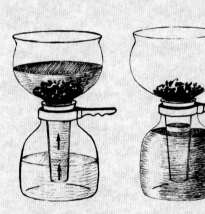

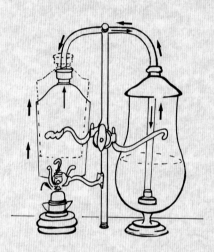

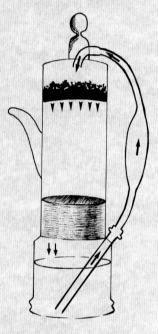

VACUUM COFFEE POT
The water is boiled and forced by steam pressure to the top. When the heat is taken away, water is drawn down by vacuum.

BALANCE
The water boiled out of the left hand compartment into the right, which changed the balance, causing the cover to extinguish the flame and the brewed coffee to be drawn back.

PUMPING PERCOLATOR
The water is pumped up to percolate through the coffee once only.

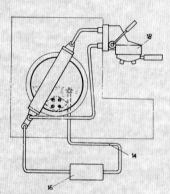

RECIRCULATING PUMPING PERCOLATOR
The water is pumped up and recirculates through the coffee many times.

PLUNGER OR FRENCH PRESS
The boiling water is poured over the coffee and the plunger pushed down after a few minutes.

LONG ESPRESSO
A long espresso is made when hot water is forced through compressed coffee with steam pressure.

SHORT ESPRESSO
A short espresso is made in a group when hot water is forced through compressed coffee by a pump or lever.

CHAPTER 7

Coffee Brewing Innovations

Brevet d'Invention
établi par la Loi du 7 Janvier 1791.

CERTIFICAT de demande d'un BREVET D'INVENTION,
délivré, en vertu de l'Arrêté des Consuls, du 5 Vendémiaire an 9,
aus C.^{ns} *Denote, pension et Mouch,*
domiciliés à *Parilly* département de *la Seine,*

THE TRADITIONAL VERSION OF COFFEE BREWING HISTORY

Previous histories of the development of coffee equipment mostly use a patent's lodgement date as a starting point. Since the French have one of the oldest accessible patent systems, most of the honour for coffee inventions has been to their credit. However, a fuller reading of the originals has shown that many of these patents, attributed to the French, were actually of German origin.

It must be remembered too, that the invention date and the date of market acceptance of the product were sometimes years apart. In some cases, the technology was simply not available to produce what the patent described, and sometimes the ideas were so revolutionary that their quality was not accepted for many years.

William Ukers' book, *All About Coffee*, written in 1922, has been the basis of most English language histories. While this book contains much useful information, it has its limitations and is by no means definitive. Ukers did not set out to evaluate or analyse trends or items and place them in an historical context. His book suffered from its author's lack of personal contact with original resources and even from a possible lack of familiarity with the machines themselves. This led to too great a reliance on patent information, rather than on the products in the market place.

Early German language sources are excellent, but dated, and do not seem to be quoted much. There is a lot of information about coffee making from the 1780s in Krünitz', *Oekonomische Encyclopaedie* of 1784 which contains a large section on coffee.[1] Boehnke-Reich in 1885 published one of the most informative books of the century, about coffee and its effects on life, *Der Kaffee in seinen Beziehungen zum Leben.*[2] There

followed many excellent references through to the 1930s, but no major analysis since that point, until Trillich's book on coffee and roasting of 1934.[3]

French books have been more descriptive than analytical. Henri Welter's book in 1868 was excellent for the history of coffee and included a reasonable account of processing at the time.[4]

The Italians have little serious literature about coffee technology prior to 1900, and much of that is reworked translations from abroad. Leonida Valerio in 1927 wrote the first really serious book on coffee processing in the Italian language, *Caffè e Derivati*, but it was not until the 1980s that other major books of quality appeared. Italians have done little research on espresso coffee history, which is unfortunate because it is the major development of the twentieth century. The lack of research seems to stem from a combination of the difficulty of finding original source documents and from the excessive dependence on verbal sources, which has not helped in the full writing of the history of coffee in Italy. The history will only become complete when companies take the trouble to compile their own detailed histories.

THE SHAPING OF COFFEE HISTORY

The political events of the eighteenth century influenced the course of coffee more than any other single factor. At the heart of the matter was the struggle for supremacy between England and France. Around the beginning of the eighteenth century tea started to become the national drink of England while coffee was continuing to establish itself as the national drink of France. In 1730 the English coffee house disappeared, to be replaced by the club. The more the British took over the tea trade, the more the French rejected it in favour of coffee.

France

In 1791 there was a slave revolt in Haiti, which was a French colony and supplied half the world's coffee. By the time the revolt was over in 1794, the slaves had totally destroyed the plantations and the coffee industry altogether. Haitian coffee was replaced by coffee imported from Java. This sudden disruption to supply must have caused an increase in price. It is significant that Jean-Antoine Chaptal, Napoleon's Minister of the Interior, wrote a book in 1801, which was the first modern, general treatise on wine, with a more scientific approach than ever before. It seems extremely likely that he raised issues which spilled over into discussions about coffee.[5]

The Continental System, instituted from 1806 to 1812 by Napoleon as a measure against England's ability to trade with Europe, was a barrier to all imports. It hence encouraged manufacturers in France to make up the shortfall. Naturally it also restricted coffee imports.

Germany

The Germans were also beginning to take more interest in coffee. During the course of the eighteenth century, tea and coffee prices fell incessantly and rapidly. In 1727, eight merchants were trading in coffee and tea in Göttingen. By 1730 coffee and tea had largely been established with the upper and middle classes, representing in numerical terms one quarter of all households liable to tax. In 1765 twenty-seven Göttingen merchants sold eleven varieties of coffee and six brands of tea.[6]

State taxation was introduced in Germany to reduce imports and deny other countries profits and hard-earned currency. Germany was not happy to see France and the Netherlands with their own colonies supplying coffee. The duties made coffee expensive and this meant that substitutes such as chicory came into favour. A more immediate effect of the taxation and import barriers, in Germany, was an increase in smuggling, so that coffee was still available, but at high prices. In 1770, chicory was introduced to Germans as a substitute for coffee which could be drunk in large quantities without the insomnia and restlessness brought on by coffee. Chicory became known as Prussian coffee and indeed was much more widely known and consumed there than in any other part of Germany. Those who drank the substitute saved money and improved their health and also helped the German economy by restricting imports. Napoleon controlled a large part of Europe and he imposed his will that coffee and chicory should pass for coffee.

SOCIAL FACTORS

In 1783 Ami Argand, a physicist from Geneva, invented the Argand lamp which gave much improved lighting, effectively improving the quality of nocturnal life. Card playing, reading, writing, sewing - everything was possible. Coffee was just the drink needed for increased sociability and nightime activity. It met the need for something to keep you awake to enjoy the extension of the day. Improvements in oil lamps and the introduction of gaslight in the 1840s meant even more hours available for drinking coffee.

The invention of safety matches to replace flint and the introduction of kerosene from 1853 were helpful in simplifying the making of coffee at the table and must have encouraged further development of table-top coffee machines.

Apart from the attractive flavour of coffee and the concomitant socialising which brought numerous adherents, there were other factors contributing to the spread of coffee throughout France so that it became a need.

One such factor was that the Age of Enlightenment created a thirst for knowledge. Botanists were interested in new species of edible plants. Anything new was tried out and became popular, at least for a time. Some fads became habits of long duration. This acceptance of novelty was assisted by the fashion for all things from Turkey and the Far East, as well as the potential which existed for high profitability in trading with the Levant and the French colonies. In France, the drinking of coffee in defiance of a number of prohibitions gave it an added attraction.[7]

Another influence involved in popularising coffee may have been a dependence on caffeine, although this has probably been over-emphasised. Most coffee was drunk with milk which puts a lining on the stomach and slows down the absorption of caffeine. In addition, the coffee was probably more dilute than is usual today, as the coffee grounds were often re-used and mixed with substitutes. Coffee was known as a stimulant, although no physical cause was apparent. However, when drunk with milk, the stimulant effect was lessened. This can be contrasted with alcohol which is a depressant but, because the effects are so mild, few people associate light drinking with feeling mildly sedated.

THE INVENTIONS BEGIN

The combination of scarcity of coffee, higher prices and the incentive to manufacture led to a rash of inventions which forever changed the way coffee was prepared.

Coffee became harder to obtain and more expensive after the revolts in Haiti in the early 1790s which destroyed the plantations. Around this time Paris had a population of half a million and eight hundred coffee houses.[8] The turmoil after the French Revolution and the increased competition between the coffee houses may have led to an interest in how to make a better cup of coffee, especially with the higher costs involved. The increasing use of milk with coffee may have caused a greater interest in how to get more flavour to make the milk coffee taste more like coffee. The quest for a good cup of coffee was really beginning and the nineteenth century was to produce a flood of the most amazing coffee inventions.

In Europe in the eighteenth century the use of coffee spread immensely. Yet, there was little technological development in the brewing of coffee. Filtering was known, but it probably made poor coffee and was not in widespread use.

The most significant development through the eighteenth and nineteenth centuries was the increased use of the grinder. Using the mortar and pestle was normal for a wide range of substances including coffee and its use was in fact much more widespread than the physical evidence today would suggest. Spices were ground in small grinders and it was a short step to use them for coffee. Large spice grinders became coffee grinders as we know them today. The developments were more in the nature of decoration than improvements in the grinding technique. Whether they were made of wood, iron or brass, the grinding mechanism stayed the same. Both grinding and crushing were used from the early days with much discussion about the relative merits.

Demachy in 1775 left a detailed description of the state of the art of coffee roasting, grinding and brewing which shows the advances to have been more of scale than technology.[9] The detailed drawings of grinders in Demachy's book show that he understood the mechanics of the grinders and that there had not been much change at all in the past two centuries. The grinding mechanism was the same but put in different covers.

The roasting was still in a sealed cylinder turned by hand. During the process an amazing thing happened - an odourless, 'obscure vapour' wet the interior of the cylinder. Even as Watt was inventing the steam engine in England, the French were unable to identify the moisture coming from the bean as steam. I am aware that 'vapeur obscure' could be translated as 'dark steam' except that the steam coming from coffee beans is definitely *not dark*. I can only conclude that Demachy meant obscure vapour. Amazingly the process was not controlled by colour as it is today, but by smell emanating from the enclosed vessel.

> When the odour is accompanied by a taste of fire, it is ready... turn the cylinder away from the fire until the vapour begins to diminish, then pour the coffee into a chest which can be closed. [English translation]

There is no mention of cooling; it was probably assumed that the aroma was better preserved in a sealed chest. Demachy said that the colour should be more reddish than brown. Obviously it was known that colour determined the quality but without a sampling mechanism in the closed cylinder, roasters were forced to use smell as the determinant.

Demachy recommended that the coffee be made by boiling the water, taking off a quarter and adding the coffee to the remainder, while giving it a little heat. The fresh heat caused the liquor to rise and by slowly pouring in the quarter portion, it caused the liquor to sink down. As soon as the coffee stopped rising, the pot had to be carefully sealed up and the coffee left to clarify. This happened slowly but could be sped up by placing the pot on marble or something very cold. Some coffee shop owners added cold water or even isinglass, but this affected the flavour and colour. Others added diluted caramel, but the gourmets did not approve.

Anything that could be roasted was used to make coffee which, as a word, was becoming synonymous with the word 'beverage' - much as we say 'beef tea' or 'dandelion coffee'. Demachy concluded by noting how unhealthy it was for the women in the marketplace to breakfast on a pennyworth of bad bread dipped in a detestable drink called milk coffee. As a propagandist, Demachy was a failure. Filtered coffee and a breakfast of bread dipped in milk coffee were destined to become features of French gastronomy. Many people feel that the quality of French coffee has not improved. I know of no other country where a cup of coffee is so mistreated - *croissants* and bread covered in butter and jam are dunked in the coffee at breakfast time as a regular habit.

THE POT

Except for filtering, there is very little evidence of innovation in brewing during the eighteenth century. Probably the most common method was to brew the coffee in a pot by pouring boiling water over the grounds - a method that remained all over Europe for more than two hundred years. The simple technique of just pouring boiling water over the grounds and letting them brew for five minutes, which makes an excellent coffee, was too simple for most. Despite the lack of pot illustrations in this book, it must be remembered that pot brewing was probably the most common method in many countries for the longest period of time. The form changed immensely over the centuries as did the ways to make the coffee. Every imaginable combination of hot and cold water with a multitude of clarifying substances such as isinglass were used to try to make the coffee clear. Reheating also played an important part in the recipes. The pot method was the starting point for innovations.

BEGIN THE BIGGIN

A biggin is a pot with a cloth bag or metal filter set in the top. The boiling water was poured over the coffee and through the mesh. When the water level rose up above the coffee level, the coffee brewed in the filter. The efficiency of the biggin depended on the fineness of the grind - if too fine, the water could not penetrate the coffee and would simply run through the sides of the filter - if too coarse, the water ran straight through, without brewing, but as the water level in the pot

Above: The Madame Bleu coffee pot was very popular especially in Scandinavia. A cotton bag was tied to the base of the filter. France - 1900s.

Right: Ash's *Kaffee Kanne* - an English coffee pot showing the filtering bag. There was a small lid at the top for hot water which kept the coffee hot in a *bain-marie*. c.1910.

rose above the coffee in the bag, the brewing process might take place then.

Before the introduction of the biggin, coffee was probably poured from a separate brewing pot and strained through a cloth bag held in the mouth of the coffee serving pot. A small leap had the coffee grounds put into the cloth bag in the serving pot and then the boiling water poured through. Ukers, however, in *All About Coffee* (1922) gives a different version of the biggin's origins:

The coffee biggin, said to have been invented by a Mr. Biggin, came into common use in England about 1817. It was usually an earthenware pot. At first it had in the upper part a metal strainer like the French drip pots. Suspended from the rim in later models there was a muslin or flannel bag to hold the ground coffee, through which the boiling water was poured, the bag serving as a filter. The idea was an adaption of the French fustian infusion bag of 1711, and other early

French drip and filtration devices, and it attained great popularity. Any pot with a bag fitted into its mouth came to be spoken of as a coffee biggin. Later there evolved the metal pot with a wire strainer substituted for the cloth bag.[10]

Ukers continues: ' ... that in all probability the word "biggin" came from the Dutch "beggelin" (to trickle or run down)'. One thing is certain, coffee biggins came originally from France, so, if there was a Mr. Biggin, he merely introduced them into England.

A History of Old Sheffield Plate offers yet another version which says that coffee biggins appeared for the first time about the year 1787. 'Biggin' or 'bagging' was a dialectal word, in the northern counties of England, for refreshment taken between regular meals. 'Bagging-time' was either 10 o'clock in the morning or 4 o'clock in the afternoon. The book goes on to describe a coffee biggin as a jug with a lip and cover, inside which is a ledge on which a round wire can rest to hold the muslin bag for straining the coffee.[11]

I am inclined to feel that there is a lot of fancy in all of the above. A good imagination is needed to flesh out what would otherwise be a boring story. I am reminded of the proponents of *pretzels* who have invented the story that the word *pretzel* comes from the Latin *pretiola* (a present). A *pretzel* is bread with salt on it and the word seems to be closely connected with the German words for bread and salt - *Brot* and *Salz*. Just saying the words quickly gives you a word very close to pretzel which could have easily been formed in one of the many dialectal forms.

The connection of the words 'bag' and 'bagging' are too close to 'biggin' to be ignored. That a basic and simple piece of kitchen apparatus could have such a definite history seems far-fetched. After all, it is nothing more than a cloth strainer and was probably used in Greek and

A Britannia metal biggin from the mid-19th century. They are very hard to find with their little cloth bags still in them.

Roman times for other products. The growth in popularity was probably connected with the production of the 'new muslins', products of the industrial revolution, which were very much in demand in England in the late 1780s and early 1790s.[12]

In spite of the biggin's broad use, early biggins are a rare find in antique markets worldwide. There must be thousands upon thousands of coffee pots, still extant, missing their little filter bags. In over twenty years of searching antique markets, I have only seen a few complete biggins. One of those is illustrated - a very common English pot with its original bag.

What can be said about biggins is that they probably appeared simultaneously, with no particular origin, in various places, eventually achieving a long-standing popularity which lasted well into the twentieth century. The biggin was, like many early inventions, probably invented for other purposes but it became the basis for future coffee brewing innovations.

PERCOLATING OR FILTERING

The word 'filter' is widely used in talking about coffee, but its meaning is very close to the word 'percolate', so close that most people use the words interchangeably. Common usage of the word 'percolate' is in the sense of water percolating at atmospheric pressure through sand. The word 'filter' refers to a cloth or filter paper being used. In the United States the word 'percolator' is used to refer to the pumping percolator, where the coffee circulates and percolates several times. This is not an accurate description and is very confusing because the American 'percolator' is different from a simple percolating device. An accurate description would be a 'pumping, recirculating percolator'. Since the word 'pumping' is superfluous, because in order to recirculate the liquid must be pumped, this book will refer to the American percolator as a 'recirculating percolator'. In Germany, the word seems to be used for just about anything - including an espresso machine.[13]

The correct use is as follows:

Percolator or filter: The water percolates through the coffee grounds or filters through grounds supported by a filtering mechanism such as paper or fine mesh.

Pumping percolator: The water is pumped up once only to filter over the coffee.

Pumping recirculating percolator: The water is pumped up, percolates and is pumped around again and again.

Each machine worked differently and had a different history.

To filter coffee is an excellent way to make clear coffee. The first filters were mostly simple meshes, but filter papers did exist. A filter is a container with some straining device. The trick to make a filter work is to have the coffee coarse enough so that it does not fall through the holes, while being fine enough for the boiling water to extract the flavour as it passes through. If the coffee is too fine, the water may not pass at all, and if too coarse, the water may fall straight through.

The main problem with brewing coffee was that the grounds floated when the water hit them so they needed to be held down. Inventors de Belloy, Rumford and Hadrot discovered that if you compressed the coffee just enough, the coffee could act as a barrier and slow down the brewing process. Unfortunately the timing only worked if the grind was correct, and if the coffee did not swell so much that the water was prevented from falling through altogether. The grind and the size of the brewing compartment had to be designed perfectly.

The twin purposes of designing coffee filters were the clarification of the coffee and the timing of the brew. The timing could be controlled through the size of the hole through which the water entered or left the compressed coffee compartment, but this technique was not widely used. Clarifying the coffee required small holes, but the smaller the hole, the longer it took for the water to pass through. It was therefore very difficult to fulfil both functions at once.

Basically the early methods were unsatisfactory and depended on grind size to work at all. For some reason, it took many decades to work out that the filter should be used for filtering, and another device should be used to control the timing.

THE EVOLUTION OF FILTERING

Filtering coffee was definitely known in the seventeenth century and probably much more widely than previously acknowledged. The paucity of evidence still does not limit the range of coffee makers that actually existed. There is even mention of a 'lawn sive' [sieve], in 1662 in England.[14]

One of the oldest filtering devices is depicted in a painting, held in the Johann Jacobs Museum, Zurich, Switzerland, dated 1780, by Jean-Etienne Liotard of Geneva in Switzerland. It clearly shows a filter machine with a tap between the upper filter compartment and the coffee pot. The tap that allowed the brewing time to be manually controlled is an improvement on the filter pots that must have pre-dated this design. It is unlikely that the filter and the tap were invented at the same time. The problem of the water flowing through too quickly would have resulted in the addition of a tap to stop the flow until the brewing process was completed.

Another filter pot is illustrated in the book *A History of Old Sheffield Plate* with the date 1795 and it is a very rare item.[15]

A silver conical filter made in Hamburg around 1785 by Johann Christopher Hellmers is in the Johann Jacobs Museum in Zurich. It is the same shape as the 'Hamburg filter' which was very popular in Germany from the end of the 1890s. Its existence in silver suggests that there were others

HB

A filter pot from a painting by Liotard. There is a small tap on the upper section to control the water flow. It is interesting to note that the pot has a metal manufacturer's nameplate. Switzerland - late 18th century.

A coffee pot and filter. The little stem in the filter is similar to the presser in the de Belloy filter. This indicates that the presser must have existed a few years before Hadrot and Rumford mentioned them. England - 1795.

Conical filter in silver. Germany -1785.

The illustration shows three filter pots. Because coffee floats, pots in Figs.1 and 2 probably made weak coffee, whilst the filter in Fig.3 made a stronger cup.c. 1825

in porcelain before it. Filtered coffee as we know it today was known in France. Demachy writing in 1775, even though a little doubtful about this method, stated:

> *Of all the bourgeois methods imagined to prepare coffee, I will only speak of the last. A funnel is placed on the coffee pot or rests on a tripod over a cup. A muslin filter bag sits in the funnel and a double dose of coffee per cup is put into it and boiling water poured over three or four times.*[16]
> [English translation]

In Germany, Krünitz reported in 1784 that the recently introduced method of brewing coffee was the best. A linen or hair cloth (coarse material for straining) or better still, a white blotting-paper filter which was only used once, was put into a filter funnel of tinned metal. It was recognised that the water must be poured on slowly. It was also stated that the brewed coffee must be filtered again if you wanted stronger coffee and that the coffee could be reheated and the spent grounds used again to make a good taste.[17] Either the coffee was very coarsely ground, or the coffee was generally very poor for this to be considered. While the idea of filtering was good, the metal filters probably rusted and the filtering mediums were unsatisfactory. Certainly filters were mentioned in Germany during the next hundred years and may well have persisted in use throughout the whole period.

Boehnke-Reich stated that the original coffee machine was discovered by Albinus in Demerary in the West Indies in 1783. It was a reversible filter pot, with a spirit flame around the lower part.[18]

A round flat filter with holes was mentioned in 1825. This used silk, wool, linen, hemp or horse hair as the filtering medium.[19] In 1861 a round filter was described which used a water spreader

which was very much the same as the Melitta filter of 1908.[20] The Melitta filter of 1908 was acclaimed and this could only have occurred if there was no similar product available. The Melitta filter can be seen to be the application of new materials - aluminium and especially filter paper - to an old idea.

Even though these mentions of filter paper from the 1780s in both France and Germany are proof of the attempts to make filtered coffee, I do not believe their acceptance was widespread. It was to be over a century before filter paper use became general in Germany.

From the little written evidence and the lack of examples, I am confident that, even though there were innovations in the eighteenth century, most of the effort had gone into making porcelain pots of increasingly luxurious and costly decoration. Coffee gave the rich the opportunity for a display of elegance and grace leaving the importance of the coffee pot contents behind. While the rich were indulging themselves with expensive tea and coffee services, which have fascinated collectors to this day, there were doubtless many others interested in the product itself. These others were to spend the next century improving the coffee.

DE BELLOY FILTER POT

The de Belloy filter pot of 1800 is acclaimed as the first filter pot even though no patent exists and we are still not sure just who de Belloy or du Belloy was. One book gives the date of 1691, but this is almost certainly wrong.[21] If we are to believe Ukers, it may have been Jean Baptiste de Belloy, Archbishop of Paris. If true, he was 91 years old at the time of the invention - surely one of the oldest inventors ever. Perhaps he could have made heavenly coffee using holy water.

There is no doubt that the sandwich was named after the Earl of Sandwich but it is unlikely that he was actually the first man to place a filling between two pieces of bread. Similarly with the de Belloy filter. It was possibly named after the Archbishop but not invented by him.

Cadet-de-Vaux, a prominent coffee scientist of the time, offers a more likely origin of the de Belloy filter. In his book he says that the filter was merely the application of the process used to leach ashes and plasters for making soap, but that the new use of an existing invention did not reduce its merit.[22]

The de Belloy filter pot consisted of a pot within a pot - *a bain-marie* to keep the coffee hot, an infuser positioned over the coffee to filter the coffee and a press to compress the coffee to stop it rising. It is hard to know exactly what the de Belloy method was, as there are no known operating instructions provided by de Belloy. Brillat-Savarin in 1825 published the *Physiology of Taste* and wrote:

> *I have tried, in my time, all these methods and all that have been proposed up until today, and I have settled for obvious reasons upon the one*

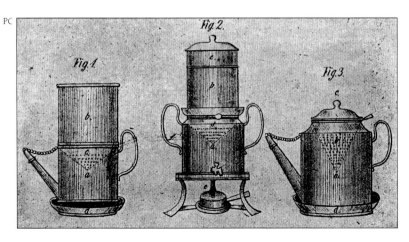

which is called à la de Belloy, which consists of pouring boiling water upon coffee placed in a receptacle of porcelain or silver pierced with little holes. This first essence is taken out, heated gently to boiling point, put once more through its sieve, and the result is coffee as clear and as good as is possible in this world.[23]

On theoretical grounds alone, any method which involves reheating, boiling or re-brewing should be rejected, let alone one using all three. This indicates that coffee in general was probably very bitter and strong in 1825. Alternatively it may have been coarsely ground and totally underbrewed.

Whatever its origin, in terms of name and inventor, this pot was certainly a development from the biggin - from a filter suspended in the pot, to a filter suspended above the pot. Importantly *time* was introduced as an intrinsic part of the coffee pot. For the first time a part of the brewing process was controlled by the pot itself or at least was supposed to be. This idea was new and important because it was to be the basis of many future inventions. The fact that the de Belloy pot would often fail to work - grind size was critical and the technology just did not exist to get a consistent grind size - was not as important as the fact that it became an object of discussion and contention. The most interesting thing about it is that even though it was found to be deficient, it was the subject of such interest and acclaim in both France and Germany.

de Belloy's Mistake

By concentrating on the fact that the timing could be slowed down by compressing the coffee grounds, de Belloy changed the course of coffee making development. However, his system could not work without stringent control of grind size, coffee density and quantity. Others tried to improve on what he had done but the basic idea was wrong - his idea could never work without a great deal more precision. Other inventors followed him down the wrong track. It was as if Leonardo da Vinci had said that the only way to fly was with flapping wings and nobody thought of gliding. The idea of separating filtering and brewing time control was not to surface for over a hundred years after de Belloy's death when Auguste Carton invented the Selecta filter in 1927. It seems incredible that it took so long for de Belloy's mistake to be rectified and even then it was by accident. Carton was trying to make a filter that was easy to clean. Even when he made a filter with timing control it was hardly noticed.

1800 is the accepted date for the invention of the de Belloy filter pot. The following century was to see enormous developments in coffee technology, leading to new directions. Considering what the words 'a cup of coffee' could mean in terms of flavour, it is a wonder that coffee became popular at all. There was no guarantee of what might be used to make it, no consistency in roasting it and fairly haphazard methods of brewing it. Coffee was literally a concoction of whatever excited your interest. Perhaps the rare and accidental good cups of coffee alerted the best minds to the existence of a good cup of coffee - if only you could find a way to produce it. The industrial revolution was in full swing and fanciful minds turned to the application of chemical apparatus and mechanical devices to make that elusive cup with the same aroma as in the beans.

Coffee aroma is exciting and attractive, even from badly and over-roasted coffee beans just freshly ground. This aroma seems to elicit a need to drink a cup of coffee, and to create the illusion that the aroma will be reproduced as the same enticing taste in the cup. This was the ever-present goal of inventors.

THE IDEA OF PATENTS IN EUROPE

In 1791 the French Minister of the Interior introduced patents. It is interesting to note that the first patent documents in France actually carried the words: *Patents of invention, improvement and importation.* The point is that the patent was often registered in the name of the importer and not necessarily in the name of the inventor. Sometimes the original inventor's name was mentioned in the patent. Without patent attorneys, it was difficult for an inventor in one country to register a patent in another country. In England patents had existed for many years but now the French inventors had their chance. The patent period was rather shorter than today's - the first patents had only two years' duration and later patents five. This short protection period had a dramatic effect on the way the inventors worked. They must have been in a real fervour to follow an existing success with another success. Only by constantly inventing new patents could inventors have a protected product. The existence of patents does not appear to have been the catalyst for all the new inventions and yet without the patent system, developments would have been totally different. In an age of passion about coffee, the patent system became the expression of new ideas.

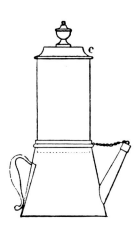

The de Belloy filter pot was the most famous but not the first filter pot. France -1800.

A de Belloy filter pot with a rammer and water spreader, with the mark Chatelain. France - late 19th century.

The French economy was very different to the English economy at the beginning of the nineteenth century. France had recently lost Canada as a colony, whereas England had lost the American States but these had been replaced by Canada, Australia and India. England was prospering enormously through its trading activities with the Empire, while France had no real empire to trade with. France was forced to develop a trade within its own borders.

Their populations were also very different. England had a population of sixteen million of whom one million lived in London. France had a population of thirty million of whom six hundred thousand lived in Paris - the pivot for the whole country. All roads led to Paris. France had an enormous population of coffee drinkers in the provinces, anxious to keep up to date with prevailing fashions such as the new coffee makers, while the British Empire colonists were more interested in tea.

Substantial duties were levied on coffee in England in 1816 - from eight and a half pence from any British plantation in America to thirty-two pence from any other country and were reduced to four and eight pence respectively in 1842.[24]

Internal tariffs had been abolished in 1790 in France but it was not until 1818 that this happened in Prussia. In 1834 the German Customs Union was established comprising seventeen States and twenty-six million people.

Even though the first German patent was in 1379 (for a water pump), it was five centuries before modern Germany, as opposed to the individual States which comprised Germany previously, began registering coffee patents. By that time France had stolen the march and registered the basic coffee equipment, much of which was invented in Germany. It was not until the twentieth century that Germany made up for lost time with some very impressive developments. For many reasons, France was the place where all the activity was going on. France had an excellent recording system, at the time, for a product which interested it - coffee. Even though the inventions were taking place in both Germany and France, they were being recorded in France.

The Italian patent system started in 1474 in Venice and each city-state had its own system. This meant that the protection of the patent was only granted for that state. Since the potential reward was smaller the interest in making patents was also smaller.

The first inventions must have caused a complete change in the way things were done. Gone were the days when there was merely discussion with no real conclusion. A patent application was a reasoned, written declaration by one person that he was right and an invitation to another to declare that he was also right .

Today we think in terms of expanding an initial idea to its limits. By contrast some of the nineteenth century French patents were nothing less than controlled lurches from one machine to another. The failure of the first idea often nurtured the desire to invent something, anything. The inventors searched for ever more exotic solutions in an attempt to invent that something, even when there was no advantage to be had. Some French patents are so enormous, so full of totally different machines that it is nearly impossible to establish just what has been invented. In some cases the solutions were so complicated that they defied economic manufacture. Through all the excitement, only the coffee makers that offered a simple solution prevailed.

HB

A probable drawing of the Henrion Pharmaco-Chemical Infusion Coffee Pot patented by Rouch, Henrion and Denobe in Paris. It was a biggin with a *bain-marie*. France - 1802

THE FIRST PATENT IN FRANCE, 1802
Denobe, Henrion and Rouch

On the thirtieth Germinal of the tenth year of the French Republic (March 1802), the Prefect of the Department of the Seine forwarded two packets containing pieces supporting the application for a patent to the Minister for the Interior. In May of the same year, a patent was granted to Messrs. Denobe, Henrion and Rouch for a period of five years - the first French coffee patent. They called it a 'pharmaco-chemical infusion coffee-pot' and they claimed, as all other inventors would claim, that their invention was timesaving, economical and that it preserved, unaltered, the taste and the precious qualities of the beans. Denobe was a quarry proprietor, Henrion was a lampmaker and Rouch was a doctor from the faculty of medicine at Montpelier. It seemed that Rouch invented it, Denobe financed it and Henrion made it. Later it became known as Henrion's coffee pot.

As the first French coffee patent it is worth describing in detail. It was a double-walled pot with a triangular sieve in the middle to hold the coffee and a lid to seal it hermetically. To make six strong cups you used three ounces of coffee, poured boiling water over it and allowed it to stand for seven or eight minutes. In a book called *Dissertation sur le Café*, J.M.A. Gubian writing in 1814 said coffee should be brewed for twenty to thirty minutes in this machine.[25] There was obviously confusion as to how long it took to brew a cup of coffee.

At the same time you poured boiling water into the outer section to keep the coffee hot. There were two taps to draw off the hot coffee and the hot water. So far so good, but then the patent goes on to describe how you could economise by adding one ounce of coffee to the already used three and make another six cups. It was in fact little more than a metal filter biggin with a tap sitting in a *bain-marie*. However its existence stirred up debate and this in itself was a catalyst for further innovations.

THE FIRST SCIENTIFIC APPROACH
Antoine Alexis Cadet-de-Vaux

Antoine Alexis Cadet-de-Vaux was probably the first person to use a scientific approach to gain an understanding of coffee brewing. Even so his book, *Dissertation sur le Café*, published in 1806, got it all wrong. His book was in fact a polemic against the de Belloy coffee pot. Perhaps de Belloy's ecclesiastical connection gave him 'pulpitations'. Nevertheless, his arguments were so logical and compelling that he was accepted and respected as an authority on coffee. So much so, that he was still being quoted ninety-five years after his book was published. As a member of learned societies of sciences, arts and letters all over France as well as learned foreign academies, it was no wonder that he attained such a position. He even called himself a missionary for domestic science. His position was not justified. His name is hardly mentioned in present-day histories of coffee.[26] Nor does his name appear among the inventors of the period.

Cadet-de-Vaux's main complaint against the de Belloy pot was the use of tin-plate, which changed the flavour of the coffee. The tin was not evenly spread, but the biggest problem was that the vertical walls of holes in the filter could not be tinned at all and could rust. Cadet-de-Vaux asked a Monsieur Nast to make a porcelain pot, with a tin filter. Porcelain was more economical because if any single part broke, it could be replaced, whereas with tin-plate the total replacement of the pot was required. It was an advance, because even with a tin-plate filter, a porcelain pot was more economical. It was to be some time before an effective porcelain filter was made. Despite his scientific approach, Cadet-de-Vaux did not see the cardinal error that Archbishop de Belloy had made, in overlooking the importance of precision in relation to the grind size, coffee density and quality.

The full name of Cadet-de-Vaux's book was, 'Dissertation About Coffee; its History, its Properties and the Procedure to Obtain the Nicest, Healthiest Drink in the Most Economical Way' [English translation]. His book is almost a dissertation on how not to make coffee and probably set the course of good coffee making back a few decades.

The Cadet-de-Vaux Solution

Cadet-de-Vaux's logical mind went back to basics to deduce a perfect coffee brewing technique. He somehow managed to reach conclusions which are almost incredible:

Coffee must be reheated because it tastes better...[27] *Coffee can be prepared one or two days in advance, even for a large house...*[28] *The water should be between fifty and sixty degrees or even a cold water infusion.*[29] *Establish the weight of coffee used as half an ounce per cup. The weight loss in roasting should be three ounces in sixteen.* [English translation]

At least he nearly got the weight loss right for roasting.

He recommended the use of a *Caféomètre* (or a hydrometer) to determine the strength of brew - it was merely a device to measure the specific gravity of the brewed coffee.[30] Results were measured in *Caféométriques*. He tried three different temperatures to determine the best temperature. The higher the number, the better the extraction. Somehow he got the following results:

Using cold water infusion 9.250 *Caféométriques*
Using hot water infusion 7.625 *Caféométriques*
Using boiling water infusion 6.125 *Caféométriques*

These results are the opposite of what I would expect, yet I have never seen any criticism of his results. It is most unusual to dissolve more from a substance with cold water than with hot water. The fact that it was quoted in 1901, in Chryssochoïdès' book, ninety-five years later, shows that it remained unchallenged.[31] Perhaps Cadet-de-Vaux owned the only *Caféomètre* and no-one could check his results.

Cadet-de-Vaux also gave instructions for coffee shop owners on how to improve their cup of coffee. His apparatus was a conical filter of porcelain or crockery with a filter of silver or pewter in the base sitting on a crockery pot. Conical filters were already in use in Germany. An infusion of tea-coloured water should be made by pouring warm water over exhausted coffee grounds. The night before use, this 'tea-water' should be heated to fifty or sixty degrees and poured over compressed coffee and allowed to filter the whole night through. In the morning this coffee should be kept at the front door and small amounts taken to the *bain-marie* as required. The infused coffee would be the same at 6 a.m. as at 10 a.m. All this was better than boiling the coffee several times during the day for fifteen minutes, clarifying it and reboiling it. He specifically advised reheating the coffee, giving assurances that this would improve the flavour.

He claimed that his machine alone would stop the coffee shop industry collapsing as people used the de Belloy machine at home. His machine made better coffee and he could prove it. He was to be the first of many who thought the proof of the scientific method would be sufficient to convince the public to make a better coffee in a better way. Simplicity was always to be a handicap in the design of a new coffee pot - a complicated design promised more. On paper, his machine may have made better coffee in a commercial environment than other commercial brewers, but it was a dead end as far as domestic brewers were concerned.

Cadet-de-Vaux did not stop with his book. He must have been active in spreading his ideas, for his name appears in the patent file for Denobe, Henrion and Rouch. In a letter to the Minister dated 26 August, 1810, Rouch complained that Cadet-de Vaux had stolen their patent. The Minister replied that the patent had run out.

Also in the patent file, there is an extract from the letters to the editor of the *Journal de Paris* of September 29, 1810. Rouch informed readers that it was his invention that made coffee without boiling. He said that this would astonish the readers and annoy Cadet-de-Vaux; but everyone knew it.

The French writer, J.M.A. Gubian in 1814 described the way that Cadet-de-Vaux suggested to make coffee:

Mix the infusion of four cups of cold water on half an ounce of coffee with the infusion of three cups of boiling water on the same coffee and heat just before you need it.[32]   [English translation.]

Cadet-de-Vaux's commercial technique had by now moved into the domestic sphere, but it lacked magic. It probably never made a really good cup of coffee, but at least it would never have made a bitter one - not until it was reheated. All these references to Cadet-de-Vaux's ideas, including Chryssochoïdès' 1901 Instruction Book, show how little was learnt or understood.[33] It is hard to know how they took him seriously when he gave instructions for making coffee using exhausted grounds. At least he admitted to its having a disagreeable taste. His ideas on cold water coffee-making were repeated in Germany in the 1840s without quoting his name and have been in vogue somewhere in the world at times ever since. It would seem that normal coffee at the time was not very good and reheated coffee the same. How else could Cadet-de-Vaux have been given credence after suggesting that coffee should be reheated?

From these beginnings, the inventions started to come forth in ever-increasing numbers. The rising level of controversy and discussion meant that people were taking coffee brewing more seriously.

The Hadrot coffee pot was another filter pot with a press to keep the coffee in place to stop it from floating. The idea was much the same as that of de Belloy and Rumford. France -1806.

THE SECOND PATENT IN FRANCE, 1806
Hadrot

Hadrot described his coffee filter as a coffee maker which operated without boiling and he claimed that others who had tried to save the aroma had failed. He complained that other coffee pots using cotton or wool bags adversely flavoured the coffee. The other makers, he complained, gave the coffee the flavour of cotton or wool socks (the bags in the biggins), or even rust.

As a solution, Hadrot used a filter of tin hardened with bismuth and a rammer to compress and level the coffee to half an inch. By measuring the compression he sought to control the flow which would slow the brewing down, but he failed to realise that the grind size, as well as the quantity of coffee, was of great importance. On the inside of the pot he placed a rim to act as a measure for the rammer, to control the compression.

Count Rumford

While he was in Paris in 1806, the American-British scientist, philanthropist and administrator, Benjamin Thompson, F.R.S., known as Count Rumford, invented a percolator with a *bain-marie*, but made no patent application. He suggested that by compressing two-thirds of an inch of coffee into something less than half an inch with a rammer, you made a better cup. Hadrot's and Rumford's inventions were basically the same, except that Rumford's was less precise, and there was no device to control the compression.

History has been much kinder in remembering Rumford and this may be due to the fact that the Hadrot patent drawings were in several parts whereas the Rumford filter was in one easily-understood drawing, requiring no explanation as to how or why it worked. All Rumford really did was to combine de Belloy's and Hadrot's inventions. Rumford's coffee pot has been remembered, but not his words. In 1812 he wrote a forty-eight page essay on coffee which he published in London.[34] In fact this was the most intelligent and complete work about brewing

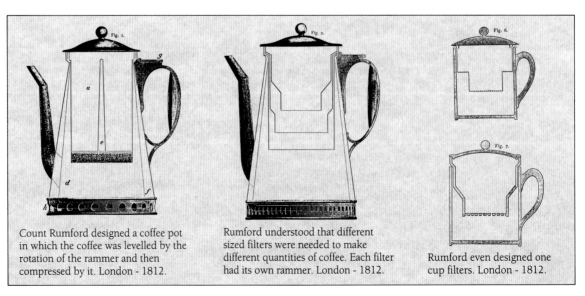

Count Rumford designed a coffee pot in which the coffee was levelled by the rotation of the rammer and then compressed by it. London - 1812.

Rumford understood that different sized filters were needed to make different quantities of coffee. Each filter had its own rammer. London - 1812.

Rumford even designed one cup filters. London - 1812.

coffee printed to that date and perhaps for many decades after. He understood levelling the coffee, pressing it, slow brewing time and that hot water made better coffee than cooler water and that a fine grind made stronger coffee than a coarse grind. He even noted that the air became attached to the small solid particles of the ground coffee and often remained attached to them, causing them to rise to the surface of the water.

Most importantly, he proposed that the depth of coffee should be the same irrespective of the number of cups brewed and that it followed that the diameter of the filter should increase as the number of cups increased. He then proceeded to calculate the diameter to four decimal places and showed different strainers for different numbers of cups.

He even invented a one-cup apparatus which took eight to ten minutes for the water to filter through. There is a precision about Rumford's statements that make him the first coffee scientist to really contribute to coffee knowledge. Rumford's influence on coffee making was like a comet - a flash of light on the subject which did not return to illuminate it for decades, but sadly, nobody noticed. His essay first appeared in 1812 and was reprinted in 1875 as part of his total works. Ukers showed a drawing of his coffee pot and gave a few quotes. If his works had been more widely read and put into practice, coffee making would have been much improved at an earlier date. However, he was writing in English and most of the innovation was in France and Germany.

Rumford was a colourful character. As well as being a Count of the Holy Roman Empire, he married Lavoisier's widow, invented Rumford soup in Germany and designed the English Gardens in Munich.

A Sheffield pot with presser to keep the coffee down. There was no water spreader. England - 1805.

THE WATER SPREADER AND THE FILTER

The most widespread innovation in coffee brewing practice in the nineteenth century was the water spreader. It was designed to prevent the water from being poured in such a rush that it would cause the bed of coffee sitting on the filter to be broken up and made to float. Slowing the pouring helped to control the timing. No date or person has been or can be reliably linked to its introduction. The earliest known example to my knowledge is the yellow pot, which clearly shows a water spreader, from the *Directoire* Period in France, nominally 1795 to 1799 but which could be as late as 1815. The lower pot incorporated a *bain-marie* with the entrance for the water in the open spout on top of the handle, and a small tap to empty it, under the handle. It is interesting that this style of coffee pot was to remain popular in France through the rest of the 1800s, even though there are few examples extant.

The Folger's Coffee Silver Collection in Cincinnati contains an 1805 percolator with a water spreader which sits just above the coffee, so its prime purpose must be to keep the rammer upright. It was not a water spreader in the conventional sense, sitting at the top of the pot.[35]

Above: Eames and Barnard silver filter showing water spreader and rammer. The rammer could not be rotated. England - 1829.

Left: Filter pot with water spreader and *bain-marie*. *Directoire* style. France - 1795 to 1799.

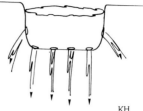

The water spreader had an important role. It broke up the flow of water so that the coffee grounds tended to remain at the bottom instead of floating. In addition, it restricted further pouring of hot water until the spreader was empty, thus ensuring a reasonable brewing time.

Left and Above: Brown earthenware
filter pot, probably French or
Dutch. c. 1820s.

KH

Above: Reversible Filter Pot or
Napoletana. The water is boiled in the
lower section, then the whole pot is
tipped up and the water filters through
the coffee which is held in the middle.

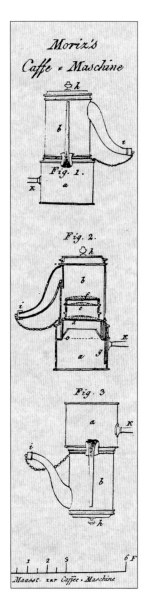

Morize patent for the
reversible coffee maker,
nowadays commonly called
a Napoletana. Paris - 1819.

The silver 1829 Eames and Barnard filter has a water spreader which sits high in the rim of the filter - its normal position at the top of the filter.[36] This filter was for coffee and sat in a teapot. In other words, it was part of a combination teapot/coffee pot. It also had a rammer which rested loosely on the coffee, its own weight acting to compress the coffee. This would seem to indicate that the scientific ideas of measuring the extent of the pressure, as in Rumford and others, had been abandoned.

The brown filter pot in the illustration, possibly made as late as 1830, also has a water spreader in the upper position. This type of pot was popular for the next hundred years with water spreaders made of different materials.

The water spreader seems to have been developed somewhere before 1800. It was in many ways one of the most significant developments in the early 1800s and is still used in modern commercial filter brewers and good domestic brewers.

THE FIRST REVERSIBLE FILTER POT PATENT
Séné

An Italian book published in Verona in 1751 describes a coffee maker which was an early reversible filter and says that it was widely used in Italy.[37] The next mention is the discovery of the reversible coffee pot by Albinus in Demerary in the West Indies in 1783. This is clearly wrong. There does not appear to be a reference to it anywhere else.[38]

The need for a clear patent drawing to secure a place in history could not be better illustrated than in the case of the French inventor, Séné, whom Ukers consigned to the scrapheap of history with the single sentence: 'In 1815 Séné was granted a French patent on a device to make coffee without boiling'.[39] Séné has never been heard of since.

Séné registered the first patient for the reversible drip coffee pot. His patent briefly describes five pieces to be assembled in sequence but he fails to explain just how the machine operates. Even worse, it is not immediately clear precisely what he did invent. His kettle has a double wall and into it fits a filter box across which the water passes to extract the coffee. The patent says:

The fourth piece is a reservoir which forms the coffee pot into which the coffee falls and which fits ON the kettle ON THE OTHER SIDE and they are closed by a little copper bar which keeps the evaporation down. [English translation.]

Both the kettle and the coffee pot were double-walled to produce a very quick boiling and slow cooling action. Séné's patent only really makes sense as a reversible drip pot because the kettle was obviously the lower part and the pot the upper. Tipping it upside down was the only way to make it function. We will never know if the Séné pot was ever marketed in France but certainly it was a new step.

ANOTHER REVERSIBLE FILTER COFFEE POT
Morize

In 1819 Morize, a tinsmith/ lampmaker from Paris, made an application for a reversible drip coffee maker. Edelstan Jardin, a French author writing in 1895, (whose book, *Le Caféier et le Café*, was a source of information for Ukers) said that the problem with Morize's coffee maker was that the grounds fell to one side of the coffee maker and the water fell straight past.[40] He also stated that in spite of the great publicity given to this utensil, it was forgotten immediately after its appearance. This in fact was not true.

Morize's original design must have been unsatisfactory because five weeks after the original application, he made another application for a filter with larger holes, to be placed between the first two, to control the speed and also a movable filter so that you could make two, four or six cups. In the light of this, Edelstan Jardin's comments do not carry much weight. After all, he wrote his critique some seventy-six years after the Morize invention was granted and, one hundred and seventy years later, the machine is still available in Italy, where it is known as the Napoletana.

In theory you boiled the water before you turned the pot over but with the level of technology at that time and using tin, you probably melted the seam in the bottom if you tried. The idea of the reversible coffee pot was to surface again in the Russian oval coffee pot and in the true Italian Napoletana, neither of which had seams in the base.

Morize had learnt from previous inventors because he claimed that his pot worked without either boiling or evaporation and that it needed only fifty-one grams of coffee instead of ninety-two. The dream of somehow getting more flavour from less beans continued for a long time. I cannot recall any inventor claiming that you made a better cup in his machine by using more coffee. In most cases you would have.

The Morize machine was certainly known in Germany and was described immediately after its invention in *Dinglers Polytechnisches Journal*.[41] The article commences with the comment that the de Belloy machine blocked up very easily, the filter rusted and you needed a lot of coffee to make a strong cup. By comparison, the Morize invention improved on this, as the filters could be taken out and cleaned and you used a third less coffee. One of the advantages claimed was that as the water boiled, the steam developed the aromatic part of the coffee which streamed out of the spout at the moment the pot was turned upside down. Dingler thought the Morize machine was the best available.

In 1841, Friedrich Reimann, a German cookery author, stated that the de Belloy and Morize machines were held in high esteem in Germany. He said that the usual method was de Belloy's, but also commented on the slowness and that the machine blocked up when a lot of water was poured on to the coffee.[42]

A later model Monnet with a much simpler filter mechanism. This model is from Paris and not Lyons - probably 1880s.

A reversible coffee pot which could be lifted out of its stand and turned by the handle. France - 1900s.

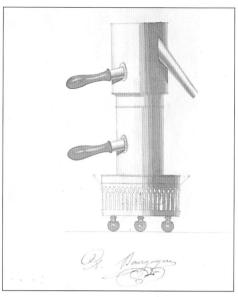

A Bourgogne reversible pot from the patent drawing. France - 1849.

The oval-shaped coffee pot could be rotated in the stand. It was called a Russian coffee pot and was very popular prior to 1900. The big advantage was the seamless base. France or England.

Above and Right:
A Monnet reversible filter pot in tin from Lyons. The fittings were very similar to the Morize original patent.
France - mid 19th century.

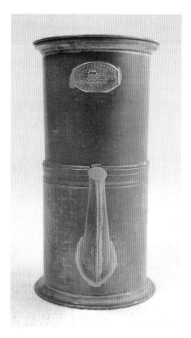

An early Napoletana, made by hand probably in the early 1900s. Italy or France.

The Bernstein brass coffee maker featured a milk jug to be kept warm on the top. Germany - 1890s.

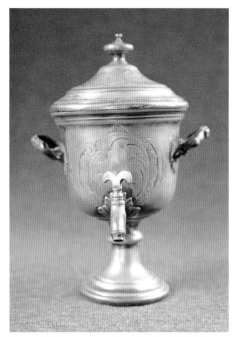

A vertical filter coffee maker. England - 1860s.

The boiling water was poured over the ground coffee in the back compartment and the coffee filtered through the vertical round filter. England - 1860s.

A pewter pot with the filter in the lid. Pewter is not good for coffee and it probably made putrid coffee. France - 1900s.

'La Precieuse' was the name given by Joseph Demaison of Lyon in 1891 to this valve filter. The valve sitting on the filter is inverted. In use, the weight of the pouring water keeps the valve open and when it has fallen through, the counterbalance on the valve causes it to close, preserving the heat and aroma. France - 1891.

This style of enamel French filter pot was very common at the turn of the century.

A German filter pot of the 1900s.

Right: The white German Karlsbad coffee pot and the brown French filter pot were very popular. They both used a ceramic filter in which the filter hole was produced by the intersection of two longitudinal slits at right-angles. The little ridge under the spout of the brown pot caught any grounds which had fallen through.

A coffee pot with a pump in the horizontal handle made for Cafés Gilbert. France - 1920s.

THE RUSSIAN COFFEE POT AND THE NAPOLETANA

In 1849, Bourgogne came out with a filter pot with a hot water reservoir which was turned upside down to filter through the coffee. The Russian coffee pot followed and it was just a reversible model on a frame, which looked very decorative and could be used at the table. Then came the Napoletana, the name given to the aluminium filter pot which was widely used in Italy in the decades after the Second World War.

PRESSURE FILTERS
Tiesset and Moupier-Pierre

In 1840 Auguste Alexandre Tiesset and René Louis Moupier-Pierre incorporated a vacuum pump into a coffee maker. It was an innovation that responded to a major problem with the filter machines - water blockage. If there was the slightest enclosure of the coffee in a fixed compartment, the swelling of the coffee could act as a barrier to water passing through. Positive or negative pressure in the form of a vacuum was needed to encourage the water to fall through. Their patent is not important for itself, but it does serve to indicate the types of problems faced in making a cup of coffee using a filter. The finer the grind of coffee, the larger the swelling and the greater the likelihood for a blockage to occur. Hence the need for the development of machines which used pressure to force the water through the coffee.

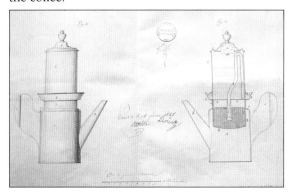

The Mahler & Durietz Patent. The spirit in the reservoir around the middle was lit and the flame boiled the water, which was forced by steam pressure through the loosely packed coffee grounds. France - 1845.

DAUSSÉ AND HIS FILTER INVENTIONS

In 1846 Daussé produced a manual for the coffee lover.[43] It was really an advertising brochure for his two inventions which must have already existed for some time. The first invention was a coffee pot, made of either tin-plate or hard porcelain, which incorporated a float to indicate how many cups had been made and also a tap to control the number of cups to be made. The models with a spirit lamp were of tin-plate or tinned copper. The models in a fountain shape were of bronze or of silver-plated Britannia metal and had a small candle in the base to keep the coffee hot. The models for coffee shops were of brass, tinned on the inside.

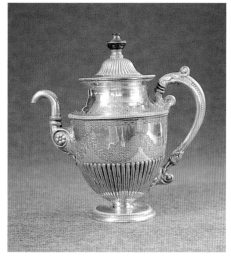

In 1886 the Royle pumping teapot was introduced in England and is rather common. The tall shape and narrow base suggest that this model was for coffee. The coffee model is uncommon. England - 1886.

The Eureka filter pot showing the woven mesh filter. Germany - 1880s.

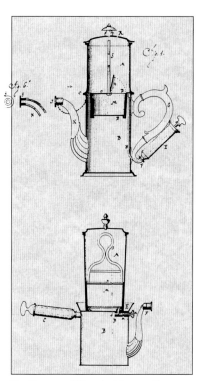

The Tiesset and Moupier-Pierre coffee pots had pumps to make a vacuum and draw the water through the coffee. France - 1840.

A Franz Dehne commercial filter pot from Basel. Switzerland - 1895.

The French liked warm brandy after their coffee. The hot coffee warmed the cup which was inverted to allow the brandy to be warmed in the bottom. France.

Left: A typical French commercial filter pot from around the turn of the century.

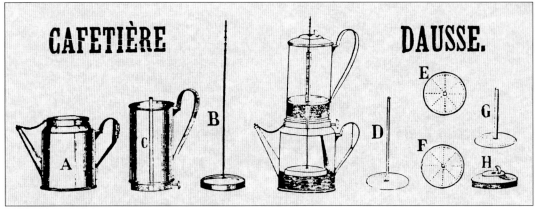

Left: A filter pot with a ridge around the top to hold spirits which were lit. When the water in the top had boiled, a little tap in the middle was turned manually to allow the boiling water to fall slowly through the little hole over the coffee. France - 1860s.

The Daussé coffee pot had a tap to control the filtering. France - 1844.

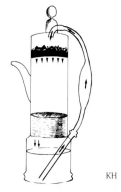

The Pumping Percolator. The water was pumped up to fall over the coffee once only.

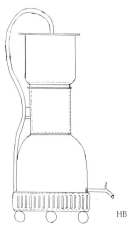

The Jones Pumping Percolator. Water is forced up the tube by steam pressure and it then falls onto and percolates through the coffee. England - c.1819.

The Morel patent for a one-cup brewer was an important catalyst in the development of the espresso machine. France - 1898.

Daussé recommended fifteen grams per *demitasse* and a ten minute infusion time before making the coffee. To make *café au lait*, sixty grams of very fine powder were allowed to infuse for at least a half hour and then the tap was opened slightly until the level in the base reached two cups. Then a few spoonfuls were added to boiling milk. Cleaning instructions were given in great detail - especially the two flannel filters which had to be boiled for an hour the first time to get rid of the sulphur odour. The filters were made of swanskin of wool - a fine-twilled flannel, from Segovia in Spain. Boiling water had to be poured into the coffee pot for the first time if it was tin-plate or tinned brass - to get rid of the taste of resin. Daussé was in no doubt that better coffee was made with water at 95 to 100 degrees Celsius. His pots allowed the use of a finer grind of coffee with the benefit of economy and avoided the use of clarifiers.

The most surprising statement made is to coffee shop owners:

After the second filtering of the grounds, the grounds are now so exhausted that those who buy grounds to make coffee again, do not want to buy grounds if they have been used in one of my coffee makers.[44] [English Translation]

There must have been quite a business in selling exhausted coffee grounds for Daussé to have even mentioned it.

SMALL ONE-CUP FILTERS

These filters, which were placed on top of the cup, were the catalysts for the espresso machine and for the German filter paper coffee makers.

The earliest patents in France for this type of coffee maker, Mahler's in 1885, Giraud's in 1895 and Morel's in 1898, came in several versions which were not significantly different from each other and not very innovative except to make one cup at a time over a glass. The development of this coffee maker was insignificant in content and yet an important step in the development of coffee makers in general. Up until the late 1800s, most, if not all, coffee makers had been designed to make

about four to six cups while shops were producing even larger quantities.

A filter to make one cup at a time was a simple concept, but one that was at the very heart of the *CAFÉ EXPRÈS* - coffee made expressly for you. Morel's large coffee pot, with a removable press to keep the coffee down, was not particularly exciting. As a small version, it helped to change the coffee world. In cafes in Paris and throughout Europe, people were soon drinking coffee made with single cup filters.

THE FIRST PUMPING PERCOLATORS

Boiling water releases steam seven times its own volume and in the confined space at the base of a percolator, this creates sufficient pressure to lift the water up a tube to fall over the coffee. The extraction is the same as for a filter. The efficiency of the pumping percolator depends on the filtering and on the speed with which the water is pumped over the coffee. There was no particular advantage except that the brewing process was self-contained and the resultant coffee a little hotter. Because the water had to be boiled, it took some time for the process to take place and in this sense, it probably made a good cup of coffee, because of the extended brewing time, which depended on the amount of heat applied. It was the first coffee maker to have a tube outside, visible to all. The magic and theatre of coffee making had begun.

The Jones pumping percolator was mentioned in print in 1901.[45] No patent has ever appeared and it was when I read the German *Dinglers Polytechnisches Journal* of 1820 that I came across the earliest reference to it.[46] The name Jones is obviously English and in fact he had a shop in The Strand, in London. On the balance of probabilities, the machine was invented in England in 1819 or before.

In the same year, 1819, Laurens was granted a French patent for a coffee pot without evaporation. This was the first patented pumping percolator but it was very similar to the Jones coffee pot. The water was boiled in the lower part and was forced up the central tube by steam pressure to fall over the coffee. From the time the boiling started, the water took three quarters of an hour to fall over the coffee. It took fifteen minutes to boil on the fire and twenty minutes on a spirit lamp. The usual claim for economy of use was of course made.

Was there any connection between Séné, inventor of the reversible drip pot, and Laurens? Both made their applications from the same address, 31 Saumon Passage, Paris. Saumon Passage was probably a gallery of similar shops where there were many tinsmiths and lampmakers.

The Laurens and Jones pots were obviously connected in inspiration. Whether the tube is on the outside or inside makes very little difference - it was just a device to raise the water.

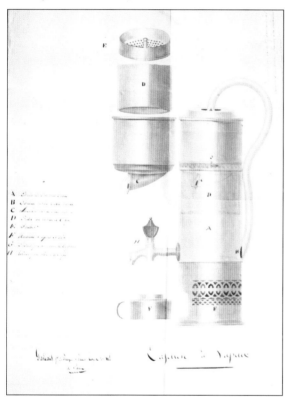

The original patent drawing for Gandais' pumping percolator. The water did not pass through the coffee until the flame had expired. France - 1827.

Laurens opened the door for such developments as that of Jacques Augustin Gandais, whose French patent came out in 1827. Gandais' patent application was for a pumping percolator with the ascending water tube on the outside (the same as the Jones machine). He referred to it as a new filter coffee pot which was called a steam coffee pot. It was really a filter machine in which the water was raised by steam. After ten minutes the water reached a temperature of 85 degrees *Réaumur* (boiling point was 80 degrees *Réaumur*) and expressed the entire essence of the coffee by the double action of the steam and the water passing through the coffee. This was the first time that the idea of needing steam and water to get the full flavour from the coffee had been conveyed. This idea was to linger for more than a hundred years, even though it had no real

substance. After the flavour had been leached out by the hot water there was nothing more for the steam to do. The fact that only a small amount of steam actually passed through the coffee at all entirely escaped Gandais.

Most importantly the patent says that the model was imported from Germany but had originally come from England, where this type of steam machine was in widespread use. Gandais was almost certainly the first to try to patent this type of machine in France.

LONG BREWING TIMES

The long and variable brewing times in the early days were an indication of the problems faced by the inventors of the early coffee makers, such as getting the water to boil quickly, or more likely the difficulty of getting the water to percolate through the coffee.

In 1814 Gubian described a slow infusion method which took two hours in the cinders of the fire and then a further fifteen minutes using isinglass, a transparent form of gelatine derived from fish bladders, to clarify the decoction.[47] In 1868 there was a book with mention of a cold water infusion of ten to twelve hours - times that seem incredibly long these days. The same book even mentioned using coffee grounds as a toothpaste and feeding old grounds to geese to make them more tasty.[48]

The Durant automatic coffee pot. Under steam pressure, hot water rose to the top compartment until the water level fell below the lower tube opening when steam went up this tube. A small amount of steam went out the upper right outlet, fell down the tube and condensed onto the lower counterbalance which caused the flame to be extinguished and opened the valve N to the lower compartment, whereupon the water fell over the coffee. *Voila!* France - 1827.

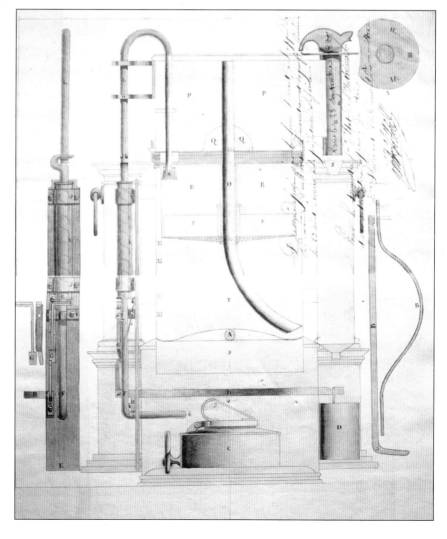

FIRST FULLY AUTOMATIC COFFEE MAKER
Durant

Three months after the Gandais patent of 1827, Nicolas Felix Durant, a manufacturer from Chalons-sur-Marne, made an application for a new patent offering the same advantages as the steam coffee pot of M. Gandais. Durant was described as making a 'percolator, employing for the first time, an inner tube to raise the boiling water for spraying over the ground coffee'.[49] In many books Durant's invention is shown but it is actually Capy's.[50] Louis-François Capy's invention just happens to be in the same patent application folder as Durant's in the French Archives. It looks as if Durant transferred his patent to Capy - probably because he could not get it to work.

What Durant in fact invented was the first automatic coffee pot - a pot that extinguished the flame when the coffee was made. This has never been recognised because of the Durant and Capy patent mix-up, perpetuated by Uker's book, which illustrated Capy's pot as Durant's.

The idea was ingenious but certainly too complicated to be a success. I doubt if it ever worked at all. M. Durant was gracious enough to suggest that if you wanted any further details you should ask M. Capy who had a model. M. Capy, a tinsmith/ lampmaker, must have been very clever to make such a complicated machine.

Capy's coffee pot was the second inner-tube coffee pot which extinguished the flame automatically. Laureys in 1828 made a simplified model of the same type. He had put the coffee pot in a *bain-marie* which emptied and probably melted if you did not turn the flame down in time. Advances brought complications. Instead of finding a solution to a problem, many inventors were finding problems to solutions.

Carl Hölterhoff made one of the more ingenious devices. The coffee grounds were in the top section and the water was forced up the central tube. By rotating the central tube, holes at different levels corresponded so that the desired number of cups could be made. In fact it was a central tube pumping percolator. Germany - 1884.

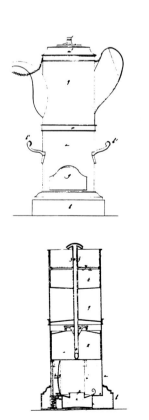

Capy's patent. Like Durant's, it probably never worked. France - 1827.

Above and Right: The Laureys percolator. The water in the outer compartment boiled up the tube and over the coffee. In theory, the patent worked. France- 1828.

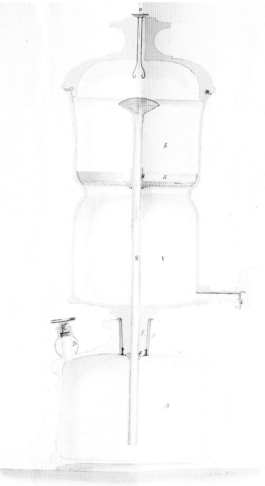

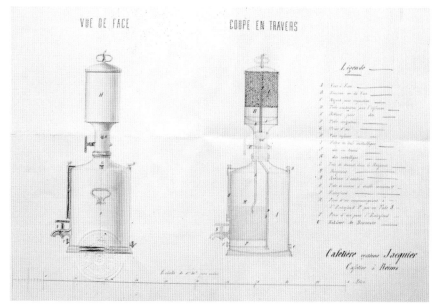

Above: A Jacquier-Jayet pumping percolator in which the coffee falls into the adjacent compartment. France - 1856.

Left: The Jacquier-Jayet pumping percolator where water falls into the middle chamber. France - 1856.

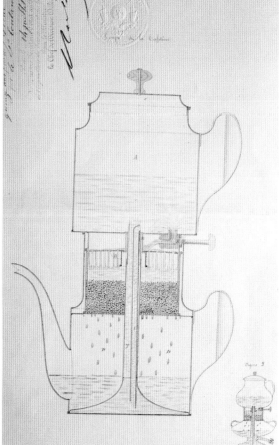

Coutant in 1855 invented a manually-controlled percolator. It may have been the inspiration for Dagand's patent three months later. France - 1855.

Kirmair invented the 'Czarine'. France - 1891.

A French gas-heated pumping percolator to make about 300 cups. The whole unit is one metre high and was probably used in a railway station or an army barracks. Invented by Prat. France - 1889.

Dagand also patented two commercial size percolators. France -1855.

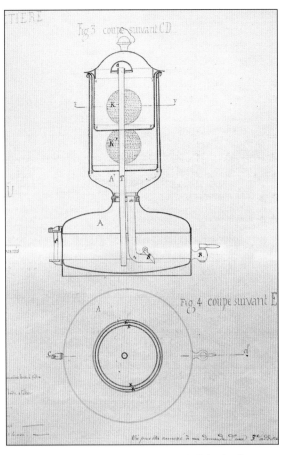

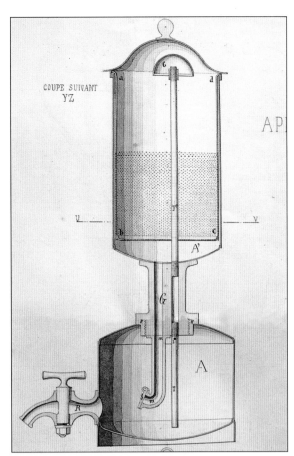

KH

Pumping recirculating percolator, commonly known as a percolator. The water was pumped up and percolated down through the coffee grounds and the coffee liquid was then circulated repeatedly through the grounds.

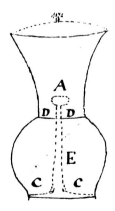

Madame Richard's patent drawing for a pumping recirculating percolator. The coffee rested on the filter D. The water boiled up the tube A, filtered through the coffee and entered through the little gap at C into the tube E to recirculate. France - 1837.

THE FIRST RECIRCULATING PERCOLATOR
Madame Richard

In a pumping percolator the water falls through the coffee grounds once, whereas in the recirculating percolator the same water passes through the coffee several times. In the base of the coffee pot there is a bell shape where the steam is formed. The steam cannot escape and forces the water up the tube to fall over the coffee grounds. The water percolates through the coffee, enters the bell and the process is repeated again and again. Because it tended to brew the coffee with water at boiling point and there was little time control, the electric version of the recirculating percolator was considered by some experts as the worst of all coffee makers ever invented.

The first recirculating percolator patent was based on a machine imported by Mme. Jeanne Richard from the inventor Mr. Van. s. Loeff of 32 Brander Street in Berlin. The water went up and then down, filtering through the coffee for as long as you liked. The patent said that the coffee pot had the form of the de Medicis bowl with continuous infusion and boiling. The simple diagram does not show just how the water in the base was kept in motion.

Mme. Richard lodged four different designs in the one patent application in 1838. The fourth was the most important of all - the recirculating percolator.

Dagand in 1855 attempted a complicated recirculating percolator with small valves. It probably was never produced because three years later he changed the patent to a simple pumping percolator, which achieved great popularity.

Above: The Dagand patent. France - 1855.

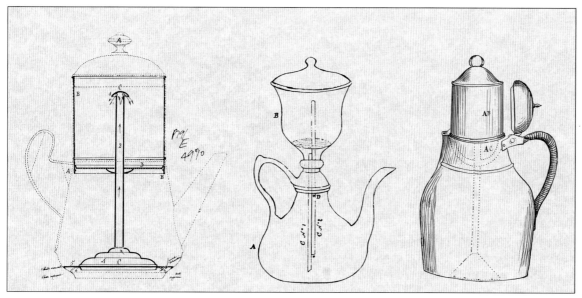

The 1865 and 1875 Pique patents incorporated a small hole in the base to allow the water to circulate. The hole is below the spout in the circular rim which supports the pumping bell 'C'.

Massot & Juquin made an interesting recirculating percolator. It was clearly derived from the vacuum pot. The water rose by the lower tube C1 and then fell and the cycle continued. This was all part of the attempt to get something more from the coffee. Where was the flavour going? Where was the aroma going? How to unlock the secret? France - 1865.

Alloncius. Note the small holes in the bell through which the brewed coffee passed to recirculate. France - 1866.

A Pique model in tin.

A French percolator using the Pique system.

An Italian percolator using the Pique system. The coffee basket in this is larger than the French model - the Italians wanted a stronger coffee than the French.

Left: The Bouillon & Siry percolator using the Malen system. France - 1900s.

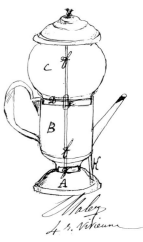

The Malen patent drawing. France - 1872.

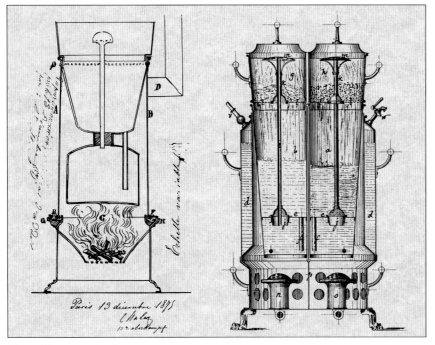

Above: The patent drawing for the Malen commercial percolator.

Above Right: Another Malen patent drawing. Paris - 1875.

NEW TYPES OF RECIRCULATING PERCOLATORS
Pique, Massot and Juquin

For some reason, in 1865 there was renewed interest in the recirculating percolator. Pique in 1865 made a model with a little hole to allow the water to fall back down. It was to be produced in a similar form for years both in Italy and France.

Also in 1865, Massot and Juquin claimed a continuous and automatic circulation. The water rose by the lower tube up to the level of the bottom of the upper tube, when the steam pressure was released and the brewed coffee fell down the lower tube. Then the whole process was repeated. Two circulations were sufficient for a perfect infusion - so they said. The same idea was

included in the same patent for a washing machine for linen. Surprisingly they did not say why this method was better than simply boiling the linen. The idea might have been satisfactory, but I doubt if it worked for coffee. Two circulations do not seem enough to have produced a flavourful coffee.

Alloncius in 1866 made another model of the recirculating percolator, which must have worked, as similar models are still made today.

Louis Malen's hand sketch in 1872 was in fact the same as the Bouillon and Siry pot. Bouillon and Siry probably used the Malen patent after it had run out. This type of percolator is reasonably common in both English and French antique markets, so presumably they were widely distributed.

Louis Malen made a recirculating percolator, similar to Pique's, in 1877. It is important to note that the tube section was held firmly in place by the pot itself.

Unfortunately, all of the variations seemed to have worked, as they actually produced some type of coffee, which is a pity, since no other coffee maker was destined to make such large quantities of bad coffee as the recirculating percolator. The water temperature was either boiling or too close to it and there was no inbuilt timing device to stop the recirculation. This left the recirculating percolator prone to overcooking the coffee and making it bitter.

The recirculating percolator's design was perfectly suited to the incorporation of electricity as it was the only type of machine which did not boil dry - at least not for a long time. Without electrical cut-outs, all the other types, which forced the water away from the element, were prone to boiling dry. What also made the dreaded

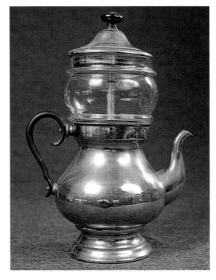

Above Left and Above: A recirculating percolator with a bell based on the Malen 1875 patent.

Left: A later model of the Bouillon & Siry percolator.

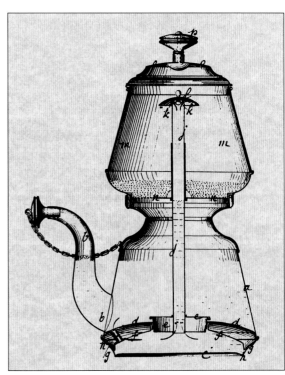

The Malen patent. France - 1877.

A recirculating percolator with three separate burners to control the speed of brewing. Germany - 1900s.

percolator popular was the fact that the later models included a glass cap in the lid. This maximised the theatrical effects of the bubbling coffee and reassuring perking noises.

In the next few years there were several different patents for recirculating percolators, all with different systems. Many of these systems have continued right to this day.

HYDROSTATIC PERCOLATOR
Edward Loysel

Loysel's hydrostatic percolator was an attempt to solve the problem of water not percolating through the coffee grounds. By utilising the higher pressure from a column of water on the coffee, the water was able to force its way through.

The same principle had been used in Germany in the Realsche Presse which was an impractical tube, 16 to 20 feet long, connected to a container of coffee. It was mentioned in Reimann's book of 1841, so it certainly pre-dated Loysel.[51] The idea was to make a very strong syrup using fine coffee for use in hot water or hot milk. The Realsche Presse was named after the French Count Real and first described in an Italian book by Luigi Annoni in 1834.

The names of Edward Loysel, Edouard Loysel de la Lantais and Edouard Loysel de Santais all appear in different books. They all belong to one and the same person. The Lantais name is correct, Santais being the result of misreading an old handwritten French L.

Edward Loysel was possibly the first coffee engineer and was the inventor of the famous large coffee machine used at the Paris Exposition of 1855. The machine had already been used in the Crystal Palace in London and used twelve grams

of coffee per cup.[52] Loysel invented a domestic version of the hydrostatic percolator, which still appears in antique shops and markets in the English-speaking world, and several other coffee makers which were triumphs of complication. He was obsessed with the principle of hydrostatic pressure and the consequence that the pressure could force the water:

> upwards through the pulverised material intended to be operated upon, and after maceration [steeping] be caused to descend through the material and thus extract or carry off the soluble or extractive matters contained in it.[53]

It was really an upside-down filter machine with a second pass, or an atmospheric pressure pot with a more complicated operation.

Hydrostatic percolators were made in England and do not seem to have been made in France. The French wanted a cup of coffee and the English wanted theatre. Loysel was very inventive. In 1854 he had the idea of grinding tea and coffee into a small container which sat on a spring balance to indicate the weight. He invented a hydrostatic pressure teapot to use the ground tea leaves and made further modifications to make his hydrostatic percolator work.

Naturally, it was an improved apparatus, but perhaps by oversight, Loysel forgot to say just how it was an improvement on any other coffee maker. I suspect it was not. The sheer mass of cold metal in his domestic machine relative to the amount of hot water was almost bound to make a cold cup of coffee. In theory, with the correct grind and just the right amount of ground coffee, you might get a slightly higher extract because of the higher pressure from the water column than could be achieved with a simple filter. In view of the problem of getting the water to actually pass through the coffee, he might have made an improvement, but only a slight one. Loysel never claimed such a thing - only that the water came up from below and then went down again.

With the commercial machine patented in 1854, he made something simple into something very complicated, but making it enormous obscured its inefficiency. Loysel brought the coffee machine from the kitchen to the serving area, probably for the first time. The theatre of coffee brewing had truly arrived.

What Loysel did was to take a normal size machine and multiply it many times to a height of two and three quarter metres, or nine feet; in the case of his largest models, eleven feet. It was as if in a world of Shetland ponies, he suddenly produced a Percheron. The effect must have been dramatic, as people who were taking minutes if not hours to make a cup of coffee suddenly saw a machine making two thousand cups per hour.

Actually the two thousand cups per hour was only partially correct. The earliest mention of Loysel seems to be by Henri Welter who said the machine made forty thousand cups per day.[54] My calculations show that achieving a figure of two

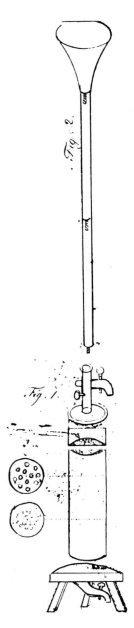

The Realsche Presse was a brass apparatus to make a coffee extract. It was 16 to 20 feet long and made in connecting screw sections. An overnight brewing of eight *Loth* of fine coffee and half to three-quarters of a jug of cold water produced an extract of strong coffee. Count Real was a Frenchman mentioned in an Italian book of 1834 by Luigi Annoni. However, this drawing appears in a German book of 1841.

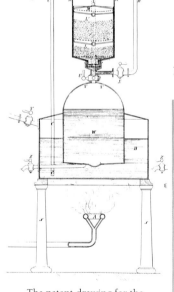

FIG. 20.

Loysel machine showing the funnel and filter. The principle was to force water through the coffee by using the pressure of the water forcing down from a height.

The Loysel machine at the Paris Exposition of 1855.

Loysel machine showing the funnel in place.

The Loysel machine at the Café du Percolateur, Place du Palais Royal, Paris, was of Brobdingnagian proportions and, at about eleven feet tall, probably the largest coffee machine ever made.

The patent drawing for the large Loysel machine, 1854. The water was boiled below and by steam pressure raised to the cistern above, whence it fell down a tube after the chain was pulled and came up through the coffee from below. The round container was sitting in the lower boiler which was acting as a *bain-marie*. At least the coffee was hot.

An English hydrostatic pressure filter machine. It was fairly certainly a derivative of Loysel. The coffee was in the cylinder filter which was put into the urn and the water filtered through it. The machine was probably as elegant as the coffee was cold.

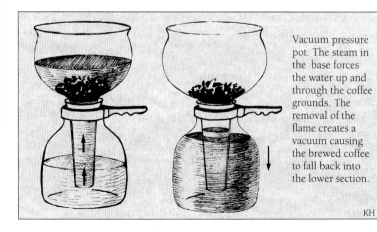

Vacuum pressure pot. The steam in the base forces the water up and through the coffee grounds. The removal of the flame creates a vacuum causing the brewed coffee to fall back into the lower section.

KH

thousand cups per hour would have required a brew cycle better than eight minutes with the large machine and three with the small machine. The cups in the illustration look a normal size. Considering the complications just in changing the coffee from one brew to the next, and handling the hot metal pieces, I believe it would have required an expert team to do the job. That is supposing you could actually boil 330 litres of water every hour and get it to pass through the grounds so quickly. Even though Loysel was the first person to use gas heating in a coffee machine, I doubt if he was able to heat that much water and get the machine to work.

Loysel specifically says in his patent that steam pressure is not used to force the water through the coffee grounds:

> *It should be understood that the pressure of steam in a boiler used for heating the liquid is not employed to force the water through the substance to be operated upon, but merely to raise the water to the required altitude to allow of its acting by hydrostatic pressure.*[55]

The fact that Loysel had to say this is significant. He had to remove any doubts that his machine had broken any of the unwritten rules that coffee could not be boiled. Loysel did not want to ruin his commercial chances by being seen as a rule breaker. His machine was not, as is often claimed, the first espresso machine.

Without actually looking at his patent, it is impossible to understand just how it operates. The machine worked by boiling water until it was pumped by steam pressure to a little reservoir at the top, where a tap controlled by a chain let the water fall, then it was forced up through the coffee. Many writers have erroneously assumed it was somehow a forerunner of the espresso machine, whereas it was really a complicated filter machine. The machine may have been used at the Antwerp Exhibition of 1885.

Loysel is significant for the fact that he was probably the first engineer to apply himself to the problems of coffee brewing. The steam engine and the railways had proved to be profitable avenues for engineering talents, but coffee was not. The Wilda'sche filter produced in Germany in 1894 can be seen as being derived from Loysel's ideas.

VACUUM POTS AND ATMOSPHERIC PRESSURE POTS

The vacuum pot shared the same idea as the pumping percolator, which was to raise the boiling water, but in the vacuum pot the water was forced through loosely packed coffee and brewed. This was an excellent method for making coffee provided that the grind was correct and that the coffee was stirred in the upper compartment and given enough time to brew.

Vacuum pots and atmospheric pressure pots may look the same but they operate very differently. In both, the water is pumped into the upper compartment. During this process, the coffee is being brewed at the correct temperature - a vital factor in brewing a better cup of coffee. In the vacuum pot when the heat source is taken away, the steam condenses in the lower compartment and creates a vacuum which draws the brewed coffee back down into the lower compartment. In the atmospheric pressure pot, after the water has gone up through the coffee, a cap on the spout is taken away which releases the pressure and lets the brewed coffee fall under atmospheric pressure.

THE FIRST VACUUM POT - *Professor Nörrenberg*

The first mention of these coffee makers appeared in 1827 with the publication of a drawing of a laboratory-glass coffee maker by the physicist, Professor Nörrenberg of Tübingen, Germany. There is a feeling from reading the text that the reader is expected to know all about this type of machine. Certainly the drawing does not seem to be primitive as if it were the first example. Nobody knows when the first one was manufactured, but Nörrenberg is the first person to have made a drawing with a date to establish the existence of the machine. It seems certain that this type of maker was known in Germany prior to 1827, the date of Beethoven's death, because Beethoven's biographer mentions that the composer owned a glass coffee pot.[56]

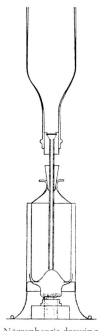

Nörrenberg's drawing. Germany - 1827.

The simple Grandin and Crepaux pot was called by the Italians a Milanese. Internally it was identical to the Grandin and Crepaux patent.

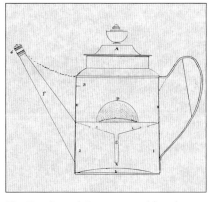

The Grandin and Crepaux pot, although described in the patent as an atmospheric pressure pot, could have been described as a vacuum pot. If the heat source was removed it worked as a vacuum pot. If the cap on the spout was removed it worked as an atmospheric pressure pot. France - 1832.

The Francesco Negretti patent was for a Milanese with a whistle in the spout in the form of a cap with a hole. As the level of boiling water progressively fell, the steam eventually reached a small tube on the underside of the spout and blew the whistle. This indicated that water had gone to the top and was brewing the coffee. Removal of the whistle allowed the brew to fall back through the grounds to the lower section. Italy - 1879.

Grandin and Crepaux

In 1832 Grandin and Crepaux made the first French patent application for a 'coffee pot with filter and atmospheric pressure.' It was really a filter by another name. Compared to other methods where the coffee was tepid, it was an excellent idea. Even though the patent does not say specifically to remove the cap, it mentions that the coffee was served boiling, indicating that the heat source was still in place so the cap must have been removed and the filter operated under atmospheric pressure as the name of the patent indicated.

Louis Boulanger

On the 8th of September, 1835, Louis François Boulanger applied for a patent for a pot made of glass, metal or earthenware. The advantages he claimed were that it could make coffee *à la minute* and that it prevented aroma loss. It must have been faster than any other contemporary coffee maker.

Pierre Beunat

On the 5th of August, 1837, Pierre Joseph Beunat applied for a patent for a 'coffee pot Atmopede infuser'. He claimed that it used a quarter less coffee, less fuel than *à la minute* makers and that its operation was a powerful distraction. Beunat's statement was the first recognition that these double bowl glass coffee makers were the first to provide a visual spectacle at the table as the coffee bubbled and brewed. The static tea making and coffee filtering processes were beginning to give way to dynamic processes with heat underneath. It was the start of the great divide where coffee machines became self-contained with their own heat source. Most tea makers remained purely as recipients of hot water.

The Atmodès and Madame Richard

In 1837 Madame Jeanne Richard made applications for several different coffee pots. One of these was an Atmodès vacuum coffee pot with a glass bowl that had a safety valve on the top. It must have required extreme delicacy in use not to snap off the tap. The fact that I have only seen one glass machine with a tap is a testament to their fragility. Madame Richard talked of having the lower bowl in glass so you could see the whole operation. One of the big advantages that she claimed for the Atmodès was that the glass bowl prevented air from affecting the brewed coffee, which of course meant that the aroma was not being lost. The patent application said that the system of Atmodès was quite simple and had been used for a long time in Germany. Two months after her first application Madame Richard made another application for an addition to the patent for the *importation* of a German Atmodès coffee pot. The notion of importation is significant.

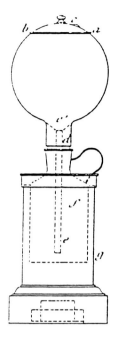

Boulanger patented drawings for glass vacuum pots. France - 1835.

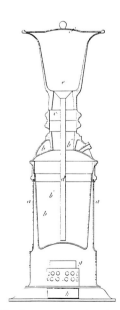

The Beunat patent drawing showed another early machine. France - 1837..

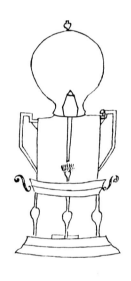

Left: The Atmodès vacuum pot drawings of Mme Jeanne Richard. The patent was for an import from Germany. France - 1838.

Below: Capette's *Myrosostique* patent. This was the beginning of the age of spectacular looking patents. France - 1837.

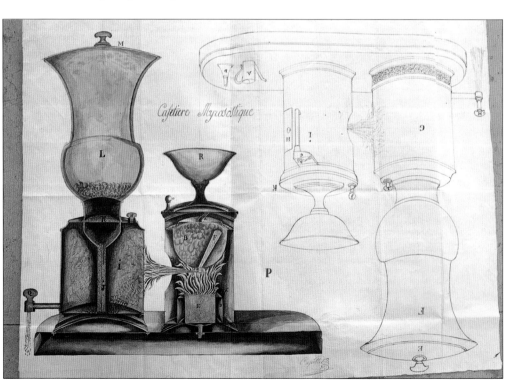

Platow and Vardy

In 1839, Mority Platow, an engineer (who signed the patent and whose name is distinctly Central European, possibly Moritz) and James Vardy, a gentleman, were granted a patent in England. Their machine was similar to that of the French Grandin and Crepaux pot of seven years earlier which, if operated as a vacuum pot, would have been a forerunner of this patent. Platow and Vardy's innovations were separating the coffee maker into two parts, having a spout and fixing the filtering surface with a screw. Altogether it was a more sophisticated machine. Under the filter there was even a spring safety valve. The French pot was controlled by removing a cap over the spout and thus releasing the pressure which kept the coffee up. The English pot was operated by removing the flame and so creating the vacuum in the lower section which sucked the coffee down. The top part was made of either glass or metal. There is little evidence that they were widely used all over Europe in the second half of the nineteenth century but quite a few of these pots are still in existence. The fact that some English vacuum pots were made of metal kept the idea alive until Cona machines made from German lime glass were commercially produced in 1910.

VACUUM POT WITH A TAP
Madame Vassieux of Lyons

In 1841 Madame Vassieux of Lyons lodged a French patent for a glass vacuum pot. She made two applications and the first had a filter at the top of a tube, very much like the Atmodès. The second filter was a much more conventional round disc filter.

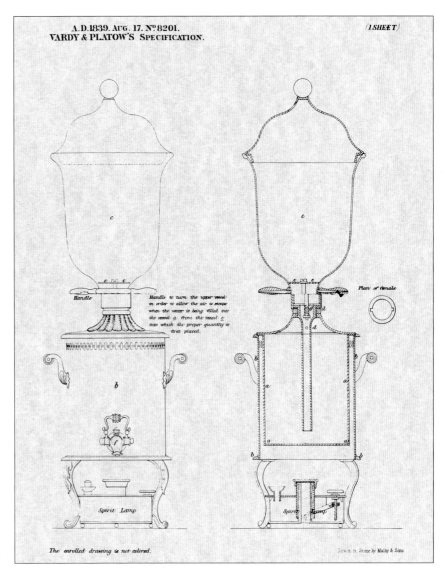

A.D. 1839. AUG. 17. Nº 8201.
VARDY & PLATOW'S SPECIFICATION. (1 SHEET)

Platow and Vardy. The patent said that the upper part was generally of glass although there were metal tops as well. England - 1839.

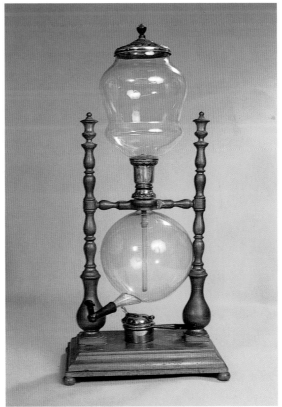

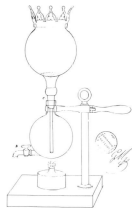

Mme Vassieux's 1841 patent. The crown on the top is for resting the glass upside down when it was taken off to allow the coffee to be poured.

Left: One of the oldest glass vacuum pots in the world. The washers under the base are old Louis coins with holes drilled in them. The operation is very similar to the Vassieux patent and it may in fact be a Vassieux machine. France - c. 1843.

Far Left: An English vacuum pot in the Platow style - turn of the century.

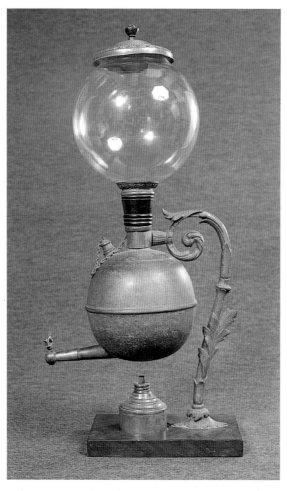

Malpeyre patent - the *Hydropneumatique*.
France - 1841.

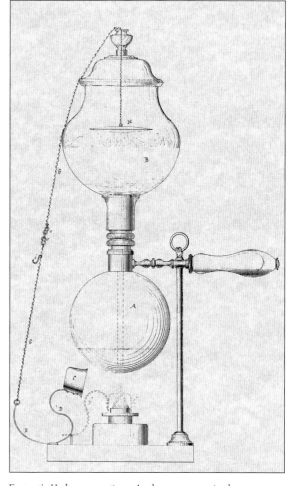

Fortant's *Hydropneumatique*. As the water rose in the top,
the float rose causing the chain to fall and the cover to
extinguish the flame. France - 1842.

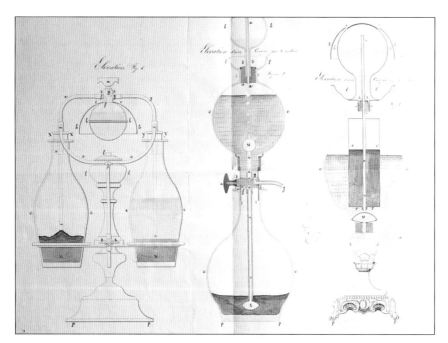

The Galy-Cazalat patent
drawings are as colourful as they
are complicated. France - 1847.

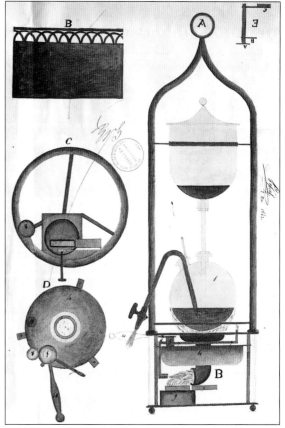

The Lepeut *Vapourisateur*.
France - 1842.

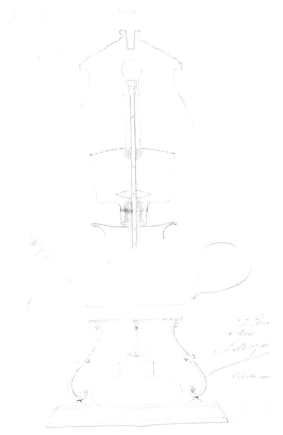

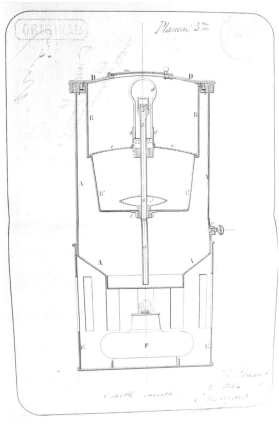

Left and Far Left:
Penant attempted ever more
complicated drawings,
but only simple machines
prevailed. France - 1869.

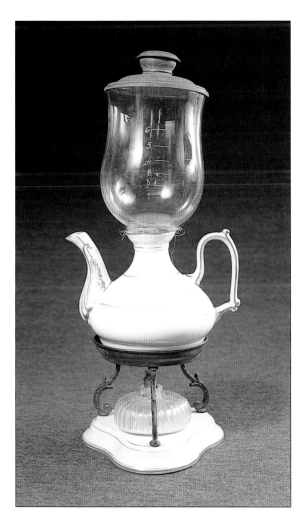

The Raparlier patent showed cup gradations on the upper
part. It was well-designed and had a simple screw-in filter.
Note the loose rope fibres which acted as a seal between
top and bottom parts. France - 1858.

ATMOSPHERIC PRESSURE POT
Raparlier

In 1858 Raparlier invented a pot with a glass upper bowl on which cup gradations were marked. This was a change from the metal bowls where it was impossible to tell how much you had brewed. There is nothing special about the Raparlier except that we know it was produced and marketed in France.

REBIRTH OF THE VACUUM POT

The English Cona Company in 1910 introduced a range of vacuum pots which was in essence as simple as the glass vacuum pot made by Madame Vassieux in Lyons in 1842. In 1890 the Englishman Stevenson invented a screw-up rod which held the filter in the upper bowl. This was a big advance and possibly the catalyst for the Cona Company's expansion, as his device was adopted by the Cona Company. Stevenson invented another rod to hold the filter and started his own company to make vacuum pots. The Silex Company introduced the system to the United States in 1909 where it became quite popular but it did not dominate the market anywhere except in Japan. There the search for excellence required that classes be set up so that coffee shop workers would know exactly how to stir the coffee before it went down into the lower compartment.

Attempts to make fully automatic vacuum pots and balance coffee pots continued through the last half of the nineteenth century, but in practical terms came to nought. In fact the attempts to make the machines automatic resulted in the

The Napier machine of 1840 was very simple. The coffee grounds were put in the open vessel and boiling water poured over them. A small amount of water was put in the globe and boiled. When the water had changed to steam, the heat was removed which created a vacuum and drew the brewed coffee back into the globe ready for serving.

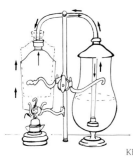

The Balance or 'Gabet'. The water container was suspended over a flame. Steam pressure forced the water to the other side; the container rose; the lid over the flame, no longer supported against the container, fell over the wick and extinguished the flame. This created a vacuum, so that the brewed coffee returned.

creation of the most incredibly complicated and exciting patent drawings. In these terms it was the most exciting period for invention in France and elsewhere.

HORIZONTAL VACUUM POT
Napier

About 1840 Napier, a Scots engineer, produced a variation on the vacuum pot coffee maker. The upper open bowl was placed to the side and the closed globe next to it. It operated by boiling a small amount of water in the globe so that when the flame went out, a vacuum would be created and the coffee, brewed in the open pot by pouring on boiling water, would be drawn into the globe. These pots were to become popular in England throughout the nineteenth century and were the basis for a whole range of 'balance' coffee makers in Europe.

THE BALANCE COFFEE MAKER
Gabet, Bascule, or Lyonnaise

On the 17th October, 1844, Adrian Emile François Gabet lodged an application for what became one of the more popular coffee makers of his time, which was sometimes called a *Bascule or Lyonnaise*. Clearly it was derived from the Napier pot - operating with the same coffee brewing principle. Steam pressure forced the boiling water to pass through the tube to the open pot where the ground coffee was brewed. The change in weight allowed the boiler section to rise and the flame was extinguished. In theory it was a practical and simple automatic coffee maker. However, in spite of its apparent simplicity, the machine did not work reliably. I do not know if similar machines existed before Gabet's, but he insisted that his machine worked without springs. The 1855 French patent of Rousselle reported that there

were frequent explosions of porcelain *Bascules*.

Other patents soon appeared. Springs and other complicated mechanisms were introduced to overcome the machine's inertia and to help extinguish the flame. Penant introduced a spring in 1851.

IMPROVED BALANCE COFFEE MAKER
Turmel

The Turmel machine of 1853 was designed to overcome problems of the seals failing. If this happened, the vacuum was released and the coffee was not sucked back to the tap side. If there was a partial vacuum and some of the coffee was left in the brewing side, or the wet grounds covered the filter, the coffee would not come out of the spout because there would still be a vacuum in the spout side.

The machine was suspended on a spring in the base and moved up and down with the change in weight. There was no counterbalance. Because each porcelain pot had a different weight, this meant that each model had to have a counterbalance specially made for it. The complicated piece on the boiler caused the returning coffee to make its own seal by filling any air gaps. Chryssochoïdès described it in 1901 and it was probably made, although I have never seen one.[57] Turmel's patents and others are evidence of the fact that balance coffee pots had many problems and possibly did not work very well.

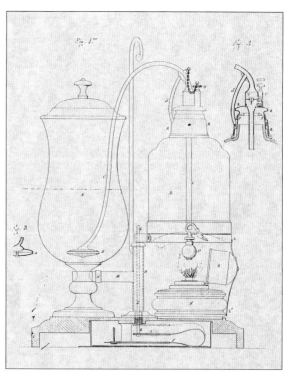

The Turmel patent drawings indicate that there were major problems in making the machine operate. The vessel over the flame was mounted on a spring to ensure that the vessel would lift, allow the cover to fall and extinguish the flame. The cap of the vessel had a by-pass tube to suck coffee into any gaps and make a tight vacuum.
France - 1853.

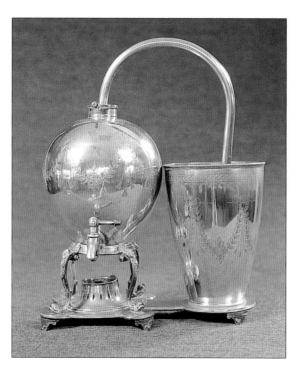

A 'Napier' horizontal vacuum pot. Scotland - 1840.

The Gabet patent drawing. It was a 'Napier' machine on a balance and self-extinguishing. France - 1844.

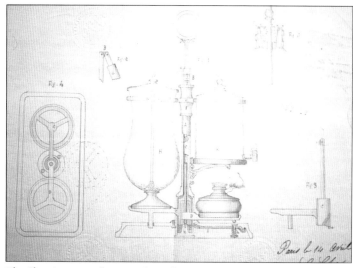

The Chevrier patent illustrates the sophistication needed to make balance coffee makers work. France - 1880.

Appolleoni Preterre lodged a patent for this design. England - 1849.

Another English balance coffee maker or 'Gabet'. England - 1849.

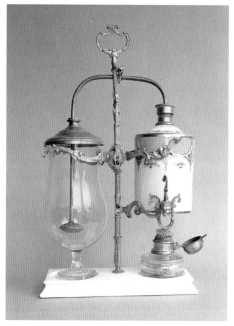

Penant invented a *Bascule* or balance with a coil spring on the central column to help the balance work. France - 1851.

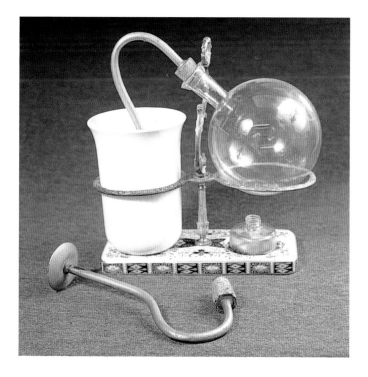

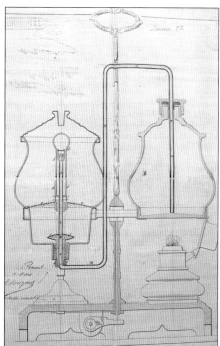

Far Left: The Robertson patent was for a 'Napier' with a glass tap. This Robertson model was sold without the tap. There was a little cane handle on the glass spout for pouring. England - 1890.

Left: The Penand [sic] patent of 1869 forced the water through the coffee from below in the same way as a vacuum pot.

This Veyron machine appeared in a Milan catalogue. Italy - early 1900s.

UB

INVERTED VACUUM POT
Veyron

From 1842 to 1876 Pierre Veyron attempted to patent many different coffee pots in his need to invent something and in doing so has created one of the largest French patent files.

All the other variations on the vacuum pot had been invented, ranging from the Grandin and Crepaux pot which looked, on the outside, like a normal coffee pot, to Madame Vassieux's glass machine with a tap in the lower section to avoid having to dismantle the machine to pour the coffee. Napier had even pre-empted the horizontal possibility.

There was only the option of inventing an upside-down vacuum pot and Veyron tried again and again. The water was boiled in the upper section and forced to the lower section. The flame went out and the coffee ended up, by vacuum, in the top section where there was a tap, which made pouring easier. It was a case of vacuum working against gravity and required a very good seal between the parts. There is one illustrated in a Milanese catalogue from the turn of the century. Trillich, a major German author who wrote a comprehensive book about coffee equipment and inventions, mentions a Veyron-type maker by Frimmel in 1880 in Vienna.[58]

Just a few months after his first patent, Veyron went back to a conventional Grandin and Crepaux pot with the variation that there was now a glass

KH

The Plunger or French Press: The ground coffee is put in, boiling water poured over, the coffee stirred, and after a few minutes the plunger is pushed down.

bell on the top so that you could see the coffee brewing. There was nothing basically against the Veyron system except that the technology of the day was not sophisticated enough to produce it.

Veyron was persistent and his last patent in 1874 was for a Veyron system patent with an automatic flame-out. Neither he nor Loysel, the hydrostatic percolator inventor, had many imitators trying to steal their inventions - perhaps later inventors were more perceptive about the problems.

THE MOVING-COMPARTMENT FILTER

This machine had a piston, at the end of which was a compartment with a filter top and bottom. The coffee was placed in the compartment and submersed in the hot water to brew. After a short time the compartment was lifted out of the water and suspended to stop the coffee brewing. Lavigne, in 1854, made a small compartment-type coffee maker. Bourdier and Houet, in 1882, made a compartment-type machine in which the compartment was held up by hooks. In 1896 Giraud made the Brasilienne where the compartment was held up by notches.

In the 1980s the Rombouts Company of Belgium tried to introduce a compartment model where the coffee was held in a pre-packed capsule, but it was not a great success. The extra pressure needed to force the water through the coffee made it too difficult to use.

THE PLUNGER OR FRENCH PRESS

In 1852 Mayer and Delforge invented the first of the plunger or French press coffee makers. The filter was forced down to compress the coffee at the bottom of the pot. The idea was very simple but the technology of the times made it difficult to make a moving filter which was fitted tightly enough to the container to ensure that the coffee grounds were separated and kept in the lower section and prevented from floating around the filter into the upper section.

At the turn of the century the French Cafeolette was well-promoted by Louis Forest and was very popular for making milk coffee. The Melior brand was introduced in the 1930s with a stainless steel filter and metal pot. Later models had a glass pot in a metal frame. In the 1970s, Bodum, a Danish company, introduced a glass pot with coloured plastic support and lid and plunger. On account of its excellent range of colours and with mass promotion, it has become a designer item, popular the world over.

The Japanese Hario Company in the 1980s introduced its own models with nylon filters and glass bodies. The luxury design of these plungers, incorporating gold and silver, became a major feature. There are several other modern brands which use plastic.

The plunger has truly been one of the prominent coffee makers of all time. Its simplicity and the fact that by its very nature it is impossible

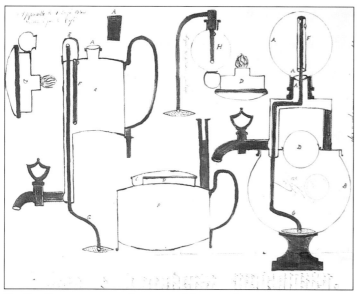

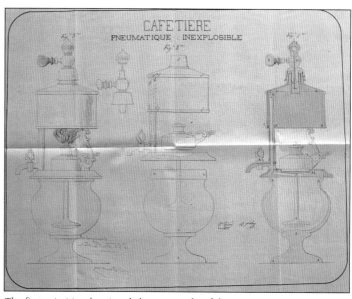

The first Veyron patent was the reverse of the normal vacuum pot. Water was forced down through the grounds to the bottom section, then the brewed coffee drawn up to the top section by vacuum. By placing a tap at the base of the top section, it was easy to pour the coffee into a cup. France - 1842.

The first primitive drawings led to more colourful drawings, but the Veyron system never became popular.

Above Left and Above:
Bourdier and Houet compartment plunger showing the compartment hooked in the 'up' position. France -1881.
The tin compartment contained the coffee between filters.

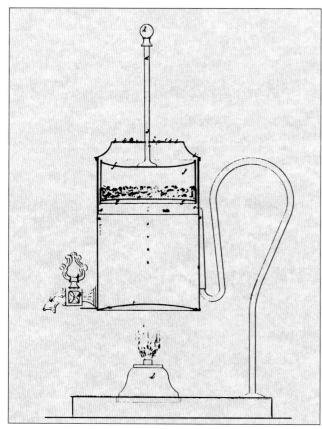

Left: The Lavigne compartment plunger. The coffee was put into a compartment which was lifted out of the liquid to stop brewing.
France - 1854.

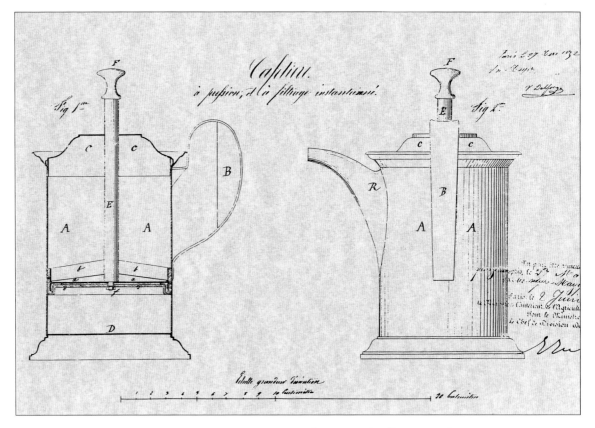

The Mayer and Delforge patent for a press. France - 1852.

Below: Patry invented a press coffee pot. When the lid was closed, a spring was forced down on the ground coffee. France - 1869.

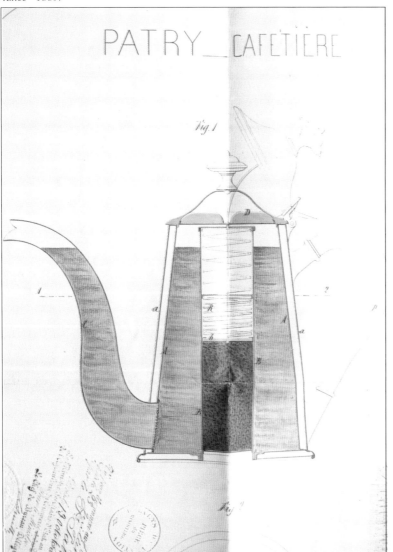

to boil the coffee and make it bitter, has made it a real alternative coffee maker. For proper extraction, the coffee *must* be stirred after the water is poured on.

It is interesting to consider the ability of the plunger to make good coffee. There do not seem to be any serious studies about its efficacy and this is probably due to the fact that it is one of the least automatic machines ever invented. The grind should vary for each model depending on the fineness of the filter. The ease of pressing the plunger down changes with the grind size - the coarser the coffee, the easier it is to push down. There does not seem to be a universally understood grind for plungers such as for espresso and filter. The brewing time seems to vary with the mood of the operator.

One of the requirements in the instructions is to stir the coffee which is more often honoured in the breach than the observance. The object of the stirring is to break up the floating coffee grounds so that they will sink to the bottom and thus help the infusion. It is my belief that the grounds should be stirred a second time, just before pushing the plunger down, so that the essence in the grounds at the bottom of the pot will come into solution.

The plunger's main advantages are simplicity and the ability to brew the coffee at the table and serve it immediately without flavour degradation. The biggest disadvantage is the inability to keep the coffee warm. In 1991 the Belaroma two-stage plunger was patented with the idea that the coffee grounds had to be totally immersed by the first filter before the second filter was pushed down.

Louis Forest was the proponent of the Cafeolette plunger for making milk coffee - the true French coffee. This machine was very popular prior to the First World War and had a removable mesh filter in the spout. France - 1900s.

INVENTIONS OF THE NINETEENTH CENTURY

The nineteenth century encompassed many different inventions, some of which were important and some of which merely showed the ability of people to invent a complicated way of doing something simple. Many of them did not go beyond the patent office, while others must have been made, because they are referred to in contemporary books, although they appear to be incapable of either economic or uneconomic manufacture. Nothing seems less likely to have been manufactured than the locomotive percolators and yet there are a few in museums and private collections.

COFFEE DIVERSITY:
EUROPE AND THE UNITED STATES

France and Germany were already major consumers of coffee. Even in the early years the consumption of coffee rose very quickly in England from one ounce per head in 1804 to one pound per head in 1840 - an increase of 1600 per cent.[59] In 1815 there were less than twenty coffee shops in London charging a minimum of sixpence per cup. Fifty years later there were a thousand shops charging a penny to threepence per cup.[60]

The inventions just described were at the forefront of technology and like the first motor cars, they were probably the toys of dilettantes and the rich. Tin rusted quickly, glass broke and porcelain was not convenient for making into complicated shapes. These were all major materials used in the new coffee brewing inventions. The masses were making coffee in simple inexpensive pots of earthenware and porcelain.

English brewing methods changed during the nineteenth century from complicated boiling processes, to pouring boiling water over the coffee. Another method was to pour cold water over grains overnight and heat (not boil) in the morning. The French were similarly occupied - one method required the coffee to stand in a pot for two hours in the ashes of a fire. Obviously the connection between brewing time and flavour was not widely known.

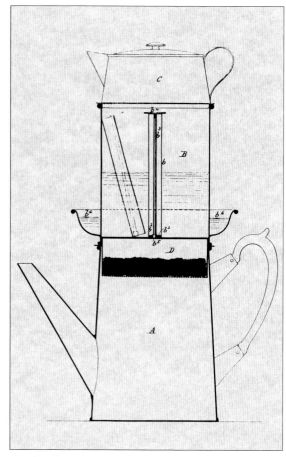

David Lindo invented an ingenious coffee pot. The flame from the spirits in the upper rim boiled the water in the whole upper section. The water in the central tube also boiled which theoretically produced enough steam to dislodge the tube from the small hole at b5. This allowed the water to trickle down over the coffee. England - 1884.

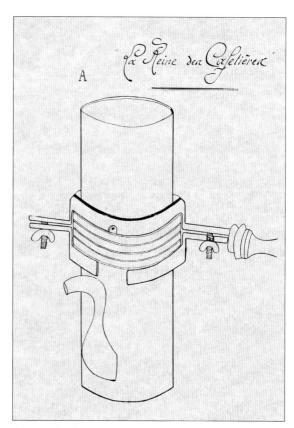

Jules Tarallo de Sant'Agostino wanted to make a name for himself and he did. His address was Rue St. Augustin. The reversible pot, 'the Queen of Coffee pots', was not nearly so inventive. France - 1899.

Eriberta Predari combined the Veyron principle with an egg cooker. Sarah Guppy in England in 1812 also combined a tea pot with an egg cooker, but left no drawing. France - 1872.

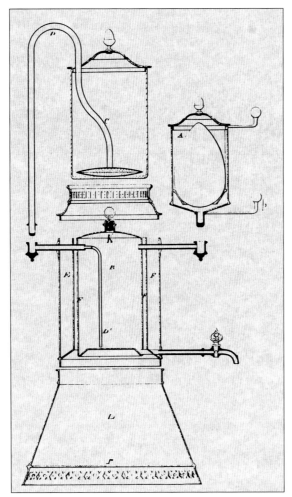

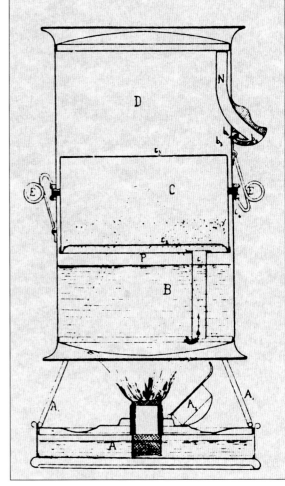

Mme Gadiffert invented a pot in which the water boiled up and over the paddle wheel which turned and rang the bell. France - 1862.

Above: Trottier made an automatic reversible coffee pot. The water boiled and was forced by steam pressure up the tube and through the coffee. The pot was suspended on c and it overbalanced (because the water was at the top). In so doing, it extinguished the flame. The little ball at b3 near the spout acted as a valve to relieve the air lock when pouring the coffee. As if this were not complicated enough, Trottier made another on the same principle which revolved twice. After the first turn, the flame went out and the top section was full of steam. As it condensed, it created a vacuum which drew the coffee back up and the whole pot turned over once more. The Trottier idea was similar to one by Meüdt in 1858 which probably did not work either. France - 1896.

Hertmann invented an automatic brewer. The alarm clock caused a match to strike, lighting the flame. The water boiled and passed up the tube where it filtered over the coffee, eventually causing the coffee container to overbalance and descend, extinguishing the flame. Germany - 1895.

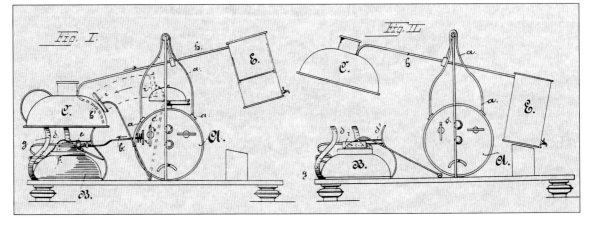

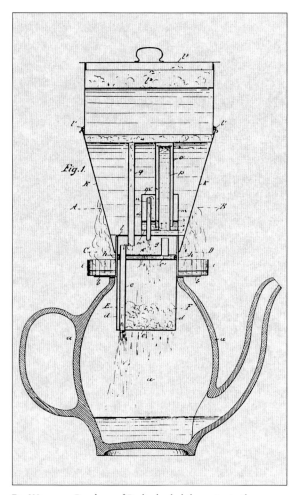

Dr. Warnerus Borchers of Berlin boiled the water in the upper section. The water also boiled in a series of interconnecting tubes. When the flame was extinguished, the steam condensed, creating a vacuum which then siphoned the hot water through the tubes and over the coffee. Germany -1895.

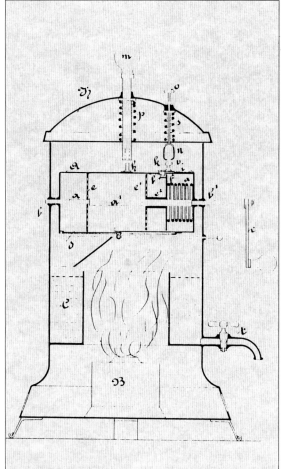

Carl Wagner of Dresden roasted coffee in a drum in which the ends were grinding blades. After the coffee was roasted, the spring near the handle was released, turning the drum into a grinder. The coffee grounds fell into the hot water contained in the annular ring in the lower section. Germany -1887 .

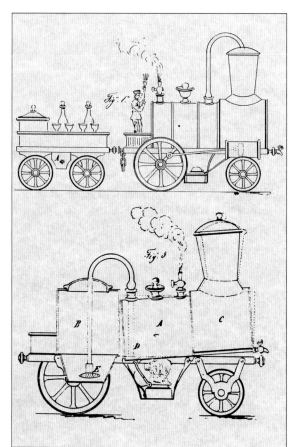

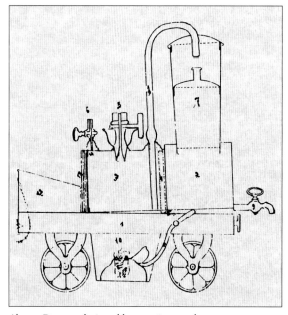

Above: Demazy designed locomotives on the pumping percolator principle. The coffee falling into the funnel caused the cover to extinguish the flame. France - 1887.

Left: Toselli made several designs for locomotive coffee makers. They operated on the Gabet balance principle. Italy - 1861.

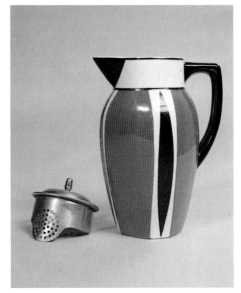

A pot using a lid with holes, patented by W.H. Smith. England -1890.

The French continued the idea of compressing the coffee by using a weighted upper filter. Other machines used small wire frames to keep the filter down.

The Caffeta was a coffee maker with a whistle to signal when the water was boiled. It was available in Germany and England in the first quarter of the 20th century. Its uselessness as a brewer and its very existence could be construed as an indication that the other systems of the era were not efficacious.

In America there was an equal lack of understanding. In 1844 *The Kitchen Directory* advised boiling the coffee in a tin pot for twenty to twenty-five minutes. By 1856 the considered wisdom of *The Ladies Home Magazine* was to put the coffee in the pot on the stove overnight and boil in the morning. The result was 'rich, mellow and a most delicious flavour'.[61] Any boiling of coffee results in bitterness, so I can only imagine that a lot of salt was being used in the coffee or in the meal before it, since salt neutralises the bitterness of coffee. In 1861 contemporary journals were recommending that boiling water should be poured over the coffee, but scenes from movies showing coffee pots boiling in the campfire indicate that this was still a widespread method of making coffee.

At the same time the latest French method of filtering the coffee was described and the biggin was approved as the best coffee maker. Right through the century the controversy over whether or not to boil raged on. One advantage of boiling coffee for a long time was that the room smelled wonderful even if the coffee tasted terrible. The anticipation must have been as high as the disappointment was deep.

German inventors were busy, but more discriminating about what could be considered useful. The Germans were wary of using metals and this was a limiting factor in the inventions they could use. Tin does not seem to have been widely used, whereas in Italy and France it was quite common. Germans did not like French machines because of the use of tin - it gave an unacceptable flavour and masked the aroma. Even when filters were used to make a light, clear brew, which was left to stand overnight, there was bluish oil on the surface and a strong metallic smell. In any case it was not good for health. Rusty tin made

things worse. Only glass and porcelain could be recommended as acceptable materials. In 1841 the de Belloy and Morize methods of making coffee were very popular in Germany.

A book published in 1864 by Rottenhöfer, the Bavarian royal chef, showed that many of the coffee machines in vogue were of French origin.[62] Rottenhöfer was very impressed with the Daussé machines and gave five pages to them. The German double-glass bowl vacuum pot was so well-known that it did not even merit a drawing in the book.

Only two early machines of German origin are described in Rottenhöfer's book and they show no major novelty except the ability to heat the milk at the same time. The first is Wagemanns and Böttgers hot-air coffee machine. This machine was very similar to Koch's coffee machine which was illustrated in *Dinglers Polytechnisches Journal* in 1838.[63]

Rottenhöfer also described a two-way tap coffee pot which was quite new in 1864. The two-way tap allowed you to draw either coffee or hot milk at will by turning the tap backwards and forwards. The hot water rose and brewed the coffee, probably in an open filter at the base of the glass. The process was controlled by taking away the lamp, letting the coffee fall one third and then replacing the lamp till the water rose again. The machine was thus a vacuum pot coffee maker.

Rottenhöfer goes on to show Gabet coffee machines, with glass containers and self-extinguishing lamps, to be useful for making tea and coffee. Surprisingly, he advises that you can make stronger coffee if you repeat the process by lighting the lamp again. One of the advantages was the ease of cleaning, an important point for the fastidious Germans.

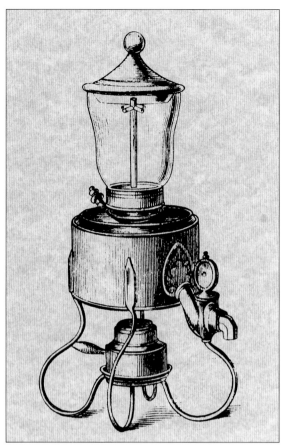

A two-way tap coffee pot. The outer compartment contained warm milk and the inner one coffee. Germany - 1864.

Because of the difficulty of penetrating the Italian patent system, it is hard to know if the Italians were inventive in the nineteenth century. It would appear that the Italians were saving all their ingenuity for the twentieth. Catalogues show 'the German filter machine' and the Milano (later to be called The Milanese) which was the Italian version of the Grandin and Crepaux machine from France in 1832. Veyron's coffee pot was also in a Milan catalogue. The Caffettiera of the Brothers Prina is shown in a publication of 1829 but it was in fact just a fancy version of Gandais' pumping percolator of 1827 from Paris. Most coffee in Italy throughout the nineteenth century was being made in filter machines.

THE QUALITY OF THE COFFEE

In Italy chicory was in general use and coffee was being adulterated as everywhere else. Turf, acorns, roots of horse chestnuts, brown coal - all were being used.

From the first mention of coffee there has been mention of the admixture of adulterants and in some cases complete replacement of the coffee itself. Pierre Delcourt wrote about coffee frauds in detail. He wrote in 1888, but what he wrote applied to a whole period in the history of coffee. The coffee was being mixed with chicory, acorns, figs, old grounds. Even chicory, one of the cheapest products you could buy, was not safe from adulteration - it was being mixed with roasted carrots and a host of other things.

Raw coffee was being coloured to hide the damage from humidity and water on the docks. Seawater gives the beans a grey bloom on the outside and a green, black colour on the inside. Fresh water gives the beans a white bloom on the outside and they swell. To remove traces of seawater damage, the coffee was put into baths of a lime solution which was then washed out. Raw coffee in transit could take on any flavour either from other products in the hold or from a fire on board a boat.

In Germany, more than half the coffee consumed was not real coffee but substitutes, although by the end of the century, a cup of German coffee was probably better than coffee served in most other countries.

The Dutch in Maastricht and the Belgians in Antwerp were considered masters at colouring coffees and had specialised factories for it. Prussian Blue and Indigo were used to make coffees take on the appearance of Martinique, Guadeloupe and Puerto Rican coffees. Using a whole range of yellow and orange dyes, it was possible to imitate coffees from Menado, Padang and all the high quality coffees. Turmeric and iron oxide were used to make yellow coffees. Roasted coffee was enrobed and polished with beef blood caramellised in sulphuric acid. There were other tricks which were trade secrets and which, no doubt, were equally horrifying.[64]

There must have been some very strange ideas of what coffee was. The existence of what were considered good substitutes easily led to the use of bad subsititutes. A German publication of 1845 gave the following recipe:

In Holland you add to half a pound of coffee, two cut-up cocoa beans, ten lemon pips, a little cinnamon and four loth [60 grams] cubed white bread. If the coffee has been damaged in any way, evidenced by false colour, take out the bread and replace with onions. When the coffee is half-roasted, take out the onions, add two cloves and one peppercorn and continue roasting.[65]
[English translation].

In spite of all this, the consumption of coffee grew. The consumers must have been most tenacious. Doubtless the rich could afford the real thing while the poor had to put up with substitutes.

'GLAZING' IN THE UNITED STATES

Joseph Walsh, writing in Philadelphia in 1894 stated:

It has been the custom for some years back to coat or glaze coffee with certain gluey or starchy compounds, ostensibly to protect the beans from the oxidising influence of the atmosphere, preserve the aroma and clarify the liquor in preparation, each roaster and dealer having a different compound for the purpose. It is most generally composed of various glues, moss and other starchy substances and is usually prepared by placing the materials composing the compound in a cask, vat or tank filled with boiling water conveyed through pipes or by injecting steam, thoroughly stirring it at the same time until it is mixed to the requisite consistency. After the solution is prepared it is applied to the coffee while hot, generally in the cylinder while revolving, which diffuses the material and imparts an even and uniform coating to the coffee, adhering and hardening as it cools. But the claims made by the roasters and others who coat or glaze coffee, that large quantities of eggs are used exclusively in the preparation of the glazing compound is simply absurd, as is also the claim that it is resorted to for the purpose of closing the pores, to protect and retain the aroma and for self-settling purposes. The real object being to conceal defects, disguise low grades and damaged coffees, as well as to add weight and colour to light, chaffy and 'quakery' coffees, the process adding all the way from five to ten per cent to the weight, according to the nature of the coffee and the character of the coffee used: light chaffy-bean coffees absorbing more of the material than the hard and solid ones, while the softer and rougher the bean the more it improves in appearance by the process.

What is known as the 'egg glaze' is prepared from eggs alone, mashed and applied after the coffee has been first cooled, and then baked on by means of a hot blast, when it forms a hard, transparent shell, protecting the coffee until it is ground and ready for use; and also serving to clarify the liquor in the pot after infusion. Another composed of one part gum arabic dissolved in water, to which is added four parts starch, with

sufficient water to make it limped [sic], the whole being boiled for upwards of twenty minutes, and which is best accomplished by inserting a small pipe of live steam from the boiler into the compound until it is reduced to the consistency of cream; then, after stirring well, it is poured on the coffee while in the cylinder as it revolves, or it may be spread over it while in the cooler, if proper care be taken to diffuse it well. Still another excellent compound for glazing coffee is prepared from one part Irish moss, one part gelatine, one part isinglass, one ounce sugar and two dozen eggs, the first three ingredients being first boiled in water, then strained and applied as in the foregoing formula. For the purpose of imparting a lustrous aspect to roasted coffee, a liquid has recently been invented, the composition of which is so far unknown. It has a specific gravity of 0.868 at 15 degrees, burning with a sooty flame and leaving no fixed residue. It is clear and oily in appearance, but entirely free from color, taste or smell, and mixes in all proportions with petroleum, from which fact it would appear to be nothing more than a highly purified petroleum oil, in which case it must be classed among the illegitimate additions to roasted coffee.[66]

The question has to be seriously put: What was the purpose in making a better coffee maker when the roasted coffee was of such varying quality? The combination of poor quality coffee, bad roasting and poor brewing, meant that the chances of getting a good cup of coffee in the nineteenth century were very low.

UB

A ship-shape coffee maker. Possibly France or Holland.

CHAPTER 8

The Espresso Coffee Machine Revolution

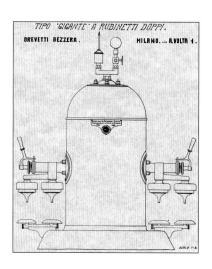

E SPRESSO COFFEE

An espresso machine forces water *through* COMPRESSED coffee so that the coffee grounds are irrigated. If the water goes *around* the grains the result is filtered coffee. The pressure needed to force the water through the coffee grains increases with the fineness of the grind and the degree of compression. The higher the pressure used, the more complete is the flavour extraction. The first espresso machines made long espresso coffees where several cups of water were forced through lightly compressed coffee. In this sense the product was somewhere between filter coffee and true espresso coffee, but probably closer to filter than espresso. Later espresso machines used pumps and were able to make short strong espresso coffee, one or two cups at a time. The ratio of water to coffee is generally higher in long espresso coffee than in short.

The use of the word 'espresso' to describe a particular type of coffee is a little ambiguous. An espresso in an Italian house, from a domestic machine, can be either long or short, but in an Italian bar, from a commercial machine, it is most definitely short and very strong.

ORIGIN OF THE WORD 'ESPRESSO'

It seems that any machine that produces steam or operates with steam pressure earns the name espresso machine. This probably arises from the confusion surrounding the origin of the word espresso. The words *express, expres* and *espresso* each have several meanings in English, French and Italian.

The first meaning is to do with the idea of 'expressing' or squeezing the flavour from the coffee using the pressure of the steam. The second meaning is to do with speed, as in a train. Finally there is the notion of doing something 'expressly' for a person.

The espresso machine originally acquired its name from making a cup of coffee 'expressly for you'. The first Bezzera and Pavoni espresso machines in 1906 took forty-five seconds to make a cup of coffee, one at a time, expressly for you. These machines forced hot water from a boiler and then steam through the coffee. As far as speed goes, they were anything but fast compared to today's machines which make coffee in a third of the time.

THE NATURE OF THE PROBLEM

From the first days of brewing coffee, inventors were confronted with the problems of grind size, water temperature and brewing time, which they never fully understood. These critical factors had to be just right for a complete extraction of the coffee flavour. Vacuum pump machines and the vacuum pot were early attempts to solve the reluctance of the water to filter through the coffee. Despite these endeavours to get all the flavour out of the coffee bean it still held something back. The pursuit of perfect extraction from the coffee bean was to continue for a long time.

Often the technology lagged behind the ideas of the inventors. The pressure from a boiler was not strong enough to make a complete extraction in a short time. Since the boiling water was never fully expressed from the coffee grounds during the brewing process, the steam was used to dry the coffee, by expelling the water from the grounds more quickly, rather than to extract any further flavour. There was also a lack of understanding of the coffee making process. For years the inventors believed that passing steam through the coffee was vital for a more complete extraction. They simply had it wrong, as once the flavour is extracted, steam can extract no more - only bitterness. Modern espresso machines never use steam in the extraction process. It is used only to froth and heat milk.

In the early days, a machine operator required a level of skill almost on par with a train driver. The primitive safety standards meant that there was a risk of explosion from the gas, electrocution from the exposed switches and the added danger of working in a busy environment with steam.

ORIGINS OF ESPRESSO COFFEE

Italians have several versions of the history of espresso coffee, all of which diverge significantly from reality. The combination of oral history and early books, without reference to the facts, has led to a story close to fable. One such version based on the best published sources is:

In truth the first attempts to make a bar machine were at the Antwerp Exhibition in 1885 where Loysel exhibited his gigantic machine, which could make tens of thousands of cups per day, but which, on account of its size, was unsuitable for public use.
A few years later came the true progenitor of the machine for the bar. In 1903, Bezzera, an Italian, invented it and patented it. His attempts to launch it on the market did not succeed and in 1905, he sold the patent to an industrialist, Desiderio Pavoni, who succeeded in commercialising the machine and his machine dominated the market for decades. [1] [English translation]

An accurate version would read more like this:
In 1855 Loysel introduced a large capacity coffee machine for the bar which was in no way a pressure coffee machine. In theory it could make thousands of cups a day but in practice it made much less.
The true progenitor of the machine for the bar came thirty years later in 1885 with Moriondo's machine. In 1901 Bezzera patented a new machine with a single-cup handle. Some time in 1902 he sold the patent to Pavoni, an industrialist, who succeeded in commercialising it in 1906.

Other Italian, French, English and American books have repeated the popular versions about the origins of the espresso machine, often giving credence to Loysel's machine as the first espresso. But Loysel specifically said, in his patent, that the steam was *not* used to force the hot water through the coffee. Confusion and error still plague the history of the espresso machine and its inventors. Many authors actually believe that steam is used to brew espresso coffee. It never was.

KH

Long Espresso coffee is made when hot water under pressure is forced through compressed coffee. When the water boils, it forms steam pressure which presses down on the water and forces it up the central tube through the compressed coffee. As the water level falls, so does the steam level until it too goes up the tube through the coffee. The steam naturally comes after the water in the most simple espresso machines.

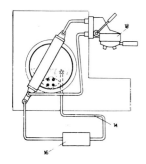

Short Espresso coffee with mousse is made when hot water under pressure from a pump is forced through finer, more compressed coffee.

THE REAL STORY OF THE COMMERCIAL ESPRESSO MACHINE

The commercial espresso machine of the first half of the twentieth century was the greatest and most exciting development in the history of coffee. The story of how it evolved, over six decades, is one of Italian persistence that finally gave birth to espresso coffee - a drink the Italians now claim as their own. It is amazing how much effort and intellect went into solving the problems involved in making a better cup of coffee.

In most histories the commercial espresso machine appeared to have been a *machina ex Deo*, or at best a heavenly birth, with Bezzera as the earthly parent. In fact its development followed a clear and well defined path.

There was no single Italian genius responsible for espresso coffee. Several inventors, from various countries, all contributed to the development of the espresso machine until Gaggia in 1948 finally conquered the bean. His machine was able to extract just the right amount of flavour to make the true espresso.

TOWARDS THE FIRST ESPRESSO MACHINE

By the very nature of their light construction and their consequent inability to withstand high steam pressure as in modern commercial machines, the first domestic espresso machines were all low pressure pumping coffee pots.

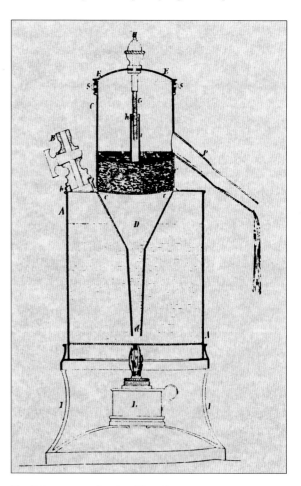

The Rabaut patent drawing: There is a filter at the end of the central rod and below the outlet tube. England - 1822.

Dr. Romershausen made a patent in Prussia for a domestic espresso machine in 1818.[2] I suspect that he was just patenting something that was widely known in a similar form in the world of chemistry. This same design could be used to process a number of products such as hops and sugar beet. Coffee was just one of them.

In 1822 Louis Bernard Rabaut, a Frenchman, lodged a patent in London for a machine which called for 'blotting paper or other unsized paper above and below the coffee to make the extract come off exceeding clear'. The machine was almost certainly an adaptation of the first Romershausen machine but was specifically for coffee. It may have worked in theory, but the blotting paper probably prevented the liquid coffee extract from passing through. The reason for Rabaut making his patent application in London and not in France may well have been that this type of machine was already known in France and he could not patent it there. Caseneuve, a Paris tinsmith, in 1824 invented a machine designed to prevent the loss of aroma, but it was probably too complicated to make.

THE FIRST ESPRESSO MACHINES
A LOW PRESSURE PUMPING COFFEE POT
Samuel Parker

In 1833 Samuel Parker, an Englishman, invented a coffee pot which pumped the water up through the coffee instead of letting it fall over it. The idea was the same as Rabaut's, the changes were simply cosmetic. Parker was well aware that the coffee's best flavour came out first and the bitter extracts last, which he specifically noted. If only later inventors had read his patent.

His mistake was to recommend a ratio of one ounce of coffee to two ounces of water - approximately four times stronger than an Italian short black espresso. This result would have been almost undrinkable. On the other hand it may have been coarsely ground coffee and very weak.

Lebrun, an optician from Paris, made an espresso machine in 1838 that worked, and became popular in southern Europe. While Lebrun did not invent the espresso machine his was probably very influential in introducing espresso coffee to Europe. In 1844 Cordier

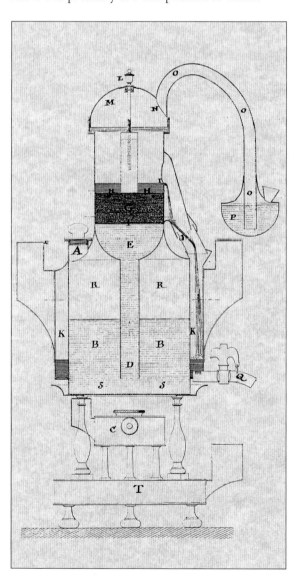

Caseneuve made a very complicated looking machine so that there would be no aroma loss. France - 1824.

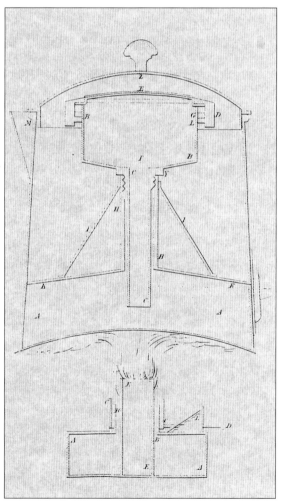

Samuel Parker's patent drawing shows the coffee compartment is screwed in. He specifically claimed that his spirit burner was better than Rabaut's. The ratio of coffee to water was four times that of an Italian short black. Without a safety valve it was doubly lethal. England - 1833.

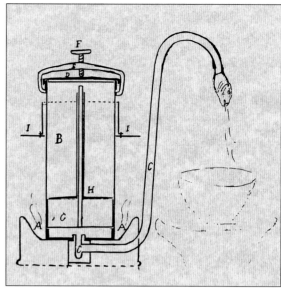

Right and Far Right: The Lebrun espresso machine was simple and practical. The machine sat in a dish of spirits. The flame burnt and boiled the water forcing first water and then steam through the coffee.
France - 1838.

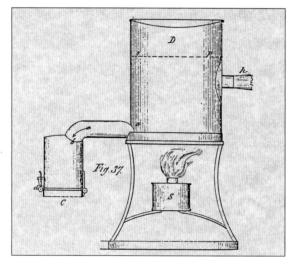

In Romershausen's practical espresso machine, the boiling water was forced through the coffee at C. Germany - 1847.

depicted every possible espresso machine in his patent application, including one with the coffee in an outside container, similar to Eicke's German machine of 1878.

Romershausen made a steam pressure pot for coffee in 1847, which was much more practical than his first invention of 1818. He stated quite clearly that using steam pressure would result in a stronger and more complete extraction of all the soluble substances. He specified coarsely ground coffee and the use of filter paper and, most unusual, by including a cup-measure, he stipulated the quantity of coffee to be used. When two-thirds of the drink had arrived the rest was to be discarded, obviously because it would have been bitter.[3]

Right: Cordier designed many possible variations of an espresso machine.
France - 1844.

Far Right: Goyot designed an espresso where the lid screwed directly onto the base.
France - 1849.

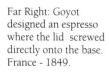

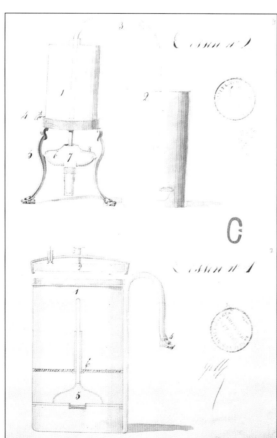

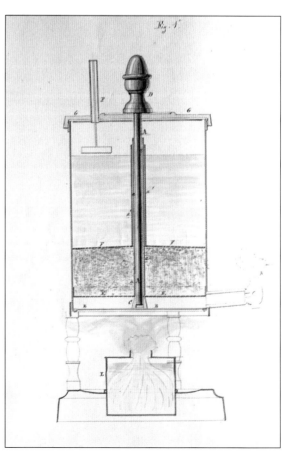

THE VIENNA COFFEE MACHINE - A WEAK ESPRESSO

Reiss in Vienna reinvented the Parker style espresso machine about 1868. The Vienna coffee machine is one of the most common nineteenth century coffee makers and is found in antique markets all over Europe, an indication of its attractiveness as an item of decoration. The fact that so many are in pristine condition is a sure sign of how little they were used to make coffee. In terms of improving the taste of the coffee, Reiss added nothing to existing ideas. The form of the invention with the glass bell and the connection with Vienna were sufficient to make it a success. Because the coffee could not be compressed very much, it was an espresso machine that could not make strong coffee but it could make something a little stronger than filter coffee. The weight of the central tube and coffee compartment was 375 grams and the diameter of the central tube 17 millimetres. This meant that it was capable of providing considerable resistance to the force of the water. The central tube in the original Reiss machine, even though it was not screwed in, ensured that the water passed through the coffee. It must be considered as an espresso machine even though it will never be known just how much the coffee was compressed or how finely it was meant to be ground. It is really a matter of conjecture as to what extent any of the early machines were espresso machines in practice.

The Vienna coffee machine came in several basic versions: tipping or with tap; metal lid or glass lid; screw-in funnel or loose funnel.

Although patents for the Vienna coffee machine certainly existed prior to 1900, the machines may not have become popular until after 1900. For instance, Chryssochoïdès' book in 1901, the most complete book about commercial and domestic machines of the time in France, does not mention a single machine in which compressed coffee was used. A catalogue page from Carlo Sigismund in Milan from the turn of the century shows only one Lebrun machine - a domestic espresso machine. The first mention I have been able to find of a commercial espresso machine is in a Florentine magazine of 1909, *La Scena Illustrata*. An Italian book about coffee pots written by Luigi Manetti in 1906 included the Eicke machine and no other espresso machine.

The Risk of Explosion

Several ideas were combined in the Vienna coffee machine which made it an attractive tablepiece. The glass lid was a necessary part of the theatre, but metal was sometimes used instead. Most of the glass tops had chains attached to stop them falling off. Some models with taps were fixed to supports, whilst others were tipped to pour. The central tube came in several versions. Some were screwed into the base ensuring that the steam pressure forced the water through the coffee. Without a safety valve there would have

An original Reiss Vienna Machine with the maker's name on the boiler. Austria - 1869.

A small Vienna. The Vienna was one of the first machines to come in a whole range of sizes.

Large Vienna with screw-in funnel.

An unusual Vienna with single support, with the marks 'Berndorf Alpacca Silber' underneath, made by Krupps, Germany.

Electric Vienna. There was no electric cut-out when the water had gone through the coffee.

Side view of the electric Vienna.

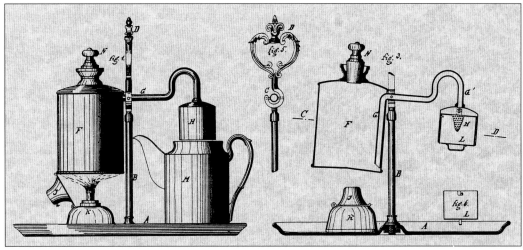

The original Eicke patent drawing.

The Eicke machine. When the water passed through the coffee, the container rose and the lid fell, extinguishing the flame. It was a solidly constructed machine. Germany - 1878.

been a high risk of explosion. The normal type used a heavy and tight fitting central tube to try and force the water through the coffee. While with this there was no risk of explosion, there was a risk of rocketing the central tube through the glass dome.

Even though the principle of making coffee through Rabaut style espresso machines must have been known during the nineteenth century, other less complicated machines and filter machines were more popular. The expense was probably the reason - the technology to make strongly engineered machines was available but the result would have been too costly or bulky for widespread domestic use. Without strong boilers, these machines would have exploded, a fate which some kitchens experienced. Safety valves existed

but were not widely used. As the compressed coffee in the brewing compartment expanded, the water stopped flowing. Pressure built until the machine exploded. There was always the temptation to make a stronger cup of coffee by putting in a little more coffee which could have caused an explosion in an espresso machine. There had to be a way to squeeze out just a little more flavour and this problem was exercising many minds.

The Spread of Ideas

With improved transportation, both goods and ideas travelled rapidly all over Europe. In 1860 there was a train from Lombardy to Vienna. In 1868, it took twenty-eight hours to go from Paris to Turin. The first sleeping car service from Paris to Vienna opened in 1873. Thousands travelled instead of just the privileged few. Ideas were literally only a day or two away. International exhibitions all over Europe tempted the curious to adapt new ideas to all sorts of new contraptions and claim them for their own.

Books, patent abstracts and journals were freely available all over Europe, which meant a wide dissemination of the latest ideas and technology. These factors made it very difficult for historians, decades later, to know who should be given credit for a particular innovation.

Right: The Kessel espresso machine. The filter for each cup revolved manually. Steam followed the hot water through the coffee. This was the first espresso machine to make one cup at a time. It was the first machine to control water and steam separately and had a bayonet fitting. Germany - 1878.

Far Right: The Kessel patent claims: 1. Coffee maker typified by having on the lower part of the boiler a tap which can operate so that boiling water and steam can be passed, one after the other, over ground coffee in the infusion cup with a sieve in the base and from which excess steam can be released.

2. Coffee maker according to claim 1 in which the infusion cup is connected by a bayonet fitting to a spreader plate with holes in it.

PATENT-ANSPRÜCHE:

1. Kaffeekocher, dadurch gekennzeichnet, daß am unteren Teile des Kessels *(a)* ein Mehrwegehahn *(e)* angeordnet ist, mit dem nacheinander kochendes Wasser und Dampf zu dem Kaffeemehl in der mit durchlochtem Boden versehenen Schale *(p)* eines Meß- und Aufgußbehälters und überschüssiger Dampf nach außen geleitet werden kann.

2. Kaffeekocher nach Anspruch 1, dadurch gekennzeichnet, daß die Kaffeemehlschale *(p)* in eine Schale *(q)* mit durchlochtem Boden *(u)* gesetzt ist, die durch Bajonettverschluß mit einer am Auslaßhahn angebrachten Glocke *(o)* abnehmbar verbunden ist, die oberhalb der Kaffeemehlschale eine durchlochte Verteilungsscheibe *(r)* trägt.

THE FIRST ESPRESSO MACHINE WITH WATER AND STEAM CONTROL
Gustav Kessel

Italian inventors Luigi Bezzera and Desiderio Pavoni are generally considered to be the inventors of the first espresso machine. However, Gustav Kessel, a German, has the honour of lodging the first patent, in 1878, for a machine with separate controls to cause the water and then the steam to pass through the coffee, held in a filter holder with a bayonet fitting. For whatever reason - too small or too clumsy or because there was not enough steam pressure to make it work effectively - the machine's use was not widespread, if in fact it was ever manufactured. There seems to be no other reference to it in contemporary sources. Kessel's machine incorporated all the ideas of water, steam and a bayonet fitting to make a single cup at a time, which were later used in the Bezzera invention. It even included a relief valve which was added by Pavoni to the Bezzera machine. It is possible that the idea originated prior to 1878, as that was only the second year of the German patent system. English inventions of a similar type were around at the same time, incorporating the use of steam power, which was becoming more common.

Kessel's was one of several machines using a combination of hot water and steam to make tea and coffee. All these patents are compatible with the idea, expressed in a French patent by Dartois in 1879, that there was a need to use steam to get full extraction. The idea of impregnating the coffee with steam before extraction was in the 1827 Laurens patent in France. The combination of water and steam in coffee brewing came from the observation of a domestic espresso machine - the coffee came out first and was followed by the steam, so it was therefore seen as being part of the process. The logical conclusion was that the brewing process needed steam to be complete. This false notion held sway for another seventy years until the 1940s. Steam is not necessary for a complete extraction of the flavour and modern espresso machines do not use steam in the brewing process. Steam has never been used to brew coffee. It is only used in modern machines for frothing the milk.

THE BEGINNINGS OF THE COMMERCIAL ESPRESSO MACHINE
Angelo Moriondo

Even if an inventor's name is known, it is very difficult to find any details of a patent in Italy, especially prior to 1900. Sheer luck led to my discovery, while searching through French patents in Paris, of a patent signed by Angelo Moriondo of Turin, lodged on the 23rd October 1885, for a coffee machine.

Angelo Moriondo's machine was a solidly constructed bulk brewer of fifty cups, with a large boiler heated by gas. It was almost certainly the first Italian bar machine that controlled the supply of steam and water separately through the coffee. Without separate controls, the large boiler would almost have had to empty its contents before any steam could be passed through the coffee.

Surprisingly, Moriondo has never been mentioned in other historic accounts of the development of the espresso machine but he was deeply involved and is certainly one of the earliest discoverers of the expresso machine, if not *the* earliest. The Italian patent system is probably responsible for his exclusion from the picture.

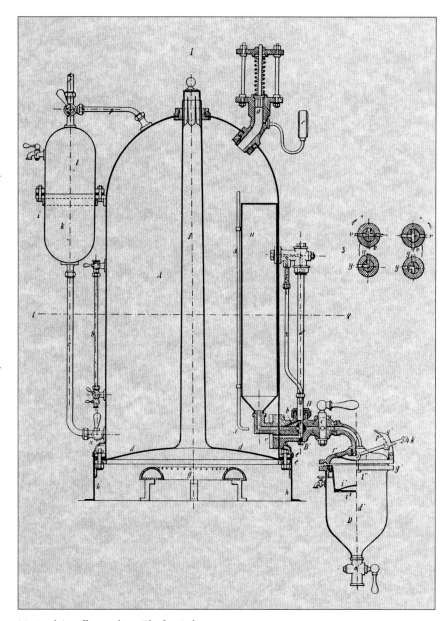

Moriondo's coffee machine. The first Italian water and steam machine patent. The whole machine could be rolled on wheels over a flame or controlled with gas as shown. The hot water was in the large tube 'u' and was pushed through the coffee by steam in the narrow tube 'x'. The coffee was in the filter basket at the top of the external fitting and was compressed by the ratchet lever. The brewed coffee fell into a receptacle from which it could be served. Italy - 1885.

Moriondo's machine was important, not only for itself but because its design could clearly be manufactured. It used the principle of forcing the water through the coffee grounds, under pressure, followed by steam to dry out the grounds. This was necessary if a controlled amount of hot water was to be forced through the coffee followed by a controlled amount of steam in the desired proportion.

Moriondo's patent claimed that his machine employed a *unique* system involving the application and utilisation of steam for instantaneous filtration and economic preparation of coffee. The unique system was really a restatement of earlier ideas that steam was necessary to make a complete extraction, but his machine was the first Italian machine to actually separate the idea of steam and water into distinct functions with a separate supply of steam and hot water. The use of the word 'unique' probably indicates that it was the first Italian coffee machine to use this idea.

Moriondo lodged many other patents about other subjects and he lodged another patent for coffee machines in 1910 which offered no significant difference in style to his first. We can therefore be almost certain that he actually made his machines over a period of at least twenty-five years.

I have in my collection an espresso machine with a bayonet fitting and a patent number, 1119, which I purchased in Turin and for which the Italian Patent Office is unable to provide the exact year of invention. I feel that the number indicates a patent date of 1900, or the 1890s. This kind of machine, with its bayonet fitting, could have been a link between Moriondo's bulk brewer and Luigi Bezzera's single-cup brewer.

THE ONE-CUP MACHINE
AN ESPRESSO MACHINE IN NAME
BUT NOT IN FACT
Luigi Bezzera

Bezzera created the 'one cup at a time' machine. But why did he want to make one cup at a time? In cafes in Paris, and probably Milan, one of the most popular ways to make coffee at that time was to place a small filter over a cup, producing *'caffè expres'* - coffee made expressly for the customer. Bezzera's machine used exactly the same brewing principle as had Moriondo, and even had a similar large sized boiler, but instead of making large numbers of cups at a time, he used a bayonet fitting of one-cup size. Bezzera lodged his patent on the 19th November, 1901, and an amendment including a steam relief valve, on the 17th January, 1902, under his name, but which was probably made by Desiderio Pavoni, a friend of his.

What exactly did Luigi Bezzera invent? He did not invent espresso coffee as we know it today. The low pressure in the boiler of three-quarters of an atmosphere was too low for the machine to be anything but a rapid filtering machine. The word 'espresso' does not appear in his patent nor does the word 'cappuccino'. (The word cappuccino possibly derives from the colour of the habits of the Capuchin monks.) What Bezzera did was to combine the idea of a single cup of coffee with an existing machine such as Moriondo's and he claimed that this was an instantaneous coffee machine. His patent says:

The other machines of the day make a large quantity of coffee, for example, fifty cups, in such a way that the coffee stays fresh and rich in aroma only for the first cups served immediately

Below and Centre: One of the first domestic Italian espresso machines with a bayonet fitting. The picture on the left shows the filter sitting on the water container and the picture on the right shows the filter locked in position. There is a safety valve on the tallest tube. Italy - c.1900.

FR

A very early machine with an external group.

after the action of the water and steam, while in the present machine the coffee is made one cup at a time. [English translation]

Bezzera's invention was the handle with the filter in it and the connecting bayonet fitting on the machine for making one cup of coffee at a time - much as we use today. This is known as a group. In operation, the handle had three positions: Off, Water and Steam, which made making a cup of coffee very easy.

Bezzera's object was not only to make the coffee faster but also to force the water through the coffee. This solved a problem that had existed for decades - if the coffee was ground too finely, the water simply would not filter through at all. In 1840 Tiesset had proposed a vacuum pump to draw the hot water down. Others had pumps on top to force the water through. The steam in Bezzera's machine was merely a substitute for air pressure, as in the vacuum pump, to force the water through. On the other hand it duplicated the action of all other pressure espresso coffee pots in that the water passed through the coffee first and then the steam forced the remaining water through. This dried out the coffee. A dry cake of coffee indicated that filtering had finished in a filter pot or a one-cup filter. There was an idea that the last drop had not been extracted from the coffee until the steam had been applied and that the steam was necessary to make a really good cup of coffee. The Bezzera machine did it all.

In 1906 an International Fair was held in Milan where Bezzera had a large stand and *Caffè espresso* was offered for the first time made in the Ideale machine which was advertised on a sign on one of the front pillars. This advertisement showed the names of both Luigi Bezzera and Desiderio Pavoni.

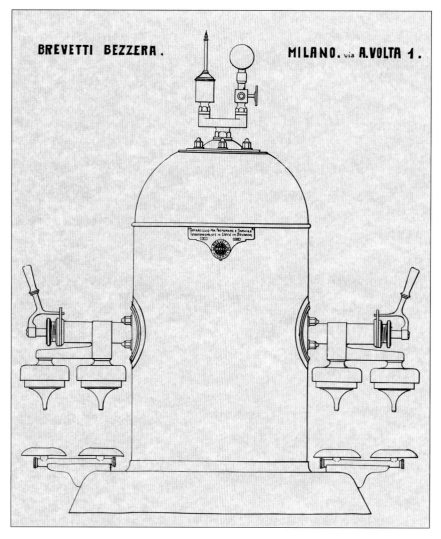

The original patent drawing for the Bezzera machine (19.11.1901). The machine was called a 'Giant type with double tap'. Each cup was made individually and there was a safety valve and pressure gauge on top of the machine.

The first Bezzera espresso machine, front and back. The back of the original photo called it 'An espresso coffee machine'. There were two steam valves, probably for heating milk.

GB

GB

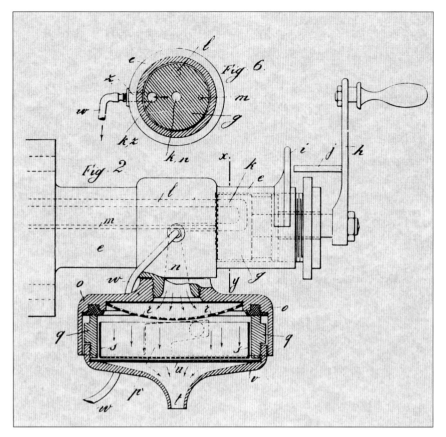

The drawing from Pavoni's German patent application in 1902. The diagonal tube is the relief valve. The same drawing (lodged in Italy on 17 January 1902) appears as an amendment to Bezzera's original patent.

The Milan Fair of 1906 showing the Bezzera Stand. Both Bezzera and Pavoni's names appear on the sign on the front left pillar advertising the Ideale machine. *Caffè Espresso* from an espresso machine is offered for the first time.

The sign on the column read as follows: *"IDEALE„* (Brevetto Bezzera). Apparecchio per preparare e servire istantantaneamente il caffè in bevanda. Desiderio Pavoni, Milano. Via Dante Ang. via Giulini. [English translation]. *"IDEALE"* (Bezzera patent). Machine to prepare and serve the beverage coffee instantaneously. Desiderio Pavoni, Milan. Corner of Via Dante and Via Giulini.

One of the first written references to an espresso machine is by Dr. A. Cougnet writing in 1909 for *La Scena Illustrata*, a magazine published in Florence.[4] In the article he referred to freshly brewed coffee as the true coffee 'made on purpose' recommended by Senator Mantegazza, a writer of books on popular hygiene. Cougnet went on to say:

> Already in many shops, so called 'expres' coffee, comes served by means of a little filter sitting on the cup. But the action of these primitive filters is so slow that the water loses its heat and the coffee arrives weak and not hot. The Ideale machine remedies this defect by preparing and serving the coffee instantaneously. The Ideale solves all these problems. It consists of a boiler kept constantly at a pressure of three quarters of an atmosphere and produces the necessary steam to make a perfect cup of coffee. It is truly the triumph of mathematical formula over the blind empiricism which persists in duping the client by serving a perfidious decoction rather than an aromatic infusion. The Ideale is a marvellous patented apparatus, the property of Mr. Desiderio Pavoni of Milan, is well-known to all gourmets ...
> and won a gold medal at the recent International Exhibition in Milan. [English translation]

By 1909 'Ideale' was the name of a machine associated with Desiderio Pavoni.

THE IDEALE MACHINE
Desiderio Pavoni

Pavoni's addition to the Bezzera machine was probably the steam relief valve. All the evidence points to this being the case. Many people have confused the machines and the achievements of both these men. (See Appendix II.) Even though the steam relief valve appeared in Bezzera's 1902 addition under Bezzera's name, it was almost certainly made by Pavoni who lodged an identical relief valve drawing in France and Germany under his name a few months later.

The traditional story is that Bezzera was in financial strife and Pavoni helped him out by buying the patent for ten thousand Lira, a considerable sum in those days. It is certain that the patent was transferred to Pavoni in 1903. Another version is that Pavoni bought the factory from Bezzera. Interestingly, La Pavoni company brochures say that the business was founded in 1905. It seems more than likely that Bezzera was manufacturing the Pavoni machine before Pavoni's factory was in production.

There is no doubt that Pavoni and Bezzera were friends - both families agree on this. Under the deal they had made, Bezzera and Pavoni must both have had rights to make the machines because both continued to make machines under

The photo accompanying the article written by
Dr. A. Cougnet about the Pavoni Ideale machine was
from the 1906 Milan Fair. This machine has 8 bolts on
top, the same number as Pavoni's version, whereas
Bezzera's had 6 bolts on top.

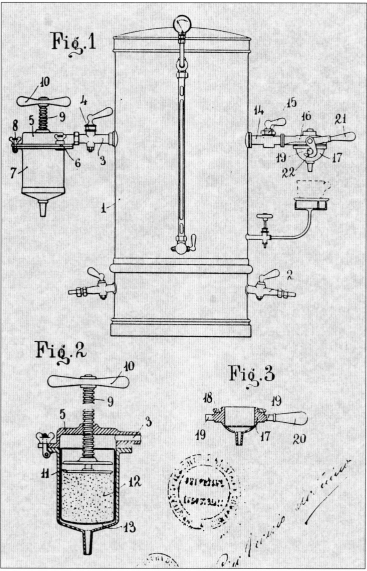

their own brand names. More than likely Pavoni
bought the patent and the rights to make the relief
valve machine while allowing Bezzera to make his
original machine. That theory would be consistent
with the fact that Bezzera did not include the valve
on his own machines. Whatever the case, Pavoni's
machine was strongly based on the Bezzera
design.

One thing is certain - the stand at the Milan
Fair in 1906, though it bore as the main sign the
name Bezzera, was in fact a stand which featured
the Pavoni machines. Pavoni's name appears on
the column in the stand together with Bezzera's. In
early Italian sources Bezzera's name was not
mentioned. Cougnet in 1909 and Leonida Valerio
in 1927 mentioned only Pavoni.[5] Both the Pavoni
and Bezzera companies were producing
throughout the period and I can only assume that
it was the Pavoni machine that dominated the
market. Certainly the pressure relief valve is on
every modern machine because with the higher
pressure from the electric pump, it is very
necessary. Perhaps Pavoni's gas control valve,
which he patented in 1905, was the critical
difference between the two machines.

AN INNOVATOR
Pier Teresio Arduino

There is one other name to join the pantheon -
Pier Teresio Arduino. An Arduino company
brochure says that in 1905 it was the first
manufacturer to use mass production techniques
with espresso coffee machines and their first
machine was presented to the world at the 1906

Milan Exposition. There does not appear to be any
independent evidence of this.

In the last days of 1906, Arduino patented a
coffee machine known as the 'Victoria'. It was not
in the Moriondo or Bezzera style but incorporated
a heat exchanger to heat the water very quickly
and the coffee was made in jugs. This original
Victoria Arduino machine had nothing to do with
the development of the espresso machine.

A second Arduino patent in 1910 was for a
machine in the Bezzera style with a single-cup
handle and also a screw press bulk filter on the
side to squeeze all the flavour out of the coffee. In
the same way that Bezzera changed the Moriondo
bulk brewer to being a one-cup brewer, so Rosetta
Scorza and Achille Gaggia more than twenty years
later had the idea to make the Arduino bulk screw
press into a single-cup press brewer.

Arduino won gold medals at fairs in Bologna
and Paris in 1909 though there is no record of the
kind of machines exhibited. The Arduino
company won other prizes in Rome, Turin and
Genoa and seems to have had a very large factory
with a large production. Other patents followed
for handles with two spouts to make two cups at a
time and even a machine with hand pumps.

Arduino tried to overcome
the problem of lack of
pressure with a screw
piston on the side in 1910.
An English patent of 1914
showed that he had already
given up the idea.

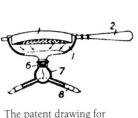

The patent drawing for the Arduino double spout espresso handle. Italy - 1918.

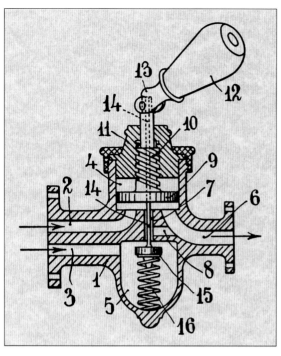

The patent drawing for the Arduino espresso control tap. Italy - 1910.

THE COMMERCIAL ESPRESSO ESTABLISHED

In 1910, Moriondo, Bezzera, Pavoni and Arduino, the fathers of espresso coffee, were making machines. Each had done something to establish the espresso machine in the world. Moriondo had invented the idea of making bulk coffee using hot water and steam; Bezzera applied a single-cup handle to the same type of machine; Pavoni probably made the relief valve and certainly commercialised the machine; Arduino made some refinements such as a two-cup spout in 1918 and successfully commercialised the machines. It was only a matter of time for the technology to catch up and solve the problem of the need for greater pressure to force the water through the coffee.

The basic machine with a boiler was a combination of groups and bulk brewers and lasted until Gaggia introduced the lever machine to the world in 1948. His was the true espresso machine which produced a coffee with mousse on it. The only connection between the new machines and the old was the existence of the boiler and the handle to hold the coffee. All the machines prior to 1948 really produced a 'quick filtered' coffee.

The early espresso machines must have been cumbersome and the result dependent on the artistry of the *barista* - the man behind the bar - who was capable of making the machine sound like a steam train with alternate bursts of hot water and steam through the coffee. In spite of the theatre - an impressive polished machine with eagles and tubes, and the sound - the coffee was in fact a pale relative of post-war espresso coffee. Pre- and post-war coffee were as alike as fried eggs and poached eggs - made from the same ingredient but with a totally different appearance and taste.

The Small Cup in Italy

There is no doubt that the cup used for a black coffee in the first half of this century in Italy was larger than the cup of today, reflecting the inability of the early machines to make good extractions. It was impossible to make a full extraction in a small cup without more pressure.

The size of the Italian coffee cup is difficult to determine. Old porcelain coffee sets seem to have very small cups and old coffee pots are relatively small, certainly smaller than the equivalent German pots. The modern cup, in a bar, is very small and contains only a small amount of coffee, around 35cc (35 millilitres, or 1.25 fluid ounces) which reflects the improvement in the extraction process of the coffee.

At first I thought that the size of the cup was dependent on the fact that when coffee is brewed, the bitterness comes out at the end. It follows that the less you brew, the less bitter the coffee is. I now feel that cup size has been determined from pre-coffee times.

Prior to coffee coming to Europe, beer and beer broth were the main food and drink of Northern Europe. Around the Mediterranean countries, wine was king. Beer was served in large jugs and glasses, while wine was served in much smaller glasses. When coffee came, it was as a substitute for the current drink and was served in the same quantity. Turkish coffee in Greece was served in little cups to replace the ouzo and wine. Italian coffee was served in small cups to replace the wine and *grappa*. In all the northern countries, the coffee was served in much larger cups as a replacement for beer. It was a substitute of hot quantity for cold quantity, perhaps even warm for warm. It was not the coffee machine that determined the cup size - on the contrary, the society determined the cup size and this in turn influenced the design of the machine which only had to make small cups. France does not fit the theory very well, but it must be taken into consideration that northern France was once very much part of the Frankish Empires, while the south has a great deal of Spanish and Italian influence. In a sense France has a foot in both camps and drinks both enormous milk coffees and small black coffees.

THE FIRST PUMP MACHINE PATENT

It was soon discovered that steam pressure was not enough to force the water through the coffee. More pressure was needed.

In 1909 Luigi Giarlotto of Turin offered a solution by adding pumps. The machine incorporated a hand-rotative pump that forced the hot water through a heat exchanger tube into the brewing chamber, then a bicycle style pump to force the coffee up into the top of the machine and a stirrer right at the top. The rotative pump idea was excellent and years before its time. It became a feature of modern espresso machines.

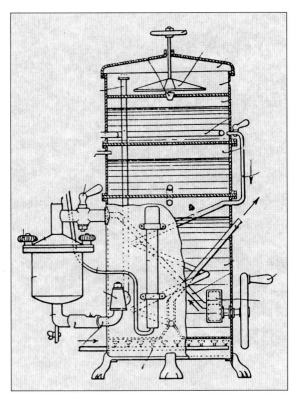

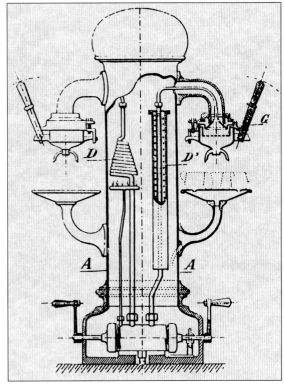

Far Left: Luigi Giarlotto's patent added a hand-driven water pump (lower right) and an air pump (bicycle shape left of centre). Italy - 1909.

Left: Marius Malaussena, in Nice, invented a gas and electric instantaneous espresso machine. The Snider machine was the electric version. Italy - 1922.

In 1922 Marius Malaussena, from Nice in France, made a patent for ideas which were later incorporated in the Snider machine, which was eventually to capture about fifteen per cent of the total pre-war market in Italy.

The Snider machine was one of the best espresso machines before the war. The pressure to force the water through the coffee came from the water reticulation system and was higher than from a steam boiler, with consequent better extraction. Although the patent drawings show two versions - cold water passing through pipes heated with gas on the left and electricity on the right - as far as I know, no gas machines were ever produced. The water flow was controlled by the handles at the base which were connected to gas and electricity at the same time. The electric Snider machine is said to have made good coffee and this is probably due to the fact that the higher pressure from the tap could force the water through finer coffee. The Snider did have a steam facility, but it is unlikely to have been as good at making steam as the conventional boiler models. A Snider machine was capable of making better espresso coffee than other machines.

The electric version is practically devoid of insulation of any type. The combination of water and electricity is always dangerous and when the machines were placed on zinc countertops, the operators would have experienced plenty of shocks. Most other manufacturers had models like the Snider - they were known as 'electro-instantaneous' coffee machines.

In 1927 the Victoria Arduino Company lodged a patent for a machine with individual air pumps on each group to force the water, which was supplied below boiling point to the group,

Front and back views of a Snider electric espresso machine. The water was heated as it passed through the small round heaters. The globe at the top was for steam.

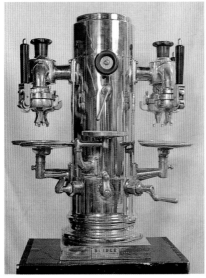

A back view of the Snider machine.

An early espresso machine which operated with pressure from the tap. The tap was connected to the water supply and electricity to the little boiler below it. In theory if the water reached the coffee at the correct temperature, this machine made excellent coffee. Italy - 1920s.

FR

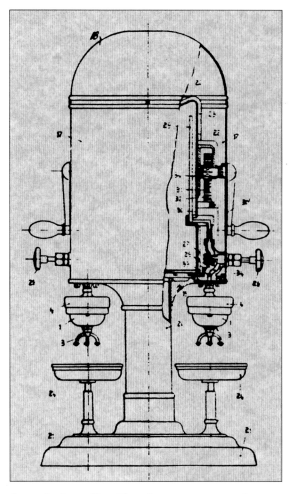

Michele Donn and the Victoria Arduino Company patented a machine with hand air pumps to compress air and operate pistons to force the water through the coffee.
Italy - 1927.

THE AUTOMATIC ESPRESSO

Some ideas of coffee brewing were constant, such as the desire to have more water pressure so that the coffee could be ground finer and a stronger cup made, but there were also many attempts to make a machine which would roast and grind the coffee as close as possible to the moment of brewing.

In 1912, two Frenchmen, Maurice-Georges Pouzot and Faust-Laurent Zambrini, lodged a patent for a machine incorporating a gas coffee roaster, an electric grinder and an automatic manual espresso brewer in which the ground coffee fell directly into the brewer. Decades before the technology was available to realise it, the espresso machine had been taken to its logical conclusion only six years after its introduction in Milan in 1906.

Mario Levi from Turin in 1913 patented a machine in which the ground coffee was portioned into a filter cup by turning a handle and the coffee was brewed espresso-style into a cup below. This machine looked capable of manufacture and was designed to speed up the operation.

The same Mario Levi improved on this coffee maker in 1919. He invented and made a roaster, grinder and coffee maker all in one, called the Standard Tipo A-7. About fifty were made and sold, but unfortunately none are known to exist today. Many patents for such ideas from around the turn of the century did not look even remotely like working. Up to the present, I do not know of any other machine produced to incorporate the whole coffee function. The Standard Tipo A-7 was truly a unique machine for its time.

In 1935 The Illetta machine appeared in Italy, invented by Dr. Illy. It was a fully automatic machine which dispensed with the manual operation of the handle. It was the first machine to

through the coffee. The object was to avoid using boiling water and scalding the coffee. The need to produce steam in the boiler in other machines meant that the temperature of the water was above boiling point which was bad for the coffee.

In 1931 Paul Ciupka in Germany wrote that the temperature of brewing in espresso machines was 103 to 108 degrees and, as a consequence, some users had over-extracted by up to six per cent.[6]

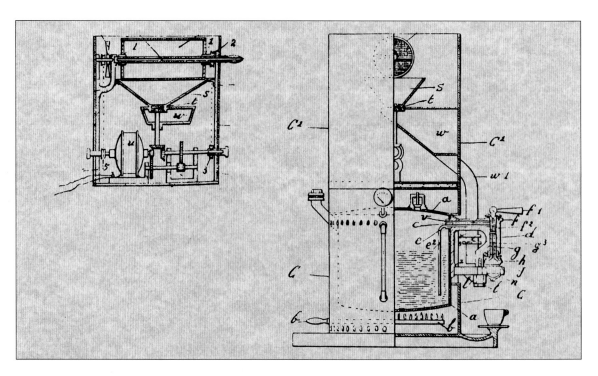

Pouzet and Zambrini proposed a coffee roaster with gas heating and an electric coffee grinder with the coffee falling directly into a revolving filter which dispensed the espresso coffee. France - 1912.

use compressed air to force the water through the coffee.

From all the attempts that were being made it is obvious that everyone had an idea of the problems of existing machines: slowness, insufficient pressure, inability to grind coffee finely enough to make a strong enough brew. Nobody in their wildest dreams could have imagined what the coffee would be like when those problems were finally solved.

ELECTRICITY AND OTHER DEVELOPMENTS

Gas was widely used but electricity was becoming more widely available and inventors quickly found new applications. In many cases the ideas were excellent, but were ahead of their time in terms of the pressure and electrical control equipment required to use them.

The Marzetti machine of 1910 conveyed the water, which was boiled in the base of the machine by electric elements, through the coffee by steam pressure. If Marzetti had allowed the water to come from the water supply directly through the boiler, he might have discovered espresso coffee with 'cream' (mousse). Electricity was used in new machines from about 1908 and this was one of the first examples in an espresso machine.

The Spaniard Adrian Vazquez del Saz in 1912 wanted the best of both worlds - to make coffee in bulk and to draw from it one cup at a time. It was very obviously a development from a Bezzera-style machine and sought to overcome the problem of the slow speed of brewing by creating the illusion that every cup was being made 'espresso'. Bulk brewers like this are used on some modern espresso machines. They do *not* make espresso coffee but much weaker quick filter coffee.

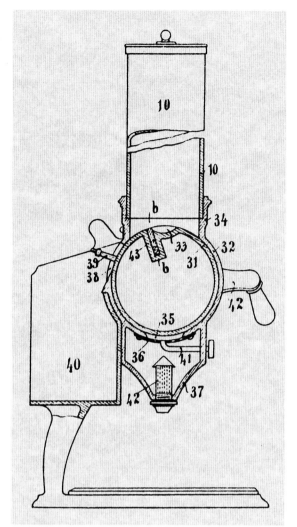

Mario Levi made a design for an automatic machine. The ground coffee in the top was transported (in 33) to the bottom of the machine by turning the handle. The water came in horizontally (41); the handle turned again and the spent coffee was brushed off by (39) into (40). Italy - 1913.

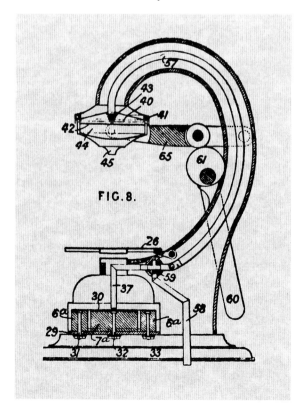

FIG. 8.

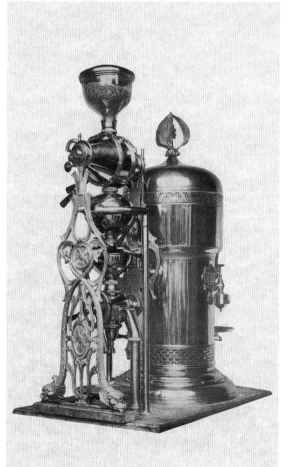

Left: Mario Levi succeeded in making a roaster, grinder and espresso machine all in one. The idea is not surprising. The surprising thing is that it worked. France - 1919.

Far Left: The Marzetti electric espresso machine. Water was boiled in the base where there were two concentric cylinders acting as electrodes. The water was then forced through the coffee under steam pressure. Italy - 1910.

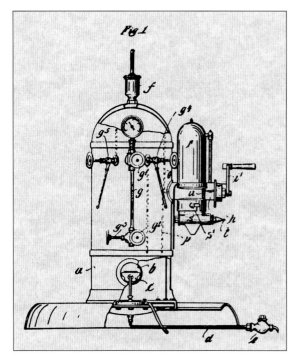

Adrian Vazquez del Saz of Madrid invented a bulk-brewing machine with a one-cup dispenser. Spain - 1912.

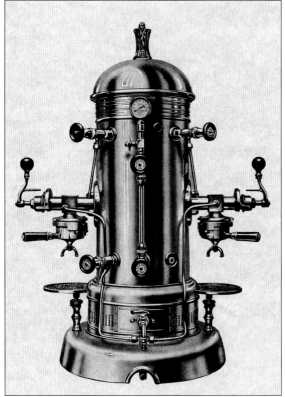

The La Pavoni Mignon was still the same basic machine in operation as the 1906 model. The relief valve to take away the pressure from the group is very prominent and still part of the group. By 1929, twenty thousand of this brand had been sold. Italy - 1930s.

IMPRESSIVE MACHINE - UNIMPRESSIVE COFFEE

In a crowded bar in downtown Milan, where the coffee grinder was going non-stop, spreading a haze of coffee aroma, and a spoonful of sugar was being stirred in the cup as if its sweetness grew with the stirring, a cup of espresso was really something, 'black as the devil, hot as hell, pure as an angel, sweet as love'.[7]

The espresso machine changed coffee drinking in Italy, Spain, Hungary, Austria, Switzerland, France and all of South America except for Brazil which even today uses methods more common last century. Not the coffee, but the espresso machines themselves, sitting on the counter with lions and eagles and other emblems adorning them, became the focus of attention. The feeling was that this machine was getting closer to solving the problem of the magic. The more elaborate the machine, the better the coffee.

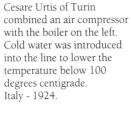

Cesare Urtis of Turin combined an air compressor with the boiler on the left. Cold water was introduced into the line to lower the temperature below 100 degrees centigrade. Italy - 1924.

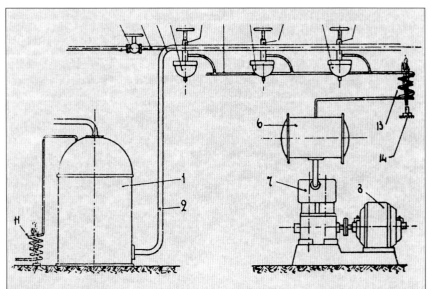

An Argentinian espresso machine. - 1920s.

The early espresso machine, despite its popularity, was still not perfect for Italy. There was an unsatisfied need to have the coffee in a cup that was even smaller, combined with a more complete extraction of the flavour. In short, there was a need to have a machine, not making the same coffee in a better way, but making a new, even stronger coffee. The search was on for the coffee grail.

GAGGIA CREATES THE TRUE ESPRESSO THE ESPRESSO MACHINE IN NAME AND IN FACT

There are stories that, before the war, Giovanni Achille Gaggia, a bar owner in Milan, was experimenting with screw-type pistons to make coffee and that after the war he tried the lever piston and it worked. Another story goes that Gaggia actually possessed a model of the screw piston and could show it to people. Yet a third story says that Rosetta Scorza, the wife of an inventor, came to Gaggia with an idea for a new machine. The idea was a little primitive and when the inventor died, his wife sold it to Gaggia for a thousand Lira (a large sum of money in those days). Gaggia made some improvements and the true espresso machine as we know it was invented.

The facts almost fit in with these stories. Rosetta Scorza of Milan was married to Sr. Cremonese who was a technician in a coffee grinder factory. He made tests to see if the coffee was ground evenly and was responsible for introducing the cone mill to Italy in the 1930s. He patented the idea of a screw piston, which forced the water through the coffee. This was not in itself a new idea, but one that had been known from at least 1909 with the Giarlotto patent. Cremonese died and Rosetta Scorza was left with a patent.

A gas espresso machine made by WMF. Germany - 1920s.

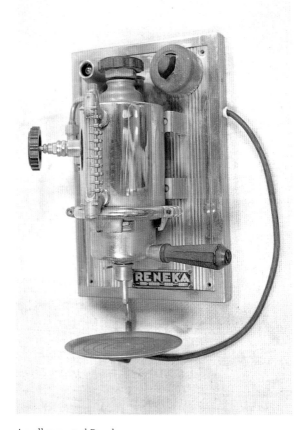

A wall-mounted Reneka machine. This was a model designed for small establishments. France - 1930s.

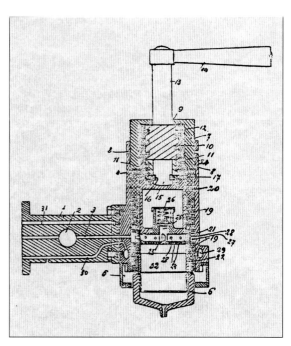

The Rosetta Scorza hand piston with screw action. As the handle was turned horizontally, the piston pushed down to force the water through the coffee. Italy - 1936.

The patent was for a screw-press piston, but the style of language used by patent attorneys to describe ideas even before they became inventions covered pistons of all types, including lever pistons. Therefore a lever piston would still have infringed the Scorza patent. The new machine was basically a one-cup version of the Giarlotto and Arduino ideas of more than twenty years earlier. It could even be said to be a combination of the 1927 Arduino one-cup piston machine and the Giarlotto and Arduino screw pistons.

The story continues that Rosetta Scorza tried to get existing manufacturers to use her invention but they were not interested. It is possible that she showed Gaggia the patent, because he lodged a patent application for a piston group, two years later.

Giovanni Achille Gaggia, born in 1895 in Milan, set himself up in a coffee bar in the same city, where he became a dedicated barman. He was not satisfied with the flavour of coffee coming from his existing machine, which scalded the coffee and made it bitter. Perhaps the coffee was over-roasted and burnt to compensate for the poor extraction. Before the Second World War, he patented and developed a rotative screw piston which he made from aluminium and brass and which could be connected to the boiler of the conventional machines of the day. The steam had been eliminated from the brewing process, but the water was still too hot. Gaggia made many attempts to make his rotative piston work, but there were problems with leaks. He tried several of these pistons in friends' bars by simply attaching them to their boilers, but they were very tiring to use.

Gaggia produced small quantities but the war came and a bomb destroyed the small stock. After the war he started in production again with brass groups and asbestos, but the system still was not perfect and he must have changed from the rotating piston to an up and down lever piston which was really his own idea, even though technically covered in Rosetta Scorza's patent.

Rosetta Scorza ultimately received a payment for the use of her patent because Gaggia's own must have infringed on it. Both the original Gaggia patent and the Scorza patent are totally different to the lever patent which Gaggia lodged in 1947. This incorporated a large handle with a spring to force the piston down on the coffee and provide sufficient pressure to actually extract the essence from it. Rosetta Scorza had the idea of using a piston in a cylinder more or less as a hand pump. Gaggia's idea was to combine this with a strong spring which acted as the force to push the water through the coffee. The combination of ideas worked. I think it can be said that the Scorza patent provided the idea for a single or double cup piston and Giovanni Gaggia provided the motive force to make it work. Gaggia's 1938 patent incorporated a rotative handle and a strong spring which he did not show in the patent drawing.

The 1947 patent incorporating gears and a spring in the group was a lot easier to use and less tiring than the rotative group. Gaggia still did not make the whole machine. He attached the groups to the old upright machines where the group position was halfway up the boiler. The old boilers were not designed for the new groups and there was too much steam which was not needed.

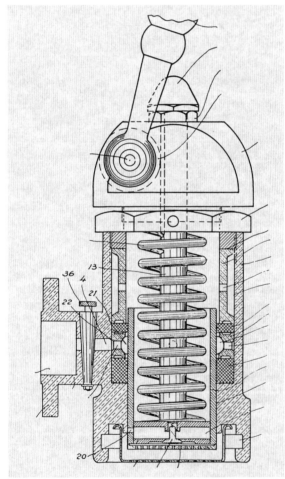

The Gaggia patent of 1947 for the spring lever group. It was an invention that led not only to a better coffee but to a new type of coffee altogether. The ground coffee was put in the U-shaped filter at the bottom of the piston. Pulling the handle down compressed the piston spring and at the same time let water into the newly-created brewing chamber. Releasing the spring allowed the piston to force the water through the coffee. The selection of the right-sized spring to force the water at the correct pressure and rate through the coffee was the crucial factor in producing the new espresso coffee.

The Gaggia patent of 1938 eventually was produced as a group which could be bolted onto other manufacturer's machines. The horizontally rotating screw produced the pressure to force the water through the coffee.

Gaggia Introduces the Spring into the Lever

Gaggia must have been very persistent to incorporate the spring into a lever-operated piston. The idea might have been relatively simple, but to make a working model required real talent. The lever without the spring would not have made espresso coffee as we know it. The spring provided the pressure and it was the pressure that forced the water through the coffee in such a short time - fifteen seconds for a short black. On the 20th June 1947, he lodged his patent for a new boiler and on the 8th August 1947, lodged his patent for the lever group.

It was a major step, perhaps the single biggest development of all time in coffee brewing. Gaggia's importance was his commercial realisation of a good idea. He made it happen. His machine made a cup of coffee that was totally different to any other coffee. By using a lever, the pressure applied to the coffee by a spring was independent of the pressure in the boiler. At the same time, the water temperature used became independent of the temperature in the boiler so that a stronger, quicker and controllable filtration was possible. The use of steam was lessened, and was only for frothing milk and not for making coffee. The boiler could be smaller and the heat loss consequently smaller. In fact the patent described a boiler with two chambers: a small one for steam and a large one for hot water, one on top of the other. The coffee could be finely ground, the water was forced through, and into the cup came coffee with a 'cream', a light coloured mousse, on the top. The coffee was made faster and had a more intense flavour and aroma - everything the market wanted. Gaggia must have been amazed - he could never have expected coffee with mousse on the top. It is possible that he did not like what he had produced. It was as if he had been trying for a better hard boiled egg and instead made a poached egg.

He offered the perfected group to other manufacturers who smiled and declined. They thought the results were strange and inferior. However Gaggia had some marketing sense and installed his groups in bars with a large sign on the window - *'Caffè crema di caffè naturale'* - coffee cream from natural coffee. People became curious, entered the bars and looked at the mousse on the coffee. Some walked away declaring it was a fraud, while others recognised that the coffee was not bitter and had more flavour. Several large and prominent bars in Milan, such as Motta and Biffi in the Galeria, adopted the system. A few sales were made outside Milan and in 1950 a total of thirty machines was sold.

Then problems started about the validity of the patent. Victoria Arduino claimed that the system of using a piston was the same as the Melior system. The claims were never resolved although there were large legal expenses.

Gaggia did not have a real workshop, but had the groups, the lever handles and filters made for him by Valente, who had a factory which made parts for hair dryers. In 1952 Valente started making his own machines, incorporating washers on the pistons, under the brand name Faema. Gaggia then set up a factory with Sr. Capsoni as

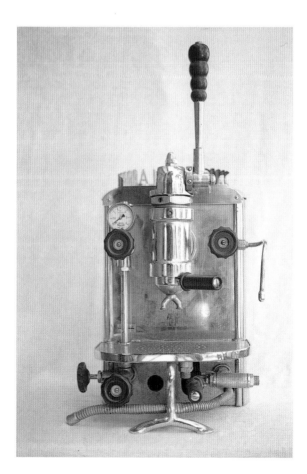

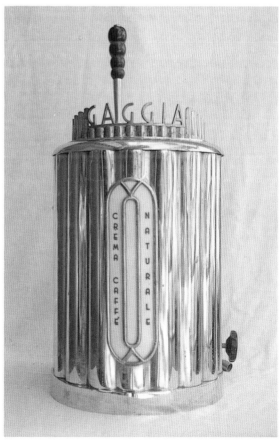

Far Left: The first Gaggia lever machine. The dial shows the pressure in the boiler. The natural coffee cream or mousse on the cup produced by this machine was the visual difference between the new and old styles of coffee. Italy - 1948.

Left: Back view of the Gaggia lever machine.

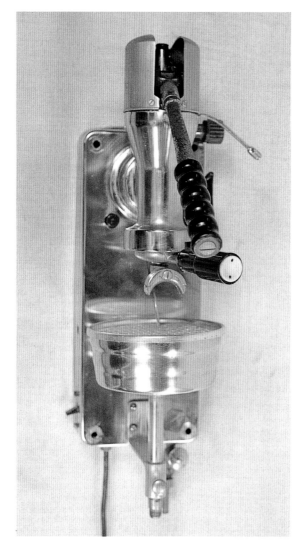

A wall-mounted WMF lever machine with instantaneous heating. There was no boiler. Germany - 1950s.

THE INTRODUCTION OF THE ELECTRIC PUMP

Beniamino Rota lodged a patent in 1950 for the Condor machine. It overcame the problem of the simultaneous drop in water temperature and pressure when cold water passed into the boiler to refill it. His machine forced the water, by tap pressure or with an electric pump operated by a foot switch, through a heat exchanger in the steam section of the boiler, and then into the boiler. The steam could still be used, as in the older machines, by using the two-way tap.

Rota's machine was a major step towards the development of the heat exchanger and electric pump that would revolutionise coffee making and supplant the lever machine. Rota had still failed to recognise that steam was unnecessary to complete the brewing process and especially if you used an electric pump. Once the water had passed through the coffee, it was in the cup. The steam had no effect on the coffee in the cup. Steam was not used in a lever machine to dry the coffee. If the coffee was packed tightly enough into the filter, it came out dry and this became the criterion for the correct packing of the coffee.

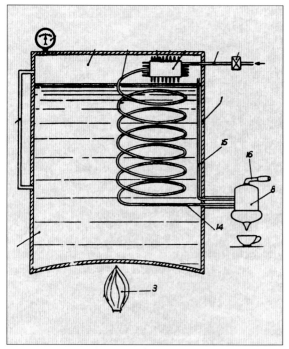

Beniamino Rota made a patent for a machine in which an electric water pump forced the water through the coffee and then used steam to dry the coffee. Italy - 1950.

engineer to make complete machines. The Gaggia Company was now ready to exploit the invention. Machines were exported all over the world to start a revolution with this new, true espresso coffee.

New machines were tried including some with steam powered groups. The piston was forced down with steam pressure but the washers hardened after a few months. The Cimbali company tried compressed air without commercial success.

Gaggia died in 1961. His significance was that he showed what happened when hot water was forced through finely ground coffee. For the first time, it was possible to extract everything from the coffee. The machine was in control of the bean. The bean could not keep anything back.

The impact was enormous. The mousse meant that the product was instantly distinguishable from the product of the previous Bezzera style machines. Overnight the large upright machines had gone, replaced by long cylindrical horizontal machines. Geralomo Spaguolo had tried horizontal machines in 1922 without success, but in 1948 they were in fashion and spread from Italy all over the world. The handles going up and down were the sign of frenetic activity as the strong essence trickled down into the cup, followed by the hissing of the steam valve to froth the milk for the cappuccinos.

The Haiti Coffee Machine Corporation in 1950 manufactured machines in which the piston was operated by a compressor under the counter. The same system was used by the Cimbali and Universal machines, but it was not considered to be a good system.

Valente and Arosio designed a new lever machine in 1952 and changed the piston design by putting washers on it.

Cimbali used a hydraulic pressure system to take the strain out of using the lever. The company introduced hydraulic piston machines in 1956

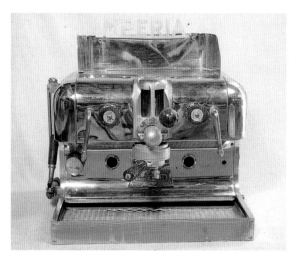

An Imperia French machine which adopted the new horizontal design of the new lever machines. This machine had no sophistications at all, merely an on/off handle. It relied on mains pressure to make the coffee and since this was greater than the boiler pressure of the pre-war machines, it made a better coffee. France - 1950s.

The Cimbali Company originated the hydraulic group. It was a volumetric group allowing precise dosing of the quantity of water to brew the coffee. Italy - 1956.

A Dorio hydraulic espresso machine. The metal tubes at the top of the group introduce pressure from the water mains and force the pistons down to make the coffee. Italy - 1960s.

which made excellent coffee and were very popular. They did not rely on electrical power, sensitive solenoid valves or electric pumps. Later on, improved reliability of electric components meant that totally electric and electronic machines became dominant in the market place.

VALENTE INTRODUCES THE PUMP TO THE ESPRESSO MACHINE

In 1955 Giampietro Saccani of Lecco made a substantial advance by keeping the temperature of the group constant. He allowed the water from the boiler to circulate through the group and in this way the coffee was the same temperature after one cup or after a break of ten minutes. Valente's name is usually associated with this discovery. Valente further developed the idea in 1960 and it was to be the basis for the Faema E61 - called after the eclipse of 1961. The electric pump was unable to pump hot water and so cold water was pumped through the heat exchanger under pressure. It was a complete reversal of the past where hot water was pressurised. Now the water was pressurised and then heated. These features made the Faema E61 machine famous and it is considered one of the best machines ever made. The Cimbali company sued the Faema company for the infringement of the Cimbali patent for heat exchangers and won, with the consequence that Faema had to pay very large damages.

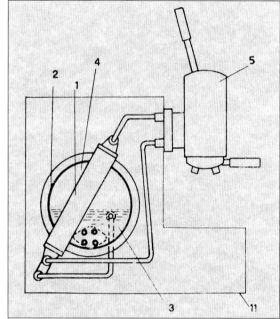

Valente's lever espresso patent. The principle of using a heat exchanger and the water from the boiler to keep the group warm could also be used in a lever machine.

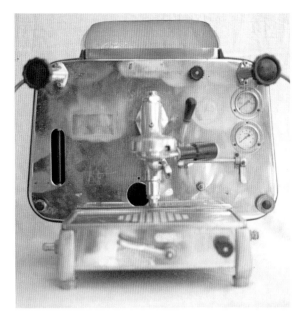

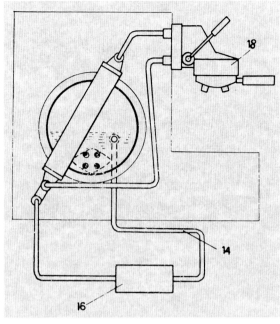

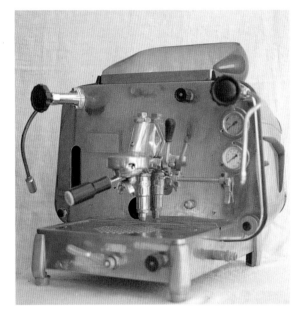

The patent drawing shows the water circulation for the Faema E61. The pump (16) forced fresh water from the mains through the heat exchanger located diagonally in the boiler. Meanwhile, hot water had been circulating through the group - in at the top and out at the bottom. This group is widely considered to make the best coffee although others make equally good coffee. The two major changes from the lever machine were the absence of the lever and the fact that there were now two gauges on the machine - one to tell the boiler pressure and the other the pump pressure.

Although the new machines with heat exchangers used the same pressure in the boiler as the old pre-war ones, the electric pumps applied a pressure to the coffee about ten times greater than before. The water in the boiler was used exclusively to supply steam and hot water for tea and other hot drinks. It was never used to make the coffee. The cold water from the pump passed through the boiler in a copper tube and exchanged its coldness for the heat of the water in the boiler, hence it was called a heat exchanger. The coffee could be more finely ground, although not without a limit to fineness. Because the pump passed a defined quantity of water at a defined rate in the new machines, and there was now control of water temperature and machine temperature, brewing temperature, time of brewing - everything - the whole process was under control.

THE ESPRESSO MACHINE PERFECTED

The heat exchanger system was used for lever machines and electric pump machines. The electric pump used was the Procon and Faema held the rights to use the pump for ten years. The espresso machine had been perfected. Everything that followed was an attempt to do it more simply, more cheaply, more easily, with more controls but always to achieve the same result. The other major innovation which would affect the way in which machines were constructed was the vibratory pump instead of the rotative pump. The cycle for the electric power to an electro-magnet was continuously interrupted to give a succession of

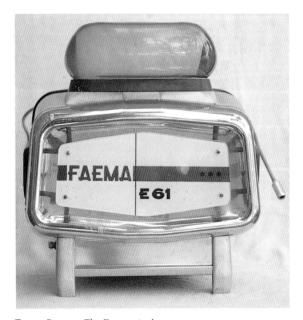

Top to Bottom: The Faema single group E61 machine was the first of a whole range of a new type of espresso machine. Italy - 1961.

A Vibiemme machine. It used the original group from the E61, which is easily recognisable by the little diagonal handle on the side. Italy -1989.

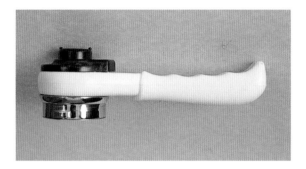

The Paoletti Handle was called a *'Boghe'*. By inserting the spring-loaded handle into the group and twisting back, the handle pressurised the coffee and ensured that it developed a cream in the cup by emulsifying the coffee. Italy - 1990.

The Futurmat electronic espresso machine. Spain - 1990.

The Spidem espresso machine showing the *'Boghe'* handle and a new milk frother. Italy - 1990.

little jerks to the piston which forced the water through the pump. These pumps are very small and have allowed espresso machines to become very small. Vibratory pumps appear in many domestic machines.

The evolution of the coffee brewing process for espresso machines had finished. Innovators were looking for different ways of doing the same thing. The basic process would stay the same but there would be many small innovations such as controlling the quantity of water going through the coffee. This was first done by using timers to control the time the pump ran. The latest devices are small turbines which give electronic signals at each revolution as the water passes through. The signals are counted electronically until preset numbers of revolutions have been achieved, at which point the cycle stops.

The other significant addition was a *gigleur* or restrictor orifice of 0.7 millimetres introduced into the water line to give better control to the water flow. All Italian machines have this. Some Spanish espresso machines are designed to work with very fine coffee but do not have the refinement of the *gigleur*. Spaniards drink their espresso coffee much stronger than Italians do - the extraction takes up to forty-five seconds and has much more mousse because of the greater use of Robusta coffee. This higher extraction level is achieved by grinding the coffee more finely. These machines make excellent *café con leche* - the Spanish coffee with hot milk, but are not designed to use the coarser Italian grind which makes a distinctly Italian style coffee.

In 1984 the Italian company Sibocaf introduced an espresso machine which brewed a normal short black espresso coffee and then sucked it back into the machine where it was cooled by a refrigeration unit and ran back into the cup as an iced coffee!

In 1984 Sr. Paoletti of Florence invented a handle which always gave cream on the coffee, but it was only used in domestic machines.

THE FULLY AUTOMATIC ESPRESSO MACHINE

The ultimate and highest form of the espresso machine for non-Italians is the fully automatic machine. This machine grinds a measured dose of coffee into the brewing chamber, brews it to the desired quantity, expels the exhausted grounds and then is ready for another cycle. The most recent machines are even capable of automatically adding the frothed milk to the coffee to make cappuccinos. The Italians seem to be extremely conservative when it comes to advanced commercial espresso machines and shun the most modern machines. The Italian relationship with a manually operated espresso machine is one of familiarity, competence and confidence. This contrasts with many operators from other

Right: The Rossi group worked with hydraulic pressure from the same pump that made the coffee and was installed in the Reneka GAV series and several other machines. The combination of solenoids, pistons and slides made it a simple machine on paper but a machine that required a lot of attention. The vertical piston on the left forced coffee into a brewing chamber in a horizontal slide which was pulled by a piston to brew in the middle. Everything was controlled by electronics and three hydraulic solenoids to operate the pistons and co-ordinate the grinder. Gino Rossi was an Italian associated with many technical developments for manufacturers from the first post-war years. Italy - 1965.

Right: The Santa Flavia group was controlled electronically and, when it worked, was like magic. The ground coffee fell into the brewing compartment where stepping motors compressed it - the compression could be controlled by the user adjusting the resistance of the compressing motor. It used plastic parts and the user could easily control the temperature of the water as well as the pump pressure. The idea was good.

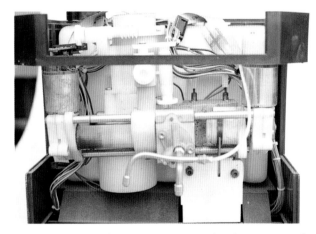

Above: The parts in the Santa Flavia were miniaturised and the water was heated in a metal block containing an electric element and a serpentine path for the water. All the controls needed to fill the normal boiler automatically and safety devices to prevent explosions were eliminated. Italy - 1990.

Right: The I.D.E.A. machine was developed by Lucio Grossi and operated mechanically. Italy - 1990.

Right: The Armellin machine crammed a lot into a small machine. A grinder was included together with a larger boiler and a volumetric quantity control for the water. As the water was forced through a tiny turbine, it revolved and the number of revolutions was counted electronically. It was one of several machines which incorporated a grinder which ground the coffee directly into the handle. Switzerland - 1986.

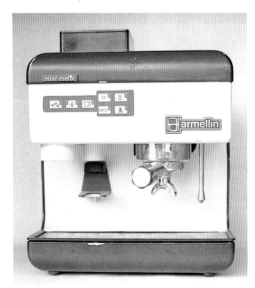

Right: The Saeco machine was based on a Swiss design with plastic parts and a simple timer to control the amount of water brewed. It sold at a low price and by 1992 had sold six hundred thousand units. It was easy to clean and a good machine for the price. Italy - 1980s.

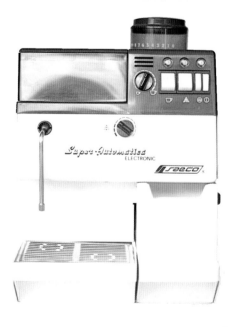

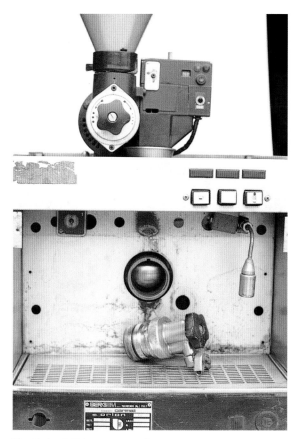

The Carimali Orion was one of the earlier pre-electronic machines and worked well provided it was cleaned scrupulously at the end of each shift. On top of the machine is the EGI grinding and dosing mechanism which dropped the coffee into a rotating brewing chamber. Italy - 1981.

The Nuova Simonelli 'Logica' was a fully automatic grind-and-brew machine with push button electronic controls. Italy - 1992.

with Swiss precision. The result is a machine which works. Swiss machines, using Italian parts, seem to be the best and most reliable.

The most modern espresso machines incorporate controls over all the variables in the machine, with small electronic displays for checking and adjustment purposes. Essentially the machines have the same operating relationships and produce the same coffee as the Faema E61, except that there is now the added certainty that this machine is operating correctly. There are many different brands of automatic machines - their difference is not in the quality of the coffee produced, which is essentially excellent, but mainly in the reliability of the components and the operation and the ease of cleaning and repairing.

ESPRESSO COFFEE AROUND THE WORLD

Decades after the Faema E61 machine of 1961, which brought the espresso process under control, one would expect that all machines would work well. It is however not so simple. Making a machine is not just a matter of putting a succession of parts together and knowing that they will work. It requires a lot of skill to make sure that the heat of the water in the group is the same all the time. Many machines have yet to solve this problem. The only test is whether or not they make a good cup of coffee.

The true espresso coffee is not designed for mass production. The operation of a four-group machine at full capacity in a busy location requires skill, plus the manual dexterity of an octopus. Many manufacturers have replaced the group on their espresso machines with a bulk brewer glass cylinder holding many cups of coffee. While this is sold as if it were a bulk espresso machine, it is in fact a filter coffee machine attached to an espresso machine and it does not make true espresso coffee. This attachment is used in Italy and France for breakfast coffee - a large cup of hot milky coffee. The only way to make espresso coffee in bulk is to use a very large group with a special large capacity filter handle.

countries who are much less competent and not long-term operators of the machine and who produce results of varying quality, even within the same establishment. As a consequence, fully automatic machines are much more attractive overseas than in Italy, where they are rarely seen.

The first automatic machine was the EGI Milan system, produced in 1965. Rossi automatic groups and other machines appeared in Italy in the 1960s. Switzerland seems to have the largest number of these machines in use and they sell for enormous prices and incorporate precision technology and the latest electronic controls performing to the very high Swiss standards. Some machines with Italian brand names actually incorporate the Swiss heart of the machine, so it is misleading to talk about Swiss and Italian machines as if they were totally made in Switzerland or Italy.

Mr. Franzolins, of Italian origin but working in Lausanne, has patented many inventions, which are operating in different machines sold under many different Italian and Swiss brand names. The machines are complicated in the number of parts which have to be co-ordinated and are the fruition of the creative flair of the Italian mind combined

This model by Giussini and Gachter, Milan, had a screw thread and was much more solid in construction. Italy - 1910s.

A very solid electric model with screw top and copper base by Leopold Giussini, Milan. Italy - 1920s.

THE DOMESTIC ESPRESSO MACHINE

There are few examples of stove-top or spirit burner espresso machines from the pre-1900 period, apart from the Lebrun, Vienna and Eicke machines. Without knowing just how tightly the coffee was packed in the coffee compartment in those days, it is difficult to determine whether these were espresso machines or filter machines operating at a slightly higher pressure. It seems likely that the coffee was much more coarsely ground than for domestic espresso machines of the same type today. The Eicke machine seemed capable of making a pot of coffee under pressure of a similar strength to a Vienna but it was not an espresso coffee.

After 1900 the history of the domestic espresso machine does not follow directly from the first commercial machines. The coffee made by the first commercial espresso machines in Italy and France led to a taste for coffee with a stronger, more concentrated flavour - a type of coffee relatively unknown. No sooner had the commercial machines been developed than Italy and France became involved in the First World War, which temporarily slowed down advances. The war was the transition stage between a basically non-electric world and an electric world. Nevertheless the taste for the new coffee grew. The commercial machines gave impetus to the domestic espresso machine market, but few domestic machines with separate control for steam and hot water appeared until the 1920s and they were very much the minority. From the 1900s until the 1950s most machines were just electric versions of earlier domestic machines and made long espresso coffee. In other words, the cup of coffee available in a bar from a commercial machine was totally different to that available at home.

Below: A 'Diana' Mignon with pop-out fuse.

The Orso model was different in that it advertised that it used no rubber seal.
Italy - 1917.

Above Right: The Aquilas models were made for both flame (right) and electricity (left). Suggestions have been made that they were designed in the shape of a Greek temple.
Italy - 1917 to 1920s.

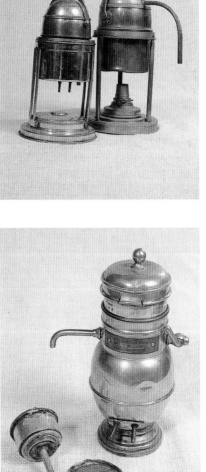

Right: A Select Electric. Many pots were not made very robustly. The washer found in this machine was not rubber but cardboard, probably a replacement of the original rubber. Note the valve opposite the outlet spout.
Italy - c.1930.

While most houses in Italy had solid fuel stoves, and gas stoves were being increasingly used, the availability of electricity meant a larger and growing market for electric models. Italy was a country with great variations in standards of living. Some mountain communities had to wait decades before electricity and gas arrived. A disadvantage was that these new gas and electric stoves made supervision essential to prevent the machines from boiling dry.

There seemed to be very few stove-top machines in the 1920s and 1930s, probably because of the difficulty of picking up a very hot machine. A wooden handle would have solved this problem, but machines with wooden handles are extremely unusual. The solution was to use spirit burners and brew the coffee at the table, where the process could be supervised. The machines were very strong and were designed to make a small amount of strong coffee. When electricity came, the machines were electrified so that the guests could enjoy the aroma of the coffee as it brewed directly into the little cups. Then the machines could be switched off immediately by pulling off the ceramic plugs to prevent melt-down. Such innovations as thermostatic control were as yet unknown.

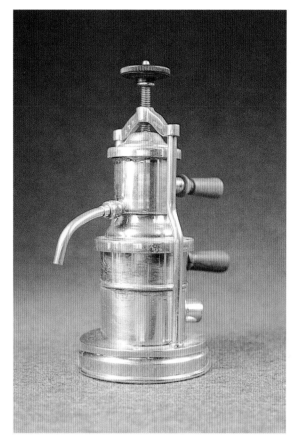

A very solidly constructed machine. With time, better methods of construction and heavier metals were used. These were needed to withstand the extra pressure which resulted from using finer coffee to make stronger coffee. Italy - 1920s.

DOMESTIC ESPRESSO MACHINES

A spirit version of the 'Diana' with automatic flame-out. When the water boiled away, a bi-metal strip in the base tripped and allowed the metal cover over the flame to fall and extinguish it.

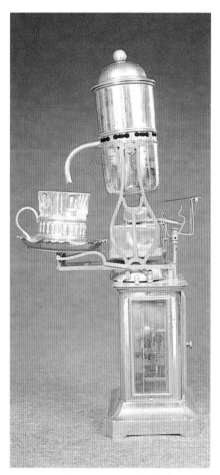

The twentieth century started with the Ardovino automatic coffee maker. When the alarm clock rang, the cover over the spirits opened revealing the wick which was lit by the match striking the emery paper. The coffee fell into the glass which overbalanced causing the flame to be extinguished. One of the features of the design was that it made two cups of coffee, but only the second fell into the cup, while the first remained in the machine to provide another cup of coffee. Patented Italy - 1906.

DOMESTIC ESPRESSO MACHINES

Above and Right: Increasingly electricity was being used as a heat source. This Spanish model illustrates the use of a separate universal element with a matching coffee pot. Spain - 1920s.

Above: One of the most popular ways to heat the espresso pot electrically was to enclose the pot in an element. Italy - 1930s.

Above: A machine with screw top, no safety valve and made of aluminium. Brauneis & Co., Vienna. Austria - 1930s.

An electric machine. Italy - 1930s.

This well-constructed model is possibly of German origin although it does appear in an Italian catalogue. It had the name 'Oikos' and the word 'patent' instead of the Italian *brevettato*. 1930.

An excellent machine for making four strong cups of coffee. Most of these machines are French or Spanish. They were possibly made in the Basque region. c. 1920s.

The Neowatt machine with external coffee holder. The temperature was lower and the coffee probably less bitter as a result. Milan, Italy -1930s.

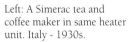

Far Left: An early Velox with a common electric fitting. By using only two of the three sockets it was possible to vary the wattage. Italy - 1930s.

Left: A Simerac tea and coffee maker in same heater unit. Italy - 1930s.

Far Left: A copper machine with separate control for steam and water. Possibly German or Austrian - 1930s.

Left: The tinning of the metal and the horizontal wooden handle indicate that this model was probably made in the 1920s. The screw thread in the middle was very unusual at this time. It was a forerunner of the Moka. Purchased in Chile.

UB

FR

An elegant brass machine from Spain - 'Fuego'. The ratio of coffee to water is very high, higher than in French and Italian machines. Spain - 1930s.

The Victoria Arduino Company made several elegant models like this. This was one of the first uses of a handle with bayonet fitting in a domestic machine. Italy - 1920s.

A pumping espresso - the pump was the little bulb sitting on the base. The hot water and coffee were put into a container and forced by air through the coffee and into the cup. Italy - 1920s.

Far Right: A portable espresso. The top fitted into the base and the solid fuel was placed in the middle. It was a Fiorenza brand, Sport model, and made in Milan. Italy - 1930s.

Right: A Femoka with an unusual compartment in the middle. The design ensured that the coffee was hot. France - 1930s.

Far Right: The Stime from Bologna had a removable element which screwed into the top. Italy - 1920s.

Right: A large French machine, the Femoka. One of the first with a steam valve for heating up milk. The French wanted *café au lait*. France - 1950s.

A portable Aquila Adele. The handles on the brass cups folded and they both fitted into the space over the lamp. Italy - 1920s.

A simple spirit model, the 'Garemo Expres'. Italy - 1920s.

A classic machine made by Snider Bros. Italy - c.1920s.

A baby Lutetia. Italy - 1920s.

Most of the spirit models were for one or two cups. The Stella on the right was for spirit and electricity. The Stella Company first made machines in 1924.

An elegant brass and copper three-cup pot, 'The Premier'. Some models made up to six cups at a time. Italy - 1930s.

This is one of the many models of the time when bakelite became more widely used for handles and electrical fittings. Italy - 1930s.

The Spanish T.E.R. machine passed two spouts through the machine with the object of making a hotter cup of coffee. Spain - 1930s.

A brass body and plastic handle formed an unusual espresso for the period - a pouring espresso machine. Italy - 1930s.

This Moka D'or machine did everything. It was electrically heated top and bottom and had a hot water heated jacket to keep the filtered coffee in the top hot. In addition it had an espresso group with individual taps for steam and hot water plus steam for heating milk plus hot water for making tea. France - 1930s.

DOMESTIC ESPRESSO MACHINES AFTER THE SECOND WORLD WAR

The espresso machines made after the Second World War fell into a number of new types which hardly existed at all prior to 1939.

- The first were the aluminium stove-top machines, which were mainly in the form of self-contained pots. In the late 1970s, stainless steel began to replace aluminium.
- In the 1950s following the success of the commercial Gaggia machine, lever machines appeared and later electric versions with steamers for frothing milk.
- In the 1960s as in the commercial world, pumps (rotative and later vibrating) were put into domestic machines.
- Fully automatic commercial machines became available in 1965 to be followed by a domestic version. The increased availability of electricity and power after the Second World War meant larger capacity machines could be made.

Alfonso Bialetti designed his first Moka Express in 1933 but it was only in the post-war years that it became really popular and sold more than twenty million. It was a strong aluminium machine with a safety valve and was designed to go on the stove. The Moka style had two major problems. The finer and tighter the coffee was packed, the greater was the resistance to the water passing through, with a consequent rise in pressure and temperature, which caused bitterness in the coffee. In addition, because there was a range of sizes, the brewing time was shorter for smaller models than for larger, which meant that the flavour changed with the number of cups to be made. Nevertheless it was generally satisfactory and sold very well. There were a large number of competing machines, most of them promising what they were unable to deliver - a better cup of coffee using less coffee.

LEVER HANDLE ESPRESSO MACHINES

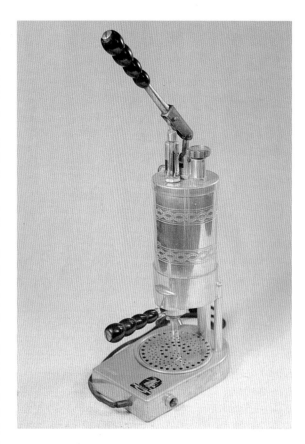

The commercial Gaggia machine created a demand for domestic models. Gaggia produced a small lever machine in aluminium. Italy - 1948.

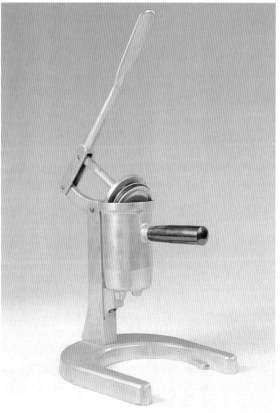

A simple machine showing the hand lever. Coffee was placed in the container which had a filter at the bottom and the piston was pushed down, but because the coffee was not compressed, it was not espresso coffee. Italy - 1950s.

Left: The Gaggia 'Gilda' electric machine incorporated a spring. The spring-loaded arms were pushed down which allowed the boiling water to fall into a little well. The handles were released which forced the water through the coffee. Italy - 1950s.

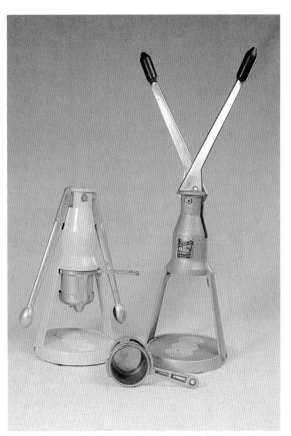

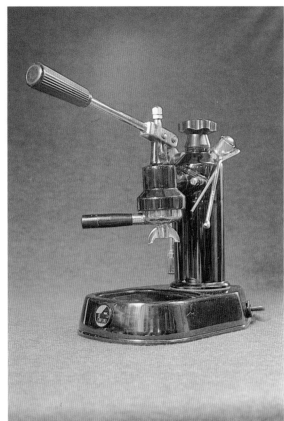

Right: The 'Baby Faemino' by the Faema company similarly made a quick plunger type infusion. Italy -1960s.

Far Right: The Pavoni machine with steamer. Italy -1970s.

The Micron Express with spring-lever handles. Italy - 1960s.

The Zerowat. Italy - 1960s.

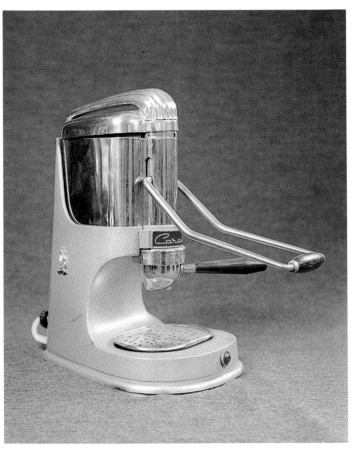

The Caravel was a more sophisticated model using a lever spring. Italy - 1960s.

The Faema machine incorporated the new piston with washers. Italy - 1952.

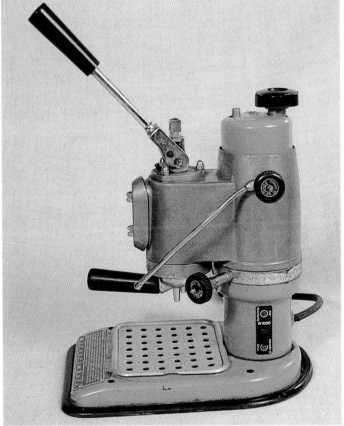

Above: Micro Cimbali by the Cimbali Company. Italy - 1950s.

Left: La Peppina. Italy - 1960s.

POST-WAR STOVE-TOP DOMESTIC ESPRESSO MACHINES

After the Second World War ended in 1945 espresso machines were very different in character to prior models. They utilised aluminium on a much larger scale for the machine bodies and plastic for the handles. The growing and prosperous European market allowed for mass production and low prices.

Below: These light-gauge aluminium models were low-pressure espressos, more in the style of the Vienna machine. They had no brand and were very cheap and very suitable for the low standard of living in the chaotic years after the war. Italy - 1950s.

Above: The Bialetti Moka was popular for decades after the war. The cartoon character welcomed you *'Ci sono Io'* (here I am). The Moka was of solid construction in aluminium with a brass safety valve and rubber gasket. It came in 1, 3, 9, 12 and 18-cup sizes to make the normal small cup of Italian coffee. While the ratio of water to coffee was the same and the strength of coffee theoretically the same, this was not actually so. The brewing time of the larger sizes was much longer than for the smaller one and hence there was more likelihood of over-extraction. Italy - 1950s.

Left: The Nora model had a new basket with three tubes designed to produce a more thorough and even wetting of the coffee. Italy - 1960s.

Above: The Nova Express espresso utilised a screw-in basket for the coffee. Italy - 1960s.

Left: The Caffexpress had a push-in basket, bayonet-fitting lid and a screw knob on the lid to make a tight seal. The Moka type machines were sometimes screwed so tightly they were very difficult to unscrew. Italy - 1960s.

Far Left: The normal Moka espresso utilised steam pressure to force the boiling water through the coffee. This Columbia Creme pump model by OMG produced steam which forced the piston up. The machine was removed from the stove and the piston used to pump the hot water up. The lower temperature water meant a coffee with lower extraction and probably a better flavour. Italy - 1960s.

Left: The Giannina Express had an unusual but effective system for sealing. Italy -1970s.

The Pezzetti Smalflon had a Teflon /PTFE coating inside to prevent the aluminium being attacked by the coffee and altering the flavour. If the machine was left on the stove and the water boiled away, the Teflon would burn and make a terrible smell which rendered the pot unusable. Italians preferred plain aluminium because it became black with use and retained the flavour of the coffee. For the same reason many English people preferred a dirty teapot. They were wrong. Italy - 1970s.

The Prima had a removable inner container for the brewed coffee which flowed up the outside walls into the container. The advantage was that it was now possible to clean every part of the machine easily. Italy - 1970s.

A porcelain model, using metal clips, made by The Bavarian Porcelain Factory for the German market. There was also an electric model. Germany - 1950s.

A Hungarian model which poured the coffee into the spout of the detachable ceramic jug. There were similar Italian models. Hungary - 1970s.

The French SEB machine was originally patented in 1968 and produced in aluminium. The filter basket contained a nylon mesh which was not really necessary because most espresso machines produced a sediment-free coffee. France - 1970s.

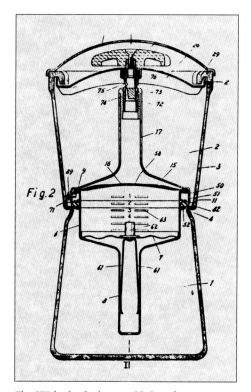

The SEB basket had a movable base for different numbers of cups.

The Puppieni espresso had a porcelain top and an alumium base. Italy - 1970s.

The Letizia by Mancioli had a separate pot in porcelain for a better flavour. Italy - 1970s.

Right: A thermos flask with an espresso machine. Italy - 1970s.

Far Right: A new type of two-position valve in the top made a simple cappuccino machine. In one position it made coffee and in another steam. It was also made in stainless steel. Italy - 1983.

Left: An ACE anodised
espresso machine in the
same style as pre-war
models. Italy - 1970s.

Above: Nova Espress 4 and 2
cup models and two
different Mignon 2 cup
models. Italy -1980s.

Above: The Mokita Ultra model put the rubber
washer into the top of a bayonet-fitting lid which
made a very nice-looking pot. Italy -1970s.

Left: The Kava was designed to make a large pot of coffee. Sweden 1960s.

Far Left: Stainless steel San
Remo with valve for coffee
and press-down valve for
steam. Italy - 1989.

Left: This aluminium model
used a round Melitta filter
paper. Switzerland - 1970s.

The Misurella used a clever design. The barrel contained an inverted cup which supported the coffee grounds and in which the water boiled. As the water boiled the steam lifted the cup which compressed the coffee. Italy - 1990.

A stainless steel TCL Milan machine with separate valves for coffee and steam. Italy - 1980s.

The Miss Italia was a cleverly designed espresso which made normal espresso and filter coffee. A basket fitted into the top and the coffee was held down by a loose filter. When the hot water came out of the outlet tube, it fell over the coffee and made filter coffee, or it could use a normal espresso basket to make espresso coffee. Italy - 1987.

A 'Happy Coffee' espresso machine with a heat-resistant plastic top and aluminium base. Italy - 1990.

Above: There were many stainless steel models with essentially the Moka design. Each new model came out with ever more stylish additions until models with gold-plated handles and knobs were common in the late 1980s. This machine is a Vev Kontessa. Italy - 1988.

ESPRESSO MACHINES WITH HANDLES
OR EXTERNAL COMPARTMENT

The Trimel was a clever design. The lower container slid into place. The handle rotated to make the water opening and the coffee could be poured as from a pot. Italy - 1960s.

The Atomic espresso was patented in 1956 by Robbiati and was very solid. The incorporation of a handle filter lent a feeling of similarity to commercial machines. It was widely exported for three decades. Italy - 1956.

An Italian machine for making a pot of coffee. Italy - 1960s.

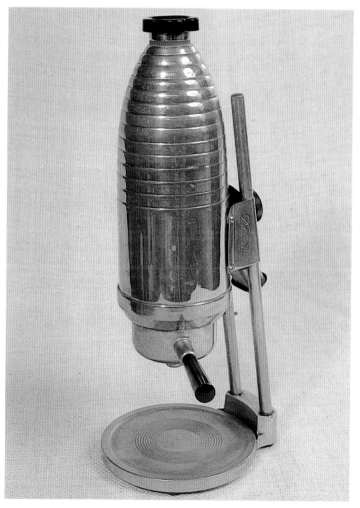

The Paluxette used the increasingly popular bayonet fitting to make a large pot of coffee. This style, with a large water compartment and a bayonet fitting underneath, was very popular in Germany. Germany - 1960s.

Right: The Stella had a screw-down lid which was opened to allow access to the coffee compartment and the water container.
Austria - 1960s.

Far Right: A French Femoka machine which makes two large cups. France - 1950s.

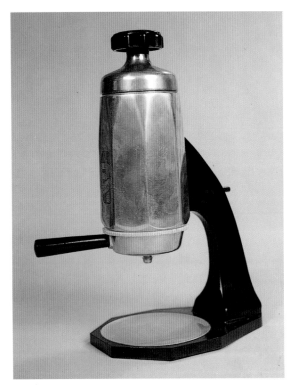

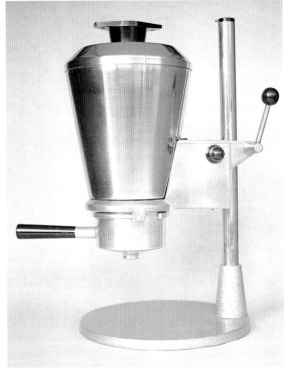

Right: An electric machine with a thermal overload button. When the machine became too hot, the button popped out and the power cut out. Germany - 1960s.

Far Right: An extremely heavy German machine. Germany - 1960s.

Right: The Marco had an unusual valve behind the handle to control the steam and water flow. It had the same design as the Italian La Venezia and was obviously a copy. Australia - 1960s.

Far Right: The AMA machine was popular for cappuccinos. Italy - 1970s.

The Poccino machine was made in Hungary for sale in the German market. It had a steam nozzle for cappuccino. Germany - 1980s.

A Karat espresso. The water in the top fell into a small compartment which was opened by turning the spring loaded knob on the side. The compartment sealed, the water boiled and the steam forced the water through the coffee. Switzerland - 1970s.

The Norkit used the same system as the Karat except that the water entry was controlled by depressing the spring loaded handle on the side. Austria - 1970s.

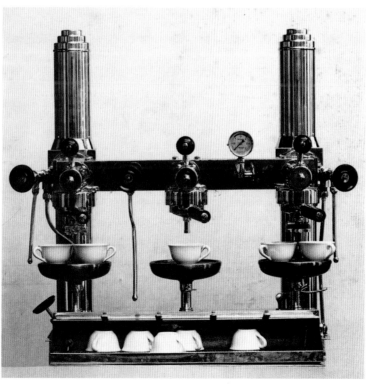

A Bezzera machine from the 1930s. The styling had changed dramatically but the performance was similar to the first machines. The large cups indicate that it was a quick filter espresso machine. Small cups were used after the Second World War with high pressure lever and pump espresso machines.

ELECTRIC ESPRESSO MACHINES

The Subiaco with built-in timer. Note the innovative clamp with a small wheel to tighten the cover. Switzerland - 1970s.

A machine to make a large pot of coffee. Switzerland - 1970s.

SEB France made an electric machine simply by putting an element into their stove-top machine. France - 1980s.

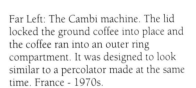

Left and Above: An Italian Sicadi butane gas espresso for making coffee anywhere, especially in the stands of an Italian football stadium in mid winter. Italy - 1970s.

Far Left: The Cambi machine. The lid locked the ground coffee into place and the coffee ran into an outer ring compartment. It was designed to look similar to a percolator made at the same time. France - 1970s.

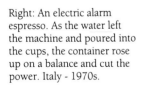

Right: An electric alarm espresso. As the water left the machine and poured into the cups, the container rose up on a balance and cut the power. Italy - 1970s.

Far Right: The Breville machine is an example of a 'badged' machine - a machine manufactured in Taiwan, Italy, Hong Kong, etc., with several different brand names - each for distribution in other countries. Australia - 1980s.

Stainless steel products, which were easily produced, increasingly dominated the market in the 1980s. Stainless steel was easier to clean than aluminium. Unless aluminium machines are meticulously cleaned, they tend to give a 'flavour' to the coffee, from burned encrustations. Electric machines were growing in popularity all the time as living standards in Italy improved dramatically. The 1950s saw the appearance of lever machines which simulated the bar machines. The electric Gilda machine with a lever was made by Gaggia in 1952 and did not have a spring. It was named after the character Gilda, portrayed by Rita Hayworth in the film of the same name. It is amazing to think that the major contribution of Gaggia was to introduce the spring into his lever machine and yet he made his first domestic machine without one. The Gilda machine with spring levers was released in 1954. In 1964 Quickmill in Milan introduced an espresso machine with a rotative pump and soon after a block heater in which water passed through a solid metal element, instead of a boiler.

It was the introduction of the small vibration pump by Stasse which really changed the domestic machine scene and made it possible for the average household to make a coffee exactly the same as in a bar. The first such machine was the Riviera. It had a cast brass boiler and brass fittings. Initially it used a diaphragm pump and then a vibration pump. The revolution was complete. These machines filled up the shelves of the shops in a proliferation of brands, shapes, sizes and complexities. They co-existed with a multitude of 'long espresso' machines and were now capable of frothing the milk as well.

There were increasing numbers of fully automatic machines which ground the coffee and brewed it directly into the brewing chamber, in imitation of large commercial machines. The high standard of living in Europe and Germany in post-war years created a market where people could spend two and three weeks' wages on a domestic coffee machine. In fact there were many who could afford fully automatic 'grind-and-brew' espresso machines from one week's salary. Just as the Americans used electric percolators to show that they were using the latest innovations, so the Italians and French were probably busy showing off their latest coffee makers which were as impressive as possible. In America, Silicon Valley was synonymous with a never ending stream of electronic and computer wizardry. In Italy the Po Valley assumed a role of similar proportions in espresso machine wizardry. The machines might have had brand names from France, Germany, Switzerland, Spain or Austria but most of the ideas and components came from the towns around Milan, Turin and points east.

The increasing availability of sophisticated espresso machines is leading to a rise in the acceptance of espresso machines in traditional filter coffee markets. Espresso machines offer strongly concentrated coffee flavour plus the facility to heat the milk, whereas filtered coffee with a lot of milk is not a satisfying drink in terms of flavour. The coffee is not strong enough and the milk is cold.

DOMESTIC PUMP MACHINES

The large rotative pump was used for commercial machines. The small vibration pump was used in some small commercial machines and all domestic machines.

The Omre Quickmill used a rotation pump attached to a small motor in the base which was reasonably effective. The water was held in the vertical tank and was heated in a solid pass-through element. It was a very innovative machine and the first of a new breed. Italy - 1964.

DOMESTIC PUMP MACHINES

Right and Far Right: The Riviera Erika machine was the first to use a tiny boiler and a pump. Originally the machine was supplied with a diaphragm pump which was not successful. This was later replaced with a vibration pump (the round cylinder on the left). In the vibration pump a tiny piston was magnetised in a continuous pulse, forcing the water through the round boiler (on the right) which was directly attached to the bayonet fitting and the handle underneath. The water was in the vertical tank at the back. Italy - early 1960s.

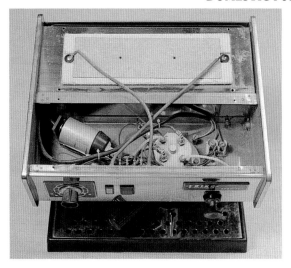

Right: A multitude of machines followed, all more or less in the same form. The Carimalina from the Carimali Company was in a metal chassis and much smaller. Italy - 1970s.

Far Right: The 'Big Bar' machine was produced *en masse* for large distribution world-wide. It used mechanical switches to control the operation. For ease of servicing, the whole operational section (boiler, pump, etc.) was set into a removable tray. Where once electrical appliances were sold in small shops with small repair departments in the back room, mass distribution required simple repair possibilities by staff who did not have the time or technical knowledge to find out what was wrong. Italy - 1980s.

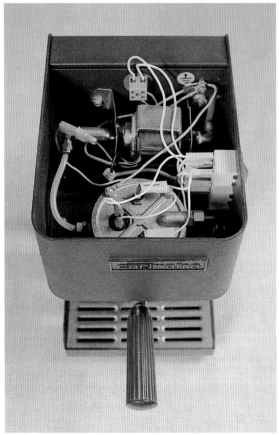
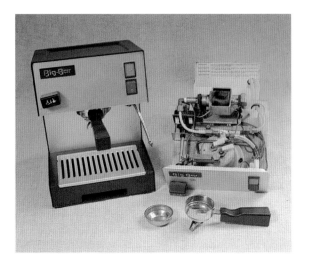

Right: The Gran Gaggia. The most noticeable thing was the light weight of the machine which had a plastic body and a metal boiler and pump. Italy - 1990.

Far Right: Douwe Egbert distributed this espresso machine which drew its water pressure from the spinning of the water chamber. It did not achieve the pressure of the vibration pump machines but certainly made a stronger coffee. It used a pressure of 1.2 atmospheres which was adequate to make a mousse on the coffee. Holland - 1990.

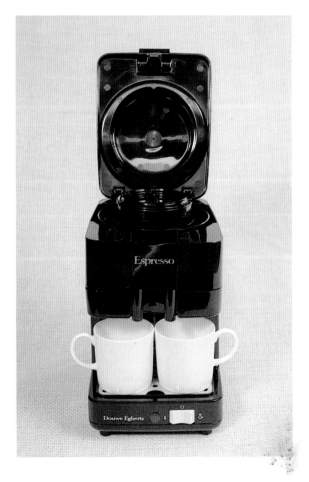

ESPRESSO COFFEE AND CAPPUCCINO

In an Italian bar there is no doubt what is meant by an espresso or a cappuccino. The Italian espresso is 25 to 30 millilitres of coffee from an espresso machine. To make a cappuccino, the same quantity of espresso coffee is put into a small cup with a capacity of about 150 millilitres and a small amount of hot milk is poured over it, with a lot of froth. The milk is traditionally steamed, the steam having the effect of coagulating the protein and in so doing making the milk thicker. The result is different from whipping hot milk and making bubbly hot milk.

To froth milk is almost an art form in itself. The frothing depends on the quality of the milk which sometimes lacks a special enzyme during drought periods. It is an easy procedure if the steam nozzle is placed just under the surface of cold milk and as the froth rises the jug is lowered to keep the nozzle just under the surface. When sufficient froth has been made, the nozzle is plunged to the bottom to heat the milk at the bottom of the jug. It is important that the milk is not boiled as when this happens the lactose or milk sugar in the milk is caramellised and the flavour of the milk changes. One of the major problems in frothing milk is that often more milk than is needed is frothed. When the leftover milk becomes cold it must be heated again and each time the milk is heated, the steam condenses into the milk and dilutes it, making a thinner, more watery milk. Many Italian domestic machines have small boilers with limited capacity to froth the milk, whereas commercial machines have large boilers and plenty of steam.

Italians do put whipped cream on the coffee and then it is called *con panna*. In many countries this is called a 'Vienna', but in Germany it is called a 'cappuccino', the Italian language version of the Austrian 'Kapuziner' which is made with whipped cream. It is likely that the *Kapuziner* was introduced to the Italians by the Austrians during the occupation of Northern Italy, including Milan, from 1815 to 1859. The Italians did not share the northern European passion for whipped cream and it was replaced by steamed milk instead of milk kept warm in *bain-maries*. This occurred probably after 1906, when espresso machines with boilers *and steamer nozzles* became more widespread.

The Italian cappuccino differs from all others, not only in the coffees used, but much more in the size of the cup. One big problem with most non-Italian cappuccinos is that the cup is larger than the Italian cup which means that the coffee is more diluted with milk and therefore weaker. To overcome this problem, many coffee shops simply put more liquid coffee in the cup by running more water through the coffee, which has the effect of diluting the coffee even more and making it even weaker. Some people think that by passing more water through the coffee grounds to make a larger cup of coffee, they are making it stronger, when in fact they are not only making it weaker but also changing the flavour. The last flavours extracted from the grounds have the characteristic of bitterness, with a wet cigarette-like taste.[8] Some French espresso machines have been improved so that the additional water does not go through the coffee but passes directly into the cup, thus overcoming the bitterness problem.

In Italy it is considered clever for the *barista* to pour the frothed milk on in such a way as to make a flower design with the brown of the mousse in the milk. By contrast there has been an emphasis outside Italy in creating Mont Blanc on top of the cup. The whole point of the exercise to make a coffee flavoured milk drink is being lost.

There are numerous variations of cappuccino outside Italy but none is an improvement on the original. Many Americans pour the frothed milk into the cup and then the coffee. It is not unknown in England and Australia to put instant coffee direct in the cup and sometimes even in the filter of the espresso machine. I have seen cold coffee mixed with cold milk and then both frothed together to make a cappuccino in York, England. I have watched the *barista* in the Milan railway station use the coffee twice, for tourists. The French do not understand the word 'cappuccino' at all and imagine that *café au lait* is in some way equivalent, which it is not. Sometimes the Moka type machines are used or even filtered coffee but the result is not the same. It is quite common to dust the frothed milk with cocoa powder or cinnamon. The original idea must have been to neutralise the sweetness of the hot milk but many bars now use sweetened cocoa powder for the sake of decoration, not flavour.

LOW PRESSURE ESPRESSO MACHINES

These machines which do not have the pumps and levers of the high pressure machines, extract about twenty-two per cent of the substances contained in the coffee and the result is stronger than filter coffee - a coffee without mousse.

THE HIGH PRESSURE ESPRESSO MACHINE AND REAL ESPRESSO

The espresso is simultaneously a solution of sugars, caffeine, acids and proteins, an emulsion of oils and colloids and a suspension of coffee particles and bubbles of gas.[9] Because of the high pressure of the extraction, about ten per cent of the oils of the coffee are emulsified and the aromas attach themselves to the fats, which explains the fragrance of the aromas. The oils are in part responsible for the body of the coffee which gives a roundness and a velvety feel. Higher viscosity is very important because it is associated with a lower surface tension of the liquid which means a deeper penetration into the taste buds thereby increasing the taste perception. The combined action of the oils and the colloids is responsible for the aftertaste of the coffee. The mousse on the surface helps to minimise heat loss and aroma loss. In short, the espresso coffee made by a high pressure pump machine is totally different to any other coffee.

OBTAINING THE MOUSSE

The mousse is the collection of the tiny carbon dioxide bubbles which have been released from the coffee. They are small because of the way the water is forced through the small interstices of the coffee. Pouring boiling water over coffee in an open pot produces froth with large bubbles. Obtaining the mousse is easy once all the variables have been controlled. The water temperature should be around ninety-four degrees Celsius but some companies say ninety-two to ninety-six degrees. Between six and seven grams of coffee should be used and the boiler should be operating at about nine atmospheres, or 120 pounds per square inch. In small domestic machines, the pressure is controlled by the pump. The correct quantity of coffee for each machine can be checked by observing the dryness of the 'cake' of coffee in the filter at the end of the process. If the 'cake' is sloppy, then not enough ground coffee has been used and the water has run straight through. If the 'cake' is dry there was too much or it was too fine preventing the water passing through. The coffee in the filter should be wet but solid so that it falls out as a solid 'cake'. Using the correct amount of coffee, time the brewing process. It should be around fifteen seconds for one short black and around twenty-five to thirty seconds for two cups. The coffee should be tamped down lightly, the object being to level the coffee, not to compress it. The correct compression is achieved by twisting the handle in the bayonet fitting which compresses as it tightens. If the time is too short, the coffee should be ever more finely ground until the correct time is achieved. If the time is too long, the coffee should be more coarsely ground. When the time is too long the result is bitter coffee.

There are other complications such as varying the grind according to the humidity and varying the temperature to a higher level when Robusta coffees are used and lower when Arabica coffees are used. These variations are not nearly as important as keeping all the filters clean - those in the machine, in the filter handle and in the group attached to the machine. A dirty filter can prevent mousse forming on the coffee. A special detergent is required to keep the filters clean. Warmed cups prevent the mousse in the cup disappearing. The colour of the mousse should be that of a milk chocolate bar. If it is too dark, this is evidence of over-extraction. There are claims that mousse from Robusta is dark brown to greyish with larger bubbles, while that from Arabica is a nutty colour with reddish reflections and smaller bubbles.[10]

Many Italian companies assert that the correct time for an espresso is twenty-five to thirty seconds and by implication that the same time is taken when two espressos are made in a two cup handle. Some diagrams show what happens when the time is too long or too short but they are in fact showing what happens when too little or too much water is passed through the coffee - not what happens when a fixed quantity of water is passed through the coffee with varying times. In fact it seems to take half the time to make one cup in a one cup handle and double for a two cup handle. In theory as well it takes a different time to make one espresso and two espressos because the characteristics of the pump basically maintain the flow rate proportional to time. My experiments show around fifteen seconds to make one espresso and twenty -five to make two. In Spain there are giant groups which make ten espressos at a time in around forty-five seconds and without bitterness. It follows that the extraction of the flavour from an espresso is both a function of the amount of water irrigating the coffee and also the time taken. It is as if the individual coffee ground is coated or encapsulated by the coffee flavour which has to be dissolved off by the water before the bitterness will dissolve.

There is no doubt that espresso coffee is more complicated to make properly, but the more care taken, the better the result.

The short black in Italy has a *mousse* on the top. The cappuccino in Italy is a short black with the addition of a small amount of hot milk and froth.

CHAPTER 9

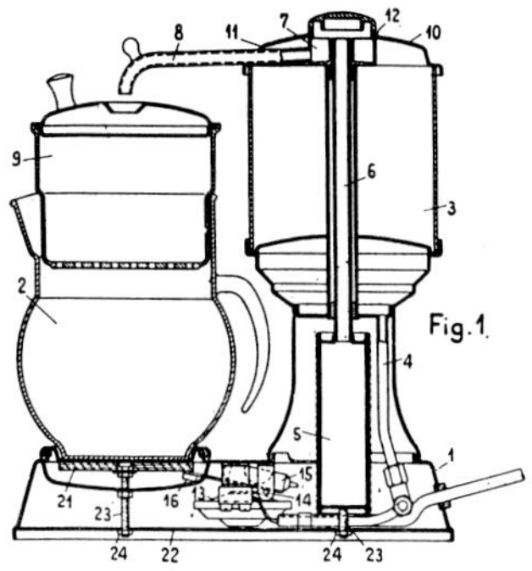

Coffee Technology of the Twentieth Century

Fig. 1.

A t the turn of the century, coffee brewing in western countries was varied and many different types of coffee makers were being used. Ideas about what made a good cup of coffee must have been slightly unrealistic when the quality of the coffee and the admixtures being used are taken into consideration.

As well as the pot and jug methods which were still being used in all countries at this time, it is possible to generalise about other national practices:

The French were making filtered coffee using a lot of chicory and milk. The filters were often of the cloth bag type.

The Germans were making a lot of filtered coffee but were intent on having a purer product and a clearer beverage with more aroma. The jug method was quite popular, particularly using jugs made of porcelain. Eicke's machine, the Vienna machine and others were in use. The German coffee industry was advanced and used more sophisticated roasting machinery than most other countries and the coffee itself was probably of a higher quality because it was hand sorted in the roasting factories. However, prior to the First World War, most of the coffee consumed in Germany was not coffee at all but malt and other admixtures.

The Italians were making filtered coffee but it was probably stronger than the French style. They had large bulk quick-filtering machines, but no espresso machines in 1900. Coffee was made stronger than in most other countries and a smaller cup was used, though not as small as today's short black cup.

The British were using a wide variety of filter and recirculating percolator machines, as well as jugs and pots. Consumption was not very high.

The Americans were using drip coffee machines and recirculating percolators. The industry at a commercial level was quite advanced and the coffee was very cheap although the quality was probably not very high.

THE PRE-ELECTRIC KITCHEN IN THE NINETEENTH CENTURY

The modern kitchen bears little resemblance to the first basic kitchens of the early 1800s which had just an open fire with hooks to suspend kettles and pots over the flames and a spit on which to cook meat. There was gradual improvement as living standards rose.[1] It took seventy years for cast iron stoves to become widely used, even though they became available soon after 1800.

THE IMPORTANCE OF HEAT CONTROL

Heat control in the kitchen was a critical factor in the design of coffee equipment. While the fire in a cast iron stove was a good source of boiling water for kettles, it was not very good for heating soldered pots which, with too much heat, would desolder. This desoldering is evident in the number of surviving metal pots which have been mended. The availability of boiling water meant that the most common methods of making coffee and tea had to be filters and pots where the water could simply be poured over the grounds and leaves. Any developments which did not use boiling water from the stove needed their own heat source.

With the introduction of gas cookers in the 1850s at last the heat source was controllable, but there were few innovations in coffee makers to take advantage of the new cookers. A few small coffee roasters appeared and some patents with automatic systems showed the use of gas. The increasing use of safety matches, which had been introduced in 1848, meant that it was very easy to light the gas as well as spirit burners under coffee makers at the table instead of using flints.

Oil cookers and paraffin stoves incorporating varying degrees of control flooded the market from the 1870s to 1930s. This did not produce much of an impact on coffee making, except for the introduction of enamel saucepans and coffee pots which could be left on the stove to keep hot.

THE SPREAD OF ELECTRICITY

As early as 1884, the Café Bauer in Berlin was lit by electric light. Although an electric stove was first used in 1889 in Switzerland and an electric kitchen was displayed at the Chicago World Fair in 1893, they did not become popular until many years later.[2]

There are two types of electricity - DC (direct current) and AC (alternating current). DC dominated the market in the early years, but from 1882 was increasingly supplanted by AC which was easier to transmit from large central stations. It was the widespread availability of AC electricity about the turn of the century at the domestic level that facilitated the introduction of domestic appliances. Among the first were coffee makers, which were introduced about 1907. Up to this point most coffee makers had been produced by specialist manufacturers of ceramic and metal products. Now this was to change, as coffee machines became part of the range of electrical products produced by the large manufacturers.

At the 1879 Berlin Exhibition, Werner von Siemens showed an electric thirty seat railway system. Five years later, in 1884, F.J. Sprague electrified the bogies of cars on the New York Elevated Railway.[3] In contrast to this progress, certainly the self-contained electric coffee maker was years behind other electric developments. Primitive machines were patented from 1881 to take advantage of the new source of power, but by modern standards they look extremely hazardous. Whether they actually went into production is doubtful. Small electric motors were produced in 1897 for coffee grinders in a very limited way at the industrial level, fourteen years after the very first electric machine of any kind, an electric coffee grinder was shown in New York in 1883.

The twentieth century was to see the full effects of the introduction of electricity in the domestic and industrial arenas. The following table gives an estimation of the production of electricity in millions of kilowatt hours over a period of eleven years.[4]

	1927	1938
Germany	12,444	55,238
United Kingdom	10,876 (1928)	30,700
France	11,388	19,300
Italy	9,770 (1928)	15,108

The interesting figure is Italy's, which in 1928 is relatively high in a country which had a much lower standard of living than the others. Car ownership in Italy in 1937 was less than a fifth that of the United Kingdom.[5] The spread of electricity was predominantly in the prosperous north. The small circuits in each house would have enabled the use of small electric coffee machines which were popular throughout Italy during this period. With a small electric coffee machine in the kitchen and a few bread rolls from the corner bread shop, it was possible to make a quick breakfast at home.

THE ELECTRIC VACUUM POT

In 1894 the English company, Compton, introduced an electrified vacuum pot. It was the first electric coffee maker made especially for the purpose. In 1897 the German Eicke machine was produced in an electric version - the spirit flame was replaced with an electric element and a switch which turned the element off when the water had left the boiling chamber. Neither machine advanced coffee brewing in any way.

Small electric machines were popular in France. An attractive machine could be placed on the table and the coffee made in front of your eyes. When the coffee was made, the small porcelain inserts holding the electric wires were pulled out.

It was in America that electricity had an enormous and early impact - far greater than in Europe. In 1900 there were two hundred and fifty suppliers of electricity in England and more than three thousand in the United States.

Electric Coffee Urn.

| 2 pint | £5 15 0 |
| 4 .. | 6 15 0 |

The honour of the first integrated electric coffee maker seems to belong to England. This illustration from the 1894 Compton's Catalogue shows the continuing English interest in the vacuum pot method. A wide range of other items was available including electric saucepans. England - 1894.

Far Right: An electric heater to be placed inside the teapot. The switch H at the top was activated by placing the heater on the pot. England - 1900.

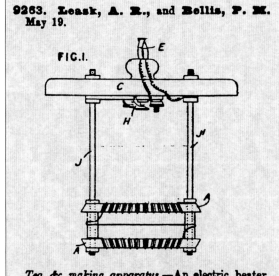

9263. **Leask, A. R., and Bellis, P. M.** May 19.

FIG. I.

Tea &c. making apparatus.—An electric heater, which may be placed in any ordinary vessel such as a tea-pot, coffee-pot, kettle, or cup, consists of resistant wire wound across one or more rings or frames A of insulating-material ; these frames are supported by nuts and distance pieces on two rods J, J¹ attached to a larger insulating piece C, which is intended to rest on the top of the vessel, and is provided with a knob. Electric connection between supply conductors E and the heating-wire is made by the rods J, J¹ and a spring switch H, which is closed by the weight of the heater when placed on the top of the vessel ; the underside of the spring is coated with insulating-material.

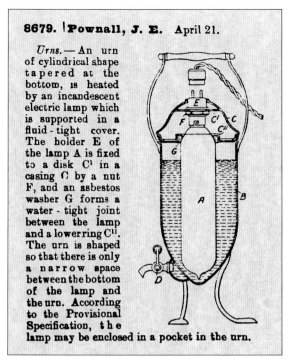

8679. Pownall, J. E. April 21.

Urns. — An urn of cylindrical shape tapered at the bottom, is heated by an incandescent electric lamp which is supported in a fluid - tight cover. The holder E of the lamp A is fixed to a disk C¹ in a casing C by a nut F, and an asbestos washer G forms a water - tight joint between the lamp and a lowering C¹¹. The urn is shaped so that there is only a narrow space between the bottom of the lamp and the urn. According to the Provisional Specification, the lamp may be enclosed in a pocket in the urn.

An electric tea urn heated by an incandescent lamp. When the globe broke, there were shocking consequences. England - 1908.

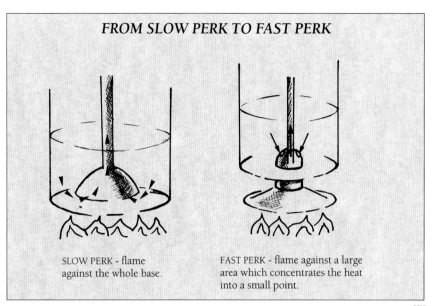

FROM SLOW PERK TO FAST PERK

SLOW PERK - flame against the whole base.

FAST PERK - flame against a large area which concentrates the heat into a small point.

KH

The very existence of electricity probably changed the development of coffee makers. The fact that electric machines without automatic controls could burn their elements out meant that the recirculating percolator, which took longer to burn out than any other machine, was a popular choice as a coffee maker even though it did not make good coffee. Most other machines boiled the water away from the element altogether and left it exposed and certain to burn out.

THE ELECTRIC PERCOLATOR —
A NEW MACHINE FROM THE UNITED STATES

The electric recirculating percolator is commonly known as an electric percolator. It is difficult to know just what made it so popular in the early years. Perhaps it was the novelty, the resultant hot cup of coffee, the fact that it was electric, the sound effects of the perking, now louder than before, or the speed. Perhaps it was the incarnation of the American dream in your cup. Perhaps it was to do with the ease of making - the machine did it for you, even if it did not do it well. Whatever it was, the adaptation of an old principle became a success all over the world.

The recirculating percolator had been known in France and Europe for three decades prior to 1900 without becoming significant. In the United States it took on a new life which was largely due to the spread of electricity. In 1890 an American company, Manning-Bowman, introduced a recirculating percolator which took about twenty minutes to begin pumping the water.

In 1891 the Carpenter Electric Heating Company advertised a simple electric tea or coffee pot. In 1901 the Western Electric Company advertised an electric teapot which was merely a kettle on an electric element and this was to be the

form of the first electric pots. The legs rested on glass marbles which were for insulation.

The slow perk system was common to all the first recirculating percolators. With a limited amount of heat, as from a spirit burner, there was a long delay before the water boiled and made the first perk and then a succession of slow perks. The fast perk system was based on concentrating the heat on a small area and boiling a small amount of water quickly and often.

The first electric percolators used a small wattage and took their power from the light circuit. Later the introduction of higher wattage electric models, gas stoves and high heat electric stoves meant that the slow perk system operated much faster and became a fast perk system.

THE FAST PERCOLATOR

In 1894 James Dunlap of Chicago, Illinois, had the idea of concentrating heat under the bell of the percolator to produce steam and elevate water up the central tube. By separating the steam manufacture from the heating of the water he devised a system capable of elevating warm, instead of hot water, up the tube. It led to his invention in 1897 of a pot which combined water heating, steam and a small concentrated heating area into one patent. This was a significant step in making the recirculating percolator one of the most popular coffee makers ever invented.

In 1904 the Sternau version of the percolator was invented. On the 29th August, 1905, the General Electric Company of Schenectady, New York, gained approval for a percolator with a self-contained element. It was for a three pint percolator based on the Sternau patent of 1904, with a polished aluminium finish and a power rating of 300-500 watts. It sold for $US20.[6]

It was described as: ' An ideal device for coffee making. The steam generated under the bell valve forces water and steam up through the tube into the glass globe, where it falls in the form of a fine spray on the ground coffee, through which the water percolates back into the coffee'.[7]

THE DEVELOPMENT OF THE AMERICAN
PUMPING RECIRCULATING PERCOLATOR

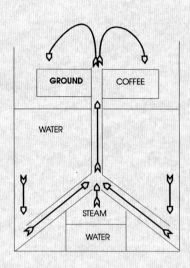

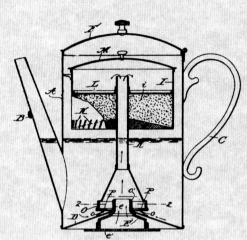

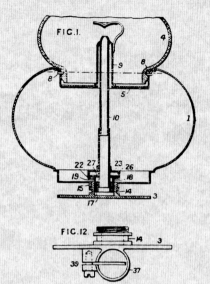

The first Dunlap patent was designed so that the water in the bottom compartment would boil and create steam which would elevate the water flowing up from the sides. The idea was ingenious but probably never worked because the percolation stopped when the water in the base was fully converted to steam.
USA - 1894.

The second Dunlap patent in 1897 showed the incorporation of the separate water chamber into the main pot with little one-way valves operated by gravity. A moderate heat concentrator was built into the base. It probably worked with moderate results and can be seen as an intermediate step to the final improvement by Alonzo Warner in 1907. USA - 1897.

The 1904 Sternau patent was not for a fast perking machine. The Sternau patent of 1908 was a wide diameter metal disc to concentrate the heat from a flame and it was a fast perking machine. The disc could be replaced with an electric element. The Stemau patent introduced a small flexible valve which alternately let the water into the heating chamber and closed with steam pressure to seal the chamber forcing the boiled water up the central tube. USA - 1908.

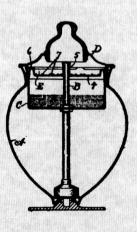

The percolator patented by Alonzo Warner encapsulated all of Dunlap's ideas and took them to finality. The heat concentrator was exaggerated and the quantity of water was minimised resulting in many fast little perks. The addition of a basket for the coffee designed specifically to give better extraction and the continuous pumping plus a glass dome in the lid made for a machine which caught the public's imagination.

The first G.E. electric percolator used the Sternau patent. USA.

The second use was in the catalogue of the American Electrical Heater Company, Detroit, Michigan in 1907.

The Landers, Frary, Clark (LFC) recirculating percolator in its spirit version is quite common. It features a large disc underneath to concentrate the heat on the well and make more perks.

An English model in copper using the fast perk system. England - 1917.

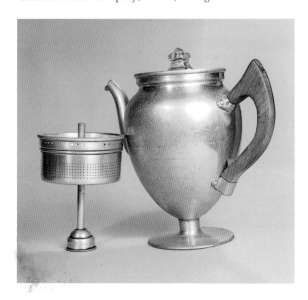

Left: The Wearever aluminium percolator showing the wide base. The pumping system was different to the LFC but the basket was an excellent copy. USA - early 1910s.

In 1907 Alonzo A. Warner of New Britain Connecticut, designed a new heat concentrator connected to a small pumping bell. At the same time he lodged a patent for a new basket to hold the coffee and allow the overflow to escape over the edges. It was designed specifically to match the water flow from the little bell. The combination was a winner and was known as the Landers, Frary and Clark Universal percolator and was an improvement on their 1901 Universal model.

LARGE NUMBER OF SMALL PERKS

This electric percolator was simply the Universal with the element around the well. Because it only had to boil a small amount of water to begin perking, it was very fast and the cold water pump percolator soon outmoded all the slower models. The change was from a small number of large, slow perks of hot water to a large number of small, fast perks of cold water. Each perk was caused by a short burst of boiling water making steam which pushed the one-way valve up against the inlet hole. This sealed the well so that the steam would now force the boiling water up the central tube. The slow perk used a large quantity of water heated by non-concentrated heat and took twenty minutes for the first perk. The fast perk used a small quantity of water in a small well, was heated by concentrated heat and took two to three minutes for the first perk.

It was a very important development in an era when the heat source was largely limited to the low heat of spirit burners or low wattage electric heaters. The other way to speed up the perking was with increased heat and this was achieved using higher wattage. The first electric percolators were powered from small light sockets and used from 300 to 500 watts. This was much less than

today's 2400 watts. The increased heat from gas and electric stoves converted the slow perk on a spirit burner to a fast perk. Thus the Warner invention made by the Landers, Frary, Clark company was a major innovation which led to the widespread use of recirculating percolators in the United States. In 1908 Sternau patented an electric percolator which incorporated the same type of fast perking system as the Landers Frary and Clark patent.

Another fast percolator was introduced by the Edison Electric Company with its Hotpoint brand which used an element in a bell. The pot carries the date July, 1914. The Metal Ware Corporation of Wisconsin patented a similar unit in 1914.

In 1915 Landers, Frary and Clark introduced a 'Safety Plug' which acted as a circuit breaker in case of burn-out. A unique gravity operated safety switch was introduced by the Robeson Rochester Company in 1924 - after inversion the pot was ready for use again.

In 1931 the Knapp-Monarch Company introduced the Therm-a-magic percolator with a timer which switched off the percolator at a predetermined time after it had reached temperature. When a device to keep the coffee hot was added there was practically nothing left to add except for cosmetic changes.

While these innovations might have been made by the companies named above, the most popular model in the 1920s was a five-cup aluminium electric percolator selling for $US1.75 from the Aluminium Goods Manufacturing Company.

The electric recirculating percolator has been described as the worst coffee maker ever invented and it probably was. The two main factors of cooking anything are to have the correct time and

Below: The Empire electric percolator made by the Metalware Corporation in Wisconsin featured a valveless double-walled pump and a three-minute percolation time. The short brewing time meant a rather weak coffee. USA - 1916.

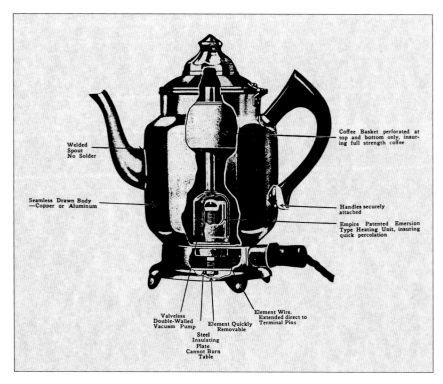

Welded
Spout
No Solder

Coffee Basket perforated at top and bottom only, insuring full strength coffee

Seamless Drawn Body —Copper or Aluminum

Handles securely attached

Empire Patented Emersion Type Heating Unit, insuring quick percolation

Valveless Double-Walled Vacuum Pump

Element Quickly Removable

Element Wire. Extended direct to Terminal Pins

Steel Insulating Plate Cannot Burn Table

Above: A GBN-Bavaria percolator. The complicated basket design was to ensure a thorough spreading of the water over the coffee and also from within the basket. This model has a normal handle but was also made with fold-away handles. Germany - 1910s.

Far Left: The Hotpoint valveless percolator used the Empire system.

Left and Below Left: The Westinghouse and larger Westinghouse automatic percolator used the LFC system. Many fancy table models appeared in this basic shape in other countries.

Middle Left: An early basic stove-top aluminium model. Hundreds of different models like this appeared through the whole of the century - an aluminium pot, an aluminium bell and a glass dome - the cheapest coffee maker of them all. USA - 1910s.

Below and Right: Three electric percolators from the Sears Catalogue. USA - 1917.

Left: An Omega. The bell had a little nick to allow the water to go beneath it. Possibly Italian - 1930s.

Corning's glass stove-top model sold from 1957 to 1971. 800,000 six-cup models were sold in 1963 and 1964.

Corning Glass produced the Pyrex Flameproof percolator in 1938. A few years earlier there was a Crystal model which looked very similar, but the glass was not suitable for the new high-output gas and electric stoves. USA - 1938.

Above: In 1960 Corning Glass introduced Pyroceram, a very strong, white, heat-resistant material. Percolators were made in both stove-top and electromatic versions. One big advantage was that they could be put into the dishwasher, a machine becoming more common and more demanding on the equipment. 'Dishwasher safe' was a new required characteristic for ceramics and glass.

A Pyrex glass percolator with plastic basket and bell. The new plastics had smooth surfaces and were easier to clean than aluminium which tended to have a rough and pitted surface. The metal trivet underneath was interposed on the electric coil element to prevent heat shock and uneven expansion which caused the glass to break. USA - 1980s.

The Westinghouse electric percolator used the Massot & Juquin system from France invented in 1865. The wide, shallow basket meant a shorter water contact time with the coffee. USA - 1970s.

The Birko used an exposed element in the base. Australia - 1970s.

This Sunbeam used a spring to keep the valve in contact with the electrically-heated well. Australia - 1980s.

The General Electric Poly Brew had an all-plastic pot. The higher level of plastics technology allowed their use in kettles. USA - 1980s.

The Sunbeam De Luxe had a bayonet-fitting lid to keep the brewing chamber and bell down. Notice the spring to keep the tension right and also the little round plastic one-way valve on the lower bell.

The Russell Hobbs was unusual in that the lid fitted tightly to the coffee basket as one piece. England - 1980s.

A glass plastic percolator by Gemco. The plastic is polypropylene, a tough heat-resistant, flexible plastic. The handle is melamine which is more rigid. USA -1990.

the correct temperature. The percolator failed on both counts. It used the wrong temperature for an incorrect period of time which resulted in coffee which was either weak, or strong and bitter.

The electric percolator grew in popularity on the same scale as the filter paper method in Germany. It is possible but unlikely that the Germans would have adopted it in the same way as the Americans had, but for the First World War. Certainly they had their own models.

America prospered and grew during the war. The use of electric articles in the domestic area grew apace and so did the electric percolator. It was as if the recirculating percolator had been designed to be electrified - there was always coffee in the pot until it was actually boiled away. These results were electrifying too! If coffee is brewed in an electric percolator for a long time, the tannin is extracted and the result is a foul, bitter brew. The percolator was extravagant with coffee, using eleven grams per cup versus six or seven with filter paper or espresso. In an attempt to reduce the over-extraction and bitterness, a coarser grind was used and this probably led to Americans developing a taste for lighter, less than full flavoured, European style coffee.

THE ELECTRIC VACUUM POT

In 1930 Frank Wolcott of the Silex Company selected restaurants as his target market. A salesman would pour the same amount of cream into two cups of coffee while the sceptical restaurateur looked on. The coffee brewed with the Silex turned much whiter. The restaurateur knew that the customer judged how much cream to use by colour and concluded that he could save money on cream by using the Silex.[8]

There were electric vacuum pots of which the most famous was the Farberware 'Coffee Robot', introduced in 1937. It brewed the coffee, shut off automatically and kept the coffee hot with a thermostat control.[9]

While sales of self-contained electric coffee makers grew in the United States, the use of gas increased in Europe. In Britain, by 1939, there were six times as many gas cookers as electric.

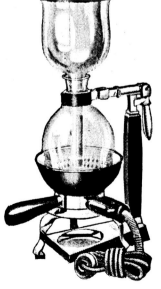

Left: The German ceramic Aromator combined a ceramic filter basket with Karlsbader-type slits and a stainless steel element. It was yet another indication of the German predelection for non-metallic coffee makers. 1950s - 1970s.

Right: This Silex was the electric version of the Silex coffee maker made of Pyrex fireproof glass - a new product from the Corning Glass Company invented in 1913. It used boron silicate for the first time, which increased the heat resistant properties of the glass. USA - 1917.

VACUUM POTS

A large copper commercial vacuum pot. England - 1920s.

The Cona was very popular in England and made a great feature of being all glass. No coffee maker has as much theatre. The base was designed so that the flame could easily be removed to let the vacuum draw the coffee down.

A vacuum pot. England - 1917.

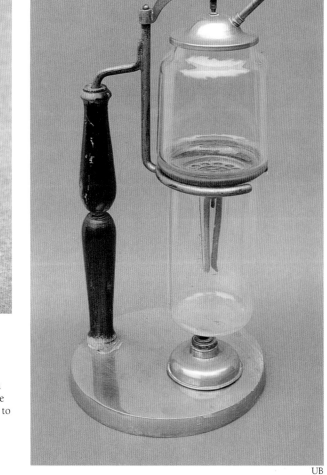

La Percola. When the coffee was ready, the top was twisted releasing the pressure and allowing the coffee to fall down. France -1920s.

The coffee brewing section swung away from the flame to cause the brewed coffee to return to the lower compartment when the brewing was finished. Germany - 1920s.

UB

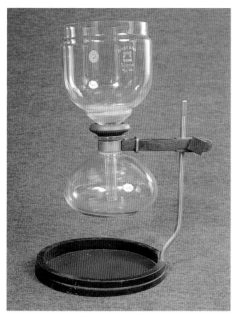

Sintrax with celluloid filter. Germany - 1930s.

The Cona Company introduced an electric element. England - 1935.

An anodised vacuum pot with bakelite handle and a metal valve. England - 1950s.

Desiderius Perlusz of Budapest patented this machine. The water boiled and rose to the top. The steam followed and blew the whistle on the lid. Then by moving the ball on the pouring spout, the pressure was relieved and the coffee fell down. Hungary - 1935.

The Cona electric. 1954.

Aluminium vacuum pot. Note the aluminium filter which could be taken apart and cleaned. USA.

Far Left; The Calor had an electric element with brewer all set into a bakelite tray. France - 1950s.

Left: The Japanese Hario Company made a wide range of siphon machines. The use of the lid was innovative. The cloth filter was put over a ceramic disc to reduce metal contact. Japan - 1970s.

Sunbeam electric automatic. USA - 1970s.

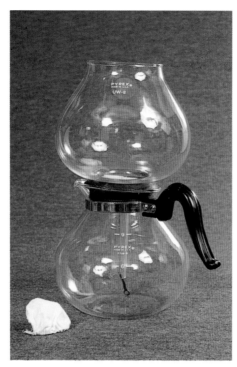

Pyrex model from the USA. Note the cloth filter to go over the central stem.

A Silex vacuum pot - USA.

A large Rowenta electric vacuum pot. Germany - 1960s.

Above: An electric balance machine. Germany - 1920s.

Right: AEG pumping percolator - NOT recirculating. The water pumped to the top and stayed there. Germany - 1930.

Right: An AEG recirculating percolator with very heavy metal pumping bell. Germany - 1927.

Far Right: An electric *ibrik* for Turkish coffee. Germany.

ELECTRIC COFFEE MAKERS
IN GERMANY AND EUROPE

It is possible that American recirculating percolators were being imported into Germany in the first decades of the twentieth century, but trade would not have been helped by the different voltages. International patents would certainly have prevented manufacture of American style recirculating percolators. It seems probable that American style percolators have not been widely used in Germany through the whole of this century.

The first electric machines in Germany were the AEG versions of the Vienna espresso and the WIKA which heated the water and coffee together. Their release coincided with the outbreak of war in 1914.

In 1926 AEG patented an electric pumping percolator in which the water did not recirculate. The completion of the brew cycle was announced when the steam caused a whistle to sound off in the central tube. The 1930 model looks very similar to American designs for recirculating percolators and the difference in operation can only be found by looking inside.

THE 1920s AND 1930s IN THE UNITED STATES

In America in 1932 the most popular methods were percolating, boiling and filtering, in that order. In 1935 Ukers showed photographs of many glass, porcelain and aluminium dripolators and vacuum coffee makers. Only some vacuum pots and percolators had been electrified.[10]

THE 1920s AND 1930s IN EUROPE

In Europe, coffee makers using small burners under the pot for heating were more popular and these seem to have been more suitable for immediate electrification. In fact, some models possibly came from the same factory with the element already inserted. There was a surge of new models using electricity, especially for domestic espresso machines. The German ceramic pour-over filter paper coffee makers did not lend themselves immediately to electrification and instead were sold in a wide range of designs, colours and sizes.

Therma electric model. Switzerland -1920s.

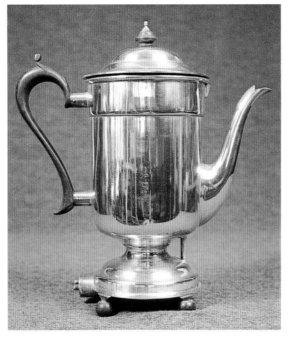

A very early percolator using the Pique system. Note the little tube under the spout. England - 1920s.

Far Left: A popular recirculating percolator. France - 1960s.

Left: The Triton used a new basket to completely immerse the coffee while it circulated the hot water. France - 1960s.

Right: An electric pumping percolator patented by Louis Marcel Pouget. It came in a stove top model as well. France - 1923.

Far Right: N.A.M. electric pumping percolator or espresso machine. The top half was connected to the lower half with a bayonet fitting and the water spreader at the top screwed down onto the coffee basket. If a small amount of coffee was used, it acted as a percolator and if too much was used, it became compressed and acted as an espresso machine. France - 1960s.

Above: The Universa was an electric reversible dripolator and came in an aluminium version and this luxury porcelain and copper model. Electric reversible dripolators are very unusual. Germany - 1954.

Above: A pumping pressure filter. The coffee was placed in a container in the base of the plastic water container at the top. The boiling water was poured in and the concertina plastic pumped up and down. Italy - 1960s.

Left: The Moccadur pumping percolator. Germany - 1950s.

THE ACCIDENTAL SOLUTION OF THE BREWING TIME CONTROL PROBLEM
August-Adrien Carton

From the earliest days of French invention there were ideas that the time of brewing had to be controlled in some way. The problem was approached mainly from the point of view that a shorter brewing time caused more problems than a lengthy one. Brewing times measured in hours were mentioned with no caustic comments. It seemed that the prime goal of de Belloy, Hadrot and Rumford was to stop the brewed coffee falling through too quickly, whereas, they should have placed equal emphasis on getting a quick brew. Had they considered making a coffee maker with a brewing time of about five minutes, consistently good coffee would have been available from the early 1800s. The idea of quick brewing was present in other brewers which had short time cycles - vacuum pots and balance coffee makers - but not filters.

On the 25th November 1927, a Frenchman, August-Adrien Carton made a patent application for a new coffee pot which was to be sold as the Selecta. The inventor's prime aim was to have a coffee pot which was easy to clean and which also allowed the coffee to filter without taking the grains with it. There was no mention of time in the patent, but Carton had accidentally solved the problem of controlling the time of flow by using three small holes at the base of the filter, rather than one large hole, which allowed water to flow faster. *For the first time*, the filtering of the coffee was a separate function to the timing. If someone, somewhere else, discovered this before Carton, there does not seem to be an example. There were many models with the hole above the coffee but not below. Certainly the Selecta is the only one I have seen. De Belloy thought that the timing could be controlled by compressing the coffee. Carton's invention allowed the coffee to be filtered without being compressed in any way so that the water could flow through the coffee freely. It was a simple but excellent idea. The French Salam coffee maker used exactly the same idea many years later.

The Selecta coffee maker, despite its excellence, passed unnoticed. It was significant in itself but hardly affected the course of coffee making at all, unless the Melitta coffee filters of 1934 were influenced by it. Marketing muscle was a real necessity if a new product was to succeed.

DOMESTIC ESPRESSO MACHINES

The domestic espresso machine was particularly suited to electrification from the 1920s because it was small and required only minimal electricity. Many models were made in Italy and France. Apart from placing the coffee in a filter compartment external to the machine, there were few significant innovations, other than electrification. The safety valve should have been important, but was not always included. Taps and steam spouts embellished numerous machines, all to increase the theatre of coffee making.

The Selecta pot by Carton. The first pot with independent timing control - a very significant development. France - 1927.

The Selecta showing the basket and the little holes in the base to control the water flow.

FILTERS AND THE FILTER PAPER REVOLUTION

In the 1980s a large and increasing amount of coffee was brewed in either an electric espresso machine or in an electric drip filter using filter paper. Neither machine could have been imagined at the turn of the century when electricity and filter paper were scarcely used.

Undoubtedly, there would have been many attempts to make a successful filter paper for coffee machines, because grounds in the cup are unpleasant. Even though these filters may have succeeded technically, none captured the imagination or favour of the public. Many different materials were used as filters, including metal, porcelain, linen and cloth as well as paper, which is mentioned in Rabaut's patent of 1822 and was certainly used in Germany in the 1780s. It was no use having a successful invention if the marketplace was neither ready, nor prepared to pay for it.

In 1885 a very significant book was published in Germany. The author was Dr. Heinrich Boehnke-Reich who brought an analytical approach to coffee preparation methods as well as a very thorough description of what was happening in the United States, England and France. Strangely, the book included a report that a potion of 30 grams of coffee in 150 grams of water had killed a dog in five and a half hours as well as quoting from Henri Welter's book published in France in 1868 that coffee was a drink for Catholics and tea for Protestants. This showed itself in the Catholics' dark complexion, which was affected by the coffee and the pale complexion of the Protestants affected by tea.

The book, as well as reporting the current practices of using filters and filter papers in Northern Germany, made favourable comments about the filtering process which must surely have influenced the further growth of filtering coffee. The author stated that in many families ground coffee was made in a filter coffee bag and that the oils made the bag rancid and the strong flavours of the coffee were held back. He described the danger of using filter paper made from old wall-paper, which contained arsenic and other dangerous chemicals.

He described a thick wool-type greyish paper which could be used in quick filtering in a conical sieve very similar to the filter devised by Melitta Bentz over fifty years later. The filter paper was not ready for use and had to be cut according to the size of the filter. In the same paragraph he discussed a filter materal made from cotton and hemp.

Boehnke-Reich's conclusions must have had an effect on future developments. There was no doubt that you could extract twenty-five per cent more from finely ground coffee than from coarse coffee. If coffee was ground very finely in a mortar and pestle, sixty per cent less coffee needed to be used and further, the aroma of filtered coffee is noticeably stronger than that produced by other methods. His comments on a wide range of brewing equipment showed that he had a real understanding of brewing and his quotations from other people with academic qualifications must have lent weight to his observations.[11]

Around 1900 metal and porcelain filters were popular over most of Europe, whether in little one-cup filters in France and Italy or in much larger domestic and commercial models. The Hamburg filter of the 1900s looks as if it is used without filter paper but a book from the 1920s states that it was.[12] Woven metal mesh was increasingly used in coffee makers toward the turn of the century, probably to avoid the problem of poor quality filter papers. The German Arndt'sche filter of 1887 used a woven mesh which was much finer than the usual punched-hole metal filters and porcelain filters of the period. Because of the small hole size a more finely ground coffee could be used with subsequently better extraction. The possibility of using more finely ground coffee now existed and this type of filter was possibly the catalyst for popularising even finer filtering devices such as filter paper. The Arndt'sche coffee filter won a gold medal at the World Exhibition in Paris in 1900.

Dr. Wiel in Zurich came to the same conclusion as Professor von Liebig that the only way to brew coffee was to pour on boiling water up to a definite limit if you wanted a healthy coffee. The extraction time approached ten minutes and there were the appropriate comments about the health benefits. The Imperial Health Office made tests and showed that the normal extraction rate from other coffee makers was 60 per cent but with the Arndt'sche filter it was 95 per cent. Over one million were in use. The German public was becoming increasingly familiar with filtered coffee.

Right: The Arndt'sche coffee filter won a gold medal at the World Exhibition in Paris in 1900. It used a woven mesh and compressed the coffee to make a good cup of coffee.

The Hamburg filter was common across Northern Germany and Holland. These three porcelain models interestingly have differing size and numbers of holes showing that there was no uniformity in the ideas of how they should operate. Germany - 1900s.

Enamel was a product for the lower classes who could not afford porcelain. The size and number of holes differ markedly. Holland and Germany - 1900s.

A brown filter pot with filter insert and water spreader. France - 1900s.

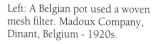

Left: A Belgian pot used a woven mesh filter. Madoux Company, Dinant, Belgium - 1920s.

A catalogue of the 1890s in Germany shows that the Wilda'sche coffee filter, patented in 1894 by Eugen Wilda, was actually being sold. It was not just a drawing in a patent but a commercial product. The illustration in the catalogue shows little similarity to the patent illustration, presenting itself as an improved model and supplied with one hundred filters. Instructions were included, and refills were available in boxes of four hundred. It looked a clumsy unit and the design suggests that it did not function well. Hydrostatic pressure was required to force the water through the coffee and filter. The patent claims a ten minute brewing time. The patent is important because it confirms that paper bag filters were in use in 1894, by declaring that it is better to use cloth filters than the paper bag filters which were expensive and easily torn.

At the turn of the century, Germany was becoming more powerful industrially and had a rising standard of living, which made little extravagances of life possible, such as real coffee. While the Germans had substitute coffees, they were not falsely labelled as real coffee. At the same time they were seeking ways of getting the most out of the expensive coffee. It was an era when coffee was being brewed in one-cup filters sitting on the cup. The time was ripe for someone to propose a new system to make a better cup of coffee, simply and more cheaply. Germany was a country where precision was a national obsession and where arguments to spend a little to save a little could be understood and implemented.

One of the foundations of Germany's powerful economy was its large chemical industry which made ever more sophisticated filter papers. Bulk brewers, using filter paper, were almost certainly in wide use when Melitta Bentz decided to make a smaller model. This was exactly what Bezzera had done to the Moriondo machine, making a one-cup machine from a fifty-cup machine. The German coffee trade magazine of 1914 discussed the use of large scale commercial coffee machines with filter paper saying they were unknown prior to 1900. The firm Gebrüder Schürmann from Elberfeld is the best known factory of this industry and in 1914 had more than two thousand complete installations of bulk-brewing machines.[13] It seems unlikely that such a large number of installations could have been made in a very short time. This firm patented a commercial bulk brewer, the Maria model, in 1906. However, it is not certain in which year commercial filter paper models were first introduced, as the firm had been in existence since 1872. Steinhauer und Sekkel was another large firm of the period which had prominent advertisements for filter paper in trade magazines of the 1920s.[14]

The Wilda'sche filter used cloth filters clamped on the base which were designed to be thrown away after each use. Germany - 1894.

A tinplate filter with removable flannel filter. From an early Munich catalogue.

A tinplate filter with supported base and sieve insert. From an early Munich catalogue.

The Tricolator. France.

Above and Right: The Hamburg filter was produced in tin with woven mesh and tin with punched holes. Germany - 1920s.

Right: A filter insert to rest on a pot - the holes were punched and very small. Perhaps French.

Far Right: The Columbus Filter had a woven mesh filter which rested in the jug. Germany - 1920s.

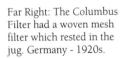

Above: A cloth filter attached to an aluminium filter. Common in Denmark.

Right: A French nickel-coated one-cup filter.

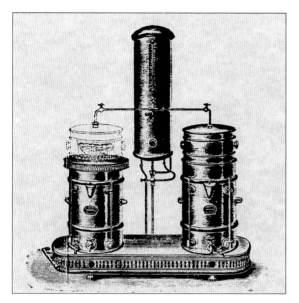

The Gebrüder Schürmann 'Maria' model for commercial use. Germany - 1914.

The filter was a water spreader supported over ground coffee sitting on filter paper. Its construction and design were very similar to the smaller domestic version developed by Melitta Bentz in 1908.

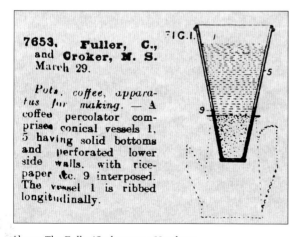

Above: The Fuller/Croker was a Hamburg filter with longitudinal ribs. When filter paper is laid against a flat surface, there is no flow. There must be a space behind the paper for the coffee to flow into. England - 1910.

In 1908 Melitta Bentz, a German housewife, successfully made a one-cup filter paper machine. She placed a piece of blotting paper in a round cup with holes in it and poured boiling water through it. Even the act of pouring boiling water through the air made it the correct temperature - just under boiling point. The important part of the design was the relatively large filter which meant that the water could easily fall through. A year later she sold 1250 aluminium coffee filter holders at the Leipzig Trade Fair. The early advertising described her filter as the best, simplest and cheapest filter in the world - an unbeatable combination. The use of aluminium would have helped to make a hotter cup of coffee than the cold, heavy porcelain filters in use at the time. The evidence indicates that the Melitta Company was active with domestic filter paper coffee makers while other larger and older firms were well established with commercial filter paper coffee machines.

Melitta's invention responded to the priorities of the German coffee drinker - clarity and aroma without bitterness. The French and Italians were not looking for these qualities, so it was more than seventy years before they responded to the idea of using filter paper and even then the Italians hardly used it. In Germany filter paper had arrived and although success did not come overnight, it was popular enough to be a commercial success. It was truly a case of the market being ready for a product and a product being ready for the market. Not only was filter paper a good idea at the time but it was properly commercialised and exploited by the Bentz family.

In other parts of the world similar ideas were being espoused. In 1905 Frederick A. Cauchois of New York brought out his 'Private Estate' coffee filter, a French drip with Japanese paper as the filtering medium.[15]

In exactly the same year as Melitta (1908), I.D. Richheimer of Chicago invented the Tricolator which was an aluminium filter device using Japanese filter paper. This was a commercial success in the United States, but not to the same degree as Melitta in Germany. The huge success of filter paper was largely confined to Germany and was not a universal phenomenon.

In 1910 two Englishmen, C. Fuller and N.S. Croker, took out a patent for a funnel with perforated lower side walls, with rice paper interposed and ribbed longitudinal walls. This was only slightly different to the 1932 and 1937 Melitta patents in which the holes were at the bottom. The results would have been comparable. This is an excellent example of a good idea in the wrong place at the wrong time.

In 1925 filter paper coffee makers were available and in favour in the United States but the market remained relatively small.[16]

It should not be imagined that the filter paper method took over the hearts and minds of Germany without a struggle. An article by Max

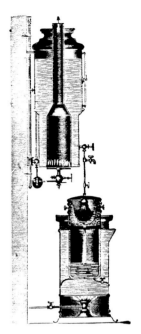

The installation was a gas boiler and filter apparatus.

The first Melitta filter incorporated all the ideas of Gebrüder Schürmann - water spreader and filter paper - except that it had a hemispherical base. After 1912, it had the more pointed base.

This one-cup polycarbonate filter had the same basic shape as the first Melitta filter.

The Brasil filter - the first quickfilter. It was the beginning of a new era for filtered coffee. Germany - 1932.

Right: 'The Bremer coffee machine is a money-spinner for coffee shops. It gives a fully automatic drink of maximum pleasant flavour without filter paper or steam pressure.' (English translation). It was made from enamel with an aluminium sieve base in the upper filter section.

Preising of Bremen in the 1926 trade magazine *KATEKA* praised the Bremer and the Karlsbader coffee machines because they did not use filter paper and complained that the filter paper left a paper flavour in the coffee. He proclaimed that filter paper was the biggest enemy of coffee lovers and should be driven out of the kitchen.[17] In 1929 Dr. Edgar Müller complained that the existing filter paper machines were sometimes slow and sometimes fast, whereas the Bremer coffee machine took eight minutes. The fact that finer coffee was needed meant a less aromatic coffee because the grinder heated up in the process and warmed the coffee. Significantly there was an advertisement for the Bremer coffee machine on the same page.[18] Articles in trade magazines are not necessarily the best sources for the truth,

because they are often written by advertisers, or as editorial at the behest of advertisers and unless you know the connection, you may think that they are unbiased. However, it may have been these criticisms which caused the Melitta Company to look to their laurels and develop better coffee makers.

In 1931 Paul Ciupka, a German coffee chemist, wrote that the brewing times using filter paper for large quantities was too long and for small quantities too short. He also mentioned a filter paper bag (eine Tuete aus Filterpapier) which indicates that such bags must have existed in some form prior to those invented and developed by Melitta a few years later in 1937.[19]

Aluminiumwerk Göttingen (now Alcan) in 1932 produced the Brasil Quickfilter which has a slightly different design to the Melitta Quickfilter of the same period. It was certainly in production before the Melitta patent which is almost identical. The connection with aluminium is that an aluminium presser was used to shape and press the filter paper into the funnel. The filter paper was in sheets and folded to make a cone. In between the wars, the Melitta company was very strong in Germany. In spite of anti-filter paper arguments the Melitta Quickfilter, which was invented in several versions from 1932 to 1937, was to be a major step in converting the Germans to filtered coffee. In spite of not being the first company with a quickfilter Melitta seems to have dominated the market for this type of filter in the years to follow. [20]

Filter paper was originally in round sheets and then in folded square sheets formed into the filter by a rammer. The formed triangular sheet was introduced to the market in 1937. It is important to note that these Melitta filters were relatively small and required several fills to make a pot of coffee. This caused the brewing time to be extended and to allow a full extraction. One of the constraints was that the mass of a large porcelain filter would have absorbed so much heat as to

The pre-war Melitta quickfilter used a square filter paper. The paper was pressed in with an aluminium shape.

This was the beginning of the Melitta 101 and 102 series filters, with ribs running right down to the bottom. The original 102 filter was for four to eight cups in Germany and Switzerland and later changed to three to six cups .

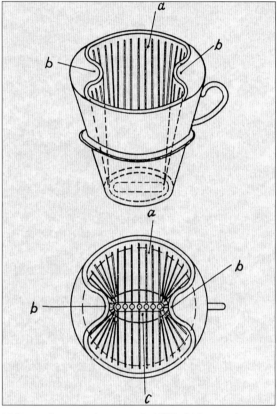

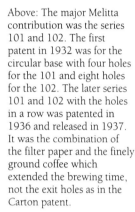

Above: The major Melitta contribution was the series 101 and 102. The first patent in 1932 was for the circular base with four holes for the 101 and eight holes for the 102. The later series 101 and 102 with the holes in a row was patented in 1936 and released in 1937. It was the combination of the filter paper and the finely ground coffee which extended the brewing time, not the exit holes as in the Carton patent.

Melitta took out another patent in 1937 which can only be assumed to be a fine example of a defensive patent to prevent other companies from taking advantage of a perceived weakness in the original patent.

make the coffee cold and so it was better to have a small filter. When lightweight plastics were used after the war, this constraint disappeared and the whole pot could be filtered in virtually one pour in a larger filter funnel. In the quickfilter the extraction rates vary according to the position of the coffee in the funnel, whereas in a level filter there is an even extraction.

While many competitors disappeared during the war years, the Melitta Company re-established itself very strongly after the War. The filter paper method has become firmly associated, world-wide, with the Melitta name because of its commercial success and due to promotional activities after the Second World War. This is indeed proof that nothing makes a product succeed like a strong company behind it.

Peter Schlumbohm, a German immigrant to the United States introduced the Chemex coffee maker in 1936. It was a one-piece, all-glass filter paper coffee maker which was successful. It was probably the first real filter coffee experience for most Americans and has lasted for many decades.

Right: In 1949 the Melitta Company produced aluminium filters. This filter clearly shows the longitudinal ribs.

FLAT FILTERS AND CONICAL FILTERS

Flat filters support a level bed of coffee and have an even extraction over the whole surface of the filter. In conical filters the coffee is washed up against the sides of the filter causing overextraction in the middle and underextraction on the sides because the water is not in contact with the coffee for as long.

The Melitta 10 series has ridges up the side to the top and a steeper angle to the sides. The most common sizes were the 101 to make up to four cups and the 102 to make up to six cups. Commercial sizes went up to 106 for making large quantities of coffee into porcelain lined containers. Filtering only takes place where there is a space behind the filter paper i.e. where there are ridges. The 10 series was a relatively small filter and required several pours to make the desired amount of coffee. Most of these filters were porcelain and it was important to have a filter as small as possible so as little heat as possible would be absorbed by the filter. After the war there were plastic and aluminium models. The series was phased out in the 1980s in favour of the 1X system.

Lighter plastics absorbed less heat and enabled the Melitta 1X series to become popular. The larger size of the filter with the ridges in the lower portion meant that a small pour was required to wet the coffee and keep it in position followed by the balance of the water in one pour. The fact that plastics were cheap, colourful and unbreakable and able to make a good cup of hot coffee simply, meant that the new shape soon dominated the way filtered coffee was made all over the world. They were widely used in domestic electric coffee makers in Europe because they concentrated the brewing in the bottom of the filter.

A Bauscher filter pot. The top compartment had a slit filter but the coffee could not flow until the top had been turned to align the filter with a hole in the saucer. Germany - 1920s.

A filter pot in which the top of the basket was screwed down to compress the coffee and control the brewing time. France - 1930s.

The Chemex filter was well promoted and popular with American coffee afficionados. USA.

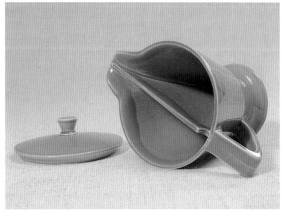

A Wedgwood Ducpour - for pouring hot coffee and hot milk together. England - 1935.

Left and Above: A French Pillivuyt filter pot. This type of pot was common in France and Germany where it was called a Karlsbader. France.

POST- WAR FILTERING METHODS

A Wear-Ever filter pot. The filter was in the vertical part of the lid. USA - 1902.

The filter screwed onto the base to compress the coffee. This was a good idea to control the flow of water but only worked well if you knew just how much to compress the coffee. France.

Aluminium one-cup filters were cheap to produce and even came with their own aluminium cup.

A portable dripolator - the spirit lamp and the filter folded up to fit into the leather case. Italy - 1950s.

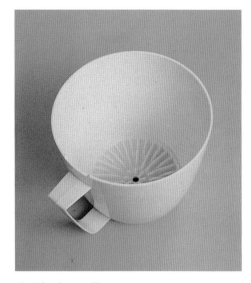

Glass was combined with aluminium. The central stem was to locate and keep the upper filter level.

This early plastic brewer shows the deformed plastic water spreader. Plastics were often used for the wrong products. Resistance to heat was one of the biggest problems to be overcome. Belgium - 1960s.

An Eduscho pot filter. Germany - 1970s.

Right: The Comforto was made by the Dutch firm Douwe Egbert for their customers who were able to purchase coffee makers with coupons from their packets of coffee. It had a plastic filter. Holland - 1968.

Far Right: Clever design combined the function of water spreading and keeping the floating coffee down in a one-cup brewer with an etched metallic filter. The brown cup was to keep the coffee down and the holes controlled the flow rate. Germany - 1980s.

Right: Aluminium filters were widely produced in the early period when suitable plastics were not available. As these became available, aluminium was replaced until, by 1990, it was scarcely used in sophisticated equipment.

Right: Danish filter, 1x6 shape, in polypropylene - a flexible heat resistant plastic which did not hold its shape very well. Denmark - 1970s.

Above: Many pots after the war were insulated with an aluminium lined felt jacket which kept the coffee hot. This was an idea first patented in the 1930s. The introduction of vacuum flasks and cheap glass jugs on electric warmers replaced them until they were rarely seen in the 1980s.

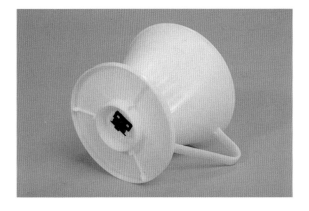

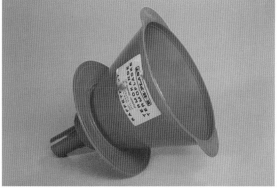

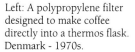

Far Left: A filter cone for use with electric machines. By moving the black button, it was possible to change the exit hole size and hence the flow rate. France - 1980s.

Left: A polypropylene filter designed to make coffee directly into a thermos flask. Denmark - 1970s.

Far left: The Art Dripper was a cardboard fold-up filter with a support to sit on the cup. Japan - 1980s.

Left: An extremely lightweight double-walled filter. Japan - 1980s.

The Fency filter had a stainless steel filter with an adjustable valve to control the time. To retain the heat during the brewing process there was a plastic float. Germany -1980s.

Left: The Coffee Mite incorporated space-age design to make a one-cup brewer with filter paper. USA - 1980s.

The Bonita filter had a woven stainless steel filter welded into the base. The welding was not completely satisfactory and later models had removable filters. Switzerland - 1980s.

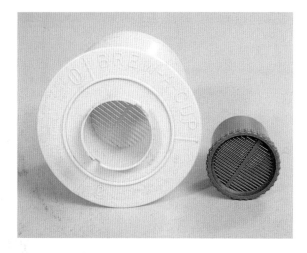

Far Left: The Brew-a-Cup used longitudinal slits as a filter, which worked for coarse coffee. The American taste for a weaker coffee might have been satisfied. USA. - late 1980s.

Left: Two one-cup filters which incorporated very fine woven nylon mesh moulded into the plastic. USA - 1990.

The Kaja was one of the first to use a nylon mesh for filtering. In 1990 nylon mesh was freely available in mesh sizes down to 20 microns. One of the disadvantages with nylon was that it discoloured after use. Germany - 1970s.

Above and Right: The True Brew by Belaroma had a polycarbonate bowl and stainless steel filter. The small hole controlled the flow rate. It made one to three cups at a time and was good for tea also. When used with coffee it was necessary to stir the coffee. Australia -1980s.

Right: The Sonja used nylon filters shaped to fit into the plastic filter funnel. The filter with two hooks was made in Hong Kong. In both cases, the nylon mesh was not sewn together but ultrasonically welded and the mesh attached to the polypropylene with a solvent. Germany -1980s.

Far Right: A gold filter one-cup brewer. Switzerland -1980s.

Right: Hivas used Swiss Elfo metal mesh (brown) and woven stainless steel mesh (black). The stainless steel mesh was much cheaper. Holland - 1980s.

Above: The Mini Minit - a one-cup paper filter bag suspended in the cup. Canada - 1990.

Left: Three permanent filters using the Elfo gold mesh. The mesh is not produced in sheets and cut to size but shaped in manufacture and then moulded into the plastic. 1980s.

172

SUCCESS OF THE FILTER PAPER METHOD POST-WAR

One of the factors in the success of the filter method after the Second World War was the development of both heat-resistant plastics and lightweight, mass-produced, heat-resistant glass jugs. The first cone filters or funnels were porcelain and were relatively heavy. Unless you took extra care to pre-heat the porcelain pot, the filtered coffee would be warm instead of hot. After the war, glass funnels in electric coffee machines were followed by the first plastic funnels, made of polystyrene, a product which, although not very heat-resistant, was light. Polypropylene and polyethylene filters followed. They were heat-resistant, light and flexible. Later, polycarbonate was much more rigid and more expensive, but did the job perfectly.

The first filter pots after the war were porcelain. They needed to be pre-heated but once they were, they kept the coffee hot and especially so when they were encased in a small jacket of felt in an aluminium cover. The introduction of lightweight, pressed heat-resistant glass jugs in combination with plastic funnels meant that without any pre-heating at all the coffee could be made and kept hot on a low flame or an electric warming plate. Filtered coffee with a filter paper could now be made easily. The light plastic funnels, because they did not absorb so much heat, allowed the filter paper to be larger. The pre-war size for six cups, the small Melitta 102, was eventually replaced by the larger 1X6 which meant that you could make six cups with two pours instead of several little pours. It no longer required the determination of a German housewife to make a first-class cup of hot coffee.

NEW DEVELOPMENTS IN MATERIALS

Aluminium became very cheap with the use of cheap hydro-electricity and was used in ever increasing amounts even though it was attacked by coffee and was essentially unsuitable. As stainless steel became cheaper and more easily mass-produced, it replaced aluminium in many coffee makers. It was only a matter of deciding which material you wanted to use and there was a machine available to work it.

Plastics were initially introduced with undesirable results - they could not stand the temperature and gave nasty flavours. Early mistakes led to better grades which were perfect. The plastics also had an important characteristic - they did not transmit electricity. This quality enabled the extensive use of plastics in the machine that was destined to sweep the world - the electric drip filter machine. These machines, while not perfect, were much better than the electric percolators they replaced and made a clear brew of good-tasting coffee which could be kept hot. Many brands appeared and they are now appearing in the countries where you could not formerly get a cup of filtered coffee.

Other developments were the replacement of the paper filter by stainless steel mesh and electroformed metal filter mesh. In 1971 the Elfo Company of Switzerland took out a patent for an electroformed filter using gold. In a process which is the opposite of etching, deposits were made in such a way that a flat metal sheet with filter holes was produced. The hole size was not as small as the holes of filter paper but, as with all filters, the coffee grounds themselves acted as the main filter.

The Rowenta Company of Germany first used this gold filter in 1975 and it has since become popular in the ranges of many different manufacturers. The principle advantage is that of cleanliness and lack of tainting. Its proponents claim that it has major advantages over woven stainless steel and nylon mesh filters which trap tiny particles in the cross-joins. From a practical point of view, I doubt that many consumers would be aware of the problem. Nevertheless many people consider gold filters to be the ultimate, as if the gold improved the flavour in some way.

THE ELECTRIC FILTER COFFEE MAKER AND A NEW ERA
Willy Brandl, Major Inventor

In Zurich, Willy Brandl's invention in 1944 was the application of a mercury float switch to a filter coffee machine. When the water ran out, the power cut out. His first machines were made under the brand name, BRA VIL OR - BRA ndl VIL ly OR likon (a suburb of Zurich). The first domestic models made one litre or six cups in nine minutes.

The first Willy Brandl patent. It had a large float switch on the water side and a boiler at the bottom of the tube and appeared as the Bravilor Baby Model A. Switzerland - 1944.

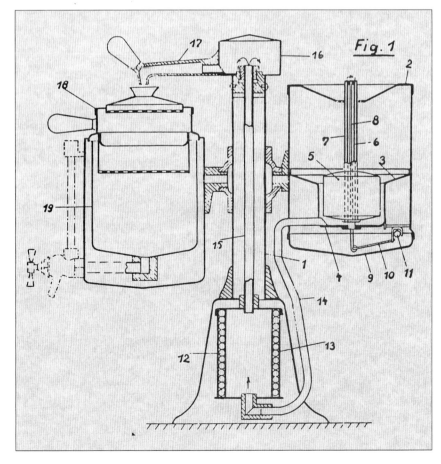

Fig. 1

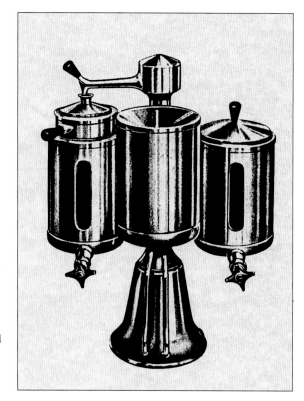

Right: The Bravilor Baby B was the first commercial machine and followed the model A which was the same as the patent drawing. The central water holder held two litres of water and there were two coffee containers. Switzerland - 1940s.

Far Right: The second Brandl patent had a small heating element under the jug. Both models used round filter paper. Switzerland - 1954.

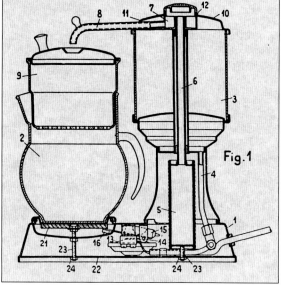

The Bravilor domestic machine - second model. Switzerland - 1949.

The improved recirculating percolators, such as the Landers, Frary and Clark machines, pumped small amounts of water often rather than large amounts of water. Brandl did exactly the same to the pumping percolator - he boiled small amounts of water to filter over the coffee rather than all the water at once.

In 1954 Brandl patented another model which was the basis for the Wigomat machine produced in Germany in 1958 by Gottlob Widman. It was the Wigomat machine which really started the electric filter coffee maker revolution. Willy Brandl made very little from these inventions and tried again with the Arbella machine which was the basis for a successful machine made by Krups. It operated with very low pressure at 100 degrees Celsius and made a first class coffee. The combination of Willy Brandl's electric coffee machine and filter paper were to make the biggest changes in the way the world consumed coffee. The Wigomat model was the first of many popular electric machines in Europe. Thirty thousand were sold in its first year of production. It was the start of a new era.

Many other machines were produced by Wigomat and other manufacturers for the mass market - a machine at a price. All these machines functioned in the sense of making coffee, but they had not been designed with the idea of making perfect coffee. They had to fight for sales and shelf space in department stores which were more concerned with the design and colours than the performance. Not surprisingly technical performance suffered and machines were produced to a wide range of standards. Whilst the consumers were prepared to accept even more magic in the guise of beautiful packaging and bright colours supported by extensive advertising showing smiling consumers enjoying the most aromatic coffee, the actual coffee produced left a lot to be desired. What was needed was a machine which brewed the coffee at 92 to 96 degrees Celsius with a brewing time of four to six minutes.

Far Left: The Wigomat machine was introduced by Gottlob Widman. It was very similar in appearance to the Brandl machine and solved the problem of an airlock in the boiler tube. In the first year 30,000 were sold. It was the start of the electric filter machine revolution. Germany - 1958.

Left: The Wigomat and the Bauknecht both used a flat paper filter in a glass filter. Germany - 1960s.

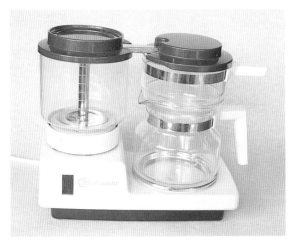

Far Left: The Bauknecht. Germany.- 1960s.

Left: The Philips Comfort brewer showed the latest style - ever more elegance. Holland - 1990.

Far Left: The Aromatic was an electric filter maker which used a small heat-sensitive valve to control the brewing. When the valve heated up, it opened, allowing the water to fall through. Denmark -1970s.

Left: The Siemens Company produced a most interesting electric pumping percolator based on a 1971 German patent by Lenschner and Schubert. The clear container floated on the water in the pot. As the water in the bottom boiled away, it was pumped up and filtered into the clear container which slid down the pot until there was only a pot of filtered coffee. Germany - 1980s.

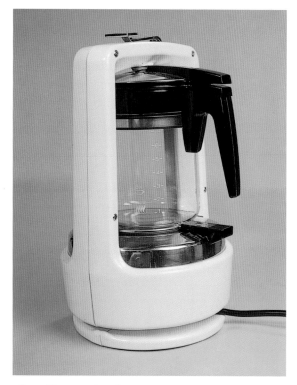

Above: Krups produced a
pumping percolator based on the
Arbella patent. Germany - 1968.

Below: The Technivorm
machine. The first domestic
filter machine to make an
excellent cup of coffee.
It brewed the coffee at the
right temperature for the
correct time and kept it hot.
Holland.

Right: The Arbella was invented by
Willy Brandl. Switzerland - 1964.

TECHNIVORM COFFEE MAKER

Gerard Smit, a Dutch engineer, who started the
Technivorm Company, set out to design a machine
to perform to the required standards. This was
very unusual - most machines were designed to
look good, not to work perfectly.

Smit had already designed a successful coffee
grinder in 1962. His Technivorm grinder had been
advertised in the catalogue of Douwe Egbert, the
large Dutch coffee company, which had a policy of
supplying coffee with high quality coffee machines
which worked well. The Wigomat electric filter
coffee maker had also been advertised in the
catalogue from 1960 to 1965. In 1969 the first
Technivorm coffee maker was advertised in the
Douwe Egbert catalogue with the words:

*Douwe Egbert automatic coffee machine. This
practical coffee machine, exclusively developed
for Douwe Egbert, offers you coffee using the
quick filter method as well as the normal [round]
filter method.* [English translation]

It was the first two-speed coffee machine in the
world, but not only that - it solved the problems of
previous models. The co-operation of an engineer
dedicated to making a better product and a large
interested coffee company was about to bear fruit.
The solution lay in determining the precise size of
the element to heat a continous amount of water at
a controlled temperature in such a way that air
bubbles were kept from the inlet. The normal

pulsating effect of other machines was avoided and a smooth flow achieved. For health reasons the machine used copper elements instead of aluminium. A special jug lid was incorporated, which mixed the coffee by displacement, instead of allowing the strongest coffee to sit at the bottom of the jug. It controlled the whole cycle to prevent too much heat at the end of the cycle and precisely controlled the warming plates to achieve the correct temperature of 83 degrees Celsius even when the jug was cold. It avoided the commonly used system of a duplex element for both the water boiler and the hot plate which was cheap but completely uncontrollable

ACHIEVING THE STANDARDS

The Technivorm machine was the first machine to achieve the absolute standards for brewing coffee set by the Norwegian Coffee Promotion Committee and their Brewing Centre in Oslo, in 1977. They were very simple and precise:

1. Brewing temperature 92 to 96 degrees Celsius
2. Brewing time 4 to 6 minutes
3. Holding temperature 80 to 85 degrees Celsius
4. A standard drip grind for the whole Norwegian coffee trade
5. A dosing of 60 to 70 grams of coffee per litre of water
6. Follow the instructions of the individual brewer.

A change in quantity of coffee per litre would change the relative strength of the coffee but the coffee itself would be brewed perfectly.

Coffee made to these standards is fully flavoured without bitterness, and contrasts with boiled coffee which has a totally different taste because cellulose and the albumen of the bean are dissolved by the boiling and, in addition, spots of oil appear on the surface of the brewed coffee.

Tests on the major European machines have shown brewing temperatures as low as 79 degrees Celsius and brewing times as long as fourteen minutes. Most cheaper models operate by boiling the water at the rate of one cup per minute which means the correct brewing time for four cups, but over-extraction when twelve cups are made. As well as the Technivorm machine some machines from Bosch, Siemens and Melitta have since achieved the required standard.

More advanced filter machines have been manufactured which incorporate electronic chips to start at set times and machines specially made to filter the coffee into vacuum flasks. Every conceivable human whim is catered for.

Larger electric commercial machines such as the Bravilor look like the earliest Gebrüder Schürmann machine but incorporate temperature control and perform correctly, because they are based on the same standards as for domestic machines.

FILTER COFFEE IN NORTHERN EUROPE — ESPRESSO IN THE SOUTH

The filter paper method eventually captured the minds of German coffee drinkers just as espresso captured the minds and palates of the Italians. Europe almost seemed to make its preferences on the basis of linguistic zones. The Swiss, Hungarians and Austrians stayed with the espresso as did the Latin countries. Holland and the other Northern countries followed the filter paper method to such a degree that in the 1970s it was difficult to find an espresso machine in them. It was equally difficult to find filtered coffee in Southern Europe. However the Northern tourists were to develop a taste for espresso coffee which was to make small inroads in their countries in the 1980s.

DOMESTIC MACHINES IN THE 1970S, 1980s AND 1990s

The 1970s and 1980s saw a great change in the way coffee was made all over the world. The electric recirculating percolator, the worst coffee machine ever invented, was in decline. The vacuum system, which was very popular in Japan, was losing its market all over the world. The hand filtering method was being replaced by the electric filtering system and because of the sophistication of these systems, this was the area of greatest change in electric filter coffee makers. The plunger system was becoming more popular although it was still a small factor in the marketplace. The advantages that plungers have are that the coffee can be made in the kitchen and taken to the table and that they are so simple and give results which are reasonably good, irrespective of the number of cups made.

The Bravilor B5E brewed five litres at a time and made excellent coffee. Holland - 1990s.

Right: The Sunbeam boiled the water in the top, a bi-metal strip opened and the water filtered over the coffee. Australia - 1980.

The Russell Hobbs filter machine used a gold mesh filter. England - 1980s.

Far Right: The two-cup Melitta had a shorter brewing time than the larger models and the coffee did not sit as long. Unfortunately the consumer preferred to buy larger models which were less suitable to make small quantities. Germany - 1980s.

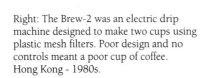

Above: The Rowenta filtered into a plastic thermos flask. Germany - 1980s.

Right: The Brew-2 was an electric drip machine designed to make two cups using plastic mesh filters. Poor design and no controls meant a poor cup of coffee. Hong Kong - 1980s.

Microwave ovens had varying wattages which meant that it was almost impossible to make one brewer to fit all microwave ovens. In the 1990s, more than eighty per cent of American households have a microwave oven and special non-metal coffee makers have been developed for use in them.

PLUNGER OR FRENCH PRESS

Two brand names in Europe are associated with the plunger or French press coffee maker Melior and Bodum. Melior was very prominent in the 1930s with a range of all metal units and from the 1950s with an upmarket range of metal units including silver and gold-plated frames with glass containers. The Bodum range, with colourful plastic handles and lids, glass bodies and stainless steel filters, became popular in the 1960s and 1970s, and has remained so.

The Japanese Hario brand used a plastic press with a fine nylon mesh. The press had diagonal flutes to stir the coffee above it as it was pressed down. Although the plunger system is very good, it does let through some sediment, which means that the coffee is best drunk immediately after being made. Because the grounds are on the bottom of the jug the coffee cannot be kept hot on a warmer. In most cases the instructions for making coffee in a plunger are to stir the floating coffee before pushing the plunger down and not to use a coffee that is too finely ground. These instructions are rarely followed by the consumer. For improved extraction it is necessary to stir the coffee twice - once to break up the floating bed of coffee after pouring on the boiling water, and a second time to mix the flavour particles in the coffee grounds at the bottom just before depressing the plunger. If the coffee is too finely ground it requires considerable pressure to make the plunger go down. Sometimes this problem can be overcome by using a pump action which breaks up the bed of coffee under the plunger.

There do not appear to be any serious studies on the efficacy of the normal plunger method probably because just about any combination of grind and time gives a result that is drinkable for non-discriminating drinkers. With care this method makes good coffee but the filter must keep out most of the grounds. This generally requires a coarser grind, more coffee per cup and a slower brewing time.

The Belaroma two stage plunger, which was invented in 1991 addresses the problem of the coffee floating. The plunger has a disc with large perforations and a filter ring as in a normal plunger. The action of pressing the large-holed ring into the pot breaks up the coffee first, which results in better extraction. Just before pressing the fine filter ring down, the coarse ring is revolved, which stirs the coffee grounds and essence into solution. As a result, the plunger can be pressed much more easily and there is a higher flavour level in the cup.

The commercial Technivorm Moccaking as well as making excellent coffee incorporated a plastic valve which closed if either the jug or filter were removed during brewing. The valve reduced mess when staff interfered with the brewing process. Holland -1980s.

MICROWAVE COFFEE MAKERS

The ground coffee was placed in the filter in the water in the cup which was placed in the microwave oven for two minutes. USA - 1990.

The Farberware microwave brewer from the USA was a pumping percolator. Water was placed in the two-cup container on the right which was sealed with the lid. Coffee was placed in the filter paper and the water container placed on top. The whole coffee maker was placed in the microwave oven. The water boiled and the resultant steam forced the water up a tube to fall over the coffee. USA -1990.

PLUNGERS

Right: Italian-made Melior plunger pots. Note the smooth edge on the press filter and also the split in the wall of the pot. Technology had its limitations. Italy - 1930s.

Far Right: A Melior pot with an expanding metal ring around the press filter. The only problem in making a good plunger was to make a good fitting filter that could slide up and down and prevent the coffee passing through the gap between the filter and the wall of the pot. Melior seems to have been the first to succeed in making good quality plungers. France.

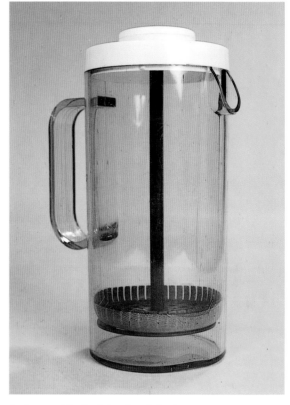

The Hario plunger with nylon mesh and plastic press filter. The ring on the press was made of plastic. The nylon mesh was very fine and kept out coarse grounds. Japan -1980s.

A plunger with plastic bowl and plastic fittings was cheap and worked well but the market preferred glass and more noble materials. Germany - 1980s.

Three plungers - green and white from Bodum, Denmark. The red model was by Prima of Germany and had a plastic moulded filter which was flexible and bent to keep tightly against the wall of the pot. 1990s.

A one-cup Filtropa plunger. The water was poured over the coffee and the plunger depressed. The handle was given a twist and removed leaving the filter at the bottom. It was a very convenient way to make plunger coffee directly into the cup. Holland - 1991.

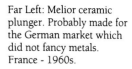

Far Left: Melior ceramic plunger. Probably made for the German market which did not fancy metals. France - 1960s.

Left: The Optima was made from polycarbonate heat-resistant plastic to be practically unbreakable. France - 1970s.

Left: The Elfo plunger filter is the result of the latest technology - it combines a springy stainless steel circumference, backed by stainless steel mesh which prevents grounds from passing around it, all moulded into a plastic frame incorporating a nut for the metal stem to screw into. Switzerland - 1991.

A BMF Primo gold-plated plastic plunger. Germany - 1991.

COFFEE MAKING IN CARS

Cars generally incorporate a cigarette lighter and the same electrical power point can be used as the source of power for making coffee while you travel. There is no sophistication involved in the coffee brewing; it is just a simple way to make filtered coffee.

COFFEE MAKING IN JAPAN

The theme of this book has been the evolution of coffee - the beans and the machines. At any point, it is impossible to know if some idea will become part of the mainstream or will be consigned to obscurity. Most of this book has been about the activities in Europe and the Americas, broadly showing a European culture and feeling toward coffee in its disparate forms.

Since the end of the Second World War Japan has prospered immensely and the Japanese have gone even further with perfecting sophisticated roasters, grinders and brewers, all in one.

Japanese admiration of Edwardian England and its use of the siphon or vacuum brewing system has been of great importance in the shaping of the Japanese coffee industry. It was and is common to have coffee prepared at a very high price in one tiny siphon at a time on individual flames in front of the customer in coffee shops. There are even classes for coffee shop workers to learn how to make coffee in siphons. In the 1980s it became more common to use drip filter machines brewing in bulk to serve coffee at a third of the price.

The Japanese desire to have the best in the world has led to their market place being different to that of the rest of the world. Japanese companies have virtually bought the entire Jamaican Blue Mountain coffee crop and the highest grades of any other crop. The prices they pay and in turn the charges to the consumer are enormous and totally out of keeping with prices in the rest of the world. On the other hand, nowhere in the world does the customer get service as in Japan. It is the normal thing for coffee to be vacuum-packed in department stores directly after grinding. Nothing has been spared to give the consumer the best possible product.

A plastic car coffee maker from Hong Kong.

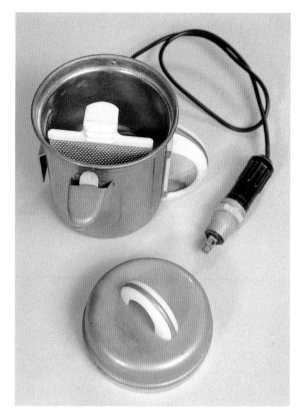

A German car coffee maker showing the plug to fit into the car's cigarette lighter socket.

The Toshiba My Cafe Mill and Drip. The beans were put in the grinding section and ground. Water passed over the grounds and fell directly into the pot. There are also grind and siphon machines available. Japan - 1980s.

The Hario iced coffee maker. Ice was placed in the container directly under the filter and the cooled coffee fell into the insulated jug underneath. Japan - 1985.

Far Left: In 1991 Mr Enomoto of the Koki Company produced a roaster, grinder and brewer. From raw bean to cup took 17 minutes. The whole process was controlled by micro-chip technology. Japan -1991.

Left: A Sunbeam removable basket coffee pot. Extraction was rarely very good in any machine unless there was a free flow of water through the coffee or tea. USA.

The Melitta IBS - Interval Brewing System brewer was designed to have repeated surges of water over the coffee. Germany - 1992.

One of the extraordinary features of Japan can be seen in the thousands of vending machines on the footpaths, selling cans of iced coffee in many combinations of brands, flavours and strengths. Coffee grind-and-brew machines are mass-produced to deliver high quality coffee. There is even a can of coffee which incorporates a system to heat the coffee, based on a separate compartment of lime and water, which, when mixed separately from the coffee, produces enough heat to make the coffee in the can hot. This is the same idea as Templeman in England in 1878.

The total Japanese scene also incorporates the technology and the attitudes of the people. Most people in the Western world see Japanese technology in the form of a host of imported electronic devices in their local stores. What they see is nothing when compared with the range of the same goods in the stores of Akihabara in Tokyo. The range of video cameras for instance, is so vast that it is almost impossible to comprehend the specifications and make a rational purchase.

The proliferation of wealth combined with conspicuous consumption and a love of technology have coalesced to form a coffee society with products unique in the world. The range includes automatic siphon machines, several different models of grind and drip, grind and siphon and drip machines which allow the coffee to fall over ice blocks and make iced coffee. The siphon machines do not operate, as in the west, with cloth filters which get dirty, but incorporate paper filters to be changed each time.

In the mid-1980s the Advance Company patented and manufactured a new roaster, a new grinder and a new filter coffee maker. I cannot recall any other company in the world doing this before.

In 1991 Mr. Enomoto of the Koki Company, after five years' study, patented and manufactured a fully automatic roaster, grinder and drip brewer. Naturally it incorporated an electronic chip to control all the processes. The coffee had to be specially treated to remove the husks before roasting and the whole process took seventeen minutes to make six cups.

All these machines, plus real gold-plated plungers, numerous Rombout-type filters and the Astoria cup filter, make Japan unlike any other market. The Japanese consumer is supplied with capsules of coffee, individually packed, at prices which are unheard of in any other country.

TYPES OF DRUM ROASTERS

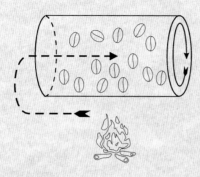

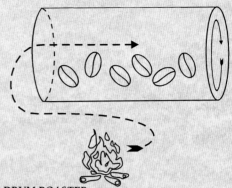

SIMPLE DRUM ROASTER.

The first simple drum roasters with the flame against the drum were improved with the introduction of the blower to take the hot air into the drum. They roasted with a combination of conduction from the heat of the wall of the drum and convective heat. Many small roasters use this system. Air temperature is in the range 350-500 degrees Celsius.

SIMPLE DRUM ROASTER WITH INDIRECT HEAT AGAINST THE DRUM.

The desire to reduce the heat of the drum wall which could scorch the beans led to the introduction of indirect heat against and around the drum, double-walled drums, and drums with one of the two walls perforated. This is the most common roaster for industrial use. Air temperature is in the range 400-500 degrees Celsius.

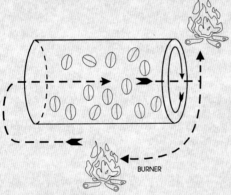

SIMPLE DRUM ROASTER WITH RECIRCULATION AND AFTERBURNER.

Pollution problems and the need for cost economies after the Second World War led to the increasing use of recirculation of the hot air which was being exhausted after going through the drum once and to the introduction of afterburners to reduce pollution. Two gas burners were needed. Air temperature is in the range 350-400 degrees Celsius.

DIRECT HEAT INSIDE THE DRUM.

The English Whitmee and UNO roasters used a gas flame inside the drum which was often of perforated metal. Air temperature is in the range 350-400 degrees Celsius.

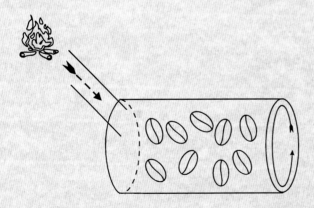

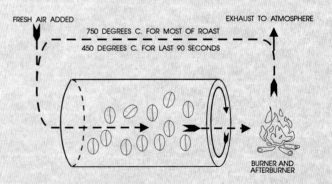

HOT AIR DIRECT INTO THE DRUM.

Another solution which was popular in German Barth and Gothot roasters and based on the Salamon patent was to introduce hot air into the drum directly without applying any direct heat against the drum at all. The heat control was direct and instantaneous. Air temperature is in the range 350-400 degrees Celsius.

THE LILLA DRUM ROASTER.

The Lilla drum roaster from Brazil used only one burner to act both as an afterburner and heat the air to roast the beans. The roasting time is normally around nine minutes with hot air at 750 degrees Celsius for most of the roast and 450 degrees Celsius for the last ninety seconds. The air was cooled by introducing cold air into the hot air stream just before it went into the roaster. Cooling takes place inside the drum for one and a half minutes with a combination of water and cold air and is further cooled outside the roaster.

CHAPTER 10

Coffee Roasting

COFFEE ROASTING

Roasting coffee is simply the application of heat to raw coffee beans. Coffee beans have always been delivered from the grower in sacks or barrels as raw, greenish or yellowish-coloured beans, about the size of small peanuts. They have a grassy flavour until heated to the desired colour at a temperature just above 200 degrees Celsius. The heat dries the coffee beans and drives off about fifteen to twenty per cent of the water content and the beans swell up just like popcorn. In the process the coffee flavour is developed. If the process is too slow, the coffee is baked. The central idea of roasting the coffee is to have the same colour in the middle of the bean as on the outside.

While the principle is simple, the process is very complex. Controlling this process so the beans are consistently roasted and removed at precisely the correct moment, has always been the problem. While a lot is understood about the roasting process, there is still a lot to be discovered.

Hundreds of chemical reactions take place during the roasting process and there are subsequent interactions between them. The method of heat transfer influences the way in which these reactions take place and also the temperature of the gases in the roasting chamber, and creates changes in the structure and appearance of the bean. Fast roasting in a fluidised bed coffee roaster produces greater puffiness. This influences the final extraction because the increased porosity allows for fuller extraction of the volatile and non-volatile components and the result is totally different to coffee roasted in a traditional drum roaster. Any differences in operation of a roasting machine will produce coffees with slightly different flavours.

ROASTING LOSS

During the roasting process, the weight loss of the coffee ranges from 14 per cent for light roasted coffees to 19 per cent for very dark roasted coffees. Most of this is moisture - the longer the roast and the darker the coffee, the greater the moisture loss. With extra fast roasting there may be a 2 per cent variation in moisture loss and 0.6 per cent variation to loss of physical bean mass which includes gas, volatiles, fat and aroma. Since the weight loss varies by the amount of water used in cooling between 3.5 per cent and 6 per cent, depending on the roaster and the country, the whole topic of weight loss is one of considerable confusion.

An open pan roaster with a
fold-up handle for ease of carrying.
Turkey - 19th century.

THE FLAVOUR COMPONENTS OF COFFEE AND HOW THEY VARY WITH CHANGES IN ROASTING TIME

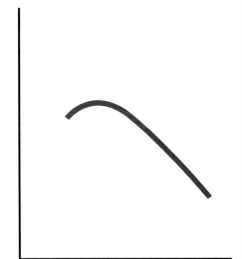

ACIDITY Acidity develops and then diminishes as the coffee becomes darker.

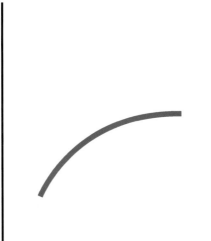

BODY The body of the brew increases as the coffee becomes darker.

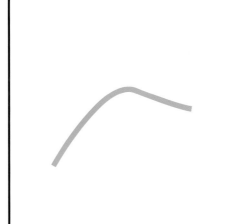

AROMA The aroma reaches a peak during the roasting and then diminishes.

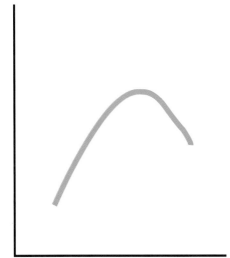

FLAVOUR The flavour or character of the coffee reaches a peak and then diminishes.

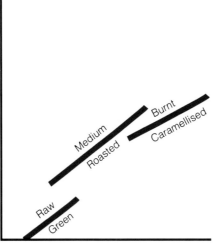

THE BASIC COFFEE FLAVOUR varies with the type of coffee. A robusta might be woody while a Kenya might have a good coffee base.

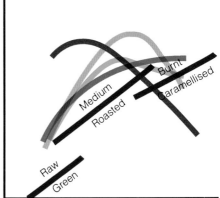

FLAVOUR PROFILE The composite picture of the components is a profile showing the development of the coffee bean during the roasting process and how, for each time of roasting, there is a different combination.

The raw bean loses moisture in the initial stages and then becomes yellow, changing to light brown, until the final brown is achieved. In the final stages, the flavour does not abruptly become caramelised but is a combination of the character of the bean and the burnt bean.

For each flavour component there will be a different graph according to the amount of roasting heat and the type of roaster. This means that each type of bean will give a different final result depending on the combination of graphs.

The final result of roasting a bean is the combination of the flavour and aroma plus the basic coffee flavour at a particular time of the roasting. This can be understood by imagining that the flavour is almond and this is added to the basic coffee flavour which varies with each bean.

A Costa Rica bean has an almondy characteristic when the coffee is lightly roasted. As the coffee becomes darker, so the almondy characteristic diminishes until it finally becomes non-existent and the burnt flavour of the caramelised bean dominates.

Because a filtered coffee is more dilute than an espresso coffee, it is possible to use a lighter roasted, more acidic bean. An espresso coffee is more concentrated and requires a darker roast to reduce the acidity and to swell the beans more to allow the water to penetrate better. Darker roasts may be used for filtered coffee but lighter roasts are not suitable for espresso coffee.

It is impossible to know what the best final colour is for a coffee without trying it in the roasting machine you intend to use. Only the general characteristics can be determined in a sample roaster.

HISTORY OF COFFEE ROASTING

The first coffee roasting equipment for coffee beans used in the Middle East, where processing began, was the open metal pan. This was very suitable for the heat coming from a small fire, but not for the high flames generated in European cooking fires. In Europe, the rotating closed metal drum seems to have been used from the first days of coffee roasting, to avoid the scorching heat of the high flames. In addition, the sealed drum was needed to trap the aroma and to prevent the flavour of the flame from permeating the roasting coffee. It is still used, domestically, in less developed parts of present-day Europe. Equipment made of many different materials has been used from time to time, including clay dishes and glass bottles.

The ideas of what constituted properly roasted coffee varied enormously and roasters employed techniques which were almost an art form. Although the French thought the coffee should be a certain colour, the operator did not need to look at the coffee - he could judge it by merely smelling for the characteristic aroma around the coffee roaster. That was if the wind was blowing in the right direction.

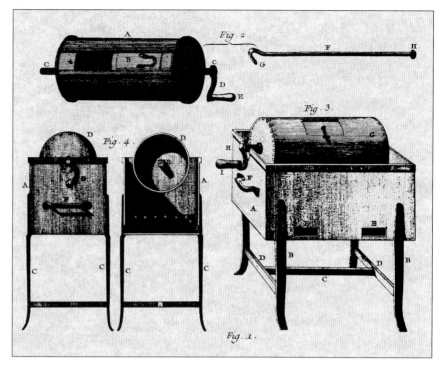

Coffee roasting in France - 1775.

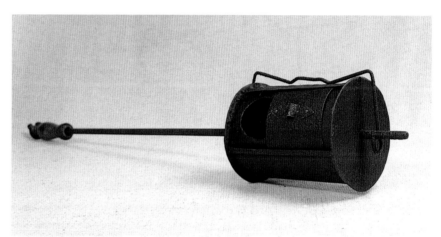

An early drum roaster to be hung over the stove.

An old roaster. Italy - early 1800s.

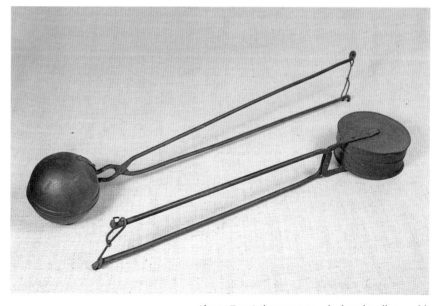

Left: A sliding-lid roaster. Sweden - mid 19th century.

Above: Two Italian roasters - the long handles would have allowed a quick release of the roasted beans without burning hands. Italy - mid 19th century.

THE RELATIONSHIPS BETWEEN THE TEMPERATURE OF THE ROASTING AIR, THE LENGTH OF ROASTING TIME AND THE QUALITY OF THE ROASTED COFFEE

THE COMBINATION OF SHORTER TIME AND LOWER TEMPERATURE IS BEST TO A MINIMUM OF 3.5 MINUTES

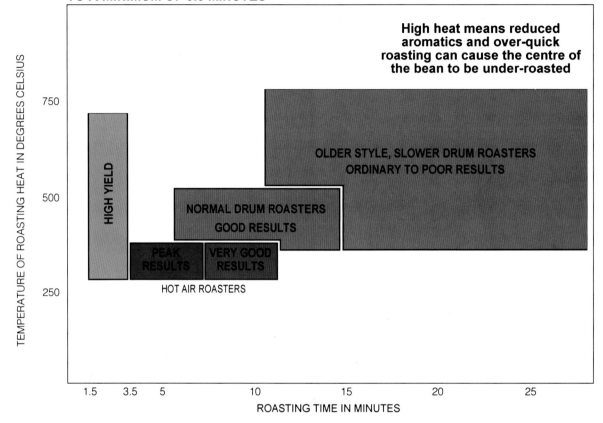

3.5 minutes seems to be the minimum time for a complete development of the acidity and flavour with Arabica coffees

Some hot air roasters operate above 320 degrees Celsius

Chart key

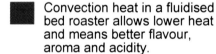

High yield is possible with high heat in a drum roaster.
High yield coffee tends to be greenish and underdeveloped.

Convection heat in a fluidised bed roaster allows lower heat and means better flavour, aroma and acidity.

Older style drum roaster with conductive heat means poor heat transfer.

The temperature of the roasting air must be above the minimum final temperature of the beans.

Drum roaster with combination of conductive and convection heat means better heat transfer, lower temperature possible.

For the same degree of roast, extended time means baked coffee which is flat with low acidity.

IDEAL ROASTING

For ideal roasting the following are necessary:

Sufficient time for the conduction of the heat to the bean and shortest possible roasting time by:
- Relative low air temperature of 260-320 degrees Celsius
- Relative high heat transfer coefficient
- A minimum roasting time not less than 3.5 minutes
- Actual roasting time as close to 3.5 minutes as possible
- Uniformity of heat transfer with good bean circulation

Cooling time should be as quick as possible with uniformity of cooling
The chart should be evaluated, keeping in mind the level of acidity desired.

All roasters are capable of adjustment to the temperature of the roasting air with consequent changes to the roasting time. A drum roaster may be used at a low temperature with increased roasting time or at a high temperature with short roasting time. It is, therefore, impossible to mark a particular spot for a roaster brand or type – only a general area within which types of roaster are normally capable of operation.

The temperature of a gas flame against a kettle may be 500 degrees Celsius while the temperature of the water inside may be only 70 degrees. A thermometer measuring the temperature of the kettle away from the flame may well show a temperature of 95 degrees. A different temperature gas flame might be possible using a thin glass beaker. Similarly, the temperature of the gas flame used in a coffee roaster may be high depending on the way in which the heat is transferred. If it is inefficient, such as through a drum with thick steel walls, a high heat will be necessary to bring the temperature of the beans up in a reasonable time. A lower heat will be possible if the hot air is introduced into a drum with thin walls. There are three temperatures referred to in coffee roasting:

ROASTER GAUGE TEMPERATURE The gauge temperature on the upper front wall of a drum roaster measures the temperature of the coffee roasting machine in that area - nothing else and certainly not the beans themselves. This temperature is only useful for knowing that the machine is ready for the coffee to be loaded and roasted in the same way as a chef waits for the oven to reach cooking temperature.

BEAN TEMPERATURE The temperature of the beans themselves during the roasting process can only be measured by a thermometer actually touching only the beans or with infra-red detectors. The final temperature will vary slightly from roaster to roaster because it is difficult to separate the temperature of the hot air around the beans from the beans themselves. The bean temperature is used for determining the final roast point, the temperature at which the beans are ready for discharge. It does not matter if the temperature varies from roaster to roaster as long as it is consistent within the roaster being used.

ROASTING AIR TEMPERATURE This is the temperature of the hot air going into the roasting drum. In general terms, a mass of coffee beans will require a higher heat to cook through, using conductive heat applied against the outer edge of the mass, than when the beans are heated individually in a hot air stream with convective heat, where they are surrounded by the hot air. The beans in the middle of a mass get hot very slowly and require a lot more heat to actually rise in temperature. It can be said that heat transfer is poor when the beans are in a drum in a mass and better when they are in a fluidised bed system. Since high heat volatilises aromatics, this means that beans can be roasted at a lower temperature heat input in fluidised bed systems with less loss of aroma than in drum roasters.

It is very important to note that the temperatures given on some of the diagrams for roasters are only indicative, especially for drum roasters of all types, because it is hard to be specific as to the exact temperature when the air comes in contact with the beans. The general theory of coffee roasting is that it is better to be gentle with the heat and to avoid heat shock as much as possible. In practice this means beginning the roast with a low temperature and raising it through the roast until the beans have swollen thoroughly and substantially crackled, then lowering the heat until the desired colour is reached, minimising aroma damage as much as possible. The final heat should be reduced so that the roasting time is extended as little as possible.

The history of coffee roasting has seen a transition from slow roasting with only conductive heat to faster roasting with a combination of conductive and convective heating as the hot air was drawn through the drum. The most recent developments are based on the exclusive use of convective heat at low temperature in fluidised bed systems.

Early Italian shop roaster. 1850s.

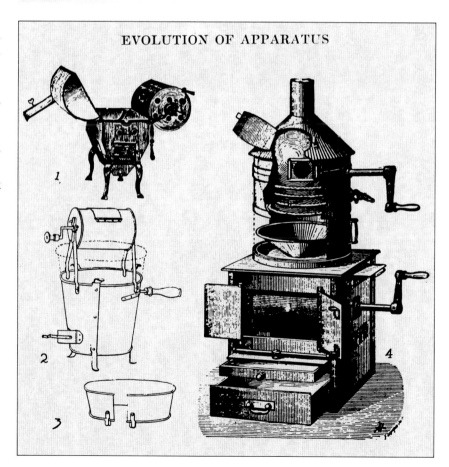

Three French roasters which showed a little more ease of use but no basic improvement in the way the coffee was roasted except for the introduction of gas heating in Postulart's 1888 roaster which gave an even and controllable heat.

COMMERCIAL ROASTING

In the beginning of the nineteenth century coffee was still roasted in small domestic and shop machines over open fires or stoves. Roasting at home was not only an aromatic treat, but it was the only way to be sure that the coffee contained nothing but coffee beans. It was a tedious job, often left to the children, so the results were variable and there was a lot of spoilt coffee. Coffee roasting requires skills, as well as a quick cooling of the coffee. There were few commercial roasters but as consumption grew so the need for more and larger roasters grew.

Daussé's French coffee roaster of 1846 was a real attempt to make coffee roasting consistent, using loss of weight as the main control. The equipment could roast two and a half kilograms, and by putting the roaster on a scale and taking away the roast loss, the dial showed just when the coffee was ready. Daussé specifically stated that Martinique coffee should have a weight loss of twenty per cent, Bourbon coffees sixteen per cent and Mocha fourteen per cent. The coffee was poured onto cold marble to cool quickly. It was not winnowed, since this would cause aroma loss. Daussé's roaster was illustrated in Rottenhofer's book in Germany in 1864 where it was included among the newest coffee machines.[1]

Daussé invented a roaster which was based on the weight loss of the beans. Beans lose up to 20% moisture during roasting - the darker the colour, the greater the weight loss. The weight loss was calculated in advance and the appropriate weight placed on the scale. When the indicator showed that the appropriate weight loss had been achieved, the roasting process could be stopped. It worked in theory, provided that a weightless hand turned the drum. France - 1846.

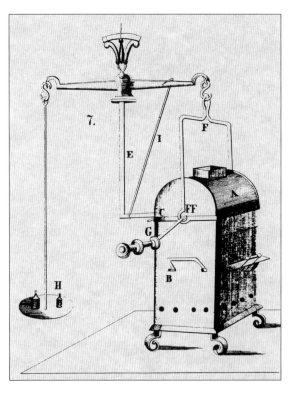

Coffee roasting in a French factory in 1886. The long vertical tube is a chute to load the coffee from the platform above. The roaster seems to be of the Carter pull-out type.

The Carter Pull-Out roaster was widely used in America for several decades after its invention. The drums were turned by belts at the back and were pulled out from the furnace when the beans were ready to be dropped. The beans were then manually stirred in cooling trays. USA - 1846.

The Burns roaster. The beans were stirred inside the drum and could be dropped out quickly for cooling. USA - 1864.

The first commercial roasters were just large cylinders. As they grew in size so did the problem of emptying the coffee out to be cooled. The American Carter Roaster of 1846 was designed to allow the whole drum to be pulled out of the roaster and the coffee cooled on the ground or in trays.

In 1864 Jabez Burns in New York invented a coffee roaster which had two real novelties. At a time when others were cooling their coffee by taking the drum away from the heat, Burns made an emptying mechanism for the coffee so that the drum did not have to be removed from the flame. In addition the drum had a double screw to ensure that the coffee beans were equally distributed inside the drum and also to allow for the beans to discharge. Burns knew the importance of speed and roast colour. In 1867 he invented a cooler, in the form of a fan under a sieve, to suck air through the coffee beans. These were the first major steps taken towards a conventional roaster which incorporated mixing vanes, cooler and the heat applied against the drum and drawn through the drum.

THE GERMAN FACTORY ROASTER

Several important factors influenced the rise of factory roasting in Germany. The first, in 1875, was the enactment of a German law forbidding the production of both raw and roasted substitute coffee beans, and their sale as coffee. While in many countries such a law would have made little difference to practice, in Germany it had real effect. The need to roast coffee beans at home in order to ensure purity disappeared with a consequent growth in the commercial coffee roasting industry.

The falsification of ground coffee came to an end in Germany in 1930. Gone were the days when a journal in Germany in 1845 which advised mothers and their daughters about coffee, recommended that the beans be washed before roasting to see if dye came out on the cloth.[2] The growth in the German coffee roasting industry was to benefit the rest of the coffee world as German ideas about quality were exported to the world's coffee markets.

German industry was producing machinery very efficiently through the last quarter of the nineteenth century and serious attempts were made to improve the technology for better roasting. The reason for German prominence probably lies in the fierce competition between roaster factories which vied with each other to make better products. Such fierce competition lasted until the Second World War when many of the smaller firms disappeared, leaving only the Probat, Barth and Gothot companies. By 1990 there were only two major companies: Probat and Neuhaus Neotec. The Germans had been very keen to make a better cup of coffee for a long time and, together with the Nordic countries, formed a huge market for quality products. Germany's

machines dominated the coffee industries of Europe for decades.

Another major component in the rise of the factory roaster was the introduction of alternative heat sources. Gas was introduced to Hannover in 1825 and Berlin in 1826 and its use was widespread in industry, being used first for coffee roasting several decades later. Where heat had formerly come from peat and coal, which imparted soot and flavour to the coffee if the roasting was done in an open cylinder, it was now possible to roast without changing the character of the coffee. Oil heating came in various forms but it too imparted taste changes to the coffee.

Electricity enabled shafts and wheels to turn without the use of long belts powered by remote steam engines and its use was not limited to electric motors. In 1903 Probat made the first electric roaster and in 1912 Gothot made a forty kilogram model. However, the high cost of electricity was a disadvantage, as was the fact that the heat could not be turned off in an instant like gas and there was little further development. Electric models were only used where there was no gas or other means of heating. The relative simplicity of enlarging the gas supply as against enlarging the electricity supply would have been a great advantage for gas. These changes to roasting technology were not universal because gas and electricity were not available everywhere. In spite of arguments as to whether the coffee tasted better, electric roasters were destined to play a minor role as small shop roasters.

SPHERICAL ROASTERS

There were many different spherical coffee roasters manufactured in France during the nineteenth century. Some sources date these from the 1840s. In 1851 at the World Exhibition the Austrian Max Bode introduced the spherical coffee roaster which applied a uniform heat to the beans with a consequent uniformity of roasting and colour. This innovation was very popular and much copied.[3] It may have been copied from American Thomas Wood's spherical coffee roaster of 1849.

In 1870 the Emmerich spherical coffee roaster, with perforations and an exhauster, was made for the first time and was extremely successful. It was invented by Alexius van Gülpen of Emmerich, a town on the Dutch-German border. Thirty-one roasters were made in the first five years, but sales rose to 333 in 1878. The first roasters used coal while gas models were introduced in 1880.[4]

The Fraser Company of New York in 1881 and Jabez Burns & Company (USA), in 1882, pursued the ideas of roasting the coffee with hot air and taking away the gases quickly to prevent the beans burning on the walls of the roaster. These companies had an agent, J. Lefeldt in Hamburg, so it was not long before the German industry further developed the idea.

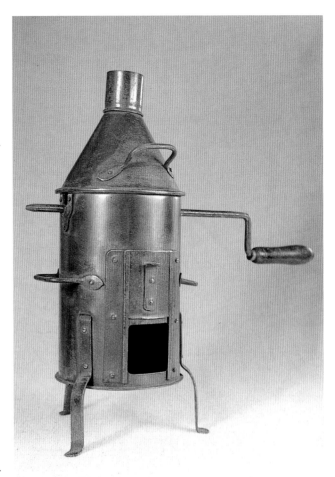

Shop roaster. France - mid 19th century.

Shop roaster. Germany - mid 19th century.

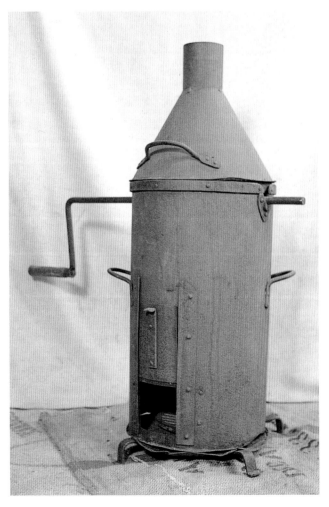

Shop roaster with removable drum. The drum was swung out when the beans were ready to be dropped and cooled. France - 1850s.

Mottant made a gas spherical roaster. The shape meant a more even distribution of heat. France - 1890.

Van Gülpen, in 1884, introduced an exhauster to draw the hot air through the holed walls of the drum or through the drum from one end to the other. He continued with developments of cylinder coffee roasters and among his inventions were a circular fan to deliver fresh air to the beans while roasting and a mixer which came from within the drum and emptied the beans onto the cooler. The introduction of the fan was the biggest change in coffee roaster design. From being a closed cylinder designed to keep the air out, the roaster now introduced the air in combination with gas.

The Ets. Legrain French gas coffee roaster won a prize at the 1894 St. Louis Fair. Note the groove in the wheel indicating that it was driven by an electric motor.

Until 1906 Van Gülpen was in partnership with Lensing and von Gimborn, and they formed the Emmerich Machine Factory. By 1883 this Company alone had sold 25,000 coffee roasting machines and it continued, as the famous Probat Company, to sell even more. The Probat Company took its name from one of its models which used gas as the heating medium.

SALOMON AND HOT AIR MECHANICAL QUICK ROASTING

It was Carl Salomon of Braunschweig in Germany who made the real breakthrough from 1889 to 1892.[5] Salomon introduced the principle of hot gas ventilation and with it quick roasting.[6] With German precision, Salomon determined the number of revolutions needed per minute so that the beans would tumble off the wall into the hot air stream being blown into the roaster. Previous roasters suffered from the fact that the beans on the walls of the drum tended to stay there if the drum turned too quickly or stayed at the bottom of the drum if it turned too slowly and hence the coffees were unevenly roasted. With the Salomon process, which used hotter air than normal, the temperature of the beans could be measured accurately and samples taken and the beans dropped out in a few seconds to be cooled quickly. Salomon certainly was not the first to use gas to roast coffee but his process removed the need to use heating oil and other smelly combustibles. To this day, there are still coffee roasters who use specially selected woods to give special flavours to the coffee. Some wood-roasted coffees are less bitter in espresso machines, probably due to the fact that the coffees roast very slowly and have reduced acidity through a baking rather than a roasting process.

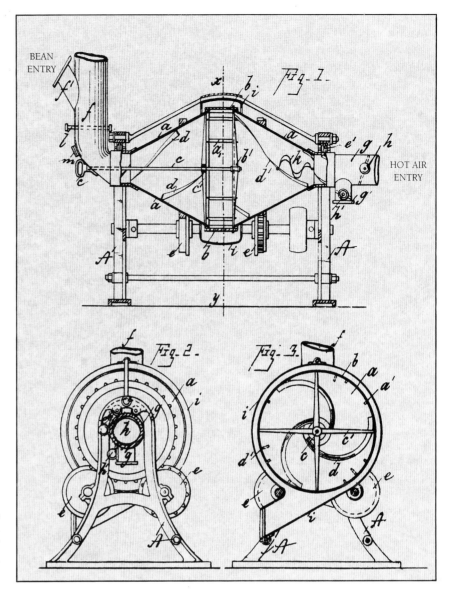

Carl Salomon's FAST coffee roaster was considered by contemporaries to be best roaster of its time. It was the first of a new type of roaster which was to be popular for the next century. The hot air was drawn through the roaster drum and the beans were thoroughly mixed. Salomon's roaster was not commercially successful. He tried to license it rather than sell it and other larger companies made similar models. Germany - 1889.

Max Thurmer's gas roaster could roast coffee in three and a half minutes which was exceedingly fast for the period. It does not appear to have been widely used. Germany - 1891-3.

Salomon tried to exploit his process by licensing users but his machine was too lightly constructed. Other manufacturers made improvements and soon Barth, Gothot and the Emmerich Machine Factory had models using similar processes with different designs. Most of the coffee roasters for the next hundred years would employ some variation of using hot air. There would be two basic types of conventional coffee roasters using heat under the drum and sucked through holes at the end of the drum, or using hot air blown directly into the drum. These technical developments meant that the commercial processes were diverging from domestic equipment which was still using heat directly against the drum or wall of the roaster with all the attendant problems of scorching through slow turning. Coffee roasted at home was becoming inferior to that roasted in a factory.

In 1892 the Emmerich Company, before it became the Probat Company, invented a coffee roaster with a naked gas flame in the roaster. This was similar to the Tupholme or Whitmee English roaster. A century later Probat was to be the largest coffee roasting machine factory in Europe. By the year 1900 Probat alone had sold 50,000 commercial roasters. As more commercial roasters were introduced there were proportionately fewer home roasters. These still exist today, but new models are extremely hard to find.

A model to roast 50 to 70 kilograms per charge. Note the small wheel at the bottom left which could be connected to a belt and pulley system.

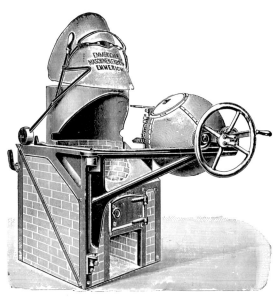

A global roaster set over a brick oven with capacity 30 to 100 kilograms per charge. The roasting chamber rolled out on a track.

The Emmerich Maschinenfabrik in Germany was one of the foremost manufacturers of coffee roasting equipment. Every one of the machines shown here was available in the 1907 catalogue for the Belgian market. What is surprising is the wide range of models, the most simple being almost identical to the earliest models of the 1870s and the most modern utilising an electric motor and gas. They depict the progression from manual spherical roasters of the 1870s through motorised spherical roasters, manual and motorised drum gas roasters to gas and electric drum roasters of 1907 incorporating husk catching cyclones. By 1907 the company had sold more than 65 000 coffee roasters. It is interesting to note that the catalogue specifically said that all Rapid roasters sold by other companies worked on exactly the same principle as the Emmerich roasters.

A small model global roaster to roast a charge of 3 to 10 kilograms at a time.

A larger model to roast 13 to 23 kilograms per charge.

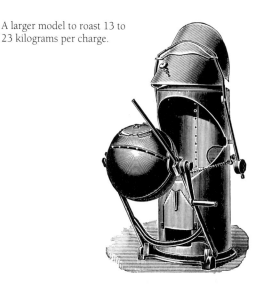

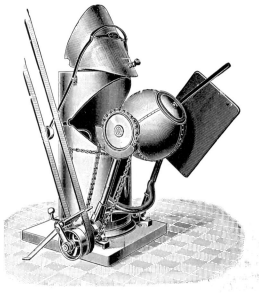

A global roaster with capacity 13 to 70 kilograms came in manual or motorised versions.

SOME ILLUSTRATIONS FROM THE 1907 CATALOGUE OF COFFEE ROASTERS FROM THE EMMERICH MASCHINENFABRIK - GERMANY.

Left: A small shop model to roast 2.5 kilograms per charge or 12 kilograms per hour. It was heated by gas and operated by a pulley. The round cylinder at the back was a cyclone to collect the husks which separated from the coffee as the beans swelled. The husks would have been previously separated by using a winnowing technique or blowing them away.

Above: A manual gas roaster to roast up to 2 kilograms per charge.

Top and Above: A global roaster set over a brick oven with capacity 30 to 100 kilograms. The roasting chamber was lifted out with the aid of a lever. It came in both hand and pulley models.

Left: Rapid Roaster. The Perfekt model came in various sizes to roast from 5 to 30 kilograms. The pulley turned the roasting drum and the cooling tray and a pump which drew hot air through the coffee and cool air tray. The drum was heated by gas. The cooling tray was emptied automatically by the brushes which stirred the coffee. The features of this roaster have become sophisticated but are basically used in all modern gas and electric roasters. While no such thing as a standard roaster ever existed, most roasters in the twentieth century used a combination of heat or flame against the drum which was then drawn through the drum by a fan which deposited the husks in a cyclone.

The first gas model roasted 5 to 20 kilograms per charge and was either manual or pulley operated. The coffee fell into the perforated tray underneath where it was cooled by agitating the coffee from side to side and allowing the air to circulate.

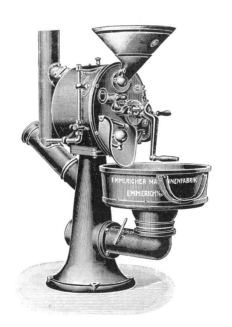

The Perfekt roaster also came in a manual model in which the drum was turned by hand.

Above: A bigger and later version of the Perfekt was the Probat which roasted 15 to 75 kilograms per charge. It was a gas heated model with an electric motor shown connected to the pulleys. The cyclone is shown in front of the roasting drum. The Probat was very popular at the turn of the century. The combination of electric motor, gas heating, a drum which mixed the coffee, a cooling tray and a cyclone were the standard features of most twentieth century coffee roasters. There were many different brands of roasters made in many countries which roasted the coffee like this, from small shop roasters to large factory machines. Germany -1907.

Right: Coolers were simple and operated by shaking the coffee which provided aeration.

A destoning machine. The beans, on account of their lighter density, were vacuumed up and separated from the stones which remained at the bottom.

Small Gülphen gas roaster. The blower C is used to blow hot air through the drum and to cool the beans. Germany - c.1920.

196

A lot of roasting equipment, even though it was specifically designed for coffee, was being made for the ersatz coffee industry, which had been legitimised. It was selling malt as malt and not as coffee. As late as 1913, when Germany was very advanced economically and had a high standard of living, the total production of ersatz coffee which included malt, rye, wheat, chicory, figs and other substances was 194,500 tonnes. This was much more than the figure for coffee at 134,394 tonnes and this for a population of nearly 68 million.[7]

A small Villedieu roaster which used a wind-up spring mechanism to turn the drum which was heated by a spirit burner. Le Havre, France -1900s.

Above: The Excelsa electric roaster by Farina. Lecco, Italy - 1930s.

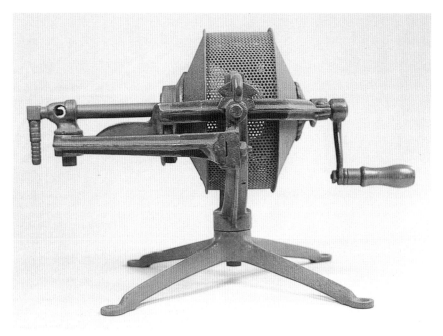

Above: Gas hand sample roaster. A small gas roaster with perforated walls. England - 1900.

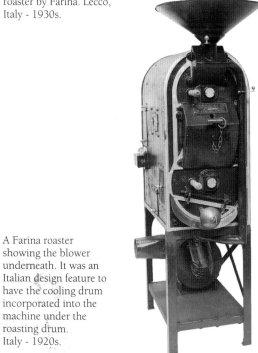

A Farina roaster showing the blower underneath. It was an Italian design feature to have the cooling drum incorporated into the machine under the roasting drum. Italy - 1920s.

The Farina hand model for use with denatured spirit roasted from 1.5 to 6 kilograms at a time. Italy - 1920s.

The Impera electric shop roaster made by Farina. Many attempts were made to develop electric roasters from the early 1900s. The high cost of electricity compared to gas was a drawback. Most electric roasters looked the same as their gas counterparts. One problem was that an electric element was slow to heat up and to cool, making temperature control a problem compared to gas which was much more responsive. Lecco, Italy -1930s.

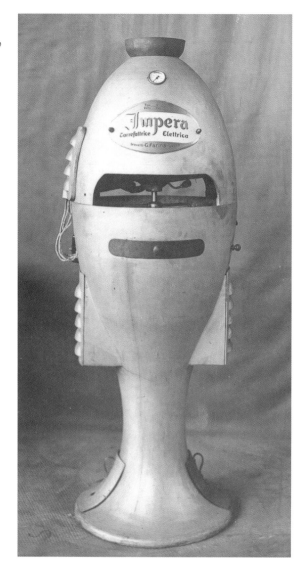

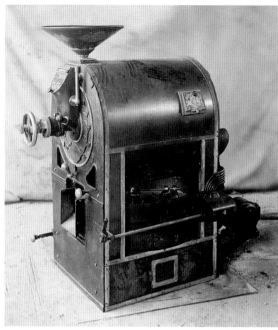

Kirsch und Mauser 10 kilogram gas model with open cooler underneath. Germany -1920s.

The Whitmee shop roaster used a perforated drum. England - 1930s.

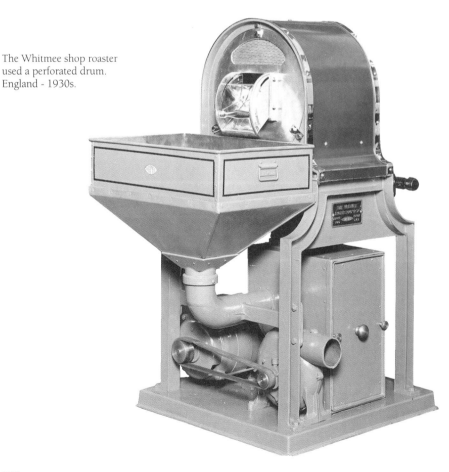

A Vittoria coke-heated roaster. The door for the oven is open. The drum was turned by the electric motor under the cooling tray. Italy -1920s.

A Probat 5 kilogram shop gas roaster. Germany - 1930s.

The Probat sample roaster generally had four barrels and roasted with gas. The barrels had openings so that the coffee could be sampled with a spoon and when ready, the barrels tipped the coffee into the cooling trays as on the right.
Germany - 1920s.

The UNO electric sample roaster was also used in small retail shops. England - 1930s.

The UNO gas roaster had the flame inside the perforated drum. For some reason the English seem to have persisted with the perforated drum roaster longer than other countries. England - 1920s.

The UNO Coffee Roaster came in small models. The smoke was exhausted into the shop and blown into the street with a fan. England - 1930s.

Above: Whitmee gas roaster for use in small shops or for sample roasting. England -1930s.

Right: UNO Infra-red roaster.'Roasted by infra-red radiant electric heat is a powerful attraction to the public'. England - 1950s.

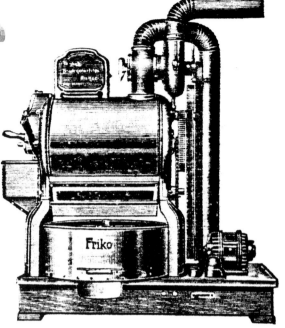

The Friko shop roaster. Germany - 1927.

Above: The Record quick *Kugel* ball roaster by Martin Falland. Germany - 1920s.

The Royal Coffee Roaster with a 25 pound charge had a perforated drum and was widely used in the USA during the 1920s.

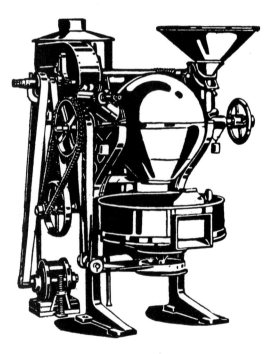

A small BARTH roaster. Hot air was drawn directly into the drum without the flame touching the walls of the drum or the beans. Many coffee roasters liked this system very much because it avoided the beans touching the hot walls of the drum. Germany - 1920s.

The introduction of low pressure gas burners in 1925 and the subsequent increase in heat enabled the capacity of coffee roasting machines to rise from 60 kilograms per charge to 240. Around this time the last electric roasters appeared on the German market. The German market produced two basic types of roaster - the "Quickroaster' which used direct and indirect heat and the 'Kugel' (ball) roaster which used indirect heat.[8]

Jabez Burns & Sons Incorporated was still a major manufacturer in the United States, making very large coffee roasters for a market which seemed to have a few large coffee companies, in comparison to Europe, which had many small companies. In 1914 Jabez Burns introduced the Jubilee Roaster in which the coffee did not come into contact with the flame - a direct gas flame in the roasting chamber was covered by a hood which prevented the beans from coming into contact with the flame which roasted the coffee at around 1100 degrees Celsius for 18 to 20 minutes.

In 1935 Jabez Burns introduced the Thermalo process. It was a major change - a large volume of hot air was blown at high velocity through the roasting drum which was still turned mechanically. The advantage was that the air could be at a lower temperature of around 550 degrees Celsius for 15 to 18 minutes which was beneficial for the flavour. Lower temperatures are generally considered better for cooking any food because less of the aromatics go up the chimney. The high speed of the air was thought to blow away an insulating air barrier around the bean. This idea was not dissimilar to the idea of fluidised bed roasters which were thought to blow away the moisture layer coming from the inside of the bean. In a major advance in 1942 Jabez Burns introduced a continuous version in which the beans were moved mechanically through a perforated drum with a rotating spiral at a temperature of 250 degrees Celsius for five minutes.

The conventional coffee roaster is operated by combining the mechanical movement of the beans with a hot air stream. All conventional coffee roasting machines can be classified according to whether the drum is single or double-walled or even perforated, whether the heat is direct or indirect against the drum, or hot air direct into the drum, or even a flame in the drum. Every manufacturer claims an advantage for a particular combination but most roasters consider indirect heat the best.

A Samiac shop roaster with husk catcher cyclone at back. France - 1990.

DOMESTIC ROASTERS

Five roasters designed for sitting on a stove. Roasting at home was very popular all over Europe. The practice began to decline at the end of the nineteenth century and was practically extinct by the 1940s.

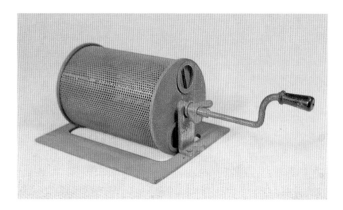

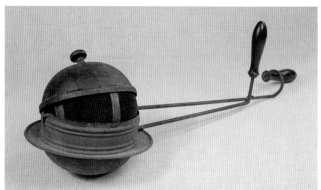

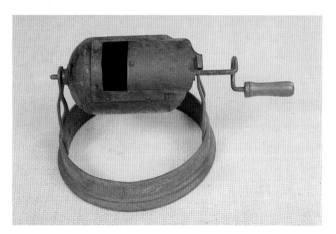

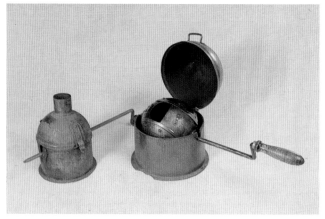

Roaster. France - mid 19th century.

HEM

HEM

Left and Right: Two electric roasters. Germany - 1930s.

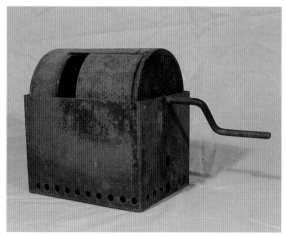

Small gas roaster. Possibly Italian - 1900s.

DOMESTIC ROASTERS

Domestic roasters were still being manufactured but with little innovation. Their design was changing to reflect the way that domestic fuel stoves were being designed, with removable rings on top to allow the insertion of roasters of different diameters into the stove. All had a stirring mechanism and were either ball-shaped, cylindrical, or dish-shaped.

At the end of the nineteenth century gas heating was incorporated into the machine but there was no basic change in the way the product was treated. The heat was directed onto the drum. A few electric roasters were invented but they are very rare. Except for one French model which worked on a clockwork spring, they were turned by hand. There have been several models using the fluidised bed process but they have been of minor importance.

HOT AIR NON-MECHANICAL ROASTERS
The Fluidised Bed Roaster

It was a well known principle that products could be heated using a fluidised bed - a stream of very hot air which heated at the same time as it elevated the coffee beans. The word fluidising in this sense means changing the beans from being in a dense solid mass supported by each other to a bed of beans separated by air and floating. If there is sufficient fluidising, the beans rise in the air and tumble. If there is too much air, the beans will fly out of the roasting chamber. The high pressure and high flow of the hot air were sufficient to eliminate the need for mechanical movement of the beans.

The first German patent for this type of roaster was produced by Caasen in 1926. Later an electrically heated, fluidised bed roaster appeared for use in a shop window - possibly based on Caasen's patent. It was the first commercial roaster of the new type to be produced anywhere in the world and was the beginning of a new era in roasting.

In 1954 the Lurgi Company of Frankfurt, Germany, invented the Aerotherm coffee roaster. Coffee roasted like this is considered to have a pure flavour as the husks are blown out and not burnt, hence there is less smoke in the roasting chamber. In a conventional roaster the husks are separated from the beans in the drum and often catch alight and create a smoky atmosphere. The fact that the beans are elevated also means that the convection heat acts on the bean more effectively and evenly. There was a limit in the Lurgi design to the speed of the air because if it was too high the beans were blown out of the roasting chamber. As the beans became darker, they lost moisture and swelled and their density became much less. This meant that it was a difficult method to control if the velocity of the hot air stayed the same. Any process involving blowing the beans straight up in the air involves the risk of not fluidising the beans and causing them to burn. It can even cause a fire, because the same velocity of air is capable, later in the roast, of blowing the beans out of the roasting chamber. It is therefore necessary to strike a balance in the velocity of the air. The heat was 240 to 270 degrees Celsius and the roasting time five minutes for a charge of sixty kilograms. The main disadvantages of the Lurgi roaster seem to have been the lack of capacity in a market which required ever larger production and the high energy cost associated with the large volume of air which was used once and not recirculated.

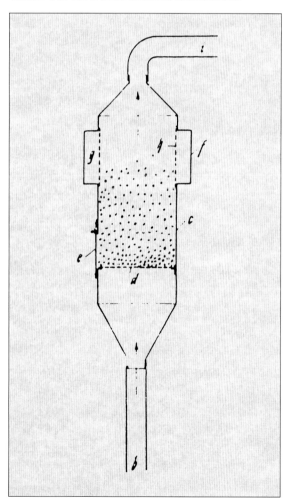

The Caasen patent for a hot-air roaster. The hot air was blown up from below and lifted the coffee beans, which were on a sieve, into the air. It is unlikely that this patent worked in this form unless the bed of coffee on the sieve was very thin. Germany - 1926.

The Lurgi Aerotherm roaster lifted the beans into the air. There was no sieve. The basic idea was very good and produced a good clean tasting coffee. There were several factory installations but none for shops. Germany -1957.

TYPES OF HOT AIR ROASTERS

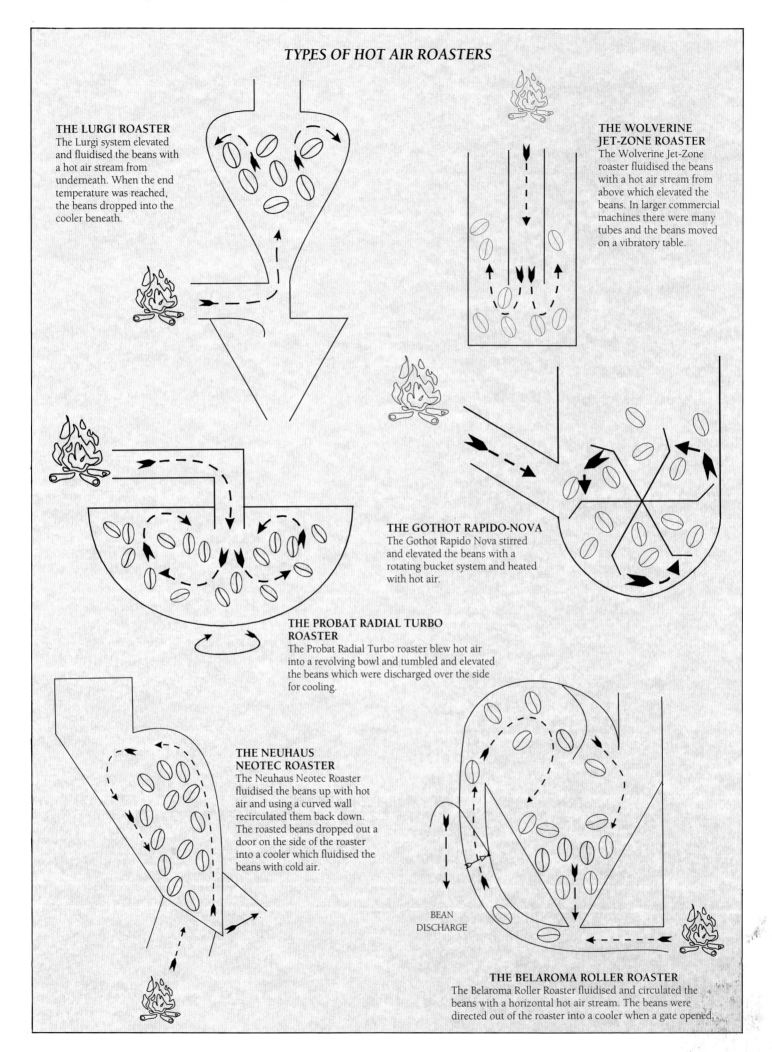

THE LURGI ROASTER
The Lurgi system elevated and fluidised the beans with a hot air stream from underneath. When the end temperature was reached, the beans dropped into the cooler beneath.

THE WOLVERINE JET-ZONE ROASTER
The Wolverine Jet-Zone roaster fluidised the beans with a hot air stream from above which elevated the beans. In larger commercial machines there were many tubes and the beans moved on a vibratory table.

THE GOTHOT RAPIDO-NOVA
The Gothot Rapido Nova stirred and elevated the beans with a rotating bucket system and heated with hot air.

THE PROBAT RADIAL TURBO ROASTER
The Probat Radial Turbo roaster blew hot air into a revolving bowl and tumbled and elevated the beans which were discharged over the side for cooling.

THE NEUHAUS NEOTEC ROASTER
The Neuhaus Neotec Roaster fluidised the beans up with hot air and using a curved wall recirculated them back down. The roasted beans dropped out a door on the side of the roaster into a cooler which fluidised the beans with cold air.

BEAN DISCHARGE

THE BELAROMA ROLLER ROASTER
The Belaroma Roller Roaster fluidised and circulated the beans with a horizontal hot air stream. The beans were directed out of the roaster into a cooler when a gate opened.

A fluidised bed roaster, probably based on Caasen's patent. The roaster was a shop window model probably from the 1930s in Germany. Since a photo exists, it must have been manufactured. It appears to be the first fluidised bed coffee roaster ever made. The coffee was roasted and cooled in the same chamber which meant slow cooling which was not good for the coffee.

The Wolverine Jet Zone roaster shop model took thirty minutes to warm up and be ready for roasting and was very large and heavy for its very small capacity. The illustration shows the small bean loading chute and the wire cage surrounding the glass roasting chamber. USA -1980s.

The increased effectiveness of convection heat enabled fluidised bed or hot air roasters to operate at a much lower air temperature than the conventional roasters and this was also considered to result in a better, cleaner flavoured coffee. Gothot introduced a roaster, the Rapido Nova, which used a bucket wheel to throw the beans into the hot air. In a sense it was a mechanical fluidised bed. The Wolverine Jet Zone Roaster was developed in the United States and the shop model operated by blowing hot air down onto the beans which were in a glass container, and elevating them. It was capable of roasting high yield coffee - swollen beans with lower weight loss and better flavour extraction. This happened when the beans were roasted very quickly - in less than three minutes. The fast roast was particularly favoured because the short roasting time preserved what little acidity existed in Robusta coffees. This enabled Robusta coffees to be used extensively in blends and because they were cheaper, considerable savings accrued to the roasters.

In 1976 Michael Sivetz of Corvallis, Oregon, invented a fluidised bed roaster in which the hot air was directed through a sieve so as to lift the beans up one straight wall of the roasting chamber. He developed this roaster with the idea of supplying the retail gourmet coffee market with a roaster with a six to twelve minute roasting time.

The Neuhaus Neotec Rotation Fluid Bed Roaster was based on the Sivetz patent and was developed from 1979. It used the idea of hot air at a maximum temperature of 315 degrees Celsius to roast quantities as large as 150 kilograms in a batch in a very short time, as little as 100 seconds and up to 8 minutes, so that the roaster had an hourly capacity of 3000 kilograms. It solved the problem of very high velocity air blowing the beans out of the chamber by redirecting the beans downwards, changing the straight wall of the Sivetz patent to a straight wall with a curve at the upper end. The Neotec roasters were combined with a cooling system using the same type of fluidised bed chamber so that the beans were cooled very quickly. The faster coffee is roasted in conventional drum roasters, the less likely the beans are to be the same colour in the centre as on the outside. Fluidised bed roasters overcome this problem easily.

Several coffee roaster manufacturers are adapting their conventionally designed drum roasters to roast in a short time by increasing the temperature and lowering the weight of the charge. They do not achieve the same flavour as the low temperature fluidised bed systems because the beans are still in a mass and have poor heat transfer, requiring a hotter temperature to compensate.

Coffee roasting machines which roast the coffee in exceedingly short times do not always do so to the benefit of the flavour of the coffee. The limit seems to be about three and a half minutes for good quality Arabica coffees and two and a half minutes for Robusta coffees. Short roasting times mean a greater volume of coffee, lower roasting

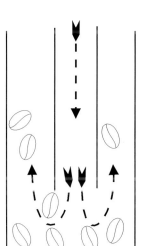

The Wolverine Jet Zone Roaster principle was used both in shop and factory models. USA - 1963.

The Gothot Rapido Nova stirred and elevated the beans with a rotating bucket system and heated with hot air.

weight loss, more extracts and free acids in the cup, but in many cases an inferior cup of coffee because the fine flavours have not had time to develop.[9] The introduction of recirculated hot air, well known in conventional coffee roasters, means a lower energy cost. The lower weight loss meant a reduced cost of production and an irresistible lure for coffee roasters. The dream of the coffee roasting industry had finally come true. The use of recirculation enabled one large German coffee roaster to achieve a reduction of gas usage of eighty-one per cent between 1980 and 1990.

The hot air principle was applied in both small domestic coffee roasters and also in small shop roasters where show was very important. These were mostly manufactured in Germany at a very high price. Although they roasted the coffee well they did not display the coffee clearly during the process because there was no light in the roasting chamber. Some German and Japanese machines were made in which the coffee was roasted in a glass tube and blown up vertically.

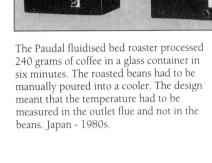

The Paudal fluidised bed roaster processed 240 grams of coffee in a glass container in six minutes. The roasted beans had to be manually poured into a cooler. The design meant that the temperature had to be measured in the outlet flue and not in the beans. Japan - 1980s.

The Neuhaus Neotec Rotation Fluid Bed Roaster was designed to roast large quantities of coffee very quickly - from 100 seconds to eight minutes per charge. The roasting chamber design solved the problem of large amounts of hot air blowing the beans out through the top. The hot air elevated the beans along the vertical wall while the beans on the diagonal wall fell into the air stream. There were shop models as well as large factory installations. The Neotec system was the first very successful fluidised bed roaster which became widely used in industry. It used recirculated air which brought major cost savings. Germany - 1980s.

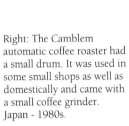

Right: The Camblem automatic coffee roaster had a small drum. It was used in some small shops as well as domestically and came with a small coffee grinder. Japan - 1980s.

Above: The Moda. A small electric fluidised bed roaster. In spite of their ease of use, these roasters were never widely used in the home. The quantities roasted were tiny. Hong Kong - 1980s.

Left: A domestic roaster for putting on a stove. The drum was turned by a small electric motor. Italy - 1990.

206

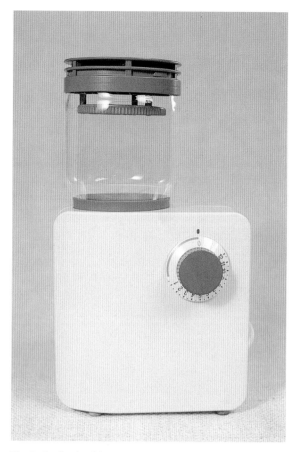

The Ender fluidised bed roaster for domestic use.
Germany - 1989.

The Belaroma Roller Roaster. This electric shop
model could roast 3 kilograms very quickly with
very little smoke. It was a fluidised bed roaster
using horizontal air flow to elevate the beans.
Australia - 1990.

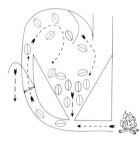

The Belaroma Roller Roaster
principle could also be used
in commercial roasters with
excellent results. Less air was
required to elevate the beans
and the roaster was very
compact compared to the
Neotec machines which
could be as high as eight
metres in large industrial
installations.

In 1990 in Australia, the Belaroma Roller Roaster was patented by Ian Bersten of Sydney and developed by Don Ebert of Brisbane, with the specific aim of allowing the consumer to see the colour changes in the beans as they roasted. This was achieved by having the beans visible throughout the roast, illuminated by a light in the roasting chamber. With a roasting air temperature of 260 degrees Celsius it was possible to roast half a kilogram (a pound) of coffee directly in front of the customer in under four minutes. It was no longer necessary for a shop to buy coffee in anticipation of orders - the coffee could be roasted to order automatically and accurately in a roaster with a blower and one moving part. The end temperature was measured by a thermocouple sitting in the beans. The same principle was applicable to larger industrial roasters. Conventional hot air roasters elevated the beans with a high pressure air stream from below. The Roller Roaster used a lower pressure horizontal air flow to lift the beans, combined with a secondary heating of the beans as they fell into the air stream. The horizontal air stream solved the problem of a fluidised bed roaster requiring a fixed amount of coffee in the chamber - the beans did not blow out the top nor fail to elevate when different quantities were roasted.

One of the major advantages of the fluidised bed coffee roasters was the possibility of using thermal sensors to measure the bean temperature very accurately and control the whole process with computers to produce consistently roasted coffee.

The most sophisticated conventional roasters also do this.

CONTINUOUS ROASTERS

Continuous roasters were first offered by the American company Burns in 1940 with the Thermalo model. Probat followed in 1980 and Neuhaus Neotec with a continuous fluidised bed roaster in 1985 and a continuous drum-type roaster in 1987. The main difference between conventional roasters and continuous roasters is the low temperature and high velocity of the heating air, resulting in short-time roasting, as little as ninety seconds and 5,443 kilograms per hour output in the largest Burns model.

NEW TYPES OF COFFEE

The Neuhaus Neotec Rotation Fluid Bed Roaster and the Belaroma Roller Roaster were both based on using heat transfer with forced convection which allows a lower air temperature of between 260 and 315 degrees Celsius to be used. The vapour from the heating bean is blown away from the surface of the bean which enables the incoming heat to be more effective. The faster the coffee is roasted, the greater is the fat content and, since the aroma sticks to the fat molecules, a coffee with strong aroma is produced.

HIGH YIELD It is possible with very fast roasting (around 100 seconds) to have puffy, swollen beans with the consequence that the greater porosity allows better water penetration and more efficient extraction of volatile and non-volatile compounds into the cup. This means that less coffee per cup can be used. This style of coffee is called high yield coffee. It is of course vital that the colour of the bean should be the same on the surface as in the centre, but fast roasting produces beans which are very different to conventionally roasted beans. If coffee roasting is too fast, the coffee may not be roasted evenly through the bean which means that the coffee may be fully roasted on the surface and under-roasted in the centre, with consequent grassy and acidic flavours. High yield roasting did not achieve general consumer acceptance.

PEAK ROASTING When the coffee is roasted around four to five minutes at a low temperature, the fat level increases, binding with the aromatics and this is coffee at its best. It is the low temperature which is most important.

JAPANESE CHARCOAL ROASTING In Japan charcoal roasted coffee is quite popular. A shelf of burning charcoal is placed under the roaster drum and the smoke drawn through the drum. The flavour is pleasantly smokey. Its popularity is probably connected to the positive ideas in Japan of cooking anything with charcoal.

COOLING

After the coffee has been roasted it must be cooled as quickly as possible to stop the roasting process. Many roasting machines speed up the cooling process with a water quench of around 2.5 per cent. Sometimes water quenching takes place inside the drum and sometimes in the cooling tray. Quick cooling is important and there is even the idea that a delayed water quench in the cooling results in less steam distillation of the volatile aromas from the hot bean.

GLAZING

Glazing coffee was a process to coat the coffee beans during the cooling process in order to protect them from the atmosphere. The most popular coating was sugar which caramellised on contact with the hot coffee beans. German legislation allowed seven per cent of sugar per one hundred parts of green coffee. Other coatings allowed in Germany were shellac, rosin, copal varnish and waxes. In the United States eggs were used. Glazing was not something done with the idea of deceiving the customer, but rather to protect the coffee from absorbing the many flavours which surrounded the beans, especially when sold loose and unprotected in the smaller shops.

Glazing was a process widely used in Europe and the Americas and also in Germany, where one book in 1929 devoted a whole chapter to the subject.[10] The practice seems to have died out after the Second World War except in Spain and South America.

The Neon Scolari Infrator infra-red roaster roasted one kilogram of coffee in twelve minutes. A Japanese model in the 1980s was very similar in design. The Japanese considered the coffee roasted in these machines to have special qualities. Italy - 1960s.

OTHER ROASTERS

In the 1960s the Neon Scolari Infrator Company in Milan made an infra-red ray roaster. Another roaster from Switzerland, the Elcalor, roasted the coffee under pressure with an admixture of nitrogen in the roasting chamber, which improved the quality of poor coffees. Neither type of roaster has had significant market influence. Microwave roasters have been tried, but without success because of problems from electric discharges, however experiments are continuing.

POLLUTION AND THE DEMISE OF THE SHOP ROASTER

As the size of coffee roasting factories became larger, pollution became a problem. While the smell of coffee roasting from a small roaster may be attractive, living downwind from a large factory was not everybody's dream. Once complaints were made to the local government officials, standards were set which had to be complied with. Smoke had to be released from the tops of buildings which were becoming ever higher. The same environmental rules for large factories were applied to small shop roasters and so the shop coffee roaster became an endangered species. Today, in most European countries, it has become virtually extinct.

Shop roasters were quite common all over Europe until the 1960s and even the 1970s, but the increasing efficiency of very large roaster companies also meant that the small shop roaster could not compete with the prices of the large companies. It was very much a case of small shops with high quality beans at high prices competing with large companies selling cheaper beans through supermarkets.

The standard way to remove the pollution was to use an afterburner which raised the temperature of the exhaust gases to a sufficient height to burn the smelly exhaust emission. The cost of the afterburner was high and the cost of the gas to run it was even higher than the cost of roasting the coffee. The competition between the giants made trade conditions difficult and the pollution problem made the small roaster's life difficult, if not impossible, among multi-storey buildings. This has not prevented the production of small coffee roasting machines, but has certainly limited the market. There are a few new roasters which use the fluid bed principle to roast the coffee, but the quantity roasted is generally small. There have been several fluid bed roasters for the domestic market but they have had an insignificant effect on the world coffee trade. The most recent afterburners use catalysts which burn the gases at lower temperatures. This type is more expensive to buy but cheaper to run.

FEWER COMMERCIAL MANUFACTURERS OF ROASTING MACHINES

Judging from the advertisements in the German tea and coffee trade journal (KATEKA) from 1913 to the 1930s the coffee roaster manufacturing industry must have been one of the most vigorous and competitive in the world with numerous brands and types. Roasters which had the gas flame inside the drum or heated the beans through perforated drum walls did not survive. It was not necessarily the process that was deficient but often the management of the manufacturing companies. The First World War did not seem to have had a great effect on the number of different coffee roasting companies, but the Second World War, which caused not only enormous physical damage to industrial areas but enormous personnel losses, was the death knell for many. By the 1990s only a very small number of manufacturers existed throughout the world. Germany and the United States dominated the market for large scale roasters while there were manufacturers in Italy, France, Spain, Greece and Brazil for smaller machines.

THE EVOLUTION OF COFFEE ROASTING

The evolution can be seen to have passed through several stages, each producing different coffees. They did not produce the same coffee in different ways. The evolution has been one from total use of conductive heat, through mixed conductive and convective heat to total convective heat.

BAKED COFFEE The early period up to the 1900s saw coffee roasted slowly which baked it and did not produce coffee with delicate acids and flavours intact. The coffee was flat and probably had a burnt smoky flavour from the husks which burned in the drum as well as flavours from oil and wood when they were used for heating. If the coffee did not bake in the roaster, it almost certainly baked in the cooling tray where cooling was very primitive and slow. The roasting was achieved with heat on the drum and little hot air.

STANDARD ROASTED COFFEE The second period began with fast roasting as hot air was introduced into the drum by inventions from the United States and Germany and perfected with the Salomon process in 1891. As roasting times diminished in the early twentieth century better flavour with more acidity in the cup was produced. Roasting times were generally six to fifteen minutes but up to twenty minutes. The roasting was achieved by a combination of heat on the drum and hot air. Cooling times were reduced greatly with the introduction of stirrers and fans to draw cold air through the coffee.

PEAK COFFEE was achieved when low temperature air was used to roast coffee in a short time in a fluidised bed. The first successful machine was the Lurgi in 1954. The Neotec and Belaroma Roller Roasters, in the 1980s and 1990s respectively, achieved the same effect with different shaped roasting chambers.

SOME JAPANESE ROASTERS FROM THE 1980S AND 1990S.

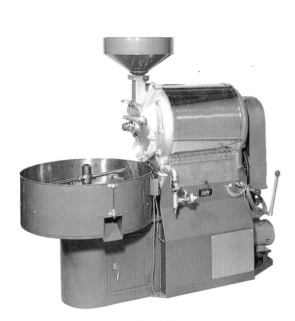

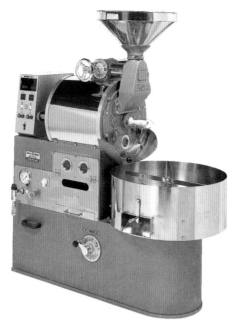

The Lucky Coffee Machine gas roaster had a capacity of 7.5 kgs and was modelled on the American Royal roaster of the 1920s with a flame against the drum.

The Fuji Royal 3 kg gas roaster was very well engineered.

The KSK infra-red roaster was closely modelled on the Italian Neon Scolari model.

The Paudal hot-air roaster had a capacity of 2 kgs. Temperature control was achieved with a probe, not in the beans, but in the hot air exhaust. There was a similar 600 gram model.

The Arakawa Jetroast was based on the Wolverine Jet-zone system.

The Bonmac electric roaster had a capacity of 2 kgs. The coffee was roasted in a drum at the top, fell into the cooler below and then into a lower drawer compartment for removal.

C H A P T E R   1 1

Grinding - The Weak Link in the Equipment Revolution

Above: A section of the grinding disc from the Colombini Ico Perfex grinder showing the machined grooves. Turin, Italy - 1990s.

W hile there has been a lot written about coffees, coffee pots and coffee roasting, very little has been written about coffee grinders or the importance of using the correct grind of coffee for a particular machine. The first discussions were on the merits of using mortar and pestle versus grinders with handles, but no facts were used to support either case, just opinions. Ciupka, a coffee consultant from Hamburg, probably introduced the first complete discussion in 1931.[1] Foot in the United States in 1925 basically understood the problems and solutions, but he gave advice which was confusing and applied mainly to large roasters. He somehow managed to deduce that the bean released different amounts of flavour, depending which end of the bean was brewed: 'nearly the full strength is exhausted from the inferior part of the coffee [the end with the germ in it], but only a small part of the virtue from the better and harder part'. The consumer, if he had read the book, would have been none the wiser.[2] Ukers in 1935 said that, 'After a long series of carefully controlled infusion tests there has been discovered a universal or all-purpose grind meaning a ground coffee which gives equally satisfactory results with any of the common brewing methods'.[3] This is exactly what every coffee roaster wanted to hear because it meant that the market could be satisfied with one grind size instead of different grinds for different machines. However, it was incorrect - different types of coffee makers require different grinds.

There has always been an inexorable desire to make a better, stronger cup of coffee and this can only be achieved by grinding the coffee more finely and brewing it correctly. It seems probable that finely ground coffee was virtually unknown except from Turkish style grinders and mortar and pestle. Since one of the main aims was to make a clear cup of coffee, it did not make sense to use coffee so finely ground that it passed through or clogged up the finest filters. Grinding coffee very finely by hand required a lot of effort but this problem was overcome with the introduction of steam and electric power. In the 1920s the common use of better designed cutters combined with electric powered grinders made finely ground coffee widely available for the first time. The first writers possibly did not understand all the principles involved in grinding but these are at the basis of making a better grinder and a better ground coffee. It is impossible to know just what grinds of coffee were available in the early 1800s, but it seems likely that very long brewing times were needed to derive any flavour at all from the coarsely ground coffee. I have tried some grinders from the nineteenth century and it is almost impossible to get finely ground coffee from them.

Very few patents for brewers precisely indicated the required grind size, instead using such imprecise words as 'fine' or 'coarse', because most inventors simply did not understand the importance of grind size. This was a grave deficiency, as their machines could not work well without the correct grind of coffee. The inventions were designed to work on paper, but not in practice. The problem arose because the inventors could not specify their grind. The word 'fine' had a relative meaning but not an absolute meaning. In addition the quality of grinders was probably such that people could not get a consistent grind, and as machinery wore, so the grind changed. There was, and is, no simple way to describe a grind and even today only the biggest companies have the special sieves necessary to measure the percentage of particles of different sizes which describe the grind in absolute terms.

THE PRINCIPLES OF COFFEE GRINDING

Finely ground coffee and correct brewing are synonymous with achieving stronger and more flavourful coffee in the cup. The fine grinding of coffee, however, involves certain principles which must be acknowledged and understood, because they are the cornerstones of successful grinding and brewing. As the coffee is ground more finely, the following fundamental relationships apply:

- the greater the friction in grinding, the hotter the coffee becomes, and the faster oxidation and staling will occur. This leads to flavour deterioration and faster aroma loss;
- as the grinder becomes hotter it causes the coffee to go through another heat process and change of flavour;
- particle sizes are more likely to be uniform, resulting in better controlled brewing;
- the surface area of the ground particles become larger, which leads to a faster and more complete extraction;
- the higher the density becomes, the more ground coffee can be fitted into a given space. A measure of finely ground coffee will contain more coffee by weight than the same measure of coarsely ground coffee. This means that the same volume of finely ground coffee will give stronger tasting coffee due to the higher extraction and the extra amount of coffee. In addition, since coffee swells about fifty per cent when wetted, this means that the extra coffee will cause increased resistance to the water in an espresso machine, extending the brewing time with consequently stronger flavour levels;
- the smaller interstices or spaces between the ground particles of the coffee bed make it more difficult for water to pass through the coffee;
- the finer the grind the greater the resistance to the water and hence there is an increased requirement for a higher water pressure to force a given amount of water through the coffee in a given time. In a pump espresso machine where the pressure is controlled, if the coffee is too finely ground, the brewing time will be extended and the coffee will become bitter.

The first grinders were made by hand and each one differed. It was impossible to tell the consumer just exactly how to grind the coffee ideally for a particular coffee maker, even in the unlikely event that the manufacturer of the coffee maker knew.

With varying grind sizes being used it was impossible to predict the results from any coffee maker. If the coffee was too fine, it might be impossible for the water to filter past it. If the coffee was too coarse, the water would pass through too quickly and the coffee would be weak. The solution to the problem of the water not passing through coffee which was too finely ground lay in inventions where force was applied in the form of pressure or vacuum. An alternative was to use coarse coffee with multiple passes of water to try to extract the flavour.

THE STANDARDISATION OF GRIND SIZES

In the 1920s, the increasing use of electric power and the resulting faster revolutions of the grinder blades led to a need for improved blade design so that the coffee could pass through the grinder faster. Shop and factory grinders became more capable of exact grinds. Even though similar technology was used, domestic grinders never gave such good results because the grinding blades were too small and became too hot.

As shops and factories began using better grinders, so standards of what was 'filter fine', 'espresso', 'drip grind', 'vacuum pot' and 'percolator grind' slowly became understood by all, even if vaguely. It was at least possible to talk about the correct grind of coffee to match the machine and its filter, if not precisely, then approximately.

Manufacturers of espresso coffee machines began to supply special coffee grinders to use with the machines. Trade associations and coffee promotion bodies, who realised the importance of grind size, were trying to establish standards with the roasting industry and retail outlets in order to give the consumer a better product. Standards were necessary so that the words 'fine', 'medium', 'coarse', 'drip grind' and 'espresso grind' would eventually have a common meaning. Whereas once the roaster supplied the coffee to the consumer to be ground and used in a variety of machines, the roaster now delivered packaged coffee, ground to suit the market demands of the various machines in that market. The lack of sophistication of the grinding processes, which had been the barrier to proper brewing practices for centuries, now received increasing attention. The bean could now be ground and brewed to specification, but it was probably not until the 1960s that the ideas were reasonably understood by some of the brewing public.

THE CORRECT MEASURE FOR GRINDING

Early grinders had a wooden drawer in which to catch the ground coffee, but these gave no indication of quantity. Most wall grinders and many electric grinders had a clear glass container, with gradations which showed the measure for the required number of cups.

Unless consumers are given a measure with the machine, they probably use a teaspoon or some other kitchen measure to determine the quantity. Germans used a measure called a *loth* which was a measure of fifteen grams. Some sources give the measure as seventeen grams, but there do not appear to be any original sources to confirm this. Since it was a volumetric measure, the weight of the coffee depended on the grind used - the finer the grind the heavier the weight. *Loth* measures have existed for nearly two hundred years and at one time were given away by the roasters in Germany and Holland to raise the standard of coffee making. In Norway they use a spoon of ten grams and recommend six to seven spoons per litre.

Many coffee makers are now sold with a coffee measuring spoon included. Italian grinders for espresso machines have a built-in volumetric measuring device.

The *loth* was a German measuring spoon for coffee. There were two volumes on the one spoon - one of fifteen grams for two cups and the other of thirty grams for four cups. The brass *loth* is the original style. The tin *loth* on the right was probably given away by coffee roasters. The porcelain *loth* is more modern and contains double the quantity.

THE HISTORY OF GRINDING

Grinders, no matter what type, hold an everlasting fascination. Antique markets are full of them at prices which defy explanation. People pick them up and turn the handles. Perhaps they form part of a folkloric memory that grinders were for the rich and are a symbol of wealth. The fascination may have to do with the aroma release associated with grinding, which makes it a pleasant activity everyone likes to be reminded of. Grinders were destined to be a central feature of the kitchen and, as such, many were richly decorated and therefore appealing.

The first mortar and pestle grinders were used for a variety of products. There does not appear to be any innovation which made one type of mortar and pestle more suitable for grinding coffee than another, although large wooden ones are often seen in photos. The controversy as to whether coffee ground in a mortar and pestle was superior to that ground in a grinder with a turning handle raged for years. The mortar and pestle was very popular and less expensive than the metal millwork grinder which was often given as a wedding present in France.

As well as the mortar and pestle type, the rotating stone wheel in a static base was used. This style of grinder has been in use for thousands of years and was mostly used for grains. There is little direct evidence that it was commonly used for coffee. Electric-powered stone grinders, using dressed stone, are extensively used in Greece and Turkey today, for making powder coffee.

The design of grinders specifically for spices, which later evolved into coffee grinders, probably came from Syria in the early 1500s. Grinders did not originate in Europe and the highest and nearest level of technology existed in Damascus, a city famous in those early days for its steel swords and expertise in smithing. These grinders were of metal and had the same basic mechanism as today's Turkish coffee grinder. The basis of the grinder was the cone-shaped millwork which is still used in domestic grinders. To grind to powder would have needed an accuracy of manufacturing technology not generally available even in the most advanced parts of Europe at the time. Ukers gives the date of 1665 as being the first time metal Turkish grinders were made in Damascus, but there is no reference for this statement.[4] In Paris I have seen one cylinder grinder from the early eighteenth century which looks identical to the current Turkish style grinders. There was no adjustment and it was incapable of fine grinding. European grinders to make powder-fine coffee were probably not available until the middle of the nineteenth century.

Left: The first coffee grinders were small spice grinders which used the same grinding mechanism as coffee grinders.

Far Left: A small wooden mortar and pestle. The result of braying or pounding coffee was a mixture of coarse and fine grounds. To make Turkish powder-fine coffee the grounds had to be repeatedly sieved through a silk scarf.

A Moroccan grinder. The diameter
is much greater.

In 1550 the cone millwork reached Europe for the grinding of spices and because of its suitability for grinding dry products, it was also satisfactory for grinding coffee. The Italians of the sixteenth century changed the form of the grinder into the grinder that we know today. The body changed from wood to metal as the shape also changed, but the grinding millwork stayed the same. The first millworks were hand-made and were inaccurately and crudely tooled. The most famous name in grinding is that of an Italian military engineer, Agostino Ramelli, who in 1588 published his ideas on the construction of the horizontal iron mill.[5] Turriano of Cremona and Veranzio of Venice were two other names involved in the development of metal cone grinders, mainly for grains. Veranzio in 1615 made the first roller mills.

It was only from 1700 that the word 'coffee grinder' was actually used in the German language and it is significant that soon after this the Arab monopoly on trading coffee into Europe was broken by imports of coffee from the East Indies. In 1700 the production of coffee grinders in series began in Remscheid, Germany. [6] Coffee was about to become the drink of the people.

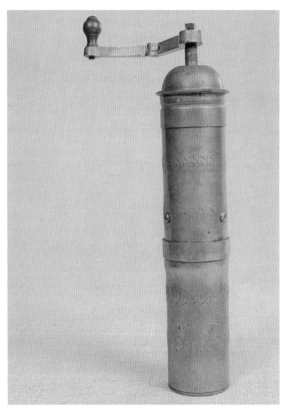

The first Turkish coffee grinders were steel
and were later replaced by brass ones in
which patterns were incised. They were
designed to grind the coffee to powder. It
took a long time to grind a small amount of
coffee and this was traditionally the job for
the woman of the house.

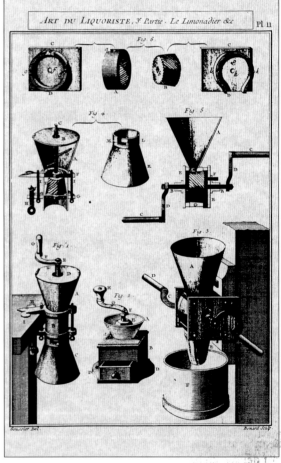

French grinders in 1775. The box model may
be of German origin.

This illustration from the 1939 Peugeot catalogue shows that the cutter design had changed greatly since the 1775 grinders. The cone itself has two distinct sections - one coarse and one fine, whereas the 1775 illustration shows only simple diagonal cuts. The 1939 grinders were said to be silent owing to this design which suppressed vibrations.

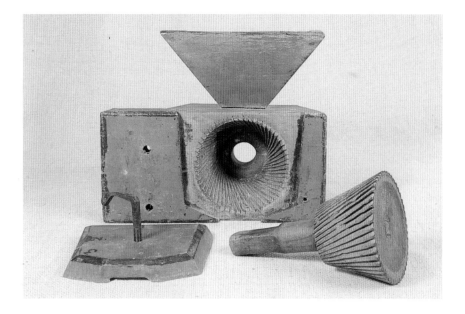

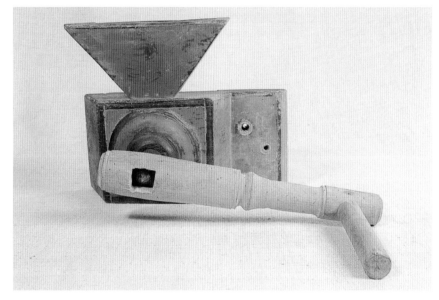

The grinder designs of 1775 published in France show exactly the same styles as are available today. At the domestic level, there were several developments. The main change was from grinders which attached to the table to grinders which were held in the hand. The central part, the grinding plates, were to be the subject of many variations in size and shape but remained substantially the same. Wall grinders, one of the many developments of form, came into being as coffee became more common, reaching the height of their popularity in the first half of the twentieth century. It does seem that many of these innovations were of such small consequence that they were almost unnoticeable and there was little development at this time. The only big development was the use of flat blades in commercial grinders.

Thomas Bruff Senior patented the first coffee grinder in the United States in 1798. It had two flat plates with coarse grooves near the centre and fine grooves near the edges. The flat plates can be considered as a flattened version of the earlier conical grinders.

In 1829 Coulaux & Cie of Molsheim, a town near Strasbourg in France, patented a new coffee grinder which had the adjustment knob, or nut for changing the grind, situated above the millwork. This was a major advance because until then most of the hand grinders had the adjustment below the millwork. The adjustment nut underneath was in the most inconvenient position for changing the grind but at least regular changes were not

Top and Above: A French domestic wooden wall grinder. Steel fillets have been inlaid into the wood. There is an adjustment plate on the back with the numbers 1,2,3. It did not grind finely. Some doubts have been expressed that this is not a coffee grinder but a grain mill. However a grinder with identical design won a medal at the Exposition de Balençon in France in 1875 and carved into the body of the grinder were the words, 'moulin à café garanti' (coffee grinder with guarantee).
France - 18th century.

Left: A wooden grinder. Germany - 1777.

A grinder for attaching to the table. These were made in small workshops. Germany - c.1800.

A grinder in a wooden housing, probably German - 1820 to 1830.

Below: An all-iron grinder, probably German - 1810 to 1820.

needed. The cutters in the new Coulaux grinder patent were brought closer together by tightening the nut, which made for a finer coffee. The patent also illustrated a two-section cone with coarse and fine cutters. It is hard to be sure if they were in fact trying to patent that because the Coulaux grinder illustrated has a different mechanism - a coarse cone section and then a flat plate with low ridges which looks fairly useless as a grinder.

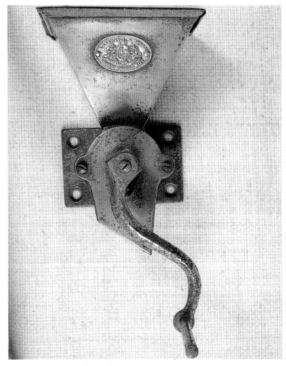

Archibald Kenrick made a patent for a wall grinder. The Kenrick name was given to many grinders which were very solidly made and are still found in antique markets. England - 1815.

A large grinder from an institution. The adjustment nut is underneath. It was quite common for bench grinders to have long extensions which the person doing the grinding could sit on. It was much less common to have the grinder incorporated into the stool itself. France - mid 19th Century.

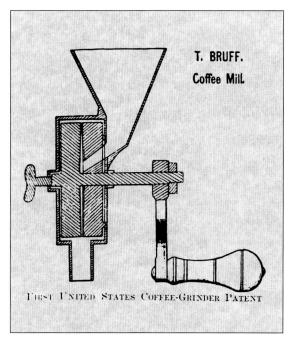

Bruff patent. USA - 1798.

The English Kenrick grinders of the time had simple cone mechanisms. The transition to the sophisticated two stage cutters shown in the 1939 Peugeot catalogue must have been under way or just starting as the machines to mill the metal were being introduced into larger workshops, away from the small artisans who up to that point had been making grinders.

A second Coulaux patent in 1831 claimed that the shaft was now centred much better than previous grinders. A German book, devoted exclusively to coffee grinders, shows only a few grinders with the adjustment knob on the top.[7] During the nineteenth century most of the German grinders seem to have kept the adjustment knob underneath.

The 1846 Japy grinder from France used intermeshing cutters, but they were not copied in domestic grinders. Many later commercial grinders incorporated this idea.

Grinders in the nineteenth century generally improved with the arrival of machines to shape the notches and surfaces on the cutters. The millworks on Turkish hand mills fit much more closely and the notches and grooves on the cutters are much finer with very small gaps for the fine grounds to fall through. The grinders were increasingly made in factories, with machine tools, so their conformity increased. As well as the large numbers made in Europe, a New England manufacturer estimated that as early as 1831, three hundred thousand coffee grinders were being made annually in the United States.[8] This figure seems high, but it must be remembered that in 1800, the wages in the United States were already one third higher than in Western Europe and the disparity was to increase through the century.[9] With a higher standard of living went a higher consumption of coffee. Reflecting the higher consumption of coffee, most American grinders seem to have a larger capacity than European grinders.

The Coulaux grinder with the adjustment above the housing instead of at the grinding end was an important development. France - 1829.

There are many collectors of coffee grinders, and whilst all the large collections I have seen contain the complete gamut of grinders, many of the grinders have the same workings with different forms. The grinding millwork is the same, whether placed vertically or horizontally and the adjustment is either from below or from on top. There were very few variations on the basic grinder.

The Mathiot grinder was one such variation. This looks to be very much a grinder that worked on paper but not on coffee. The final grind size was determined by the closeness of the rims of the plates to each other. A modified Mathiot grinder was sold in Sweden from 1909. It had a rotating mill surface like a rasp which forced the beans against a grooved surface, but there do not seem to be any advantages. The adjustment is not very good and the coffee comes out rather coarse, which was suitable for boiling, in the Swedish method of the day.

In Scandinavia, coffee grinders were the preserve of the upper classes. Farmers and the lower orders used a wooden trough with a wooden roller which broke the coffee into coarse pieces. One example exists with the date 1815 marked on it. It seems likely that these grinders were used from the late 1700s to the early 1900s.

Right: The Japy patent showed the innovation of intermeshing teeth and incorporated the Coulaux adjustment. The design of the teeth shows that machines were available to cut the teeth with precision. France - 1846.

Far Right: A grinder using a roller ground the coffee coarsely and had poor adjustment. The Swedes used coarsely ground coffee and boiled it. Sweden - 1900.

The Mathiot grinder. France - 1890s.

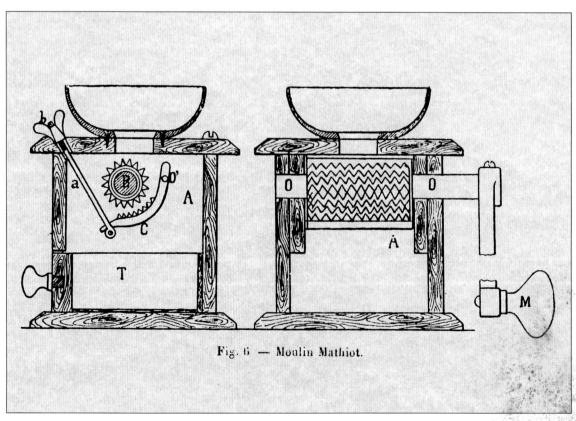

Fig. 6 — Moulin Mathiot.

A grinder made of wood. This style of grinder dates from 1785 and was used as late as the early 1900s. It was also used in Norway and probably other Northern European countries. Sweden.

Below Left: A metal wall grinder. France - c. 1850.

Below: Monitor grinder, named after the submarine used in the American Civil War. USA.

Left: Kenrick cast-iron grinder. England - 1860s.

Far Left: An Austrian grinder - 1900s.

Right: Peugeot grinder with slot underneath to fix the grinder to the table. There were 42 models in the 1899 Peugeot catalogue. France - 1900.

Far Right: An American grinder with an adjustment on the front, popular on the trek to the west.

Below: Coffee grinder from Venice. Italy - 1880.

Below Centre: Cast-iron Kenrick grinder England - 1900.

Below Right: Universal grinder. USA.

A French grinder. c. 1900.

A very unusual table model Turkish grinder. Italy - 1900s.

A small table grinder. England.

The Elma made in Guipuzcoa, Basque country. Spain - 1920.

A grinder with a scene from Savoy. There are several series of French grinders with illustrations of provinces and other scenes. France - 1920s.

A Mocca grinder with the KYM brand. Bakelite generally came in three distinctive colours - red, green and black. Germany - 1935.

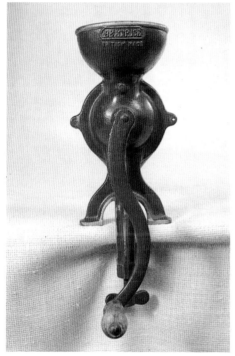

Table grinder. England.

Beatrice table grinder.
England - 1900s.

A PE-DE brand bakelite grinder in the form of a knight with a visor, made by the firm Peter Dienes. Germany - 1935.

Far Left: A grinder for the soldiers of the Great War 1914-1918. France.

Left: An unusual metal covered grinder.
Germany - 1900s.

A bakelite grinder by KYM. Germany - 1930s.

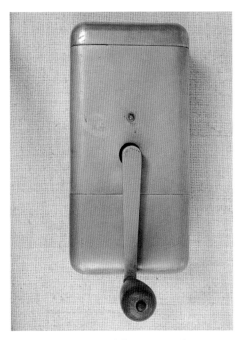

This wall grinder was of aluminium and had a removable handle as well as an unusual grinding mechanism. France.

The HOP grinder in aluminium had wide grinding plates to the very edge and grinding control underneath. France - 1950s.

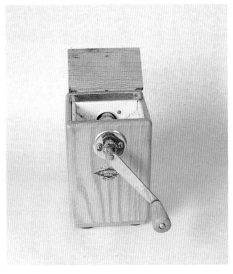

A Leinbrock Ideal grinder with horizontal handle. Germany - 1950s.

A metal grinder with a clip lid. Italy - 1950s.

A spherical grinder. Italy - 1950s.

Right: Hachhaus HaHa grinder with horizontal adjustment lever. Germany -1950s.

Far Right: A plastic Turkish grinder and a grinder with plastic adjustments. Czechoslovakia - 1980s.

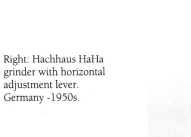

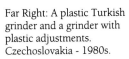

Far Left: A plastic grinder
with unusual sliding door.
Czechoslovakia - 1980s.

Left: The Moulux had a solid
aluminium body and a novel
grinding mechanism.
France - 1960s.

Brevetti is not the name of an Italian manufacturer,
but is the word for patents. This Italian model has the
container in the form of a cup underneath.

An illustration of grinders from a
French coffee factory. The adjustment
is underneath. France - 1886.

CONSEQUENCES OF THE GERMAN LAW ABOUT COFFEE

In 1875 German legislation was changed to prevent the sale of coffee that was not pure or was adulterated. Coffee was to contain only coffee, without any admixtures. The resultant change in public confidence enabled the market to change from one where the householders roasted and ground their own coffee to one where the coffee was factory roasted and ground either in the factory, in a shop or at home. This change was the impetus for an interest in improving large capacity grinders.

SHOP GRINDERS AND FACTORY GRINDERS

Shop grinders were generally just larger versions of domestic grinders. The size of the wheels, handles and mechanisms was all that differentiated them from their domestic cousins. The mechanisms were either the traditional conical or flat plate grinders. Grinding in shops was done by hand and this must have been a tiring business. Factories would have used shop grinders driven by steam power.

The introduction of steam power changed the form of industrial mills. The shafts were turned by broad belts running over flat wheels connected to the driving wheels of the steam engine. The rims of the wheels were later grooved for Vee belts when electric motors were introduced. With the increasing use of electric power, there was a big improvement in technology and it became possible and necessary to develop new high production grinders. Larger capacity coffee roasters in larger factories needed larger and faster mills with increased output to supply a growing market. Large scale industrial mills generally used rollers, a system where horizontal and vertical grooves on the rollers crushed and cut the coffee. The increased power and speed of electric motors meant that it was now possible to grind larger amounts and sophisticated grinders were needed if the grinder was not to choke up. Large cone grinders with precision-machined grooves for shops were developed in Denmark, Sweden and Germany.

An English shop grinder. The design of the cutters seems to have been constant for decades. Cone cutters had a large grinding surface and this meant that production was high even though the grinder was hand-operated.

Large counter or wall grinder for a small shop. England - 1900s.

Right: A Peugeot electric shop model. The use of a separate motor allowed motors of different voltages from all over France to be attached to the grinder. France - 1923.

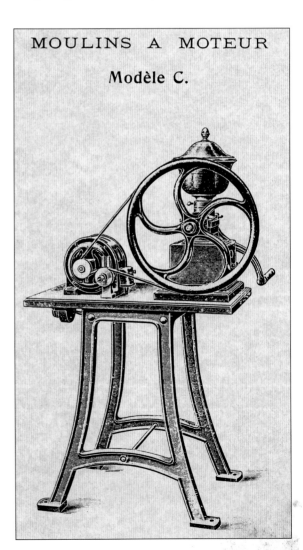

MOULINS A MOTEUR

Modèle C.

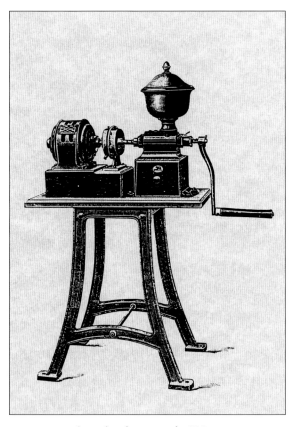

A Peugeot grinder with reducer to make 130 to 140 turns per minute. France - 1923.

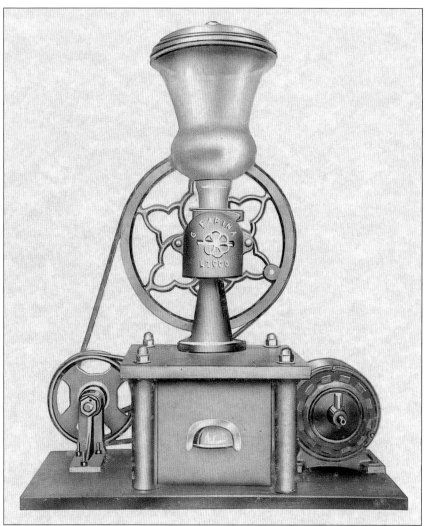

A tall elegant Farina shop grinder. Italy - 1920s.

Above: A Farina counter model. Italy - 1920s.

Left: The Enterprise Manufacturing Company, Philadelphia made a series of store grinders which were very widely used in the United States from 1870.

Right: A European grinder for a shop.

Far Right: A counter or factory grinder. The flat edge on the wheel indicates that it was intended to be attached to a belt and pulley system. France - 1900s or before.

An English grinder for mounting on the counter. The Vee groove on the rim of the wheel indicates that the grinder was probably attached to an electric motor under the counter. It had a coarse cone mechanism. England - 1900s to 1920s.

A hand grinder for mounting on a box. Most unusually the coffee fell though the air into the drawer. France or Italy - late 19th century.

A counter grinder with Vee groove for electric motor. France - turn of the 20th century.

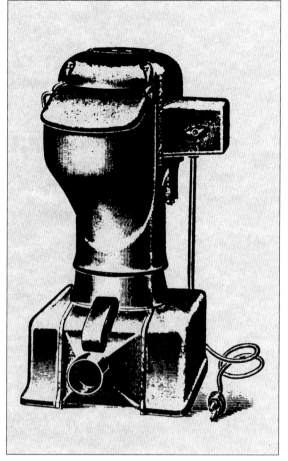

Paul Kaack coffee grinder with an enormous motor for industrial production. Hamburg, Germany - 1925.

A PE DE brand electric grinder from the 1939 Kaiser-Bazar catalogue. The motor appears to be mounted behind the bean inlet at the top. With a 1/6 h.p. motor the output was 18 kilos per hour and with a 1.1 h.p. motor 72 kilos per hour. Germany.

The Zellweger Perl showed a much improved design and a smaller motor. Germany - 1930.

Right: The Fabke 'Rapid' shop grinder also had a very large motor. Germany - 1925.

Left: The Voigt shop grinder was one of the first grinders with the motor vertical instead of horizontal. Germany - 1932.

Far left: The Voigt electric grinders from Walter Voigt, Dresden were innovative. The fineness adjustment on the large double mill seems to be on the side and work with an heloidical screw motion. Germany - 1932.

A small French electric grinder made by Ets. Legrain, Paris - 1920s or before.

An elegant shop model. USA - 1920.

A small Mahlkönig shopgrinder - Germany 1940s.

A Dayton shop grinder. The half horsepower motor is enormous by modern standards. USA - 1920s.

The Hobart was a powerful grinder. The large shop model had two different sets of blades for grinding - one was for medium and the other for very fine grind. This small shop model has a heavy grinder system which is in front. USA .

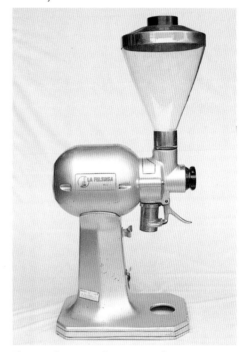

The La Felsinea grinder was one of many grinders, all with the same basic design - a grinding head attached to a motor on a stand. The only variation was in the size of the motor and in the diameter of the cutters. Italy - 1990.

Different cutters had different results. In most cases the coffee was coarsely treated in the centre and progressively ground finer as it was moved by centrifugal force towards the edge. 1920s - 1960s.

Left: A modern grinder blade uses harder steel with sharply-defined edges for cutting the coffee which reduces the friction and the consequent loss of aroma. Precision machining means that the grind size can be more closely controlled. The Swiss Ditting was very accurately cut and the blades could be resharpened. The Italian company Ico Perfex of Turin used sintered hard metal which gave a very long life in factories. The design of the blade was very similar to the Ditting blade. 1970s - 1980s.

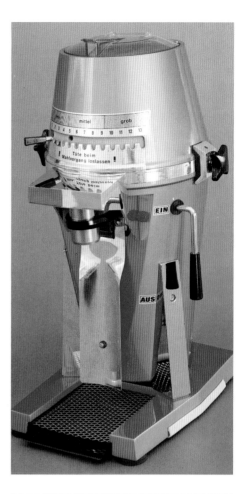

Left and Above: The American Duplex pot shape grinder is very rare. USA - 1950.

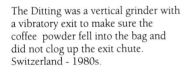

A Sik-Flex grinder used the cone grinding system. Denmark - 1950s.

The Ditting was a vertical grinder with a vibratory exit to make sure the coffee powder fell into the bag and did not clog up the exit chute. Switzerland - 1980s.

Below Left: A set of cone grinders. They produced very evenly ground coffee without heating and were widely used in Scandinavia and Northern Germany. The coffee produced was not as suitable for espresso machines as that from flat blade grinders. One of the problems with this type of grinder was that a technician was required to change the cutters whereas with flat blades it was quite simple for the shopkeeper to change them. The conical shape of the grinding blades required accurate fitting. The precise machining meant that they were quite expensive.

Top and Above: Two Mahlkönig shop grinders. Germany - 1990s.

ELECTRIC GRINDERS

The first electric machine of any type ever used was an electric coffee grinder in New York in 1883.[10] Electric grinders, for shop use, were first introduced into the United States in 1897 by the Enterprise Manufacturing Company. They were followed by the Hobart Manufacturing Company in 1898 using belt and pulley arrangements. The first electric grinders were hand grinders, with a groove for the Vee belt to the electric motor replacing the wheel and handle. Then followed motors with gear drives and later the drive shaft from the motor going directly to the cutters. The cost of making the cutters was a determining factor in their design. Whilst it is certain that conical cutters made a very even and cool grind, it was far easier and cheaper to make a machined flat cutter.

The secret of a successful grinder was to have accurately cut grooves becoming progressively shallower as they led to the grinding exit faces which determined the final particle size of the grounds. The fineness of the grind was controlled by the closeness at the exit point of the grinding faces. Better blades could be made by milling them on modern machines and lathes, rather than by using cheap and inaccurate casting methods. With improvements in metal technology, the blades were made of harder metals with sharper edges to cut the coffee. Electric grinders were to take on a life of their own in the twentieth century.

An Ajco cone grinder.
Denmark - 1920s.

The Ohlsson grinder used the cone system and ground the coffee very evenly.
Sweden - 1980s.

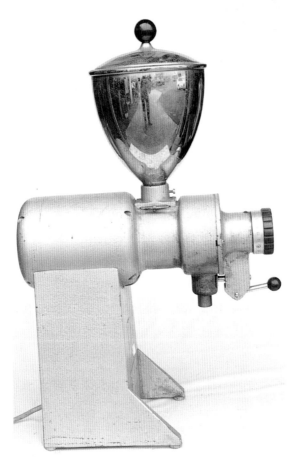

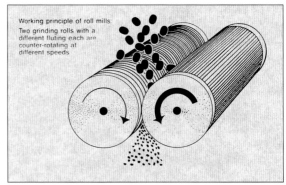

The Lepage System of grinding was used in large factory grinders. Gump grinders used the Lepage System.

For high output, the size of the grinding faces was increased, so that the heat from the friction could be dissipated. Some grinders utilised water cooling to keep the coffee cool. In factories, a different system could be used, such as the Le Page Roller Cutter Mill of 1916, which was an American invention to cut the coffee and not grind it. This invention is at the heart of most large commercial grinders of today and the method is very effective for grinding the coffee evenly and accurately. It is extensively used in large factories throughout the world where outputs of up to four thousand kilograms per hour are required. The word *Walzenmühle* or roller mill was first used in Germany in 1899.[11]

DOMESTIC ELECTRIC GRINDERS

From the first days there was a wide range of electrical appliances available but with very limited distribution. A table fan was available in 1881, and in 1883, at an exhibition in Vienna, dental drilling machines and sewing machines were on exhibition. It was not long before electric vacuum cleaners, sewing machines and massage equipment were available. Initially there were very few electric domestic grinders because of the low wattage available from a light circuit and the lack of small motors. Indeed with poor quality cutters, it required a relatively powerful motor to grind coffee at all.

In 1911, the German AEG Company, produced an electric motor of one-eighth horsepower which turned at eighty revolutions per minute. This Company began as DEG, the German Edison Company, but a few years later, changed its name to AEG. The AEG motor was used to power many domestic items. One of these was an electric grinder but it was only a table model attached to the motor. It was not an integral electric coffee grinder.

The Alexanderwerke in Germany introduced an electric grinder with a one-eighth horsepower motor in 1913.[12] It probably had a short market life on account of the war which started the next year. Other than a brief mention in a book, there are no details of this grinder, but in 1926 the same company had a grinder using a universal motor, much the same as the AEG motor. Neither the AEG nor the Alexanderwerke grinders were integral. The electric grinder had not yet taken on a separate life of its own. It would seem that the first purpose-designed electric grinders were either the Italian Simerac, or the French Peugeot which was introduced in 1932. Both used a belt-driven system.

Above: The AEG grinder was simply an electric motor connected to an existing grinder. Germany - 1911.

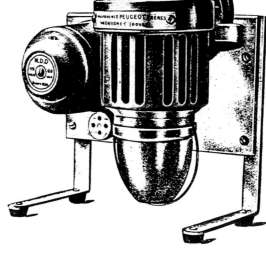

The Peugeot domestic grinder had a 60 Watt motor and output of 2.5 kilos per hour. France - 1931.

The Simerac was initially produced with the motor behind the grinder and later with the motor under the grinder. The motor turned a small pulley attached by a cloth belt to a cog inside the lid which revolved the vertical shaft attached to the grinders. Coffee beans require a large amount of force to grind, not only during the grinding process, but particularly at the start-up of the motor. This is one of the first domestic electric coffee grinders ever produced. Italy - late 1920s or early 1930s.

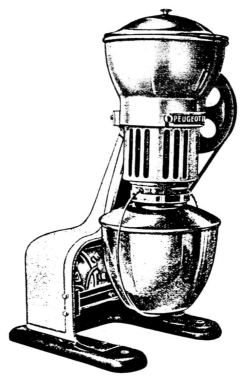

The Peugeot hotel model had an output of 5 kilograms per hour. France.

The problem of the motor strength necessary to grind coffee can be seen in this domestic electric Italian grinder. The grinding kernel has a diameter of two centimetres - in other words a tiny amount of coffee is actually ground. The problem relates to the hardness of the bean and to the fact that stale coffee beans are oily and do not grind easily at all. They can easily turn into a slurry which does not exit from the grinding chamber.
Italy - 1960s.

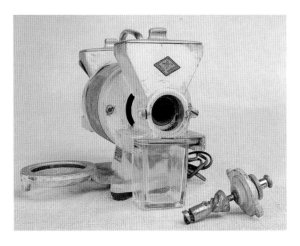

The Voigt domestic grinder had a vertical motor underneath the cutters and was a totally new style.
Germany - 1932.

The first German electric domestic grinder without a belt seems to have been manufactured by Walter Voigt GmbH of Dresden in 1932. It was the smallest of a range of commercial grinders. In the same year, the Irus Factory of Düsslingen produced a wall grinder with stone millwork to produce powder fine Turkish coffee which enabled a fifty per cent saving in the use of coffee. This, in combination with the new quickfilters, also introduced in 1932, marked the beginning of a new era. The rising popularity of the filter paper method probably caused the increase in interest in electric grinders, because it was a tedious job to grind coffee finely by hand. In 1934 the German ATE Company made an electric wall grinder with a capacity of six pounds per hour. During the whole period manual grinders were the most numerous by far and new models were constantly being introduced. In Germany a wall grinder was introduced which had two compartments - one for especially good coffee for Sundays and festivals and the other for a cheaper blend with malt coffee for the other days.

The Moccafina. Germany - 1930s.

HEM

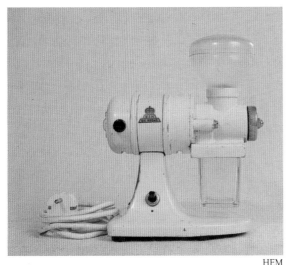

HEM

The Krone had a small but powerful motor which was excellent for grinding filter-fine coffee. Germany.

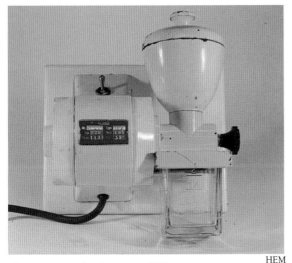

HEM

The Erpees grinder. Germany - 1930s.

In 1937, the Hobart Manufacturing Company in the United States as well as Swiss and German companies were increasingly introducing small electric domestic grinders which had the motor directly connected to the cutters without a belt. The size of the motor was appreciably smaller for the same power.

The German Kaiser-Bazar catalogue of 1939 shows only one electric grinder with a one-sixth horsepower motor at a cost one hundred times that of a simple hand grinder. It was actually sold as a shop grinder in spite of the size of its motor. A powerful motor was really required to grind the coffee but there was little interest in buying larger and more powerful grinders for the home until the 1960s and 1970s. The fact was that fresh coffee beans were crisp but took quite a lot of power to crack. Stale coffee beans were oily and soft and the ground up powder turned into an emulsion which did not flow from the grinding chamber at all.

There were relatively few electric domestic grinders between the wars. However there was a large growth in the market for electric appliances but it was nothing like the surge that occurred in the 1950s with improving standards of living.

Mass production, after the Second World War, saw technology improve and prices drop as the mass market grew. In the late 1950s in Germany and France prices became attractive for domestic grinders and this was the start of the mass market for the electric grinder. Italian electric grinders started in 1948. The AEG (German) grinder of 1952 had a plastic body, a very strong motor and was very durable. Much more important was the introduction in France in the 1950s of the much cheaper and more durable grinder with small whirling blades which sold in vast numbers throughout Europe.

AEG produced a plastic mill for filter-fine coffee. Germany - 1952

Wigomill. Germany - 1970s.

233

Right: The Braun KMM1.
Germany - 1980s.

Far Right: The Bosch grinder
had a 110 Watt motor.
Germany - 1980s.

Right: The Philips grinder
had a 80 Watt. motor.
Holland - 1980s.

Above: The Bosch grinder had a
160 Watt motor. Motors were
getting smaller and more
powerful. Germany - 1980s.

Ico Perfex of Turin, Italy made high quality
industrial grinders. The grinding channels
were accurately machined and the metal
sintered. The result was an exceedingly durable
precision grinder capable of producing ground
coffee to accurate specifications.

WALL GRINDERS

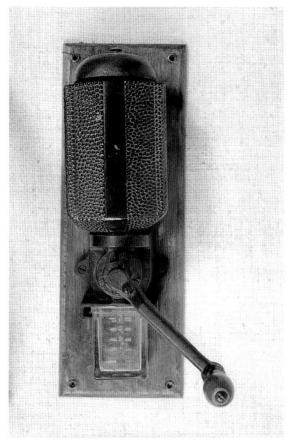

Most wall coffee grinders had this general shape. They have a whole history of their own but basically had little influence on mainstream grinders. The Peugot company and others in France made delightful scenes on the ceramic from the 1930s to the 1950s. Goldenberg and Peugot in 1920 made a grinder in the shape of a letterbox. One collector in Paris has three hundred different wall grinders.

A wall grinder. The size of the glass container is enormous by European standards. USA.

Far left: A grinder with a large container.
USA - 1900s.

Left: The Paris Rhône was very similar to the Hobart grinder made in the USA.
France - 1950s.

235

SEB wall grinder.
France -1970s.

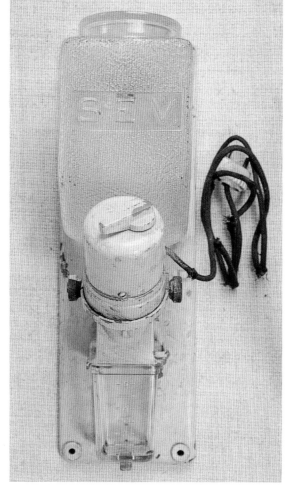

The motor for this grinder was the same
as used on a car windscreen wiper.

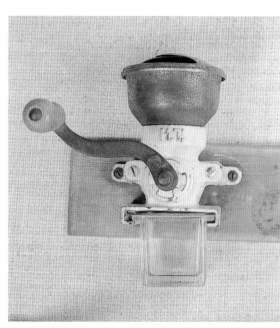

A wall grinder with a small container.
Germany - 1930s.

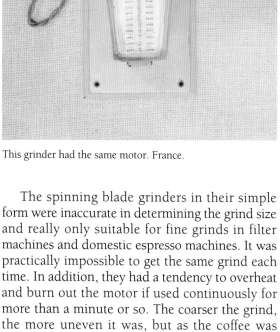

This grinder had the same motor. France.

The spinning blade grinders in their simple form were inaccurate in determining the grind size and really only suitable for fine grinds in filter machines and domestic espresso machines. It was practically impossible to get the same grind each time. In addition, they had a tendency to overheat and burn out the motor if used continuously for more than a minute or so. The coarser the grind, the more uneven it was, but as the coffee was ground more finely, friction increased the temperature of the coffee.

The idea of spinning blades probably came from equipment used for other purposes, such as pulping fruit and making milk shakes. The variations on this theme seem to be the last in the evolution of the coffee grinder at the domestic level. The first of these were made by the French Peugeot Company and date from 1952 with the Lion model and 1954 with the Ecureuil bakelite model.

The spinning blade grinders revealed their inadequacies very quickly and were improved by models such as the German Wigoplus and the French SEB which sieved the particles of coffee as they were ground, but sometimes the coffee particles got stuck in the sieve. The Technivorm grinder by Gerard Smit of the Netherlands was introduced in several models from 1962 to solve the problem of the sieves easily clogging during the grinding procedure due to the electrostatic and fatty properties of the coffee. This grinder solved these problems by introducing a radial ventilator and specially bent tips on the cutter blade which made a powerful airstream so that the sieve was kept clear. A portion-control model was introduced in 1965 and in 1972 the final version, with a flow-through system.

Some time in the 1920s, improved quality of grinding was achieved at the factory and shop level and in the 1960s at the domestic level. It was this availability of coffee ground for particular machines which allowed the introduction of the most sophisticated brewing machines all over the world. Just as domestic grinders were being perfected in the 1970s, the roasting industry was introducing vacuum-packed, pre-ground coffee in flexible plastic packaging to fill the supermarket shelves. There were many more packs containing pre-ground coffee than there were containing beans, which required special packs with valves. To a large extent the grinding problem was overtaken by the widespread marketing of factory-ground vacuum packed coffee.

SPINNING BLADE GRINDERS

The 'Lion' model from Peugeot was introduced in 1952. It was the beginning of a completely new type of grinder. A small rapidly spinning blade cut the coffee. The longer the process went the finer the coffee became. The motors were smaller and stronger and could not burn out when faced with a difficult bean. However they could burn out if kept running for more than one minute. Clips held the celluloid lid on. France - 1952.

The Peugeot 'Ecureuil' bakelite grinder with a spinning blade. France - 1954.

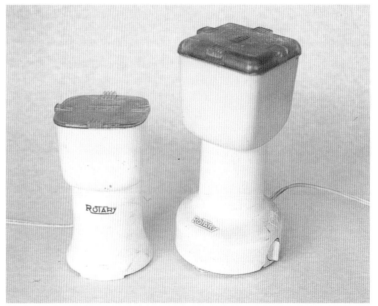

Below: Two rotary grinders with different voltages. France - 1950s.

Left: Moccador Matador. Germany - 1960s.

Above and Below: The SEB also used a safety switch in the lid. The beans fell from the top where the spinning blade propelled them through the sieve and then out into the container below. France -1970s.

The Wigoplus had a simple sieve system. The drawback with the spinning blade grinders was the unevenness of the grind and the fact that the heat generated by the friction warmed the coffee and caused flavour deterioration. Germany - 1960s.

The Philips plastic grinder incorporated a safety switch in the lid so that the motor could not be switched on without the lid in place. Holland - 1970s.

The Technivorm grinder was based on Gerard Smit's 1962 patents and solved the problem of the grounds clogging the sieve. Holland - 1960s.

The Snider grinder for an espresso machine was designed to portion the ground coffee directly into the espresso handle. The lid of the container had a micro-switch to stop the grinding when enough had been ground. Italy - 1928.

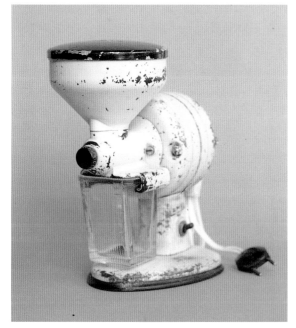

The Lamel electric grinder. France - Late 1940s.

THE AVAILABILITY OF BETTER GRINDERS

A higher standard of living in the large coffee-consuming countries has created a demand in their domestic markets for larger, stronger grinders with flat cutters. The problem of achieving perfectly ground coffee with ease has been solved, even though the solution has been restricted to those with sufficient interest and the will to spend a lot of money on the right grinder.

The evolution in grinders meant that, with the introduction of electricity, a more accurate and finer grind was attainable every time. Coffee brewing machines and pots would have evolved in an altogether different way if these ideal grinds had been available earlier.

The Oerre was designed to allow the special measuring spoon for espresso coffee to be put into the grounds container. Italy -1970s.

The metal Quick Mill by Omre was designed to grind coffee for espresso machines. Because the coffee was fine it tended to clog up in the throat, hence the inspection plate. Italy -1960s.

This grinder for espresso coffee was much bigger and the container had a dispenser mechanism to measure the coffee. It was apparent that a large motor was necessary for a reliable and effective fine grind. The large scale of production and the low cost of plastic components meant that prices were relatively low and sales high. Grinders such as this were considered domestic grinders. Italy - 1980s.

The Hario glass container grinder was hermetically sealed. The sharp cutters inside were machined and expensive in contrast to cheap cast cutters from Taiwan. Japan - 1980s.

The Gemco plastic and glass grinder did not work very well. The plastic cutters were not hard enough or sharp enough to cut the beans. USA - 1980s.

The Anfim grinder for espresso machines. There are many different bar grinders in Italy. The Anfim is the most popular in Milan. All bar grinders combine a fine adjustment for the grind and a volumetric dispenser to deliver exactly one dose into the handle of the espresso machine. Italy - 1990.

A plastic acrylic grinder with cast cutters. Taiwan - 1980.

CHAPTER 12

Packaging and the Wider Distribution of Better Coffee

C offee begins to stale from the moment it leaves the roaster - the higher the humidity, temperature and amount of oxygen present, the faster the staling.

Roasted coffee releases a large amount of carbon dioxide which can make a sealed airtight container swell to the point of explosion. The gases must be dissipated prior to packaging, so that the coffee may be packed into plastic bags or tin cans without swelling them.

In the early days of packaging there were few of these problems because the coffee was sold in small quantities and it was only necessary to keep the coffee fresh for a short time. Bags were made with greaseproof paper liners, invented in 1890 by Sigmund Kraut of Berlin. These liners acted as a barrier material to prevent the air from getting in - satisfactory for carrying coffee from the shop to the home but not for long term packaging. Ineffective packaging allowed the air to enter and the gases to escape through the imperfect seals and pores of the bag and so the coffee deteriorated.

To paint a global picture of the history of packaging is almost impossible, because markets were in different states of development, using different types of packaging. Some factories were supplying directly to the shops while, in other places, small shops were roasting and supplying direct to the consumer. When large scale distribution systems, including supermarkets, were created, sophisticated packaging became more economical and practical.

MARKET DOMINANCE BASED ON IMPROVED PACKAGING

The coffee world in the eighteenth and nineteenth centuries was very different to that which exists at the end of the twentieth century. Small growers and large plantation owners sold their crops to exporters in the growing countries who sold it to importers and traders in the consuming countries. The coffee was then sold to distributors in the cities who sold it to small factories and small shops where it was either roasted or sold to the household for roasting at home.

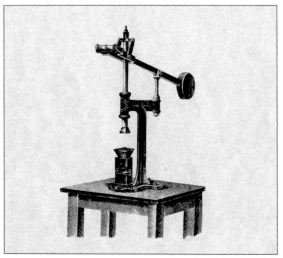

Far Left: An automatic filling machine operated by hand in Germany - 1900s. The comparable machines of the 1990s form the bag from a reel of material, weigh the coffee into the formed bag, vacuum the oxygen out or flush an inert gas such as nitrogen or carbon dioxide into the bag and seal it. One person operates several machines which can make hundreds of packets per hour.

Left: A packing machine to compress the coffee in the packet. Germany -1900s.

241

Industrialisation changed the nature of the trade. The coffee was sold to large factories which processed and packed it for distribution to small shops and restaurants. As these amalgamated into chains and grew in size, the factories expanded to produce the enormous quantities required in standardised packages which could be delivered to any part of the country in a fresh condition. Larger customers meant larger suppliers. Larger suppliers had to deal with larger importers who ended up financing growers and traders with the enormous amounts of money needed to support the industry. All these factors have caused a concentration of the coffee processing industry in the most advanced countries with ever larger capacity roasting and packing machines. For instance, coffee roasting machines exist with the capacity to roast 4 000 kilograms in one hour. Packaging machines of similar capacities exist. The basis of improved packaging was the use of vacuum packaging and improved packaging materials.

Vacuum packaging was first used in the United States in 1900.[1] As a technique it depended on getting a high vacuum in the packet with an almost total absence of oxygen. The development of vacuum packaging was the first step to delivering the roasted coffee, either beans or ground, to the customer, from large factories. A content of around one half per cent oxygen seemed acceptable to minimise staling. The swelling of the coffee bags and cans, which occurred even with vacuum-packed coffee, was solved by allowing the coffee to stand for periods of up to several days to ensure degassing, but the longer the standing period, the staler the coffee; the darker the coffee, the more gas released and the finer the grind, the faster the release of gas. A complete release of all the gas from the beans would take one hundred days, but most of the gas comes out in the first few days. Degassing times may be as little as thirty minutes for ground coffee. Degassed coffee has a different brewing time and flavour to coffee that has not been degassed. The degassing slows the penetration of the water into the grounds at atmospheric pressure as in a filter machine. In an espresso machine where the pressure of the water is much greater than the pressure of the gas escaping from the ground beans, the penetration factor is of minimal consequence.

Whatever the drawbacks, vacuum packed coffee is likely to be better than unprotected coffee. Degassing can be considered a controlled process of partial staling before the coffee is packed, which means that there is a lot of vacuum packed, partially staled coffee sold all over the world. A properly sealed soft vacuum pack is an indication that the coffee has been packed before it has been allowed to completely degas and is therefore fresher than coffee in a hard pack. In the absence of the possibility of most consumers to get freshly roasted coffee, vacuum packed coffee is the

best compromise. The increasing use of more finely ground coffees for filters and espresso machines has enabled better coffees to be delivered to the consumer because of the faster degassing times.

The other technique to protect the coffee was to replace the oxygen with gas such as nitrogen or carbon di-oxide. Oxygen was vacuumed out and replaced with nitrogen or simply flushed out with nitrogen. The coffee still had to be degassed.

The Japanese have developed a product called 'Ageless'. A small sachet which absorbs the gases is placed into the package of coffee. This absorption sachet uses iron, which rusts, and concurrently attracts and removes both the oxygen and carbon dioxide. The absorption of the gases means that the swelling of the packs is avoided.

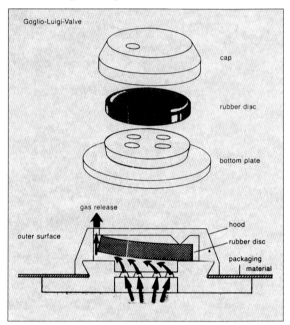

The Goglio one-way valve - Italy.   BR

In 1935 the Illy Company introduced a one way valve on cans. In the 1960s the Goglio Company of Italy invented a plastic bag with a one-way valve which allowed the gases to escape after building up to a predetermined pressure. In conjunction with the development of plastic packaging materials the coffee could now be packed into a container and sealed straight after roasting. The Goglio valve, which was a raised valve set in the film of the bag, differed from other valve systems, which were mostly set flush with the bag. This invention was the most significant development in the history of coffee packaging.

In many of the more developed markets of the world, coffee roasters lend machinery to commercial users at no cost, on the basis that the machinery is used to brew the coffee they supply. The range of machinery extends from four-group espresso machines for a weekly consumption of fifty kilograms to an automatic filter machine required for a consumption of five hundred cups per week. The range of deals that customers can negotiate is extensive and depends on market factors and competition. Commercial honesty being what it is, the commercial world has long dreamed of actually producing a pack of coffee which fits only into the machines supplied by that particular company, so no other company can supply the coffee. This has been the main goal of developing the most sophisticated packaging imaginable - ostensibly to give the consumer a better cup, which actually happens, but mainly to limit the extent of competition. There are actually machines which only operate after the insertion of a card, with an electronically coded metallic strip, which is delivered with each box of coffee.

THE SINGLE-CUP FILLED DISPOSABLE PLASTIC FILTER

The name Rombouts is normally associated with the disposable plastic filter cups, containing coffee, which sit on coffee cups and are often seen in Belgian cafes. Belgium is considered the birthplace of these filters and there are three major brands - Rombouts, SAS and Miko, which appear in many different countries with different names.

The idea of a portion-coffee filter was an excellent one and was first seen at the Leipzig Spring Fair on the 25th August, 1935. Wilhelm Tangermann from Hamburg invented a waterproof paper cup containing a quantity of coffee in a paper filter pack at the bottom. After the water was poured on and had run through, the used filter was thrown away. Twenty years later, on the 29th September, 1955, Georges Karageorges in Belgium made a patent for a plastic throw-away-cup filter. Rombouts followed with his own two years later and made a commercial success of this old idea.

The Japanese have copied the Belgian filters with sophisticated versions of their own where a small coffee capsule is inserted into the plastic cup. The same idea has been used by Douwe Egbert. The Japanese made another type altogether, the Astoria, which was unfolded and placed on the cup.

The Tangermann patent drawing of the first disposable coffee filter. Germany - 1935.

A disposable plastic filter cup. They are sold in millions in Belgium and are slowly becoming popular in other parts of the world.

The Astoria filter cup. The folded filter is packed in a flat sleeve. By carefully unfolding, the coffee is revealed in the filter and the filter can be rested on the rim of the cup. Japan - 1980s.

Douwe Egbert makes a plastic filter and the coffee capsule is replaced each time. Holland - 1987.

The Astoria filter was possibly based on an idea from Costa Rica in 1964.

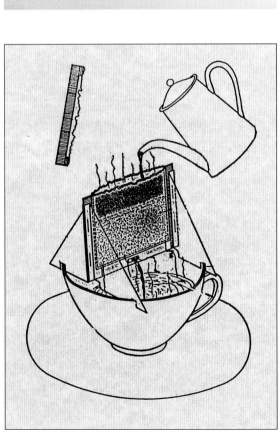

The Dimension 3 coffee filter for use in an office machine. The capsule has a plastic water inlet which directs the hot water over the coffee packed in a filter inside the bag. The force of the water is sufficient to break open the base whence the coffee filters directly into the cup. England - 1990.

Idee and Jacobs sell pods of coffee which can be placed into espresso machines. There are many manufacturers of pods sold separately or in long strips which are fed automatically into the group of a commercial espresso machine. Illy of Italy and many other companies are supplying similar pods. Germany - 1990.

THE INDIVIDUAL CUP, SPECIALLY PACKED

In bulk deliveries, the cost of the packaging is a small percentage of the total cost. With the use of sophisticated packaging, this has increased to multiples of three and four times the cost of the coffee and as much as ten times in Japan. Examples include individual filters and capsules to fit into an espresso machine and individual sachets on reels designed to fit into automatic espresso machines. The benefits for the consumer are convenience, avoidance of mess and a perfectly fresh coffee. Cost is virtually the only factor preventing this form of packaging from delivering the perfect cup of coffee to the mass market. There seems to be no limit to what can be manufactured to make a better cup. One of the most important developments in the 1990s has been the growth of pods - specially shaped compressed coffee pods wrapped in filter paper for direct insertion into espresso machines with specially fitted handles. These were a development from similar pods which were sold in strips of fifty or sixty to make real filter coffee in automatic machines made by the Rudd-Melikian company in the USA.

The development of the coffee industry over the last three hundred years has gone from consumers having to roast and grind the beans, to the finality of consumers being able to buy the product roasted, ground and packed in its own brewing compartment - a package specially designed so that it fits only specific machines.

The Maxwell House four- cup filter pouch to use in a domestic filter machine. USA - 1990s.

PACKAGING PROBLEMS

While the problems of packaging have involved ever more sophisticated plastic films and better and stronger packaging to withstand buffeting and handling on the way to the supermarket shelves, a problem of another type has arisen. In the late 1980s the world became alerted to the problem of the use of plastics which are not bio-degradable. Calculations show that from 1 000 kilograms of coffee up to a total of 1 600 kilograms of rubbish is generated. This figure includes the coffee grounds as well as significant amounts of packaging materials and the coffee industry is under some pressure to minimise this. The industry has not yet solved this problem, but if it gets bad enough, it may involve a total rethink and a change back to shop roasting or bulk deliveries. The fact that so much of the spent grounds are fibre may even mean their eventual use in other foods.

The Ueshima Coffee Company in Japan (UCC) introduced a pack of two separate cups of coffee in individual filters. The bag hung over the side of the cup and water was poured over the exposed coffee. The principle of pouring water onto the coffee directly is better than through a filter paper. Japan - 1991.

Above: Lavazza, the largest Italian coffee company, developed a small capsule to fit into a special espresso handle. It was packed into a small sachet. (left)
Nestlé, the large Swiss coffee company, developed a self-contained aluminium capsule. Loading the capsule into a special handle broke the protective seals and allowed the water to enter the capsule and produce a perfect espresso coffee. (right) 1991.

Left: The Delectel filter fits into a special handle on an espresso machine. France - 1988. (top)
The foil packet contains a vacuum packed aluminium foil container of coffee with perforations in the lid and bottom ready to put into a three-cup Bialetti Moka espresso coffee machine. Italy - 1989. (bottom)

CHAPTER 13

The Flavour of Coffee

WHICH IS THE BEST COFFEE?

There are two major types of coffee - Arabica and Robusta. Undoubtedly, the finest coffees are Arabicas, but not all Arabicas are fine coffees. Acidity is very important if the coffee is to have refreshing flavour characteristics and Arabicas display acidity. Kenyan, Tanzanian, New Guinea, also Colombian, Costa Rican and other Central American coffees are noted for their acidity. Robusta coffee is very flat, has little acidity, has double the caffeine of Arabica and a woody taste, but possesses plenty of body. Robusta coffees were only discovered in the 1870s in West Africa and were not widely used, except for instant coffee manufacture, until well after the Second World War.

Sensorial analysis comparing Robusta and Arabica coffees shows that they have very different flavour characterisics. Arabica possesses significantly more acid, wine, sour, lemon and blackcurrant flavours while Robusta possesses more motor oil, rubber and ashes flavour.[1]

The flavour of Robusta coffees is much improved if the raw coffee is processed in the same way as Arabica coffees. Its cheaper price has made it irresistible. From 1972 to 1986 the usage of Robusta in Italian coffee rose from ten per cent to forty-one per cent, which has made Italian coffee industry leaders very concerned about the drop in quality. A strong case can be made that the decline in coffee consumption in the United States from 1962 was the result of the introduction of Robusta coffee. Robusta coffees are also widely used in instant coffees.

Many countries produce both Robusta and Arabica coffees, so the country of origin gives no certain indication of type. With experience it is possible to recognise Robusta beans - they tend to be small and have rounded tips while Arabica beans are longer with pointed tips. While most Robustas are small, WIB is a grade of Indonesian Robusta which can be very large with a plump body and rounded ends. Robustas have traditionally been traded on appearance rather than taste but this practice is changing, as increasing use forces roasters to be more discriminating.

Libericas also exist. The beans are very large and extremely unlikely to be sold to you unless you are buying coffee from Singapore, Malaysia, or the Philippines. Libericas have a strange flavour and are renowned for their strength. Before 1939, they found favour in Norwegian fishing villages. Two brands were used by fishermen to keep themselves awake for three and four days at a time in bad weather - 'Hurricane', which was a pure Liberica and 'Gala', which was a mixture. Very coarse ground coffee was boiled in large kettles and more coffee and water added until the boat returned to port. It was thought that cleaning the kettle would destroy the flavour.

THE NAME OF A COFFEE AND ITS CHARACTERISTICS

The perception of a coffee is a combination of its intrinsic qualities, its historical reputation over decades and its advertising image. It is pointless to ascribe characteristics from the past to a coffee when the processing methods today have changed so much and new fertilisers are now being used. For instance, United Nations agricultural specialists have been 'improving' the processing of Ethiopian coffee so that it now resembles Kenya coffee in appearance but has lost the flavour characteristics of Ethiopian Mocha coffee.

For decades scientists have been improving the genetic stock of coffee, tea, corn, wheat, potatoes, tomatoes - everything. Some of these products are almost unrecognisable from their progenitors. In fact it is pointless to describe coffee with simple geographic and quality descriptives. Every product has a range of quality from poor to excellent and coffee is no exception. French wine, English beer, American cars, Indian tea are words which are meaningless as an indication of quality. The range of qualities and prices for them are enormous. The best Darjeeling tea at auction would command one hundred times the price of the poorest quality tea.

QUALITY COFFEE IN 1893

A sample of Bolivar coffee from 1893. It is unsorted by modern standards. The glass container was sealed with wax. Purchased in Belgium.

Coffee has undergone such a radical re-evaluation in one hundred years since the following statement appeared in 1893:

It is a well-established fact that the quality of coffee - that is, its flavour and aroma - is improved by keeping, and it is thought to be at its best at eight years, provided it has been kept in a perfectly dry place and atmosphere. As it is sold by weight, and as it loses by the evaporation of the water contained in the freshly prepared beans, dealers prefer to sell it as green as possible. When at its best, its color should be a pale yellow, for the usual variety; and greenness of color is an evidence of immaturity or of artificial coloring. Such coffee should be avoided.

The same source went on to say,

The truth is that no coffee anywhere in the world

is superior to the Brazilian, which is sold everywhere as Java, Mocha, Maracaibo, etc, at the fancy of the dealer and the whim of the consumer. Every plantation in the country produces the Java and Mocha of the markets of the United States, and it is only an affair of the sieves of differently sized meshes to classify the products of Brazilian plantations into the falsely named kinds, in order to demand a higher price from the buyer.[2]

In the 1990s, when a green colour in raw coffee is favoured and Brazilian coffee of practically all grades is considered inferior in the gourmet market, today's opinions show a total reassessment of what makes a good coffee.

In fact harsh coffees become mellow with age but good coffees do not improve - they lose their acidity and also become mellow.

EVALUATING COFFEE COMMERCIALLY

The flavour of wine is in every way comparable to that of coffee.

With experience we learn the rightness or wrongness of the colour, appearance, taste, odour, and texture of each wine for its type. We easily learn to discriminate against wines of excessive sweetness or deficient acidity. With experience we also learn the most enjoyable balance between tastes and between odours. [3]

The main difference between coffee and wine is that coffee is served hot and wine cold. The other difference is that wine is poured from a bottle which, provided it has been well stored, has the same flavour all over the world at the same time. Coffee from the same origin has different flavours depending on the degree of roast, the dispersion of grind, the temperature of the water, the brewing time, the quality of the water, the type of apparatus used, the ratio of water to coffee and how long, after preparation, it is served. A much more complex description is needed to determine just what a particular cup of coffee actually is.

THE PURPOSE FOR EACH COFFEE MUST BE DEFINED

If precise descriptions are extremely difficult to make, then how is coffee to be evaluated? There is only one criterion - the purpose for the coffee must be defined and the coffee measured against this. Just as differing varieties of grapes are suitable to make whites, reds, ports and brandies so it is with coffee. Turkish coffee served Greek style needs to have low acidity when lightly roasted and, for the Lebanese palate, to have a nice flavour when burnt. The coffees used in Germany should have high acidity to complement the sweeter and creamier processed milk specially developed for coffee. Italians require their espressos to have a cream, a mousse, which stays on top of the coffee and for this you need a blend with a little Robusta. American coffee needs to be light in flavour to be drunk long, black and often. A coffee must be evaluated with its final purpose in mind.

BREWING EXTRACTION CURVE WITH DIFFERENT GRINDS, TEMPERATURES AND TIMES

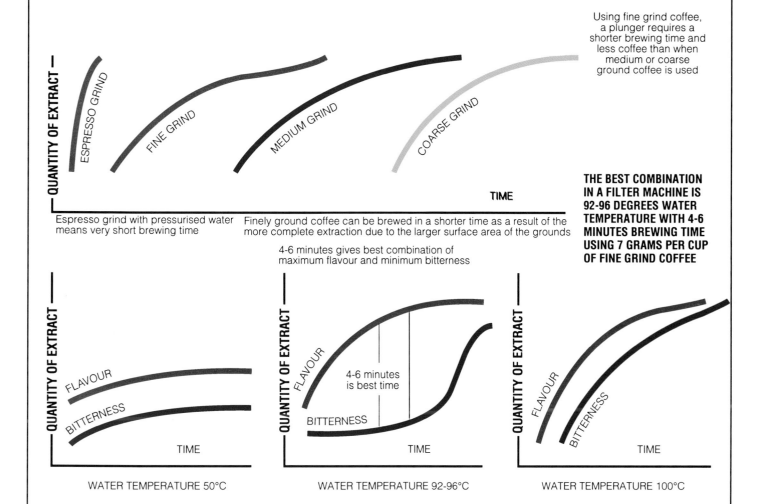

Using fine grind coffee, a plunger requires a shorter brewing time and less coffee than when medium or coarse ground coffee is used

QUANTITY OF EXTRACT

ESPRESSO GRIND

FINE GRIND

MEDIUM GRIND

COARSE GRIND

TIME

Espresso grind with pressurised water means very short brewing time

Finely ground coffee can be brewed in a shorter time as a result of the more complete extraction due to the larger surface area of the grounds

THE BEST COMBINATION IN A FILTER MACHINE IS 92-96 DEGREES WATER TEMPERATURE WITH 4-6 MINUTES BREWING TIME USING 7 GRAMS PER CUP OF FINE GRIND COFFEE

4-6 minutes gives best combination of maximum flavour and minimum bitterness

QUANTITY OF EXTRACT

FLAVOUR

BITTERNESS

TIME

WATER TEMPERATURE 50°C

QUANTITY OF EXTRACT

FLAVOUR

4-6 minutes is best time

BITTERNESS

TIME

WATER TEMPERATURE 92-96°C

QUANTITY OF EXTRACT

FLAVOUR

BITTERNESS

TIME

WATER TEMPERATURE 100°C

EXTRACTION IN AN ESPRESSO MACHINE WITH A PUMP

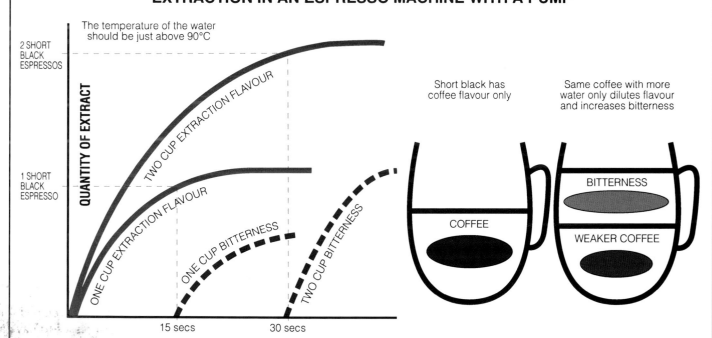

The temperature of the water should be just above 90°C

2 SHORT BLACK ESPRESSOS

1 SHORT BLACK ESPRESSO

QUANTITY OF EXTRACT

TWO CUP EXTRACTION FLAVOUR

ONE CUP EXTRACTION FLAVOUR

ONE CUP BITTERNESS

TWO CUP BITTERNESS

15 secs   30 secs

Short black has coffee flavour only

Same coffee with more water only dilutes flavour and increases bitterness

BITTERNESS

COFFEE

WEAKER COFFEE

In theory, an espresso, using 7 grams per cup, should take 25 seconds but, in practice, one espresso takes 15 seconds and two espressos take 25-30 seconds. The explanation is that the water irrigating the coffee for two espressos can only saturate to a certain point and the water volume after 15 seconds has only dissolved half the flavour. Until the rest of the water dissolves the remaining flavour, then, and only then, does the bitterness come out. The bitterness only comes out of the coffee after the coffee flavour is extracted. It is as though the bitterness is wrapped in flavour which must dissolve first.

Characteristics

Once the purpose has been defined we are able to declare the characteristics that we are looking for. These characteristics are: *Flavour, Acidity, Body, Aroma, and Appearance and Grading.*

FLAVOUR The flavour of coffee varies from country to country, area to area and time to time. It is subject to many factors such as when the rains come, the amount of sunshine, the soil, processing - just about everything has some effect. Some coffees have very little flavour. Others have flavours which range from chemical tastes to lightly honeyish to almondy to flavours of wine, cheese, even onions. It is the character in the bean that makes it worthwhile to drink provided that the character is pleasant. The possession of character makes one bean more valuable than another. As with all other characteristics there is a wide range within a geographic region. All coffee roasters regularly get samples with great variations from the same country. The only way to assess flavour is to taste. No amount of looking at the beans or descriptive matter can beat tasting the beans for an honest assessment. The first thing a taster looks for is a clean taste to ensure that no strange by-flavours, from processing, transport or warehousing have affected the coffee.

The roasting process at some point will maximise the flavour. Before and after that point the beans will have less flavour. Only trial and error will indicate the point of maximum flavour.

ACIDITY Lemonade is refreshing because it contains bubbles of carbon dioxide or carbonic acid. It is the acidity that makes the palate fresh. Flat lemonade fails to refresh. The same acidity gives life to a Hock or Riesling which is drunk with a meal to refresh the palate. Port does not have acidity - it lacks the life of a Riesling and it is never drunk with a meal.

To make a cup of coffee attractive it must have refreshment value. When a food is too acidic it becomes sour and so it is normally complemented by cream. Two examples are quinces and rhubarb which are normally served with cream or ice cream. Where a processed and sweeter milk, as used in Germany, finds favour, the coffee should be more acid than usual to counteract the sweetness. The main purpose of drinking coffee is as a refreshment.

If acidity is present in a coffee, the darker the coffee is roasted, the lower the acidity.

BODY The tongue is very sensitive to the thickness of any liquid. It feels the particles in chicken noodle soup. The tongue tells the brain that clear chicken soup is thin and that the addition of noodles makes it thicker, more flavourful and more enjoyable. Tomato soup made from tomato pulp is thin and watery. The addition of flour, sugar and cream thickens it and sends a message that the soup is now thicker and richer. In fact the tomato flavour is now diluted and masked to such an extent that it no longer exists. The point is that soup manufacturers have discovered that body is important. It is just as important for coffees to have body. Colombian, Kenyan and Indonesian Arabicas have good body, as do Robustas. Some Central Americans and Brazils are thin and watery. The more body a coffee has the longer the aftertaste remains in the mouth. If this taste is good, body is a positive characteristic.

Darker roasting will increase the body of a coffee.

AROMA One of the great attractions of coffee both in ground form and in the cup is the aroma. Its very existence heightens our sense of expectation. 'If only coffee could taste like it smells', is a common statement. The simple explanation for this non-event is that from a packet of coffee we are smelling up to fifty cups of coffee and comparing it to the aroma from one cup. In addition the brewing process only dissolves some of the aromatics and transports them into the cup while some disappear into the atmosphere. The aromatics from the ground coffee and the cup are similar but different.

Nevertheless we must make both a qualitative and quantitative analysis of the aromatics of any coffee. A knowledge of coffees gives us certain expectations and if these are answered, then the coffee is true to character. From Costa Rica coffee we expect a light, almondy aroma. From Colombian coffee we expect a honeyish smell. Indonesian Arabica has a sulphury smell while Ethiopian Mocha can have a winey smell. Other coffees have more or less aromas and the quantities vary with individual samples.

Both the time and temperature of roasting may vary the quantity of aroma in a coffee. High roasting temperatures and longer roasting tend to diminish the aroma.

APPEARANCE AND GRADING The roasting process works best when all the beans are the same size. Large beans cook more slowly and small ones more quickly. Broken beans and misshapen beans tend to overcook and become scorched and burnt. Most countries grade their coffees on the basis of size or the number of black beans, sticks and stones in a given sample. This grading is no indication of cup quality but low-graded coffees are unlikely to taste very good.

Appearance is important where the customer buys coffee as whole beans. The largest beans of all are known as Marogogipes and they are produced in Guatemala, Nicaragua, Mexico and Colombia. My experience has been that they have less flavour and thinner liquor than ordinary coffees. Nevertheless they command a premium price far beyond their actual worth because of their size. It is human nature to pay more for large apples than small ones.

Many countries produce a grade of coffee known as peaberry or maleberry which is a small round coffee bean. Most coffee cherries produce two beans or halves, but some will produce cherries with a single bean, and this is known as a peaberry or maleberry. Some Kenyan and

Tanzanian peaberries possess a nice flavour and pungency. Kenya coffee has an excellent peaberry. Peaberry coffee can be sorted by placing all the beans on a sloping conveyor belt. The round peaberry beans roll down and are collected at the bottom.

The grade attached to a coffee is no indication of absolute quality but generally a higher grade of the same coffee will produce a better liquor. The grading at best indicates that the coffee has been sorted.

A sorting table from the Emmerich Maschinenfabrik catalogue of 1907. Hundreds of women sat in German coffee factories sorting coffee on these machines. The beans fell slowly onto a moving belt which was operated by a treadle. Germany - 1907.

Sorted Coffee is Better Coffee

German coffee roasters from the turn of the century used specially designed sorting tables operated by diligent women to select defective beans and other imperfections from the coffee by visual means. In 1947 Gunson-Sortex, an English company, developed a machine for sorting the coffee which recognised both visible colours and colours invisible to the human eye. Modern technology allows sorting machines to sort foreign bodies such as stones and wood from the coffee; also discoloured beans caused by over or under-fermentation, grassy green or black beans which

were under or overripe at the time of picking. The machines operate by measuring the intensity of light at particular wavelengths reflected from the surface of the coffee. Since this light can be ultra-violet fluorescence or infra-red, the machines can see colours invisible to the naked eye. Ultra-violet light is used to measure the fluorescence in coffee beans to determine whether their growth has been affected by insect attack or over-fermentation which causes the beans to be 'stinkers'.

The sorting process which is now carried out by many different brands of machines has probably done more to improve the quality of coffee than any other single technological advance in roasting, grinding or brewing. The intrinsic quality of the coffee can now be evaluated. Sorting is never mentioned in describing a coffee. If the coffee is clean in appearance it is assumed to have been sorted.

Tasting the Coffee

Even with these characteristics the same coffee will still taste different, depending on the conditions in which it is drunk. This is where an understanding of the physiology of tasting is important.

From a physiological viewpoint, there are four primary tastes. Sweet and salt are tasted at the tip of the tongue, acid at the sides, and bitter at the back. There may be other primary tastes, for example the fullness of monosodium glutamate; and there are the tastes of alkaline and metallic flavours. Gilbert Phillips reported that if two people were connected to opposite poles of a battery and the circuit was completed by touching tips of tongues, the cathodal subject would experience an alkaline metallic taste, and the anodal subject an acid-sour taste. Salt applied to one side of the tongue increases perception of sweetness on the other and vice-versa. Grandpa had a clue when he used to put salt on his tart apple.[4]

There are many old tales based on fact, that coffee is improved by the addition of salt, eggshells, fishbones or mustard. When salt is added to coffee, it reduces the bitterness. The addition of eggshells and fishbones, which are alkaline, acts in the same way by neutralising the acidity. Mustard has an anaesthetising effect on the taste buds.

To make the palate clean for coffee tasting, it would be necessary to clean your teeth, eat a dry cracker biscuit without salt, rinse your mouth and wait a while for the palate to settle down. Tasters do not do this because they, like the customers, live in the real world where people are drinking coffee with a wide variety of foods not to mention varying quantities of milk, cream, sugar and sweeteners. Nevertheless, a taster must have a basically clean palate to make some sense of the tasting process. For instance, a meal of anchovies could render the palate insensitive to coffee for some time on account of saltiness. Because the quality of saliva is changing all the time, the results of tasting are varying all the time. Tasting the same coffee thirty minutes apart is likely to give two slightly different results.

Other senses besides taste and smell are important in the appreciation of flavour - for example the visual inspection of colour and condition.[5] Italians judge the quality of the cup by the amount of mousse in the cup in the same way that many people judge the strength of tea by the colour. Greeks judge the coffee by the amount of *kaimaki* - froth on the cup.

Only too often do wine experts disagree about the qualities of different wines. Coffee experts have the same problems because they are only expressing their own preferences after all. This means that the evaluation of coffee is a very personal thing and if you think that one coffee is better than another then there is no doubt that, for you, it is the best coffee. On the other hand experts do speak the same language and apply similar standards, but only when their palates are clean and unaffected by extrinsic factors. Tea tasters like to taste tea at the same time in the morning in front of the same window to get a constant light. But tea tasters are always looking for a bright appearance in the liquor whereas coffee tasters are not so interested in the colour of the liquor.

With all these complications, it is obvious that the flavour of coffee is an individual thing and yet we all seem to have an idea of what makes a good cup of coffee. There is no absolute to tell us what we like but there is an absolute which distinguishes coffee from other hot beverages. The coffee only has to answer two questions, both of which are calculated to evoke individual responses.

THE TWO MOST IMPORTANT QUESTIONS:

1. Does it taste like coffee ?
2. Is it pleasing to the palate?

No matter how you drink your coffee, it must still be recognisable as coffee, whether prepared as a strong short black espresso, Greek coffee or filtered.

Many coffee roasters defending their coffees will raise the point that taste is a personal matter but these questions cannot be evaded by discussion about 'personal taste'. A cup of coffee which can be confused with any other hot brown beverage is by definition not a good coffee. The fact that a person likes a cup of coffee without coffee flavour does not make it a good coffee. In each country of the world there is a body of experts which must be able to make sensible statements about coffee. No matter how coffee is made, the first criterion must be its characteristic to be recognised as coffee. Coffee does have an identifiable flavour distinct from hot ale, hot beer, hot chicory and a whole host of substitutes. Instant coffees must also answer these questions. Not only the first sip, but the rest of the cup as well.

Both questions must be answered in the affirmative if the coffee is to be considered 'good'. If it is pleasant without tasting like coffee, it is simply a pleasant beverage.

TASTING NOTES

Using these tasting techniques it is possible to evaluate all coffees. Many writers on coffee tend to write as if all the coffees from one country have exactly the same attributes. While this is never true, it is possible to make sensible statements about coffees using their geographical origin as a description. Some coffees are sold as coming from unique areas or processors and may have characteristics that make them atypical to their region or country.

The following notes are generalisations which apply to the better quality grades. Poorer grades lose their individuality and are virtually nondescript. It is the possession of a distinctive and desirable character which differentiates good coffees from the ordinary.

COSTA RICA A well-prepared coffee with bluish-green colour when raw. The aroma is light almondy with a matching flavour. Unfortunately the body is a little on the thin side, but it has a very good acidity when lightly roasted. Using twenty-five per cent more coffee per cup gives a delicious cup of coffee. Dark roasting Costa Rica causes the coffee to lose its character but it still makes a pleasant coffee.

MEXICAN, GUATEMALAN and *EL SALVADOR* coffees are not so distinctive, but make a nice cup.

COLOMBIA The best grades include Medellin Excelso and Armenia Excelso. It is a well-selected and prepared coffee. Lightly roasted it has a slight honeyish characteristic in both aroma and flavour. It has good acidity and good body. It becomes very mellow and rich in a darker roast. Colombian Marogogipe (very large size) is of superior appearance but inferior flavour to other Colombians.

KENYA Kenya coffee is renowned for its acidity, good flavour, body - everything. It is a well-rounded coffee but still must be cupped and tested. Some samples are very ordinary. The gradings are to do with size rather than cup quality. There is no doubt that a fine liquoring Kenya AA is one of the finest coffees in the world. Kenya Peaberry in a darker roast is a fine coffee but only in selected lots.

NEW GUINEA This coffee is liked by the German trade on account of its excellent acidity. It has a fruity flavour and is a pleasant self-drinker when medium roasted. It loses its fruitiness when dark roasted and makes an excellent coffee for espresso blends.

JAMAICAN BLUE MOUNTAIN Highly prized on account of its scarcity, but over-rated. I once tried ten different samples from Japan and the conclusion was that the best grade, which is only about ten per cent of the crop, was, in money terms, worth about five per cent more than the best Colombian. All the lower grades were fairly ordinary. I have tried it on two other occasions and was disappointed both times. It is delivered in wooden barrels and sells at an enormous price. Its scarcity and price probably make it far more revered than it ought to be. In 1893 the Americans had a totally different appreciation of it and thought that 'The coffee of Jamaica, like that of Haiti, is of fair quality, a little stronger than Java and milder than Rio.'[6] I suspect that a century ago this coffee was perhaps better than most but that the other coffees have caught up in quality. Certainly the quality deteriorated greatly until after the Second World War when quality control procedures were instituted and the quality improved greatly. Rarity, attention to quality and marketing since the 1950s have been instrumental in Jamaican Blue Mountain being regarded as a top quality coffee and accepted by the consumer as a luxury.

BRAZIL Around a quarter of the world's coffee is supplied by Brazil, but it is of very modest quality. It has a straw flavour, low acidity and in general is fairly uninteresting. Because its flavour level is low, it is a good blender. Its lower price makes it an even better blender for some. Brazilian coffees can be very harsh. There are probably good coffees in Brazil, but the exporters are not generally interested in selling small quantities of high quality coffee, although some European and American importers are now trying to identify good grades.

KONA Comes from Hawaii in small quantities at high prices. It is a nice mild coffee produced at high cost on delightful mountainside plantations and sold at a high price which makes it totally uneconomic for blending. It is not quite as spectacular as the Hawaiians would have you believe.

INDONESIAN Mostly Robusta, but the Arabica from Sumatra is rather special. Known as Lintong or Mandheling, it is very good coffee, with a heavy body and a sulphury flavour, derived from the volcanic soil on which it grows. It is a difficult coffee to roast - slight variations in roast colour produce large variations in flavour. A range of colours from the same bag makes it a little difficult to colour match when it is being roasted. Java and Celebes Kalossi are other well known Indonesian Arabica coffees which have excellent flavour and body. Kalossi has an enormous price which cannot be justified - it is three times that of Sumatran Arabica.

INDIAN Plantation A has a nice smooth flavour with little acidity. Mysore is hard to come by but has a nice hemp rope flavour. A really good Mysore coffee is one of my favourites. Indian coffee blends very well with acidic coffee such as New Guinea. Select carefully - some Indians look good but are flavourless. They are generally light roasted. Some Indian coffees are excellent in dark roast blends for espresso.

TANZANIA Similar to Kenya. Very good coffee at its best. Excellent peaberry. It generally has good acidity. Sometimes the name Kilimanjaro is used.

MOCHA Two regions supply Mocha - the Yemen and Ethiopia. Mocha takes its name from a port on the coast of the Yemen which no longer functions. Most of the Yemen coffee now goes to Saudi Arabia and Japan and is generally unavailable in Europe and the United States. The most famous Yemen coffee was Mocha Mattari. Certainly by reputation it was something extra special possessing a chocolatey flavour and every descriptive that could enhance a product's value. To all intents and purposes it is a mythical coffee, although it does exist in very small quantities.

Ethiopian Mocha exists and has excellent flavour characteristics in its best grades. Generally coffee cherries, when they are the right colour, are picked from the trees but Ethiopian coffee is allowed to fall on the ground whence it is swept up with stones and sticks. The cherries are not collected immediately and so they deteriorate somewhat. The combination of beans in varying states of ripeness and over-ripeness and primitive processing methods results in a very rough coffee of varying size with a range of green and yellow beans. Ethiopian Mochas are difficult to roast on account of the varying bean colours which make it difficult to match the roast sample with the beans in the roaster. The yellow beans retain their colour after roasting and have a peanutty flavour. It must have been the rough processing that gave the coffee its very definite winey, cheesey flavour because modern technology has now intervened in the form of colour sorters to produce a finely sorted coffee with the appearance and grading of Kenya coffee. In the process the individual flavour that made it so interesting has also disappeared in some grades, although most of the coffee is in the original unsorted form.

The most common Mocha is Djimma which comes in a variety of grades. It is difficult to buy this coffee and be certain of what you are getting on account of the variations between bags. Longberry Harrar is much prized but very difficult to find. It is a large bean with a pronounced cheesey, winey flavour.

The word Mocha is very widely misused. It is often used to denote a dark roast such as Mocha espresso. It is also used as a mixture of chocolate and coffee such as in Mocha icing on a cake. Its very name in a coffee connection evokes everything attractive about coffee and therefore its use is very widespread. In Germany it means a small after-dinner cup of coffee. It is also used for an after-dinner coffee blend. The fact that the word is used in so many different contexts sometimes makes it difficult to know which particular meaning is being referred to.

If the coffee you are offered is actually Mocha then try it. It is different and ten to twenty per cent can make quite a difference to a bland blend.

Flavoured Coffees

During the 1980s flavoured coffees became increasingly popular in the United States and especially in gourmet coffee shops where they achieved thirty per cent of sales. Many European and some American coffee experts regard flavoured coffee as in some way inferior; however there are numerous flavoured teas and brandies and these are respected drinks. I believe that for this reason flavoured coffees have to be considered legitimate, even if there is little recognisable coffee flavour. The most popular flavours are based on chocolate, vanilla, cinnamon, hazelnuts, almonds, macadamia nuts and various combinations thereof.

THE MECHANICS OF TASTING

The Coffee Development Group in Washington, D.C. has produced the most complete approach to tasting coffee.[7] The central fact is that coffee comes from many different origins, arrives in differing conditions, is processed after varying lengths of time, roasted to differing degrees, ground to varying degrees of fineness and brewed with varying quantities of water at different temperatures for different times at different pressures. In short, an enormous vocabulary is needed to describe precisely just what it is that is being tasted so that professional tasters can communicate with each other sensibly. It is most important that consumers and professional tasters talk the same language. For instance, when the word 'strong' is used, it is used to denote strength of character rather than bitterness.

Coffee samples are normally cupped by taking a 7.25 gram sample of carefully and consistently ground coffee and pouring over it 150 millilitres of freshly boiled water. Then follows the sensory evaluation of the brew in which the fragrance, aroma, taste, nose, aftertaste and body are checked.

FRAGRANCE - this is recognised by vigorous sniffing of the ground coffee. The fragrance is the set of gases released slowly by the heat of grinding. The 'character of the fragrance indicates the nature of the taste : Sweet scents lead to acidy tastes, and pungent scents lead to sharp tastes. The intensity of the fragrance reveals the freshness of the sample, meaning the time that elapsed between roasting the sample and grinding it'.[8]

While whole coffee beans do have some fragrance it is minimal compared to that of freshly ground coffee. Depending on storage conditions, ground coffee can lose up to sixty-five per cent of its fragrance within twenty-four hours of grinding.

AROMA - this is evaluated by sniffing the gases formed in the cup. They are evaluated by the taster referring to a memory bank of many different substances and attributing a level of intensity which relates closely to the freshness.

TASTE - this is done by slurping the coffee from a spoon in such a way as to spread the coffee all over the tongue. The taste of the coffee will vary with the temperature.

NOSE - as the liquid is slurped it aerates and goes into the nasal passages where it can be analysed. 'The simultaneous assessment of the taste and nose (vapours) gives the sample of coffee beans a unique flavour.'[9]

AFTERTASTE - this is done by swallowing a small sample and then pumping the vapours into the nasal cavity. The flavour compounds found may resemble chocolate, tobacco smoke or cloves. The word aftertaste has a totally different meaning to the average person. It simply means the taste that is left in the mouth after the coffee has gone down.

BODY - the oiliness of the brew is an indication of the fat content while the thickness measures the fibre and protein content. Together the sensations of oiliness and thickness are the body.

Evaluating the Coffee

All these terms are professional terms but they do have meaning for regular consumers who know whether they like the coffee, but not the reason why. A professional analysis is able to establish what the factors are in that decision. In a sense the professional taster is removed from the real world where people do not generally get the product in the same condition as the taster. The consumer is more likely to notice acidity or sourness, bitterness, burnt flavour and smoothness and the flavour after mixing with sugar, cream and milk.

The taster thinks he has an idea of what the market is looking for or will tolerate as a compromise for a lower price. He also thinks he has an understanding of what the consumer is tasting and also, by tasting competitive products, the actual profile of the market place.

A small sample of coffee is delivered from the agent to the dealer or the roaster whose job it is to evaluate it. A small roasting machine which can handle about one hundred grams is used to roast the sample to approximately the desired colour and then the sample is cooled. In most cases the coffee is evaluated by taking a small weight of the coffee, grinding it and pouring just-boiled water over it then letting it stand for five minutes. The coffee is stirred to allow the grounds to be wetted thoroughly and then the liquor is decanted into the tasting cup. After cooling a little, the taster takes a spoonful of the coffee, sucks it in with gusto and proceeds to evaluate it for flavour, aroma, body and acidity. Where the coffee is to be used in espresso machines, the coffee is tasted after being brewed in an espresso machine. The coffee is then compared with coffees from different suppliers and a decision made as to which represents the best value or fits the blending needs of the roaster.

How do you know what to do with a new coffee? Make three samples - light, medium and dark roast - and decide if there are any interesting characteristics. If yes from one, make another three roasts around that sample and taste again. Try again and soon it will become apparent that one particular roast elicits the best characteristics from the coffee. As new samples arrive the roaster will know from experience approximately the colour the coffee should be roasted for the particular market. It may be that a coffee can be used as a light roast and a dark roast. Colombian coffee is excellent as a light roast and also a dark roast. New Guinea has a nice fruity flavour in a light roast and makes a very good dark-roast caramellised coffee.

BLENDING AND THE THEORY BEHIND IT

Before a blend can be made, the roaster has to have some idea as to what the end result should be like on the palate, in the same way an artist should have some idea of the final picture before mixing paints on the palette. Priorities have to be established. Will the coffee have a price limit, or will it be quality at any price, or will it be the cheapest coffee that will be acceptable?

A taster and blender might be requested to make a blend for espresso machines with no burnt taste, a rich flavour and good cream in the cup, in the middle cost range, or alternatively a blend for filter machines with low acidity, chocolatey flavour, good body and ability to take milk. Experience says that certain coffees will play a part in the blend. Price consideration says that only certain coffees can be considered. From all the possible coffees, various combinations are made in varying proportions and with different roast colours. Each sample is evaluated until the desired result is obtained. It is important to note that no prescriptions can be made - the characteristics of the water differ from place to place.

The theory of making a blend is simple. Take the individual evaluations of several different coffees and give points for acidity, aroma, body, flavour, and type of flavour. Then state what your aim is in the same terms. A few mathematical calculations will tell you what proportions of the coffees should go into the blend. Blenders do not actually give points like this. Over a long period, experts have developed specific solutions to particular problems. These they can retrieve from their memory bank, and apply when necessary.

Blending is really trial and error. It is theory and failure. For instance experience may say that a blend of three coffees will give the desired result. Suppose the blend lacks body and flavour. Try ten per cent Robusta to give extra body. The flavour has deteriorated. Add some dark roast. Too dark. Add some medium dark roast. Flavour improved and good body. Reduce Robusta to five per cent. Nearly there! Add ten per cent Kenya to give acidity. Too dear. Replace Kenya with some Costa Rica. Very nice. Right flavour. Right price. Success.

Once a blend is decided upon and given a fancy name, a roaster will try to keep very close to it. The roaster has given the customer expectations and these should be satisfied.

CREATING BLENDS

Serious companies take ages to establish a new blend while less professional roasters merely combine coffees with exotic names at random as if something special can be created by chance. Some years ago, I defined a new blend as being suitable for both filter and espresso and having a rich flavour and heavy body. It took three months to perfect it.

Some roasters create blends for each restaurant as required and others have over forty blends in their books created in their heads or by the spin of the wheels on a poker machine.

BUYING COFFEE

Simply put, there is no way to judge a coffee except by tasting. The blend names, such as Mocha Kenya and Mocha Java, are famous but largely meaningless. There may be subtle flavours lurking in the background that you did not detect that now make the blend a masterpiece or a disaster. There may be off-flavours which are masked in the blend in some chance fashion. In short you cannot be certain just what you will end up with until you cup or taste the blend.

All this is happening in an ideal world where the roaster is testing and tasting regularly. Theory is unfortunately different to practice. The larger companies have testing facilities such as colour spectrometers and grind analysers and trained tasters to evaluate the coffee.

Giant companies also have other priorities. When you sell enormous quantities of coffee, it is important that you include in the blend only coffees which are available in vast quantities continuously through the year as the base for the blend. No matter what the quality, it would be silly to base a blend on a small crop such as Haiti if you could not get continuous supplies. This factor enables smaller companies to use more exotic coffees in their blends.

Smaller specialists, unless they have a long history in the coffee trade, will not have the skills to do all these jobs. It is likely that the coffees will be bought on description from traders who have also bought on description. Such a description might be as simple as Kenya AB or Indian Plantation A or Costa Rica SHB - strictly hard bean. The roaster then ascribes to the bean a textbook description of the coffee such as 'Fine Kenyas have a clean, bright-flavoured style and a solid body and taste that sometimes approaches a most attractive sappy or winey character. Poor Kenyas can be sour.'[10] Textbook descriptions are not noted for their accuracy - they never mention the range of flavours associated with a coffee. The coffee is then roasted to approximately the right colour and, without being tested, is sold. It is not easy to buy good, quality coffee and it is not easy to get the best out of good, quality coffee.

It must be stated that those coffees which are considered gourmet coffees are generally in a different class altogether to ordinary coffees.

THE BEST COFFEE
FROM A CONSUMER VIEWPOINT

The answer to the simple question, 'Which is the best coffee?' is not simple at all. In fact it is very complicated and involves all our senses and perceptions. The people asking the question want a definitive and simple answer, which will enable them to go out and buy the best in the same way they would go out and buy the best bottle of wine. But coffee, unlike wine, is subject to variations in roasting, grinding, brewing and freshness. Unfortunately, many people in the coffee trade have answered the question as if an absolute answer exists and they know it.

Any discussion about quality is necessarily personal. It matters not whether we are talking about the quality of a painting, a horse or a car. What can be analysed are the factors which make up the object, the end use and our evaluation of the factors. There can be a rational discussion of whether something can be better than something else and eventually a body of self-appointed experts will determine what makes one thing have quality and another less of it.

Some people like acid drops, an indication that their palates have a high threshhold for acidity. Other people are indifferent to lightly burnt toast and in fact even prefer it. Such a palate would probably tolerate burnt coffee and accept it as normal.

For each person there is a best coffee and the choice is often based on extrinsic factors such as price, origin, pleasant coffee experiences in the country of origin, and the packaging.

There is no best coffee. There are several excellent coffees which have more coffee flavour than many others and any one may be the best for you.

Ripe coffee cherries on the tree.
North Coast, N.S.W., Australia.

HOW TO DEFINE A GREAT CUP OF COFFEE

The normal amount of coffee for both filter and espresso machines is seven grams per cup. If coarser ground coffee is used in other machines, more coffee will be required.

An excellent cup of Colombian coffee *might* be defined as being from a selected shipment of Colombian Excelso and :

1. roasted to 220 degrees Celsius in a particular fluid bed roaster in eight minutes. All roasters operate at slightly different temperatures. Because of slight differences they can roast the coffee to the same colour even though the temperature is different.
2. ground in a disc grinder with forty-five per cent of the particles around sugar size and fifty-five per cent of the particles no more than ten per cent larger by weight.
3. the water filtered in a water softener to remove calcium carbonate and magnesium carbonate.
4. brewed in a filter coffee maker using a polyester mesh filter with the water at 96 degrees Celsius for five minutes and served immediately. This could be varied to be made by hand pouring hot water around 94 to 96 degrees Celsius over a cone filter holder and using a clean filter paper.
5. the ratio of water to coffee - 160 millilitres of water to ten grams of coffee.
6. served in a cup with no milk or sugar and allowed to cool to 60 degrees Celsius.

This description is not meant to be definitive but is included to give some idea of the precision necessary for two cups of coffee to be made identically.

Few people ever go to that much trouble to make a cup of coffee. Most coffee is prepared in a kitchen and suffers many variations on the way. The important thing is to know what is happening in the brewing process and also how we are reacting to the flavours as individuals.

The fact is that with all the variations possible, provided care is taken, a reasonably good cup of coffee will be prepared.

CHAPTER 14

Instant Coffee and other Substitutes

From the first days of coffee in Europe, a whole range of substitutes in one form or another was used. With varying success these substitutes replaced the form of the bean and the colour in the cup but they never replaced the aroma, the unique thing about coffee that gives it its universal attraction. It must have been the aroma from the ground coffee which kept people drinking it when the brew itself must have been so poor. It is possible that the flavour of coffee was so bad that many substitutes were tolerable and may have been in fact improvements on the coffee. There must have been an underlying idea that the components of coffee, which could not be understood in those early days, could in some way be replaced by substitutes, no matter how outlandish, perhaps the more fantastic the better.

Adding this background to the lure of convenience, the attraction of instant coffee is understandable. Just add water and all of the 'coffee' before you can be consumed. There is no waste.

THE VALUE OF USED COFFEE AND TEA

Coffee and tea are the only foods which have basically the same form when you buy them as when you are finished with them. All others are consumed or thrown out in an obviously diminished form. Perceiving the change in value of something that does not appear to change after 'using' is difficult. Our minds are more comfortable when the before and after process is clear and coffee and tea seem to release their flavours by a process similar to osmosis. Fresh and spent coffee and tea may be equated in value to the difference between today's newspaper and yesterday's.

In a world where saving is a virtue, discarding coffee grounds which a few minutes ago actually had value, seems difficult. This probably explains the early French habit of selling spent grounds and of using spent grounds to brew water for the next pot of fresh coffee. The consumer's reaction is to minimise wastage by finding cheaper ways to do the same job and this involved admixtures or using the same coffee twice. Stale bread is thrown out. Cold toast is discarded, but cold coffee is reheated and fresh hot water is poured over old tea leaves.

CHICORY

Chicory is mostly thought of as a substitute for coffee, but historically the opposite is true, for chicory was well-known in the ancient world. Charlemagne recommended its cultivation and the Abbot of Wahal-Leck in the Netherlands grew it in the ninth century. Industrial production commenced at the end of the seventeenth century in the Netherlands, and in France from 1765 to complement what must have been a large domestic production. It was a drink in its own right and the introduction of coffee was really a pleasant addition to chicory.[1] The bitterness of the chicory neutralised the sweetness of the hot milk, used in large measure in hot milk coffee. In 1688 Dufour said that chicory refreshes.[2]

Chicory substitutes in powder form, often for mixing with coffee, were made from beet, carrots, parsnips, mangold-wurzel, or other saccharine roots. The first English patent for this substitute for a substitute was lodged by J. Howard in 1870. The sugar was extracted from the beet, and the residual pulp was dried in a kiln, roasted and reduced to powder. Enormous amounts of supposed coffee were being sold as coffee and chicory, malt coffee and the like. In Paris in 1862 the consumption of chicory was 300 000 kilograms.[3] Even in Germany, a country with

Above: Coffee and chicory essence was probably the most popular coffee substitute in the British Empire until the 1950s.

255

knowledge of the highest standards of coffee, more than half of all 'coffee' drunk, in 1913, was artificial.[4] Very high consumption figures were present in other countries and remained high until the prosperous times of the 1950s.

A RANGE OF SUBSTITUTES

Thirty-nine different recipes for coffee substitute beverages were listed in a French book by Henri Welter and this was only for the period from 1761 to 1849. There was apparently no reason why any substance, no matter how unlikely, could not be considered a component.[5]

The English were equally inventive and talented and some of the concoctions in the patents verge on the horrific. Adulteration was commonplace in England and probably in other countries. In England:

> *coffee damaged by sea-water is also commonly washed, first with water, then with lime-water, dried and roasted, or sometimes coloured with an azo-dye to give it a bright appearance. Imitation coffees or coffee substitutes are manufactured on a large scale in America, Hamburg and also in this country.*

Various combinations of coffee, bran, molasses, chicory, wheat, oats, buckwheat, wheat flour, sawdust and pea hulls were pressed and moulded into berries.[6]

> *At a meeting in 1851, a grocer from Shoreditch [London] having produced at the meeting a compound of burnt peas, dog-biscuit, prepared earth, and a substance which, he said, "I shall not describe, because it is too horrid to mention", went on to affirm that several tons of the same material were in existence, and that it was used as a substitute for chicory and snuff.* [7]

In Germany there was also a history going back centuries, of falsification in other products. In the fifteenth century at Ulm, every tavern keeper had to swear that he had not mixed with wine, 'woad, chalk, mustard-seed, clay, *Scharlachkraut*, must of apples, lead, mercury or vitriol'.[8] Doubtless there was coffee adulteration until the law of 1875 forbade it.

In 1872, H. Warry suggested that a strong infusion of tea, coffee and cocoa be poured into a steam-jacketed evaporating pan. When the substance in the pan had dehydrated, it was removed into an atmosphere as dry as possible, allowed to cool until brittle, and then reduced to powder. This was a sensible approach to making instant coffee and if convection drying had been used instead of boiling away the water, would have produced a better product. In 1873 Francis and Addiscott suggested that the roasted stone of tamarind should be ground as a substitute for coffee. In 1874, D. Nicoll suggested that a tube of isinglass or gelatine be filled with a preparation of cream, milk, or sugar, either separately or in combination, and sealed. The tube was then combined, by pressure, with dried tea, ground coffee, or crushed cocoa, so that upon the addition of hot water the tube dissolved and the beverage was ready for use.

C. Morfit in 1876 added condensed milk to animal gelatine and coffee and added chocolate, vanilla, essence of lemon, orange-flower water or other flavouring. The heated milk contained 'powdered borax in order that the finished product may be remelted or dissolved as required' and the finished product was cooled in thin sheets.

In 1880, W.P. Branson had the idea to take a solution of filtered coffee and pass it through a series of refrigerators and take off a film of ice free from coffee. The operation was to be repeated until the solution had the desired strength. Had he continued the refrigerating, he would have discovered freeze-dried instant coffee. Instead he boiled water with animal charcoal, strained and distilled it, mixed it with the coffee extract, aerated it and bottled it. A few patents existed for machines which dosed some form of coffee concentrate with boiling water into the cup.

Certainly coffee and chicory essence was popular and with the minimal labelling requirements of the day, no one could really know what it contained. In actual fact, during the second half of the century, sophisticated scientific techniques were being developed to detect adulteration. Many of these patents from England attempted to somehow pass off the most incredible and unlikely substances as being part of a legitimate coffee product. Doubtless similar ideas were being patented all over Europe. The sheer number of these patents and the official reports complaining about fraudulent practices suggest that some of the products must have been marketed. Certainly the inventors thought that a market existed for their product. The ultimate aim was to make a quick cup of coffee. The development of one-cup filters in the 1890s was one result of this aim; the other was instant coffee, as we know it today.

Far Right: Le *Trablit* essence for coffee, milk coffee, hot or cold. Coffee essences or concentrates were very popular from the 1860s until the 1930s and are still used in some countries. They are suitable for making milk coffee because the hot milk masks the flavour to a large extent. Many extracts contained chicory. The bitter flavour of the burnt chicory was made palatable by the sweetness of the hot milk. France.

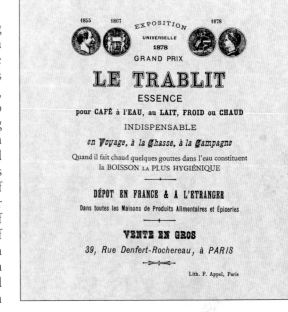

Café au lait instantané was made of pure coffee, milk and sugar and came in a little box with five portions. France.

THE DEVELOPMENT OF INSTANT COFFEE

Instant coffee is reconstituted coffee made from highly concentrated brewed coffee. It resembles real coffee but does not have the same aroma and taste and rightly should be considered a substitute. Instant coffee is manufactured in the same way as powdered milk - the coffee is brewed, under pressure, into a strong solution and then spray-dried by spraying out the droplets into a stream of very hot air which extracts the moisture from the droplets and leaves the instant coffee powder to fall. It is not just ordinary domestic coffee with the moisture removed but coffee beans brewed at high temperature with twice as many soluble solids extracted as in regular coffee.

In 1899 Dr. Sartori Kato from Japan invented a soluble coffee which was sold in 1901 in the United States at the Panamerican World Fair, but it was not a commercial success.[9] Many earlier English patents mention drying the solution in heated pans but they were not successful. I suspect that many other instant coffees were marketed in Europe but their appearance has never been recorded. Dr. Kato owes his fame to having launched his product in the United States and being recorded in Ukers' books which described the American trade history.

In 1910, George Washington, a Belgian living in America, introduced another instant coffee and started a factory which was to last for over thirty years. Several American firms developed instant coffee and it was widely used for the troops in the First World War but seems to have been of minor importance in the years following.

Cefabu instant coffee was made in Germany during the First World War but seems to have left no trace of its existence except for an advertising booklet.[10] None of the conventional histories mention Cefabu or any other factories which may well have existed in Europe.

Cefabu Coffee is not a substitute. The solubles in the coffee bean in powder form are guaranteed pure. There is an opener with each box. [English translation]

The brochure went on to say that Cefabu coffee was not dearer than normal coffee because it extracted substances from normal coffees that could not be had by normal methods. It was soluble in hot and cold water.

A short pause in the fighting is sufficient for officers and soldiers to refresh themselves with a quickly prepared cup of coffee and to regain strength for further exertions. Warships and cargo ships will in future not go to sea without being stocked with Cefabu coffee. Germany - 1910s. [English translation]

It is interesting historically that apart from the pages from this Cefabu advertising brochure there does not appear to be any evidence in coffee books or elsewhere that Cefabu instant coffee was ever manufactured. The company is never mentioned in the history of instant coffee and yet must have been one of the first manufacturers.

In 1938 the Swiss, Dr. Max Morgenthaler, of the Nestlé Company developed new methods for making instant coffee. The first Nestlé product was half coffee and half carbohydrates - maltose and dextrin, but later the carbohydrates were withdrawn to leave a product completely based on coffee. The American company General Foods, with its Maxwell House brand, was another company which was in the forefront of new developments in instant coffee manufacture in the 1940s. During the Second World War, American troops were introduced to instant coffee and developed a taste for it. This led to a substantial world-wide market growth and popularity, with a marked improvement in quality. In the traditional tea-drinking countries of Britain, Australia, New Zealand and South Africa, instant coffee held the larger share of the market over roast and ground coffee, at times more than eighty per cent. In the United States it reached a level of nearly thirty per cent, but in other countries the level was much lower. For instance in Sweden, a high quality real coffee market, the consumption of instant coffee hardly made any impact.

Freeze-dried coffee was introduced in 1965. To process this, the coffee concentrate is placed into a chamber which has a high pressure vacuum and the moisture is frozen off. The result is sold as a powder which looks like coarsely ground coffee and is considered to be more coffee-like in taste. It is a very expensive process and the spray-dried manufacturers, in an attempt to retain their market, responded in 1967 with a process of agglomerating instant coffee powder into a granular product which looked more like real coffee grounds.

The instant coffee market stagnated in the 1980s. Electric filter machines were largely responsible for this, because they were capable of brewing a good coffee with minimum fuss. The most recent use of instant coffee is in coffee bags. Patents for coffee bags with real coffee appeared in the nineteenth century but never worked. Coffee bags float and do not brew properly. In the 1970s several brands were available using burnt caramellised sugar which gave a very quick colour to the cup but not much coffee flavour. The 1990s have seen the emergence of a coffee bag which contains real coffee for aroma in the pack and instant coffee giving quick colour and some coffee flavour in the cup. Many of the customers are probably unaware that there is any instant coffee in the bag at all.

Instant coffee seems to have saturated the world market but no doubt technological developments will lead to new techniques and a better product. Research is proceeding on producing instant coffee by osmosis, and if this succeeds, it will probably produce a realistic product.

There has been an evolution from the first basic powder product produced in open surroundings and with little aroma, to a technologically sophisticated product, in which the aroma is either added back or retained. It is packed using modern techniques to stop the hygroscopic product turning into a solid mass and to ensure that there is aroma in the glass jar, at least at the moment of opening, if not later. As well as the characteristic odour, it is often possible to recognise instant coffee by the bubbles which form around the rim of the cup and also the greyish colour when milk is added .

In normal domestic brewers the extraction rate of solubles from the coffee beans is around twenty per cent while modern extraction techniques for instant coffee, using high pressure water well over boiling point in special machines, extract up to fifty per cent of the solubles. In effect instant coffee is the dried powder form of a drink which is totally different to that normally brewed at home.

CAFFEINE AND DECAFFEINATION

Caffeine is one of the many components of coffee. It has caused much controversy because of the mild stimulation it provides and because it is classified as a drug, as are alcohol and nicotine and a host of harmful drugs. It has become common to regard all drugs as deleterious to health, irrespective of the facts and there has been tremendous exaggeration of the ill-effects of coffee. For this reason there have been many attempts to remove caffeine from it.

The effects of caffeine on the human body have been greatly overstated by those who make a living from selling non-caffeine products and decaffeinated products. Caffeine does act as a mood elevator and improves mental performance in comparison to alcohol, which acts as a depressant. There is a wide range of individual reaction to caffeine but 'Overall the undesirable effects are modest by comparison with the positive ones'.[11] After a while, tolerance to caffeine is built up and there are few noticeable effects, unless excessive quantities, (three Italian short blacks in a minute) are consumed. Most people following a policy of moderation by drinking two to three cups of coffee per day will not suffer any ill effects at all.

Caffeine affects sleep but, 'Caffeine differs, however, from many other substances in that it scarcely affects the dream phases of sleep, which are psychically of such great importance ... Caffeine can be regarded rather as something that keeps you awake than as an inhibitor of sleep. It seems quite feasible that caffeine can improve mental performance by five to ten per cent'.[12] Medical research is full of claims about the damage from caffeine but these claims are rarely substantiated. It is important to note that, while many tests in the laboratory reveal all sorts of potential problems, biomedical statistics do not show any significant correlations between coffee consumption and health problems. Scandinavians have the highest consumption of coffee in the world but do not appear to suffer any significant health problems except longevity.

In 1901, Chryssochoïdès said in his book, 'Caffeine volatilises at 150 degrees Centigrade and as a consequence it disappears during roasting, therefore the exciting properties of coffee cannot be attributed to it'.[English translation][13] He could not have been more wrong.

The Germans were more concerned about what they consumed in a whole range of foods and knew that caffeine was still in the coffee. Decaffeination was attempted for years before Dr. Ludwig Roselius and Dr. Karl Wimmer in 1905 finally achieved it in Germany. The crucial step was to treat the coffee with a preliminary steam wetting prior to extracting the caffeine with various solvents and this has remained intrinsic to the process.[14]

The decaffeinated coffee was promoted with a wide range of advertising claims. From 1913 until 1929, these were the subject of several long court processes between Kaffee HAG, the company connected with Roselius, and the Association of Hamburg Coffee Roasters, the Cologne Coffee Roasters and others.[15] The net result was that Kaffee HAG had to withdraw some of its claims.

One decaffeination process, called the chemical process, works in the following way: The coffee is wetted with steam and then combined with a solvent which dissolves many of the natural chemicals in the coffee. The caffeine is selectively removed from this solution and then all the remaining chemicals which were originally in the coffee are put back into it.

The water process in the 1980s became the favoured process for decaffeination. Its chief difference lies in not using 'chemicals' in the process. It was explained to me by the manager of a decaffeination factory that the major reason for the change was on account of the safety of the workers who were operating a 'chemical' process plant, rather than for any health benefits for the drinkers of the coffee.

There is no particular advantage from either decaffeination process, water or chemical, nor from another process called critical carbon dioxide although the consumers have shown a preference for the water process. In fact there is virtually no chemical residue in the decaffeinated coffee from either type of process. Public opinion sees any product in a preferred light when it is not treated with chemicals, even though they may be harmless or undetectable in the final product. The same chemical solvents, which leave no traces in the chemically decaffeinated bean, are actually present and used in many places in normal everyday life - commonly in dry-cleaning shops for removing stains. I feel there is a mild hysteria affecting the consumer's attitude to chemically-processed decaffeinated coffee. The water process eliminates pre-steaming[16] but there is no reduction of supposed irritants (as in the chemical process) and the natural wax layer on the coffee beans is only partly removed.[17] There may be a case for saying that chemically processed decaffeinated coffee is better for some people than others. What is certain is that the consumer is paying a higher price for a product with illusory benefits. It appears that there is less flavour with water process decaffeinated coffee than with chemical process, although recent developments may be changing the situation.

In Germany there is quite a market for coffees which have been steam treated to remove the wax on the surface of the green bean before roasting. The German Lendrich process of subjecting the green coffee to a treatment of oversaturated steam was invented in 1933 to make coffee supposedly more digestible by removing the wax. The question as to whether the basic premise is correct is still under debate because some of the medical results of tests are contradictory.[18] Fluidised bed coffee roasters may also make more digestible coffees.[19]

In the past, the mere existence of substitutes seemed a sufficient reason to adulterate coffee. The twentieth century has seen an increasing public concern about health and this, combined with a need for convenience, fosters a host of instant product substitutes. While the purists may not wish to consider instant coffee as a product to compare with real coffee, it has to be considered as a product in its own right to be served when and where convenience is the priority. Improved technology and processes may eventually produce a soluble product with all the attractions of real coffee and none of the perceived drawbacks.

APPENDIX I, UKERS

Most of the historical books in English about coffee development have been based on the two editions in 1922 and 1935 of *All About Coffee* by the American writer, William Ukers. However these books have many mistakes. Ukers did not check the information supplied to him carefully enough. One instance is the name of Edward Loysel de Lantais written as Edward Loysel de Santais (p.629, first edn.). As a result, these names appear in different books as Edward Loysel de Lantais, de Santais and Edward Loysel - all were the one person.

The Durant drawing (p.624, first edn.) is actually Capy's. The Vassieux patent of 1842 is shown as the first vacuum pot patent (p.627, first edn.) when it was in fact pre-dated by several others. The Raparlier pot is described as a percolator on page 624, first edn., but is the same machine as the 'glass filter pot' illustrated as no.7 on page 625, first edn. It was neither - the Raparlier machine was a vacuum pot with atmospheric pressure. I am fairly confident that the French patents which supplied this information were not read carefully, if at all. Madame Richard is not mentioned even though she patented an importation from Germany, the first recirculating percolator.

As far as Count Rumford is concerned, Ukers totally misunderstood what Rumford said. Rumford described the rammer as follows:

four projecting bars ...fastened to the underside are made to level the coffee. (p.636, first edn.)

Ukers states that the projections were to restrict the pressure of the rammer to compress the coffee into a half-inch thickness.(p.622, first edn.)

These particular mistakes and others do not seem to have been discovered or written about before. The book appears to be all-encompassing, but does not, in the second edition in 1935, refer to the 1934 German book by Trillich or the Ciupka book already published in Germany in 1931or the Italian book by Leonida Valerio in 1927. These were major books about the evolution of equipment. The result is that information about German and Italian contributions is almost absent or underweighted. The Melitta paper filter phenomenon in Germany is not mentioned at all even though it was already a force in Germany. Similarly the Bezzera/Pavoni espresso machine was mentioned in passing when it had already changed the face of coffee making in Italy and many other countries.

Ukers writes, '...the best work in the line of improvements that have survived the test of time was done in England and the United States' (p.623, first edn.). I do not believe this was a balanced assessment in 1922 or even in 1935. Burns made a major contribution with coffee roasters; the recirculating percolators were an American phenomenon as were the Le Page roller mills, but it is difficult to find any innovation from England that would fit his statement either in 1935 or more than fifty years later.

As a reference book, *All About Coffee* is really a book with a lot of information about coffee but some of it is wrong. The fact that it has been the basis for so many other books means that there are major distortions in coffee history both in English and in other languages.

Books in the French language are particularly satisfactory about French coffee history. German language books are full of information about German facts, but the information does not seem to be integrated either within Germany or with respect to the outside world. Ukers, by not going just a little further, ended up writing a book which is sometimes inaccurate because it reflects its author's reliance on second hand information and his lack of understanding of original sources.

It is not the object of my book to write a critique of Ukers, but I will simply say that Uker's books must be treated with caution. It is unfortunate that his lack of understanding of the whole roasting, grinding and brewing process prevented him from doing more analytical work on the subject and impeded his evaluation of the information sent by his correspondents. On the other hand, much credit must be given to Ukers for his work in an era when postal communication was slow and there were no photocopiers, computers or fax machines.

APPENDIX II, BEZZERA PAVONI AND THE IDEALE COFFEE MACHINE

Bezzera patented the first espresso machine while Pavoni manufactured the first machine, the Ideale. Pavoni's addition to the Bezzera machine was probably the steam relief valve. All the evidence points to this being the case. Yet many people have confused the machines and the achievements of their inventors - Desiderio Pavoni and Luigi Bezzera.

The two biggest difficulties in establishing a clear history of the espresso machine are extracting information from the Italian patent system and obtaining solid information from other sources. To find a patent, you need a number and to find that number, you need the reference book, but the book for the years 1901, 1902, and 1903 has been lost by the Rome Patent Office, where all the old patents are stored. Other source documents which might add to the story do not appear to have been found.

By sheer luck, I found the necessary information in a later year book. It showed that the date on the first patent application by Luigi Bezzera was the 19th November, 1901 and this was followed by an addition on the 17th January, 1902, the patent being granted on the 5th June, 1902. The addition was for a relief valve to stop the explosion of steam when the handle was removed. Even though the relief valve is in the 1902 Bezzera patent it apparently was never used in an early Bezzera machine, but it was used in the Ideale, the first Pavoni machine.

On the 1st October, 1903 there was a registration in the Italian Patent Office of a total transfer of the patent to Desiderio Pavoni, but Pavoni had already registered the patent in his own name in France on the 17th May, 1902 and then in Germany on the 19th September, 1902, with drawings almost identical to those in the Bezzera patent. The transfer must have taken place in deed prior to the registration of the transfer of the patent.

A possible explanation is that Bezzera's first patent for a machine without a relief valve (19th November,1901) was his own and that Pavoni suggested a relief valve that Bezzera included in his patent of 17th January, 1902.

What is strange is that Bezzera said in his patent: '...when you take away the lower part of the doser, it erupts with force blowing and spraying, which is an inconvenience but not damaging.' [English translation] He clearly understood the problem but apparently did not include the solution - the relief valve - in his own machine.

On account of the low pressure, the explosion of steam when you removed the handle was probably not a major problem but it would have been a nuisance to have had a little burst of steam every time you released the handle. Many pre-war machines of other brands also did not have the relief valve and I can only assume that it was not a major factor.

An explanation for Bezzera not including the relief valve on his own machines may have been by agreement between the two friends. When Pavoni bought the patent and rights to make the relief valve machine, he helped Bezzera out financially and Bezzera continued to make his original machine without the valve.

Photographs of the two machines clearly show that Pavoni's has a pressure relief valve (the bent tube going down from the group) which meant that when the handle was removed, the steam pressure which was still in the group would be released and there would be no explosion of steam. There does not appear to be any evidence of a relief valve on a Bezzera machine. Two patents lodged by Bezzera in 1904 and 1912 show no relief valve, whereas a Pavoni patent, lodged in 1911, clearly has a relief valve. They were definitely two different machines - the photographs show that they had different handles and valves; Pavoni's had eight bolts on the top while Bezzera's had six. Whatever the case, Pavoni's machine was strongly based on the Bezzera design.

The confusion between Bezzera and Pavoni continues with an examination of the records of the Exposition held in the Castello Sforzesca in Milan in 1906. They hold no mention of Pavoni. There are the photos of the Bezzera stand at the same Milan Fair but none of a Pavoni stand. However, close examination of the photo of the Bezzera stand reveals a placard on the front pillar which actually shows Pavoni's name. It is certain that the Bezzera stand was actually displaying the Ideale Machine of Pavoni which would be consistent with Pavoni winning the gold medal. A 1930s brochure from La Pavoni says that the 'house was established in 1905'. My guess is that the Bezzera factory was manufacturing machines for Pavoni until at least 1906, while the Pavoni factory was being set up.

In the early Italian sources, Bezzera's name was never mentioned. Cougnet in 1909 talked only of Pavoni and Leonida Valerio in 1927 mentioned only Pavoni. Both the Pavoni and Bezzera companies were producing throughout the period and I can only assume that it was the Pavoni machine that dominated the market. Certainly every modern machine has a pressure relief valve, because with the higher pressure from the electric pump, it is very necessary. Perhaps Pavoni's gas control valve, which he patented in 1905, was the critical difference between the two machines.

APPENDIX III, COFFEE AND HEALTH IN THE SEVENTEENTH CENTURY

Most statements in the seventeenth century about coffee and the body's reaction to coffee seem to be without foundation by modern standards. There was a basis but it was totally different to anything we can imagine today. Medical practice was based on humours and theories which had been held for over a thousand years. Galen in the second century demonstrated that lack of heat had resulted in women retaining genitalia inside that were outside on men. It could be shown, organ for organ, that female genitalia was simply male genitalia turned inside out.[1] Avicenna asserted that women lacked the vital heat to convert food to sperm.[2] Excess heat [in men] could be assuaged by cutting back on spicy foods, suppressing 'images of a desired woman' or not sleeping on one's back which led to warmer kidneys, which increased the production of excrement generally and therefore also of semen.[3] Thomas Laqueur's book is full of examples of how the human body was understood before the microscope was discovered and the hitherto invisible revealed.

In 1706 Dr. Duncan of the Faculty of Medicine in Montpellier in France, wrote a book of wholesome advice against the abuse of hot liquors, particularly coffee, chocolate and tea. The book is 280 pages long. I can only give a few statements to show the general line of thinking.

Suppose Coffee, Chocolate and Tea to be either Cold or Hot, which of them you please, it cannot be but destructive to such as are Cold or Hot enough already, if Coffee be subtil it must needs be hurtful to Cholerick Persons whose Humours and Spirits are too subtile already; and if it be thick or gross those that are of Phlegmatic and Melancholic Constitutions, over whose Humours and Spirits that Quality has too much Power, can never have any Benefit by it.[4]

Coffee occasions this [the hindering of sleep] *by kindling in the Humours and Spirits too great a Heat, through the excessive Motion it gives them, and the sharpness wherewith it arms 'em, and by the rapidity of their Circulation, to which a great Dissolution is a new Spur.*[5]

Those who are not Amorous nor given to Courtship, are called cold, Witness the Title de Frigidis &c. The Cold of Winter quenches the Heat of Love. Beasts seldom Couple but in hot seasons.[6]

Just as medical experiments on rats today are assumed to have relevance to human behaviour, there was a similar assumption that the behaviour of beasts was reflected in human behaviour.

I have the feeling that the pamphlet, *The Maidens Complaint*, written by Merc. Democ., referred to in Chapter 5, has some hidden implications or is part of a continuing argument somewhere else. In a reply called *The Coffee-Mans Granado Discharged upon the Maidens Complaint against Coffee*, which I found as this book was almost being printed, the title page continues, 'In a dialogue between Mr. Black-burnt and Democritus; Wherein is Discovered severall Strange, Wonderful, and Miraculous Cures performed by COFFEE with the names of the persons.cured when left off by the Physitians.'

Democritus was a Greek philosopher known as the Laughing Philosopher who lived from 460-370 B.C. He could never have imagined how funny his theories seem today.

Then, as warmth and pleasure [through intercourse] *build up and spread, the increasingly violent movement of the body causes its finest part to be concocted into semen - a kind of foam - which bursts out with the uncontrolled power of an epileptic seizure, to use the analogy Galen borrowed from Democritus.*[7]

This opinion still held sway at the time of the publication of the pamphlet, 1663, because, 'indeed up to the early 1840s almost all authorities believed that coitally induced ovulation in humans as well as in other mammals was the norm.'[8] They believed that just as semen was produced during orgasm, so the female equivalent was produced during orgasm. In other words, no female orgasm - no ovulation.

These medical theories of the time must have had a lot to do with the *Maidens Complaint*, already quoted. It is difficult to know if the pamphlet was written purely on medical grounds or medical grounds were being used to justify a genuine complaint against coffee.

GLOSSARY

Ambergris - secretion of the sperm whale, used chiefly in perfumery.

Bain-marie - cooking vessel containing hot water used to heat contents of vessel resting in it.

Badged - machine manufactured in one country but distributed to others with different brand names.

Barista - espresso machine operator in an Italian coffee bar.

Bayonet fitting - a round section with two opposite lugs which fits tightly into a cavity so that the two parts are locked together.

Biggin - pot with a filter suspended in the mouth to hold coffee grounds or tea leaves.

Braying - pounding or crushing finely as in a mortar.

Britannia metal - a white alloy of tin, copper and antimony used for tableware.

Brobdingnag - mythical country in 'Gulliver's Travels' where people were 20 metres (60 feet) tall.

Bunnu - Arabic name for the raw coffee bean.

Caddy - tin, box or chest for holding tea.

Café au lait - French milk coffee drink.

Café con leche - Spanish or Portuguese milk coffee drink.

Caffeine - a crystalline alkaloid obtained from tea and coffee.

Capuchins - an order of Franciscan Friars.

Casein - a milk protein which neutralises acidity.

Cezve - triangular, open-mouthed boiler, with a broad base for Turkish coffee.

Chicory - roasted, powdered roots of endive used as a coffee additive.

Coffee cherry - fruit of the coffee tree.

Dervishes - members of ascetic Muslim orders who dance or pirouette violently, also known as *Sufis*.

Ewer - a pitcher or vessel with a spout and handle.

Facing - colouring green tea with chemicals to maintain appearance.

Faïence - painted and glazed earthenware.

Fines - the very finest particles of ground coffee.

Finjan - cup for Turkish coffee.

Fluidised bed roaster - machine which roasts coffee by elevating beans in a stream of very hot air.

Grappa - a coarse spirit distilled from skins, pips and stalks of grapes after pressing for winemaking.

Green coffee - the seeds of the coffee cherry after fermentation and separation from the outer skins.

Group - espresso machine handle incorporating a filter compartment and connecting bayonet fitting.

Haj - annual Muslim pilgrimage to Mecca.

Handle - lever to exert pressure on the water in an espresso machine.

Hydrostatic pressure - downward pressure exerted by the weight of the water.

Ibriq - traditional Turkish coffee pot.

Infusion - liquid extract obtained from a substance by steeping or soaking in water.

Isinglass - a pure form of gelatine derived from fish bladders.

Kahveci - a person skilled in the preparation of Turkish coffee.

Kahwa - Arabic word for coffee.

Kat - leaves of evergreen shrub chewed or brewed for narcotic effect, in North Africa and Arabia.

Kishr - a drink prepared from the boiled, toasted flesh of the coffee cherry.

Lactose - milk sugar.

Levant - lands bordering the eastern shores of the Mediterranean and the Aegean seas.

Lever - handle to exert pressure on the water in an espresso machine.

Maceration - steeping.

Mamelukes - former fighting slaves of Egypt. Overthrew their rulers in 1240. Remained influential until 1811.

Mangold-wurzel - a coarse variety of the common beet.

Millwork - crushing mechanism in a grinder.

Moulinet - stirrer in a chocolate pot.

Pantheon - the gods of a particular mythology considered collectively.

Perk - action and sound of water rising briskly up the tube in a recirculating percolator.

Porcelain - Fine, hard earthenware baked at high temperature.

Posset - a drink made of hot milk curdled with ale, wine, etc.

Privateers - private armed vessels commissioned by government in war to fight and capture enemy commercial ships.

Pyrolysis - decomposition of organic compounds at very high temperatures.

Qahwa - Arabic word for coffee.

Qat - Leaves of evergreen shrub chewed or brewed for narcotic effect, in North Africa and Arabia.

Qishr - a drink prepared from the boiled, toasted flesh of the coffee cherry.

Raw coffee - the seeds of the coffee cherry after fermentation and separation from the outer skins.

Self-drinker - a coffee from a single origin which can be drunk without blending.

Sinter - to agglomerate metal or glass particles by heat, usually under pressure, to just below melting point.

Slurry - a suspension of a solid in a liquid.

Sufis - mystical religious sect including Turkish dervishes.

Tannin - a bitter compound present in tea and coffee.

Teflon/PTFE - a non-stick lining made from polytetrafluoroethylene.

Tisane - a herbal tea.

Winnow - to free a product from chaff or refuse particles by means of wind or driven air or tossing in the air.

Zarf - ornamental metal holder for handleless coffee cup used in the Levant.

END NOTES

INTRODUCTION

[1] Meinhardt, Peter, *Inventions, Patents and Trade Marks,* Gower Press, London, 1971, p.21.

[2] Trillich, Heinrich, *Rösten und Röstwaren,* Heller, Munich, 1934, p.38.

CHAPTER 1

[1] Rumford, Count, [Benjamin Thompson], 'Of the Excellent Qualities of Coffee and the Art of Making it in the Highest Perfection', *Essay No. XVIII,* in the *Complete Works,* Vol. 4, Boston, 1875, pp.633-634.

[2] Sandon, Henry, *Coffee Pots and Teapots for the Collector,* John Bartholomew & Son Limited, Edinburgh, 1973, p.67.

[3] Heise, Ulla, *Coffee and Coffee-Houses,* Schiffer, West Chester, Pennsylvania, 1987, p.61.

[4] Desmet-Grégoire, Hélène, 'Le Café en Méditerranée', *Provence Historique* fascicule 151, 1988, p.80 quoting G. Arnaud d'Agnel, *La Faïence et la Porcelaine de Marseille,* Marseille, 1910, p.534.

[5] Desmet-Grégoire, *op.cit.* p.77.

CHAPTER 2

[1] Browne, Edith A., *Tea,* Adam & Charles Black, London, 1912, p.55, quoting Fortune, Robert. *Wanderings in China,* J. Murray, London 1843.

[2] Kazuko, Okakura, *The Book of Tea,* Angus & Robertson Limited, Sydney, 1932, pp.89-97.

[3] *Leigh Hunt's London Journal,* no.15, July 9, 1834 p.11.

[4] Maitland, Derek, *5000 Years of Tea,* CFW Publications, Hong Kong,1982, p.53.

[5] *The Penny Magazine,* Society for the Diffusion of Useful Knowledge, London, February 22, 1840, p.72.

[6] Thurber, Francis B., *Coffee from Plantation to Cup,*11th edn., American Grocer Publishing Association, New York, 1885, p.285.

[7] *The Art of Tea Blending,* W.B.Whittingham & Company, London, [n.d.,c.1885], pp.37,41.

[8] Alcott, William A., *Tea and Coffee: Their Physical, Intellectual and Moral Effects on the Human System,* Heywood, London,1886, pp. 27,29.

[9] *The Leisure Hour,* London, Nov.19, 1857, p.752.

[10] *The Penny Magazine,* London, Nov.14, 1835 p.447.

[11] Burke, James, *The Day the Universe Changed,* British Broadcasting Corporation, London, 1985, p.221.

[12] Keable, B.B., *Coffee from Grower to Consumer,* Sir Isaac Pitman & Sons Limited, London, [n.d.], p.122.

[13] Marquis F., *Taschenbuch für Theetrinker,* Voigt, Weimar, 1836, p.163.

CHAPTER 3

[1] Dufour, Philippe Sylvestre, *Traitez Nouveau et Curieux du Café, du Thé et du Chocolat,* Deville, Lyons, 1688, p.310.

[2] Dufour, *op.cit.,* pp.364-370.

[3] Soyer, Alexis, *The Pantropheon or A History of Food and its Preparation in Ancient Times,* Paddington Press, New York, 1977. Reprint of 1853 edition, published by Simpkin, Marshall, London.

CHAPTER 4

[1] Moseley, Benjamin, *A Treatise Concerning the Properties and Effects of Coffee,* 5th edn., Pr. for J. Sewell, London, 1792, p.28.

[2] Hattox , Ralph S., *Coffee and Coffee Houses,* University of Washington Press, Seattle, 1985, p.26.

[3] Kennedy, Paul, *The Rise and Fall of the Great Powers,* Random House, New York, 1987, p.7.

[4] Private letter from Palace Museum, Beijing, China, 31 January, 1990.

[5] Ukers, William, *All About Coffee,* Tea and Coffee Trade Journal Company, New York, 1st edn., 1922, p. 16.

[6] Hattox, *op.cit.* p.27.

[7] Hattox, *op.cit.* p.83.

[8] Johnson, Hugh, *The Story of Wine,* Mandarin, London, 1989, p.171.

[9] Daum, Werner, (ed.), *Yemen, 3,000 Years of Art and Civilisation,* Pinguin [sic.] Books, Innsbruck, 1988, p.137.

[10] Hattox, *op.cit.* p.84.

[11] Hattox, *ibid.*

[12] Ukers, *op.cit.* p.264.

[13] Samrowski, Dietrich, *Geschichte der Kaffeemühlen,* Munich, 1983, p.57.

[14] Lewis, Raphaela, *Everyday Life in Ottoman Turkey,* Batsford, London, 1971, p.139.

[15] Heise, Ulla, *Coffee and Coffee Houses,* Schiffer, West Chester, Pennsylvania, 1987, p.14.

[16] Wrigley, G., *Coffee,* Longman Scientific & Technical, New York, 1988, p.21.

[17] Ukers, *op.cit.* 2nd edn., 1935, p.21.

[18] Plebani, Tiziana. 'Aque Negre, Acque Salse, Acque Levantine, il Caffè, Venezia e l'Oriente' in d'Orsi, Angelo (ed.) *Il Caffè Ossia,* Silvana, Milan, 1990, p.14.

[19] Schnyder-von-Waldkirch, Antoinette, *Wie Europa den Kaffee entdeckte,* Jacobs Suchard Museum, Zurich, 1988, pp.38, 45, 51.

[20] *Tarih ve Toplum* [journal], Istanbul, vol.2, 1984, p.370.

[21] Ukers, *op.cit.* p.26.

[22] Private letters from Ahmet Mentes, Director, Topkapi Palace Museum, Istanbul, 8 Temmuz, 1992 and 7 Ekim, 1992.

[23] *Leigh Hunt's London Journal,* no. 16, July 16, 1834, p. [121].

[24] White, Charles, *Three Years in Constantinople. Domestic Manners of the Turks in 1844.* H. Colburn, London, 1845.

[25] White, *op.cit.* p.278.

[26] Houts, Sandra S., 'Lactose Intolerance', *Food Technology,* March 1988, p.111.

[27] Hourigan, J.A., 'Nutritional Implications of Lactose', *Australian Journal of Dairy Technology,* Sept. 1984, p.118, quoting Pastore M., *Latte,* vol. 4, no. 7/8, 1979, p.1297.

[28] Rowling, Nick., *Commodities,* Free Association Books, London, 1987, p. 49.

[29] Rowling , *op.cit.* p.102.

[30] Mintz, Sidney, *Sweetness and Power,* Penguin, New York, 1986, p.32.

[31] Mintz, *op. cit.* p.33.

[32] Mintz, *op.cit.* p.39.

[33] Mintz, *op.cit.* p.160.

[34] Heise, *op. cit.* p.15,93.

[35] Schnyder-von Waldkirch, *op.cit.* p.143.

[36] Heise, *op. cit.* p.15.

[37] Plebani, *op.cit.* p.18.

[38] Plebani, *op. cit.* p.22.

[39] Massimo, Costantini. 'Venezia, Capitale del Caffè', in d'Orsi (ed.) *op.cit.* p.32.

[40] Lansard, Monique, 'Der Kaffee in Frankreich, in 17. und 18. Jahrhundert : Modeerscheinung oder Institution ?' in Ball, Daniela, (ed.), *Kaffee im Spiegel europäischer Trinksitten,* Johann Jacobs Museum, Zurich, 1991, p.128.

[41] Lansard, *op.cit.* p.130.

[42] Lansard, *op.cit.* p.127.

[43] Cadet-de-Vaux, Antoine Alexis, *Dissertation sur le Café,* Paris, 1806, p.22.

[44] Lansard, Monique, *op.cit.* p.138.

[45] Ellis, Aytoun, *The Penny Universities,* Secker & Warburg, London, 1956, p.30.

[46] Ciupka, Paul, *Kaffee: Kaffee-Ersatz und Kaffee-Zusatz,* Bd.1, Meissner, Hamburg, 1949, p.42.

[47] Ukers, *op. cit.* p.46.

[48] Johnson, Hugh, *The Story of Wine*, Mandarin, London, 1992, p.193.

[49] Rowling, *op.cit.* p.104, quoting Rumsey, Walter, *A Defence of Coffee*, London, 1657, p.9.

[50] Schivelbusch, W., *Das Paradies, der Geschmack und die Vernunft*, Ullstein Sachbuch, Frankfurt/M., 1985, pp.32,35.

[51] Ellis, *op.cit.* p.19.

[52] Heise, *op.cit.* pp.64-65.

[53] Heise, *op. cit.* p.59.

[54] Italy. Ministero dell'Istruzione Pubblica. *Relazioni sui lavori della Missione Archeologica Italiana in Egitto*, Torino, 1927. 'La Tomba intatta del Architetto chi nella Necropoli di Tebe', vol. 2, Torino, 1922. [This publication was found in the library of the Museo Egizio, Turin, Italy.]

[55] Dufour, Philippe Sylvestre, *Nouveaux et Curieux Traitez du Café, du Thé et du Chocolat*, Deville, Lyons, 1688, p.58.

[56] [Chamberlayne, J.] *The Natural History of Coffee, Thee, Chocolate and Tobacco*, Pr. for Christopher Wilkinson, London, 1682, p.6.

[57] Dufour, *op.cit.* p.142.

[58] Bradley, R., *The Virtue and Use of Coffee*, Pr. by Eman. Mathews , London, 1721, pp. 23-24.

[59] Dufour, *op.cit.* pp. 64-65.

[60] Originals at Harvard University Library. Pamphlets copied by permission of the Houghton Library.
A sanitised version of the 'Men's Petition' and the 'Women's Petition' is printed in *Old English Coffee Houses*, Rodale Press, London, 1954.

[61] Teixeira De Oliveira, José, *História do Café*, Kosmos, Rio de Janeiro, 1984, p.144.

CHAPTER 5

[1] Rybczinsky, Witold, *Home, A Short History of an Idea*, Penguin, New York, 1986, p.96.

[2] Ukers, William, *All About Tea*, vol. 1, Tea and Coffee Trade Journal Company, New York, 2nd edn.,1935, p.33.

[3] Ukers, *op. cit.* p.35.

[4] Welter, Henri, *Essai sur l'Histoire du Café*, C. Reinwald, Paris, 1868, p.13.

[5] Pratt, J.N., *Tea Lovers' Treasury*, 101 Productions, San Francisco, 1982, p.50.

[6] McEvedy, C., *The Penguin Atlas of Modern History*, Penguin Books, Harmondsworth, Middlesex, 1972, p.59.

[7] Rybczynski, *op.cit.* p.105.

[?] Rybczynski, *op.cit.* p.106.

[9] Ogg, David, *England in the Reigns of James II and William III*, Oxford Press, 1955, p.297.

[10] Ogg, *op. cit.* p.312.

[11] Jacob, H.E., *The Saga of Coffee*, Allen & Unwin, London, 1935, p.161.

[12] Trevelyan, G.M., *English Social History*, Pelican Books, London, 1967, p.312.

[13] Wedermeyer, Bernd, *Coffee de Martinique und Keyser Thee*, Hubert & Co., Göttingen, 1989, p.99.

[14] Wedermeyer, *op. cit.* p.64.

[15] *Leigh Hunt's London Journal,* no.16, Wed., July 16, 1834.

[16] Ukers, *op.cit.* p.734.

[17] Dufour, Philippe Sylvestre, *Traitez Nouveaux et Curieux du Café, du Thé et du Chocolate,* 2nd edn., Deville, Lyons, 1688, pp.300,301.

[18] Dufour, *op.cit.* p.139.

[19] Welter, *op.cit.* p.355.

[20] Welter, *op.cit.* p.227, 357.

[21] Ciupka, Paul, *Kaffee: Kaffee-Ersatz und Kaffee-Zusatz.* 2nd edn., Otto Meissners Verlag, Hamburg, 1949. Bd.1, p.45 quoting Bontekoe, Cornelius, *Tractaat van het Excellenst Kruyd Thee...,* s'Gravenhage, 1678; erweiterte Auflage mit Kapiteln über Kaffee und Schokolade, s'Gravenhage, 1679. *Drey Neue/Curieuse Tractatgen/von dem Tranke Cafe...*Budissen, 1868, pp.112-114.

[22] Drummond, J.C. and Wilbraham, A., *The Englishman's Food*, Jonathon Cape, London, 1957, p.194 quoting Smollett, T., 'The Expedition of Humphrey Clinker', 1771.

[23] University of East Anglia, Norwich. Climatic Research Unit. Private letter from Dr. John Kingston to Ian Bersten. 6th March 1991.

[24] Thirsk, Joan, (ed.) *The Agrarian History of England and Wales*, vol. 5, 1640-1750, Cambridge University Press, Cambridge, 1985, p.21.

[25] Thirsk, *op. cit.*, vol. 6, 1750-1850, p.166.

[26] Walker, R. and Roberts, D., *From Scarcity to Surfeit*, University of New South Wales, Kensington, Sydney, 1988, p.5.

[27] Mintz, Sidney, J., *Sweetness and Power*, Penguin, New York, 1986, p.39.

28 Mintz, *op.cit.*, p.189.

[29] Wassenberg, Karl. 'Kaffee In Wien. Ein Versuch zur socialen Genese des Kaffee-Trinken in Wien'. Unpublished paper from symposium, *Coffee in the Context of European Drinking Habits.* Zurich October, 1990

CHAPTER 6

[1] Welter, Henri, *Essai sur l'Histoire du Café*, C. Reinwald, Paris, 1868, p.336.

CHAPTER 7

[1] Krünitz, Johann Georg, *Oekonomische Encyclopaedie*, vol. 32, Pauli, Berlin, 1784, p.172.

[2] Boehnke-Reich, Heinrich, *Der Kaffee in seinen Beziehungen zum Leben*, Thiel, Berlin, 1885.

[3] Trillich, Heinrich, *Rösten und Röstwaren*, Heller, Munich, 1934.

[4] Welter, Henri, *Essai sur l'Histoire du Café*, C.Reinwald, Paris, 1868.

[5] Johnson, Hugh, *The Story of Wine*, Mandarin, London, 1991, p.335, quoting Chaptal, J.-A., *Traité Théoretique et Pratique sur la Culture de la Vigne*, Milan, 1801.

[6] Wedermeyer, Bernd, *Coffee de Martinique und Kayser Thee*, Hubert, Göttingen, 1989, p.99.

[7] Lansard, Monique, 'Coffee in France in the 17th and 18th Centuries. Fashion or Institution?' Summary of paper delivered at Symposium *Coffee in the Context of European Drinking Habits,* Jacobs Suchard Museum, Zurich, October 1990.

[8] Heise, Ulla, *Coffee and Coffee Houses*, Schiffer, West Chester, Pennsylvania, 1987, p.172.

[9] Demachy, Jacques François, *L'Art du Distillateur Liquoriste*, France, 1775, pp.111-115.

[10] Ukers, William, *All About Coffee*, Tea and Coffee Trade Journal Company, New York, 1st edn., 1922, pp.696-699.

[11] Bradbury, Frederick, *A History of Old Sheffield Plate*, London, 1912, p.259.

[12] Ashton, T.S., *The Industrial Revolution*, Oxford University Press, London, 1964, p.74.

[13] Mielke, Heinz-Peter, *Kaffee, Tee, Kakao*, Müsers-Grafik-Druck.-KG, Viersen, 1988, p.129.

[14] Ukers, *op.cit.*, 1922, p.696.

[15] Bradbury, *op.cit.* p. 259.

[16] Demachy, *op.cit.* p.114.

[17] Krünitz, *op.cit.* p.172.

[18] Boehnke-Reich, *op.cit.* p.111.

[19] Ciupka, Paul, *Kaffee-Ersatz und Kaffee-Zusatz*, Bd.1, Meissner, Hamburg, 1949, p.47 quoting Jöcher, *Gemeinnützige Magie*, Heft 17, Kaffee, Thee und Chocolade, [n.p.] Leipzig, 1825.

[20] *ibid.*

[21] Desmet-Grégoire, Helene, *Les Objets du Café*, Presses du CNRS, Paris, 1989, p.48.

[22] Cadet-de-Vaux, Antoine Alexis, *Dissertation sur le Café*, Paris, 1806, p.71.

[23] Brillat-Savarin, Jean Anthelme, *The Physiology of Taste*, Knoft, New York, 1972, p.105.

[24] Keable, B.B., *Coffee from Grower to Consumer*, Pitman, London, [n.d.], p.121.

[25] Gubian, J.M.A., *Dissertation sur le Café*, Imp. Didot Jeune, Paris, 1814, p.29.

[26] Cadet-de-Vaux, *op.cit.* p.115.

[27] Cadet-de-Vaux, *op.cit.* p.74.

[28] Cadet-de-Vaux, *op.cit.* p.66.

[29] Cadet-de-Vaux, *op.cit.* p.97.

[30] Cadet-de-Vaux, *op.cit.* p.76 ff.

[31] Chryssochoïdès, N., *Nouveau Manuel Complet du Limonadier*, New edn. Encyclopédie Roret, Paris, pp.29-32, 1901.

[32] Gubian, *op.cit.* p.29.

[33] Chryssochoïdès, *op.cit.* p.31.

[34] Ukers, *op.cit.* 1922, p.698.

[35] Procter & Gamble Company, *The Folger's Coffee Silver Collection, Antique English Silver Service and Accessories*, [ed. Ross E. Taggart] USA, [n.d.], pp.53, 71.

[36] *ibid.*

[37] Dalla Bona, Giovanni, *l'Uso, e l'Abuso del Caffè*, presso Giuseppe Berno, Verona, 1751, pp.9-10.

[38] Boehnke-Reich, *op.cit.* p.111.

[39] Ukers, *op.cit.* 2nd edn., 1935, p.582.

[40] Jardin, Edelstan, *Le Caféier et le Café*, le Roux, Paris, 1895, p.287.

[41] *Dinglers Polytechnisches Journal*, 1820, p.340.

[42] Reimann, Friedrich, *Kaffeebüchlein und Kaffeekochbuch*, Coburg, 1841.

[43] Daussé, Aîné, *Manuel de l'Amateur du Café*, l'Auteur, Paris, 1846.

[44] Daussé, *op.cit.* p.57.

[45] Chryssochoïdès, *op.cit.* p.62.

[46] *Dinglers Polytechnisches Journal,* 1820.

[47] Gubian, *op.cit.* p.28.

[48] Welter, *op.cit.* pp.343,345,346,347.

[49] Ukers, *op.cit.* 2nd edn., 1935, p.585.

[50] Ukers, *op.cit.* p.582.

[51] Reimann, *op.cit.*

[52] *Dinglers Polytechnisches Journal*, Bd. 139, 1856, quoting *Cosmos*, Paris, August, 1855, p.127.

[53] Letters Patent to Edward Loysel, London, 1854, No. 393, pp.11-12.

[54] Welter, Henri, *Essai sur l'Histoire du Café*, Reinwald, Paris, 1868, p.336.

[55] Letters Patent to Edward Loysel, London,1854, No. 393, p.2, lines 32-35.

[56] Schindler, Anton, *Biographie von Ludwig van Beethoven,* Leipzig, 1970, p.436.

[57] Chryssochoïdès, *op.cit.* p.82.

[58] Trillich, *op.cit.* p.548.

[59] *The Leisure Hour*, London, no. 308, Nov. 19, 1857, p.752.

[60] Timbs, J., *Curiosities of London*, Virtue, London, 1867, p.273.

[61] Ukers, *op.cit.* 2nd edn., 1935, pp.642,643.

[62] Rottenhöfer, J., *Der Elegante Wohlservierte Kaffee - und Theetisch*, Braun und Schneider, Munich, 1864, pp. 74-79.

[63] *Dinglers Polytechnisches Journal*, Bd. 68, 1838, p.454.

[64] Delcourt, Pierre, *Ce qu'on Mange à Paris*, Libraire Henri du Parc, 1888, pp.38-46.

[65] *Küchen und Wirtschafts Zeitung für Deutsche Hausfrauen und ihre Töchter*, no. 3, Nov.1, 1845, p.13.

[66] Walsh, Joseph, *Coffee*, The John C. Winston Company, Philadelphia, 1894, pp.195,196.

CHAPTER 8

[1] Capodici, Salvatore and Invernizzi, Carlo, *Cognoscere il Caffè*, Eusebianum, Milano, 1983, p.364.

[2] Bramah, Edward & Joan, *Coffee Makers*, Quiller Press, London, 1989, p.74.

[3] *Dinglers Polytechnisches Journal*, vol. 105, (Figure 34), 1847.

[4] Cougnet, A., *La Scena Illustrata*, Florence, 1st November, 1909, p.14.

[5] Valerio, Leonida, *Caffè e Derivati*, Ulrico Hoepli, Milan, 1927, p.383.

[6] Ciupka, Paul, *Taschenbuch des Kaffee-Fachmanns*, Meissner, Hamburg, 1931, pp.216-217.

[7] Prince Charles Maurice de Tallyrand-Perigord, (1754 -1838).

[8] Petaracco, Dr. M., *Tea and Coffee Trade Journal*, December 1989, p.23.

[9] Illy, F. and R., *Dal Caffè all'Espresso*, Arnoldo Mondadori Editore, Milan, 1989, pp.166,168.

[10] Illy, *op.cit.* p.184.

CHAPTER 9

[1] de Haan, D., *Antique Household Gadgets and Appliances*, Poole, Dorset, 1977, p.1.

[2] de Haan, *op.cit.* p.7.

[3] Willams, T.I., *The Triumph of Invention*, Macdonald Orbis, London, 1987, p.178.

[4] Clough, Shepard Bancroft, and Cole,

Charles Woolsey, *Economic History of Europe*, 3rd edn., D.C. Heath & Co., Boston, 1968, p.774.

[5] Clough, *op.cit.* p.776.

[6] *Electrocraft Illustrated List,* [U.S.A.], 1907, p.122.

[7] *Pay-out*, Catalogue of Stuart-Howland Company, U.S.A., 1907, p.496.

[8] *Gaffer*, Corning Glass Works magazine, New York, 1978, p.5.

[9] Lifshey, Earl, *The Housewares Story*, Chicago, 1973, pp.245-246.

[10] Ukers, William, *All About Coffee*, Tea and Coffee Trade Journal Company, New York, 2nd edn.,1935, p.634.

[11] Boehnke-Reich, Dr. H., *Der Kaffee in Seinen Beziehungen zum Leben*, Berlin und Leipzig, 1885, pp.107-20.

[12] Holzborn, Adolf, *Der Eisenwarenhandel*, Heinrich Killinger Verlagsgesellschaft, Nordhausen, [c.1928] p.977.

[13] 'Maschinen zur Herstellung des Kaffee-Getränkes für Grossbetriebe', *KATEKA* (Kaffee, Tee und Kakao Zeitung), Hamburg, no.25, Dec.1914, p.7.

[14] *KATEKA*, 1925, p.701.

[15] Ukers, *op.cit.*, 1935, p.617.

[16] Foot, F.N., *Coffee the Beverage*, The Spice Mill Publishing Company, New York, 1925, p.116.

[17] Preising, Max, 'Kaffeefilter oder Papierfilter', *KATEKA*, no.34, 1926.

[18] Muller, Dr. Edgar, *Kaffee und Rösten*, KATEKA, Hamburg, 1929, p.357.

[19] Ciupka, Paul, *Taschenbuch des Kaffee-Fachmannns*, Meissner, Hamburg, 1931, pp.214,218.

[20] *Die Schaulade Vereinigt mit Kunst und Kunstgewerbe*, 8 Jahrgang. Heft 1, Jan. 16, 1932, p.34.

CHAPTER 10

[1] Rottenhöfer, J., *Der Elegante Wohlservierte Kaffee - und Theetisch*, Braun und Schneider, Munich, 1864, p.77.

[2] *Küchen und Wirtschafts Zeitung för Deutsche Hausfrauen und ihre Töchter*, no.3, Nov. 1, 1845, p.13.

[3] Heise, Ulla, *Coffee and Coffee Houses*, Schiffer, West Chester, Pennsylvania, 1987, p.54.

[4] Rotthauwe, Helmut, *The Heavenly Inferno*, Probat-Werke, Emmerich, 1968, p.14.

[5] Franke, Edwin, *Kaffee, Kaffeekonserven und Kaffeesurrogate*, A. Hartleben's Verlag, Vienna and Leipzig, 1920, p.70,74.

[6] Trillich, H., *Rösten und Röstwaren*, Heller, Munich, 1934, p.39,297.

[7] Trillich, *op. cit.* p.4.

[8] Ciupka, Paul, *Taschenbuch des Kaffee-Fachmanns*, Meissner, Hamburg, 1931, p.85.

[9] Rothfos, Bernhard, *Coffee Consumption*, Gordian-Max Rieck GmbH, Hamburg, 1986, pp.123-125.

[10] Müller, Dr. Edgar, *Kaffee und Rösten*, KATEKA, Hamburg, 1929, Chapter 9.

CHAPTER 11

[1] Ciupka, Paul, *Taschenbuch des Kaffee-Fachmanns*, Meissner, Hamburg, 1931, p.151.

[2] Foot, F.N., *Coffee the Beverage*, The Spice Mill Publishing Company, New York, 1925, p.86.

[3] Ukers, William, *All About Coffee*, Tea and Coffee Trade Journal Company, New York, 2nd edn., 1935, p.248.

[4] Ukers, *op.cit.* p.577.

[5] Samrowski, Dietrich, *Geschichte der Kaffeemühlen*, Munich, 1983, p.41

[6] Samrowski, *op.cit.* p.57.

[7] von Walderdorff, Elizabeth, *Alte Kaffeemühlen*, Callwey Verlag, Munich, 1982.

[8] Lifshey, Earl, *The Housewares Story*, National Housewares Manufacturers Association, Chicago, 1973, p.253.

[9] Kennedy, Paul, *The Rise and Fall of the Great Powers*, Random House, New York, 1987.

[10] Rybczinski, Witold, *Home, A Short History of An Idea*, Penguin, New York, 1986, p.151.

[11] Samrowski, *op. cit.* p.46.

[12] von Walderdorff, *op.cit.* p.50.

CHAPTER 12

[1] Ukers, William, *All About Coffee*, The Tea and Coffee Trade Journal Company, New York, 1st edn., 1922, p.471.

CHAPTER 13

[1] Chabouis, Lucette, *Le Livre du Café*, Bordas, Paris, 1988, p.122.

[2] Bureau of American Republics, Washington, *Special Bulletin*, 'Coffee in America', 1893, pp.9,31.

[3] Lake, M., *The Flavour of Wine*, Jacaranda Press, Sydney, 1969.

[4] Lake, *op. cit.* pp.3,4.

[5] Lake, *op.cit.* p.9.

[6] Bureau of American Republics, *op.cit.* p.35.

[7] Lingle, T.R., *The Coffee Cupper's Handbook*, Coffee Development Group, Washington, 1986.

[8] Lingle, *op.cit.* p.27.

[9] Lingle, *op.cit.* p.28.

[10] Quimme, P., *The Signet Book of Coffee and Tea*, New American Library, New York, 1976, p.85.

CHAPTER 14

[1] 'La Chicorée', *Epicier du Nord*, Paris, May 1988, p.3.

[2] Dufour, Philippe Silvestre, *Traitez Nouveaux et Curieux du Café*, Deville, Lyons, 2nd edn., 1688, p.70.

[3] Riant, Dr. A. *Le Café, le Chocolat, le Thé*, Paris 1875, p.41.

[4] Trillich, H., *Rösten und Röstwaren*, Verlag B. Heller, Munich 1934, p.4.

[5] Welter, H., *Essai sur l'Histoire du Café* Reinwald, Paris 1868, pp.430-434.

[6] Wynter Blyth, A. and Wynter Blyth, W., *Foods : Their composition and analysis*, Griffin Press, London, 6th edn., 1909, p.353.

[7] Wynter Blyth, *op.cit.* p.18.

[8] Wynter Blyth, *op.cit.* p.13.

[9] Rothfos, Bernhard, *Coffee Consumption*, Gordion-Max Rieck GmbH, Hamburg, 1986, p.364.

[10] Cefabu-Werk, Mainz. *Cefabu Kaffee*.Ludwig Utz, [n.d., 1916?], [advertising booklet].

[11] Battig, Karl, 'Coffee from a scientific angle', *Swissair Gazette*, January 1988, p.45. [Karl Battig is a Professor of comparative physiology and behavioural biology at the Swiss Federal Institute of Technology.]

[12] Battig, *op.cit.* p.46.

[13] Chryssochoïdès, N. *Nouveau Manuel Complet du Limonadier...*Encyclopédie Roret, Paris, new edn., 1901, p.12.

[14] Rothfos, *op.cit.* p.335.

[15] Müller, Dr. Edgar, *Arabiens Vermachtnis*, Hamburg 1931, p.149.

[16] Katz, S.N., 'Decaffeination of Coffee' in Clarke, R.J. and Macrae (eds.), *Coffee*, vol. 2., Technology, London, 1987, p.64.

[17] Rothfos, *op.cit.* p.347.

[18] Rothfos, *op.cit.* pps.349 and 358.

[19] Rothfos, *op.cit.* p.356.

APPENDIX III

[1] Laqueur, Thomas, *Making Sex, Body and Gender from the Greeks to Freud*, Harvard University Press, Cambridge, Mass., 1990, p.4.

[2] Laqueur, *op. cit.,* p.40.

[3] Laqueur, *op. cit.,* p.101.

[4] Duncan, Dr., *Wholesome Advice against the Abuse of Hot Liquors,* Pr. for H. Rhodes, London, 1706, p.33.

[5] Duncan, *op. cit.,* p.53.

[6] Duncan, *op.cit.,* p.63.

[7] Laqueur, *op.cit.,* p.46.

[8] Laqueur, *op. cit.,* p.184.

SELECT BIBLIOGRAPHY

These are all in my private collection unless indicated as follows:

H.U. = Houghton Library, Harvard University, Cambridge, Mass. USA

J.J.= Johann Jacobs Museum (formerly Jacobs-Suchard Museum), Zurich, Switzerland

U.B. = Courtesy of Ursula Becker, Cologne, Germany

V.A.= Victoria Arduino Company, Varese, Italy

BOOKS

ABRIDGMENTS OF SPECIFICATIONS RELATING TO TEA, COFFEE, CHICORY, CHOCOLATE, COCOA &c.
A.D. 1704-1866. Eyre & Spottiswoode, London, 1877.

ADRIAN, Hans G. *Alphabet des Kaffeehauses.* Schrader, Bremen, 1971.

———— *Bilderbuch zum Tee...mit zwölf Chinesischen Aquarellen des 18. Jahrhunderts.* Georg Westermann Verlag, n.p.,1967.

———— *Tee über den Ozean.* Schrader, Bremen, 1978.

————, Teming, Rolf L. & Volkers, Arend. *Das Teebuch. Geschichte und Geschichten Anbau, Herstellung und Rezepte.* Bucher, Munich, 1986.

AGIUS, Pauline. *China Teapots.* (Antique Collectors Pocket Guides) Lutterworth Press, Guilford, Surrey, 1982.

ALCOTT, William A. *Tea and Coffee: their Physical, Intellectual, & Moral Effects on the Human System.* New edn., rev. and condensed by T. Baker. Heywood, London, 1886.

ANDERSON, Kenneth. *The Pocket Guide to Coffees and Teas.* Muller, London, 1982.

ANNONI, Liugi. *Cenni Sopra le Diverse Macchine per fare l'Infusione di Caffè.* Gaspari Truffi e Comp., Milan, 1834. (J.J.)

THE ART OF TEA BLENDING. A Handbook for the Tea Trade. Whittingham, London, (n.d.).

BALL, Daniela.(ed.) *Kaffee im Spiegel Europäischer Trinksitten/ Coffee in the Context of European Drinking Habits.* Johann Jacobs Museum, Zurich, 1991.

BAXTER, Jacki. *The Coffee Book.* Burlington Books, London, 1985.

BELLI, B. *Il Caffè.* Manuali Hoepli. Ulricho Hoepli, Milan, [1910]. (J.J.)

BENESCH, Kurt. *Koffiebrevier voor allen die de Kunst van het Koffiezetten en Koffiedrinken beminnen.* Twaalf meditaties voor Nederland bewerkt door Georg. A. Brongers. Donker, Rotterdam, 1974.

BLAKE, John. *Tea Hints for Retailers.* Williamson-Haffner Engraving Company, Denver, 1903.

BLEGNY, Nicolas de. *Le bon Usage du Thé, du Caffé et du Chocolat,* Paris, 1687. (J.J.)

BLOFELD, John. *The Chinese Art of Tea.* Shambhala, Boston, 1985.

BOEHNKE-REICH, Heinrich. *Der Kaffee in seinem Beziehungen zum Leben.* Verlag von Fr. Thiel, Berlin, 1885.

THE BOOK OF TEA. Flammarion, [Paris, 1992] Trans. from French by Deke Dusinberre.

BONDÍ, Claudio. *L'Italia dei Caffè.* Lucarini Editore, Rome, 1988.

BRAMAH, Edward & Joan. *Coffee Makers. 300 Years of Art & Design.* Quiller Press, London, 1989.

BRAMAH, Edward. *Tea & Coffee. A Modern View of Three Hundred Years of Tradition.* Hutchinson, London, 1972.

BROWNE, Edith A. *Tea.* (Peeps at Industries.) Black, London, 1912.

BUREAU OF AMERICAN REPUBLICS, Washington. *Special Bulletin.* October, 1893. 'Coffee in America. Methods of Production and Facilities for Successful Cultivation in Mexico, the Central American States, Brazil and Other South American countries and the West Indies.'

BURGERT, Helmut. *Das Wiener Kaffeehaus.* Heimat Verlag Brirlegg, Tirol, (n.d.).

CADET-DE-VAUX, Antoine-Alexis. *Dissertation sur le Café; son Historique, ses Propriétès, et le Procédé pour obtenir la Boisson la plus Agréable, la plus Salutaire et la plus Economique...suivé de son analyse par Charles-Louis Cadet.* Paris, 1806. (J.J.)

CAPODICI, Salvatore. *Conoscere il Caffè.* Eusebianum, Milan, 1983.

————- *Guida al Caffè.* Centro Luigi Lavazza per gli Studi e le Ricerche sul Caffè, Milan, 1991.

CARBÈ, Antonio. *Il Caffè nella Storia e nell'Arte.* Lavazza, Milan, 1981.

————. ———— 2nd edn., 1986.

————- *Incontro con il Caffè nell'Interpretazione di 28 Pittori.* Lavazza, Milan, 1987.

CASTILE, Rand. *The Way of Tea.* Weatherhill, New York, 1971.
———————. ———— 2nd. pr., 1979

CAVE, Henry W. *Golden Tips. A Description of Ceylon and its Great Tea Industry.* 3rd.edn. Cassell, London, 1904.

IL CENTRO LUIGI LAVAZZA PER GLI STUDI E LE RICERCHE SUL CAFFE. *Il Caffè.* Publirel, Milan, 1980.

————- Quaderni Lavazza. Publirel, Milan, 1982.

1. *Introduzione al Caffè.* Massimo Alberini.
2. *Il Caffè Espresso al Bar. Il Macinadosatore.*
3. *Il Caffè Espresso al Bar. La Macchina Espressso.*
4. *Cocktails al Caffè.* Antonio Piccinardi. 1984.

CHABOUIS, Lucette. *Le Livre du Café.* Bordas, Paris, 1988.

CHALMERS, Irena. *Tea.* Published in Cooperation with Gill's First Colony Coffee and Tea. Potpourri Press, Greensboro, 1978.

CHEVALLIER, A. *Du Café. Son Historique, son Usage, son Utilité, ses Altérations, ses Succédanés et ses Falsifications...*Baillerie & Fils, Paris, 1862. (J.J.)

CHOW, Kit. & KRAMER, Ione. *All the Tea in China.* China Books and Periodicals Inc., San Francisco, 1990.

CHRYSSOCHOÏDÈS, N. *Nouveau Manuel Complet du Limonadier, Glacier, Cafetier et de l'Amateur de Thés et de Cafés, comprenant la Description des Meilleurs Appareils...*a l'usage des débitants et des ménages par Chaufard, J. de Fontenelle & F. Malepeyre. new edn., Encyclopédie Roret, Paris, 1901.

CIUPKA, Paul. *Kaffee. Ein Lehrbuch in enger Anlehnung an die Praxis,* Meissner, Hamburg, 1937.

———— *Kaffee: Kaffee-Ersatz und Kaffee-Zusatz.* 2 Bde., Meissner, Hamburg, 2. erw. u. Aufl.,1949.

————. ————3. erw. u. verb. Aufl. 1956; III Teil.

——— *Kaffee im Gastätten-Gewerbe.* Meissner, Hamburg, 1937.

——— *Kaffee-röstkursus.* Hamburg, 1950. II Teil. Spezialfragen der Praxis.

———. ——— 1954.

——— *Taschenbuch des Kaffee-Fachmanns.* Meissner, Hamburg, 1931.

CLARK, Garth. *The Eccentric Teapot: Four Hundred Years of Invention.* Abbeville Press, New York, 1989.

CLARKE, R.J. & MACRAE, R. (eds.) *Coffee.* vol. 2. Technology. Elsevier Applied Science, London, 1987.

CLEMENTS, Robert L. *A Chromatographic Study of some of the Compounds in Roasted Coffee.* (Publication no. 26) The Coffee Brewing Center, New York, 1966.

COCOA. The Story of its Cultivation. Cadbury, Bournville, 1927.

COLLECÇAO DAS TRES PRINCIPAES MEMORIAS SOBRE A PLANTAÇAM, CULTURA E FABRICO DO CHÁ. Typographie liberal, Sao Paulo, 1851.

CORNELL, Rolf & SULLIVAN, Steven. *Esprit d'Espresso. A Guide to Making and Enjoying Espresso and Cappuccino at Home.* Dastro Publishing, London, 1991.

DALLA BONA, Giovanni. *L'Uso, e l'Abuso del Caffè.* Presso Guiseppe Berno, Verona, 1751. (J.J.)

DAPHINOFF, Helene, (comp.) *Kleine Bettlektüre für wahre Kaffeegemiesser.* Scherz, (n.d.).

DAUSSÉ, (Aîné). *Manuel de l'Amateur du Café, ou l'Art de Torrefier les Cafés Convenablement.* l'Auteur, Paris, 1846. (J.J.)

DAVIDS, Kenneth. *Coffee. A Guide to Buying, Brewing and Enjoying.* Rev.ed., 101 Productions, San Ramon, 1987.

——— *The Coffee Book. A Guide to Buying, Brewing and Enjoying.* Whittet, Weybridge, 1976.

DE ARAUJO CORRÉA DE MORAES, Joaquim Manoel. *Manual do Cultivador do Chá do Commercio ou Resumo dos Apontamentos, que Acerca de Tão Importante e Facil Cultura, foram Publicados no Preterito Annode 1881.* Martins, Lisboa, 1882.

DE HAAN, David. *Antique Household Gadgets and Appliances c. 1860 to 1930.* Blandford Press, Poole, Dorset, 1977.

DE MERS, John. *The Community Kitchens Complete Guide to Gourmet Coffee.* Simon and Schuster, New York, 1986.

DELCOURT, Pierre. *Ce Qu'on Mange à Paris.* Libraire Henry du Parc, Paris, 1888.(J.J.)

DEMACHY, Jacques Francois. *L'Art du Distillateur Liquoriste: Contenant le Brûleur d'Eaux-de-Vie, le Fabriquant de Liqueurs, le Débitant, ou le Cafetier-Limonnadier.* Paris, 1775. (J.J.)

DESMET-GREGOIRE, Hélène. *Il Caffè e i suoi Oggetti.* Ulisse Edizione, Turin, 1989. [Translated from French by Laura Rovero.]

——— *Les Objets du Café dans les Sociétés du Proche-Orient & de la Méditerranée.* Presses du CNRS, Paris, 1989.

D'ORSI, Angelo.(ed.) *Il Caffè Ossia. Brevi e Vari Discorsi in Area Padana.* Silvana Editoriale, Milan, 1990.

DUFOUR, Philippe Sylvestre. *Traitez Nouveau & Curieux du Café, du Thé et du Chocolate...*2nd edn., Lyon, Deville, 1688. [for first edn. <u>see</u> *TRACTATUS NOVI DE POTU...*]

DUNCAN, Dr. *Wholesome Advice Against the Abuse of Hot Liquors, Particularly of Coffee, Chocolate, Tea, Brandy and Strong-waters...done out of the French.* Rhodes, London, 1706.

DUTTA, Arup Kumar. *Cha Garam! - The Tea Story.* Paloma Publications, Assam, 1992.

EICHLER, Prof. Dr. O. *Kaffee und Kaffein.* Springer Verlag, Berlin, 1938.

ELLIOTT, E. C. & WHITEHEAD, F.J. *Tea Planting in Ceylon.* Times of Ceylon Co., Colombo, 1926.

ELLIS, Aytoun. *The Penny Universities. A History of the Coffee Houses.* Secker & Warburg, London, 1956.

EMMERSON, Robin. *British Teapots and Tea Drinking 1700-1850. Illustrated from the Twining Teapot Gallery, Norwich Castle Museum.* HMSO, London, 1992.

FERRÉ, Felipe. *L'Aventure du Café,* De Noel, Paris, 1988.

FOOT, Frederick N. *Coffee the Beverage.* The Spice Mill Publishing Company, New York, 1925.

FORD, Cathy. *The Coffee Lover's Handbook.* Ed. by Dona Sturmanis. Intermedia, Vancouver, 1979.

FOREST, Louis. *L'art de faire le Café au Lait à l'Ancienne à l'Aide de la Caféolette Louis Forest.* 17th edn. Chauveau, Paris, [1913] (J.J.)

FORREST, D.M. *A Hundred Years of Ceylon Tea, 1867-1967.* Chatto & Windus, London, 1967.

FORREST, Denys. *Tea for the British. The Social and Economic History of a Famous Trade.* Chatto & Windus, London, 1973.

——— *Tee und die Engländer.* Schrader, Bremen, 1980.

FRANKE, Erwin. *Kaffee, Kaffeekonserven und Kaffeesurrogate.* (Chemische-technische Bibliothek, Bd.297.) Zweite vermehrte Auflage, A. Hartleben's Verlag, Vienna & Leipzig, 1920.

FRANKLIN, Aubrey. *Teatime.* Fell, New York, 1981.

FUKUKITA, Yasunosuke. *Tea Cult of Japan. An Aesthetic Pastime.* Board of Tourist Industry, Japanese Government Railways, Tokyo, 1934.

FUMAGALLI, Ambrogio. *Macchine da Caffè. Coffee makers.* (Itinerari d'Imagini, no. 36) Be-Ma Editrice, Milan,1990.

50 JAHRE MELITTA IN MINDEN. Die Geshichte eines Ostwest Fälischen Unternehmens. Melitta-Werke Bentz & Sohn, Minden, 1979.

GENTIL, M. *Dissertation sur le Café, et sur les Moyen Propres à Prévenir les Effets qui Résultent de sa Préparation Communement Vicieuse.* l'Auteur/Pyre, Paris,1787.

GOODWIN, Jason. *The Gunpowder Gardens. Travels through India and China in Search of Tea.* Chatto & Windus, London, 1990.

GORDON, Bob. *Early Electrical Appliances.* (Shire Album 124) Shire Publications, Aylesbury, 1984.

GROSSER, Helmut. *Tee fur Wissensdurstige. Das Fachbuch vom Deutschen Teebüro.* Albrecht, Munich, 1987?

GUBIAN, J.M.A. *Dissertation sur le Café.* Imp. Didot jeune, Paris, 1814. (J.J.)

HAARER, A.E. *Modern Coffee Production.* Hill, London, 1962.

HADWIGER, Peter. *Kaffee Gewohnheit und Konsequenz.* Edition Dia, St. Gallien, 1989.

HAMBURGISCHE ELECTRIZITÄTS-WERKE, AG. *Das Museum der Elektrizität.* HEW AG., Hamburg, 1987.

———. ——— 2nd edn., 1990.

HARDY, Serena. *The Tea Book*. Whittet, Surrey, 1979.

HARLER, C.R. *The Culture and Marketing of Tea*. OUP, London,1933.

———— *Tea Growing*. OUP, London, 1966.

———— *Tea Manufacture*. (Oxford Tropical Handbook) OUP, London, 1970.

HATTOX, Ralph S. *Coffee and Coffeehouses. The Origins of a Social Beverage in the Medieval Near East*. Seattle, University of Washington Press, 1985.

HEISE, Ulla. *Coffee and Coffee-houses*. Trans. by Paul Roper. Schiffer, West Chester, Pennsylvania, 1987.

——- *Kaffee und Kaffeehaus. Eine Kulturgesichte*. Olms Presse, Hildesheim, 1987.

HESSE, Eelco. *De Oogleden van Bodhidharma. Thee*. Hesse, Amsterdam, 1973.

——- *Tea: the Eyelids of Bohidharma*. Prism Press, Dorchester, 1982.

HEWITT, Robert, Jr. *Coffee: its History, Cultivation and Uses*. Appleton, New York, 1872.

HOLZBORN Udolf. *Der Eisenwarenhandel. Ein Lehr-und Nachschlagewerk für den Handel mit Eisenwaren und Haus-und Küchengeräten*. Heinrich Killinger, Nordhausen. (n.d.) (J.J.)

HOUSSAYE, J-G. *Monographie du Thé*. l'Auteur, Paris, 1843.

HUXLEY, Gervas. *Talking of Tea*. Thames and Hudson, London, 1956.

IGUCHI, Kaisen. *Tea Ceremony*. Trans. by John Clark. Osaka, 1975.

ILLY, Francesco e Riccardo. *Dal Caffè all'Espresso*. Mondadori, Milan, 1989.

——- *From Coffee to Espresso*. Mondadori, Milan, 1990.

IMHOFF, Hans. *Kakao. Das wahre Gold der Azteken*. ECON Verlag, Düsseldorf, 1988.

ISENBÜGEL, Ewald. *Der Kaffe und seine Fachgemässe Bereitung*. Ostern, Essen,1931. (J.J.)

ISRAEL, Andrea. *Taking Tea. The Essential Guide to Brewing, Serving and Entertaining with Teas from around the World*. Weidenfeld & Nicolson, New York, 1987.

JACOB, Heinrich Eduard. *Sage und siegeszug des Kaffees. Die Biographie eines Weltwirtschaftlichen Stoffes*. Rowohlt, Berlin, 1934.

——- *The Saga of Coffee. The Biography of an Economic Product*. Trans. by Eden and Cedar Paul. Allen & Unwin, London, 1935.

JARDIN, Edelstan. *Le Caféier et le Café: Monographie Historique, Scientifique et Commerciale de cette Rubiacée*. Leroux, Paris, 1895.

JOBIN, Philippe & VAN LECKWYCK, Bernard. *Le Café*. (Le Gout de Vie) Nathan, Paris, 1988.

JUNGER, Wolfgang. *Herr Ober, ein' Kaffee! Illustrierte Kulturgeschichte des Kafeehauses*. Goldmann, Munich, 1955.

KAKUZO, Okakura. *The Book of Tea. A Japanese Harmony of Art, Culture and the Simple Life*. A & R., Sydney, 1932.

———— *The Book of Tea*. Ed. by Everett F. Bleiler. Dover, New York, 1964.

KAZUO. *Coffee Technique*. 8th edn., Tokyo, 1981. (In Japanese)

KEABLE, B.B. *Coffee from Grower to Consumer*. Rev. by H.S. Sanderson. Pitman, London, (n.d.).

KNAPP, Arthur W. *Cocoa and Chocolate. Their History from Plantation to Consumer*. Chapman and Hall, London, 1920.

KOLPAS, Norman. *Coffee*. Murray, London, 1979.

LAUTWEIN, Jurgen. *Espresso Mokka, Cappuccino & Co*. ECON Taschenbuch Verlag, Düsseldorf,1988.

LAVAZZA BAR. *L'arte dell'Espresso Italiano*. n.p., (n.d)

LAVAZZA COFFEE TRAINING CENTER, Milan. *Il Caffè nel Mondo. Testo del Corso Audiovisivo del Coffee Training Center per il Settore Specializzato Bar*. Lavazza, Milan,1986.

La Lavazza e la Lavorazione del Caffè.

Le Miscele e il Macinadosatore.

La Macchina del Caffè Espresso.

LILLYWHITE, Bryant. *London Coffee Houses. A Reference Book of Coffee Houses of the Seventeenth, Eighteenth and Nineteenth Centuries*. Allen & Unwin, London, 1963.

LINGLE, Ted R. *The Basics of Cupping Coffee*. Coffee Development Group, Washington, 1986.

———— *The Coffee Cupper's Handbook. Systematic Guide to the Sensory Evaluation of Coffee's Flavour*. Coffee Development Group, Washington, 1986.

LOCKHART, Ernest E. *Calculations and Tables Relating to Urn Risers and Coffee Water Baskets*. (Publication no. 57) The Coffee Brewing Center, New York, 1967.

———— *Characteristics of Coffee Relating to Beverage Quality*. (Publication no.40) The Coffee Brewing Center, New York, 1967.

———— *Chemistry of Coffee*. (Publication no. 25) The Coffee Brewing Center, New York, 1966.

———— *Coffee Grinds II. Classification and Analysis*. (Publication no. 39) The Coffee Brewing Center, New York, 1967.

———— *The Coffee Hydrometer*. (Publication no. 43.) The Coffee Brewing Center, New York, 1967.

———— *The Effect of Water Impurities on the Flavor of Brewed Coffee*. (Publication no. 6) The Coffee Brewing Center, New York, 1966.

———— *Grind Analysis and Quality Control*. (Publication no.55) The Coffee Brewing Center, New York, 1967.

———— *Roasted Coffee Color Measurement and Classification*. (Publication no. 53) The Coffee Brewing Center, New York, 1967.

———— *The Soluble Solids in Beverage Coffee as an Index to Cup Quality*. (Publication no. 27) The Coffee Brewing Center, New York, 1966.

———— *Storage Properties of Vacuum Packed Coffee*. (Publication no.30) Coffee Brewing Center, New York, 1967.

———— *Water, Coffee and Beverage Preparation*. (Publication no.56) The Coffee Brewing Center, New York, 1966.

LUBBOCK, Basil. *The China Clippers*. Century Publishing, London, 1984.

LUSSANA, F. *Il Caffè*. vol.1 (Piccola Bibliteca Igienica, vol.iv) Padua, 1872. (J.J.)

MC COY, Evin & WALKER, John Frederick. [QUIMME, Peter, (pseud.)] *Coffee and Tea*. 3rd.rev.ed. New York, 1991.

MC GEE, Harold. *On Food and Cooking. The Science and Lore of the Kitchen.* Unwin Paperbacks, London, 1988.

MAIER, Hans Gerhard. *Kaffee.* (Grundlagen und Fortschritte der Lebensmittel-untersuching und Lebensmitteltechnologie. Bd. 18) Parey, Berlin, 1981.

MAITLAND, Derek. *5000 Years of Tea. A Pictorial Companion.* CFW Publications, Hong Kong, 1982.

MANETTI, Luigi. *Manuale del Caffettiere e Sorbettiere.* (Manuali Hoepli) Ulrico Hoepli, Milan, 1906.

MARQUIS, F. (Jeune). *Du Thé, ou Nouveau Traité sur sa Culture, sa Récolte, sa Préparation et ses Usages.* Paris, 1820.

————- *Taschenbuch für Theetrinker, oder der Thee in Naturhistorische, Culturlicher, Merkantlischer, Medicinisch-Diätetischer und Luxuriöser Hinficht.* Boigt, Weimar, 1836.

MASSIEU, Gulielmo. *Caffaeum Carmen.* Turin? [1718]

MATTHES, Sonja. *Das kleine Tee-Brevier.* Verlag Wolfgang Hölker, Munster, 1989.

MERRITT, Mabel C. & PROCTOR, Bernard E. *Effect of Temperature during the Roasting Cycle on Selected Components of Different Types of Whole Bean Coffee.* (Publication no.46) The Coffee Brewing Center, New York, 1967.

————- *Extraction Rates for Selected Components in Coffee Brew.* (Publication no. 47) The Coffee Brewing Center, New York, 1967.

MIELKE, Heinz-Peter. *Kaffee, Tee, Kakao. Der Höhenflug der drei "warmen Lustgetränke".* (Bd. 41 der Schriften des Museumsvereins Dorenburg e V.) Müsers Grafik-Druck-KG, Viersen,1988.

MINDENER MUSEUM. *Kaffee. Kultur eines Getränks.* Minden, 1987.

MINTZ, Sidney. *Sweetness and Power. The Place of Sugar in Modern History.* Penguin, New York, 1986.

MORTON, Marcia & Frederic. *Chocolate. An Illustrated History.* Crown, New York, 1986.

MOSELEY, Benjamin. *A Treatise Concerning the Properties and Effects of Coffee.* 5th edn. pr. for J. Sewell, London, 1792.

MÜLLER, Edgar. *Arabiens Vermächtnis Tatsachen und Dokumente über den Kaffee aus Ernährungswissenschaft und Rechtssprechung.* I teil. Carl Holler, Hamburg, 1931.

MÜLLER, Edgar. *Kaffee un Rösten: Ein Handbuch über die Beurteilung der Kaffeesorten, über das Rösten und die Zubereitung von Kaffee, Getreidekaffee und Kaffee-Ersatzstoffen sowie über die Wichtigsten Fachfragen des Kaffeehandels.* KATEKA, Hamburg,1929. (J.J.)

NIVEN, W.W (Jr).& SHAW, B.C. *Critical Conditions for Quality Coffee Brewing.* (Publication no.19)The Coffee Brewing Center, New York, 1967. *OLD ENGLISH COFFEE HOUSES.* Rodale Press, London, 1954.

O'MEARA, John P. *Free Radicals in Roasted Coffee.* (Publication no.18) The Coffee Brewing Institute, New York, 1957.

PAN-AMERICAN COFFEE BUREAU. *Coffee brewing workshop manual.* (Publication no. 54) Rev. 1974. Coffee Brewing Center, New York.

PICARDI, Gaetano. *Del Caffè. Racconto Storico-Medico.* Gaetano Nobile, Naples,1845. (J.J.)

PRATT, James Norwood. *The Tea Lover's Treasury.* 101 Productions, San Francisco, 1982.

PROCTER & GAMBLE COMPANY. *The Folger's Coffee Silver Collection. Antique English Silver Service and Accessories.* [ed. Ross E. Taggart] n.p., (n.d.)

QUIMME, Peter. *The Signet Book of Coffee and Tea.* New American Library, New York, 1976.

REATO, Danilo. *The Coffee-House: Venetian Coffee-Houses from the 18th to 20th centuries.* Arsenale Editrice, Venice, 1991.

REIMANN, Friedrich. *Kaffeebuchlein und Kaffeekochbuch.* Coburg, 1841. (U.B.)

RHOADES, John W. *Analysis of the Volatile Constituents of Coffee.* (Publication no. 52) The Coffee Brewing Center, New York, 1967.

————- *Sampling Method for Analysis of Coffee Volatiles by Gas Chromatography.* (Publication no.34) The Coffee Brewing Center, New York, 1967.

RIANT, Dr. A. *Le Café, le Chocolat, le Thé.* Paris, 1875. (J.J.)

RILEY, Noel. *Tea Caddies.* (Antique Pocket Guides) Seven Hills Books, Cincinnatti, 1985.

RODEN, Claudia. *Coffee.* Penguin, Harmondsworth, 1977.

ROLNICK, Harry. *The Complete Book of Coffee.* Melitta, Hong Kong, 1982.

ROTHFOS, Bernhard, (comp.) *Coffea Curiosa Seltene und Amüsante, Kuriose und Interessante.* Gordion-Max Rieck GmbH., Hamburg, 1968.

———— *Coffee Consumption.* Gordion-Max Rieck GmbH., Hamburg, 1986.

———— *Coffee Production.* Gordion-Max Rieck GmbH., Hamburg, 1980.

————-. ————- 2nd.edn., 1985.

ROTTENHOFER, J. *Der elegante Wohlservierte Kaffee-und Theetisch.* Braun und Schneider, Munich, 1864. (J.J.)

ROTTGER, Dr. W. *Genussmittel-Genussgifte? Betrachtungen über Kaffee und Tee aus Grund einer Umfrage bei den Aerzten.* Staude, Berlin, 1906.

ROTTHAUWE, Helmut, (called Lons). *The Heavenly Inferno.* Probat-werke, Emmerich, 1968.

ROWLING, Nick. *Commodities. How the World was Taken to Market.* Free Association Books, London, 1987.

RUBINSTEIN, Helge. *The Chocolate Book.* Penguin, Harmondsworth, 1983.

RUMFORD, Count. (Benjamin Thompson). *Complete Works.* vol.4. Boston, 1875. (U.B.)

RYBCZINSKI, Witold. *Home, a Short History of an Idea.* Penguin, New York, 1983.

SAMROWSKI, Dietrich. *Geschichte der Kaffeemühlen.* Munich, 1983.

SABONDIÈRE, William. *The Coffee-Planter of Ceylon.* 2nd. edn. Spon, London, 1870.

SANDGRUBER, Roman. *Bittersüsse Genusse. Kulturgeschichte der Genussmittel.* Bohlaus, Vienna, 1986.

SANDON, Henry. *Coffee Pots and Teapots for the Collector.* Bartholomew, Edinburgh, 1973.

SCHAFER, Charles & Violet. *Teacraft.* Yerba Buena Press, San Francisco, 1975.

SCHAPIRA, Joel, David & Karl. *The Book of Coffee & Tea. A Guide to the Appreciation of Fine Coffees, Teas and Herbal*

Beverages. St. Martin's Press, New York, 1982.

SCHIAFFINO, Mariarosa. *Cioccolato & Cioccolatini*. Idealibri, Milan,1985.

—— *L'Ora del Tè*. 4th edn. Idealibri, Milan, 1985.

—— *Le Ore del Caffè*. 2nd edn. Idealibri, Milan, 1984.

SCHIVELBUSCH, Wolfgang. *Das Paradies, der Geschmack und die Vernunft. Eine Geschichte der Genussmittel*. Ullstein Sachbuch, Frankfurt am Main, 1985.

SCHLEINKOFER, Otto F. *Der Tee*. Beckstein, Munich, 1924.

SCHNYDER-VON WALDKIRCH, Antoinette. *Wie Europa den Kaffee entdeckte. Reiseberichte der Barockzeit als Quellen zur Geshichte des Kaffees.*(Zur Kulturgeschichte des Kaffees. Herausgegeben von Holger Hasenkamp. Bd.1) Jacobs Suchard Museum, Zurich, 1988.

SCHOELLER, Hannes W.A. *Tee, Kaffe, Kakao*. Wilhelm Heyne Verlag, Munich, 1967.

SEGALL, Stanley & PROCTOR, Bernard E. *The Influence of High Temperature Holding upon the Components of Coffee Brew.* (Publication no.41) The Coffee Brewing Center, New York, 1967.

SESTINI, Fausto. *Il Caffè*. (Ser.3a. La scienza del popolo, vol.14) Florence, 1867. (J.J.)

SHALLECK, Jamie. *Tea*. Viking Press, NewYork, 1972. 136p. illus.

SIVETZ, Michael. *Coffee. Origin and Use*. Coffee Publications, Corvallis, Oregon,1974. (abstract)

SIX CUPS OF COFFEE. Prepared for the Public Palate by the Best Authorities on Coffee Making. Maria Parloa, Catherine Owen, Marion Harland, Juliet Corson, Mrs. Helen Campbell, Mrs. D.A. Lincoln. Good Housekeeping Press, Springfield, Mass., (n.d.) (J.J.)

SÖHN, Gerhart. *Kleine Kaffee Kunde*. Cram, De Gruyter & Co., Hamburg, 1957.

—— *Von Mokka bis Espresso*. Cram, De Gruyter & Co., Hamburg, 1957.

SOYER, Alexis. *The Pantropheon or a History of Food and its Preparation in Ancient Times*. Paddington Press, New York, 1977. [Reprint of 1853 ed. pub. by Simpkin, Marshall, London.]

SPANG, Gunther. *Rotes Herz und Braunes Trank*. Angelsachsen Verlag, Bremen, 1956.

SPRIESTERSBACH, Hans. *Rohkaffee von A-Z*. Verlag Gordian-Max Rieck, Hamburg, 1955.

STAVEACRE, F.W.F. *Tea and Tea Dealing*. 2nd. edn., Pitman, London, 1933.

STRASSBURG, Horst. *Das Kaffee und Teebuch*. Matthaes, Stuttgart, 1982.

STREET-PORTER, Janet & Tim. *The British Teapot*. A & R., London, 1981.

TEA [12 Chinese paintings on rice paper. Bound and boxed] n.p.(n.d.)

TEMMING, Rolf L. *Vom Geheimnis des Tees*. 3rd edn. Dortmund, 1988.

TEXEIRA DE OLIVEIRA, José. *História do Café no Brazile no Mundo*. Kosmos, Rio de Janeiro, 1984.

THURBER, Francis B. *Coffee: from Plantation to Cup*. 11th edn.

American Grocer Publishing Association, NewYork, 1885.

TRACTATUS NOVI DE POTU CAPHE DE CHINENSIUM THE ET DE CHOCOLATA. apud Petrum Muguet, Paris, 1685.

TRAITÉ DU CAFÉ, contenant l'Histoire, la Description, la Culture et les Proriétés de ce Végétal. Paris, 1798. (J.J.)

TRILLICH, Heinrich. *Rösten und Röstwaren*. Verlag B. Heller, Munich, 1934 (J.J.)

UKERS, WIlliam. *All about Coffee*. Tea and Coffee Trade Journal Company, New York, 1922.

——. —— 2nd.edn. NewYork, 1935.

—— *All about Tea*. 2 vols.Tea and Coffee Trade Journal Company, New York, 1935.

—— *Coffee Merchandising*. Tea and Coffee Trade Journal Company, New York, 1924.

—— *The Romance of Coffee; an Outline History of Coffee and Coffee Drinking through a Thousand Years*. Tea and Coffee Trade Journal Company, New York, 1948.

—— *The Romance of Tea. An Outline History of Tea and Tea-Drinking through Sixteen Hundred Years*. Knopf, New York, 1936.

UKERS' INTERNATIONAL TEA AND COFFEE BUYERS' GUIDE. A Work of Reference and an Index to Sources of Supply for Buyers in the Coffee, Spice and Allied Trades. 22nd. edn. Tea and Coffee Trade Journal Company, NewYork, 1964-5

URIBE COMPUZANO, Andrés. *Brown Gold. The Amazing Story of Coffee*. Random House, NewYork, 1954.

URTEL, Peter Martin. *Die Kunst Tee zu trinken*. 9 Auflage. Kochbuch Verlag, Munich, 1969

——. —— BLV, Munich, 1984.

VALERIO, Leonida. *Caffè e Derivati. Industrie-Commercio-Usi Sfruttamenti Nuovi e Razionale*. (Manuali Hoepli) Ulrico Hoepli, Milan,1927.

VANIER, Michel. *Le Livre de l'Amateur de Café*. Laffont, Paris, 1983.

LE VERITABLE ELIXIR. Des Propriétés, Qualités et Effets du Café. Avec la Manière d'en User tant pour la Santé que pour Certaines Maladies. Meyer, Breslau, 1754. (J.J.)

VOM KAFFEE IN FRÜHEN REISEBERICHTEN mit Beiträgen von Urs Bitterli und Antoinette Schnyder-v.Waldkirch. Jacobs Suchard Museum, Zurich, 1988.

VON WALDERDORFF, Elizabeth. *Alte Kaffeemühlen. Geschichte, Form und Funktion*. Callwey Verlag, Munich, 1982.

WALSH, Joseph M. *Coffee - its History, Classification and Description*. The John C. Winston Co., Philadelphia, [1894] (J.J.)

WEDEMEYER, Bernd. *Coffee de Martinique und Kayser Thee. Archaologisch-Volkskundliche untersuchungen am Hausrat Gottinger Burger im 18 Jahrhundert*. Bd. 1. Hubert, Gottingen, 1989.

WELTER, Henri. *Essai sur l'Histoire du Café*. Paris, Reinwald, 1868. (J.J.)

WIELER, Prof. Dr. A. *Kaffee, Tee, Kakao und die übrigen narkotischen Ausgussgetränke*. (Aus Natur und Geisteswelt sammlung wissenschaftlich-gemeinverständlicher Darstellung. 132 Bd.) Teubner, Leipzig, 1907.

DAS WIENER CAFÉ. Austellung im Jacobs Suchard Museum.

[Zurich] Jan.-Mar.,1989.

WEINREICH, Moira. *The Tea Lover's Handbook.* Intermedia Press, Vancouver, 1980.

WOMEN'S INSTITUTE OF DOMESTIC ARTS AND SCIENCES. *Beverages, Canning, Drying, Jellymaking, Preserving, Pickling.* (Women's Institute Library of Cookery) Scranton, Pa. 1929.

WOODWARD, Nancy Hyden. *Teas of the World.* Collier, New York,1980.

WRIGLEY, Gordon. *Coffee.* Longman, Harlow, Essex,/ Wiley, NewYork, 1988.

WYNTER BLYTH, Alexander & Meredith. *Foods: their Composition and Analysis. A Manual for the Use of Analytical Chemists and Others.* 6th edn. Griffin Press, London, 1909.

YI, Sabine. *Le Livre de l'Amateur de Thé.* Laffont, Paris, 1983.

YU, Lu. *The Classic of Tea.* Trans. by Francis Ross Carpenter. Little, Brown & Co., Boston,1974.

275 Jahre Wiener Kaffeehaus. Vienna, 1959.

PAMPHLETS

BRADLEY, R. *The Virtue and Use of Coffee, with Regard to the Plague, and other Infectious Distempers.* pr. by Eman. Matthews, London, 1721.

CEFABU-WERKE, Mainz. *Cefabu-Kaffee.* Ludwig Utz, Mainz, (n.d., c.1916?) (advertising booklet)

CENTRO LUIGI LAVAZZA PER GLI STUDI E LE RICERCHE SUL CAFFE. Milano. (n.d.) (folder)

[CHAMBERLAYNE, J.] *The Natural History of Coffee, Thee, Chocolate, Tobacco ... with a Tract on Elder and Juniper-Berries...and also the Way of making Mum...collected from the Writings of the Best Physicians and Modern Travellers.* pr. for Christopher Wilkinson, London,1682.

HOUSSAYE, J-G. *Instructions sur la Manière de Préparer la Boisson du Thé.* Delanchy pr., Paris, 1841.

[LAVAZZA] *Estratto da Civiltà del Bere.* n.p., (n.d., c. 1980?)

LAVAZZA COFFEE TRAINING CENTER, Milan. [Information on coffee production and processing] 1989? (20 loose sheets in folder)

LENDRICH, Prof. Dr. K. *Vortrag...uber Neuere Beobachtungen und Erfahrungen auf dem Gebiete der Chemie des Kaffees.* n.p., (n.d.)

MASCHINENFABRIK BREMEN GmbH. *Die Zubereitung des Kaffees ist ebenso wichtig wie die Qualität! Bremen* (n.d.)

THE MENS ANSWER TO THE WOMENS PETITION AGAINST COFFEE, vindicating their own Performances, and the Vertues of that Liquor, from the Undeserved Aspersions lately cast upon them by their Scandalous Pamphlet. London, pr.1674. (H.U.)

MERC. DEMOC., (pseud.) *The Maidens Complaint against Coffee. Or the Coffee-House Discovered, Beseiged, Stormed, Taken, Untyled and Laid open to Publick View.* pr. for J. Jones, London, 1663. (H.U.)

PICTURE STORY OF PREPARING TEA. n.p.,(n.d.) (Foldout booklet)

[TEA CATALOGUE-DAMAGED TEA]...per *Favorite* in the sale-room of the subscribers, on Friday, 14th July, 1837 at one o'clock... Teas ...from George Aitchison & Co.

TEA FOR SALE at the Exchange Sale-Room, Leith, on Tuesday, 13th June, 1837 at 10 o'clock. James Duncan & Co. Leith, pr. by William Reid & son. (Catalogue)

UNO COMPANY LTD. London. *A Casual Talk on Coffee.* 3rd.edn., London, 1935.

UNO COMPANY LTD. London. *Some Information on UNO Specialised Coffee Machinery.* n.p.,(n.d.)

LA "VICTORIA ARDUINO". Per Caffe Espresso dal 1905. Varese. (n.d.)

———— *Catalogue.* 1923 (V.A.)

———— *Catalogue.* 1955 (V.A.)

A WELL-WILLER, (pseud) *The Women's Petition against Coffee. Representing to Publick Consideration the Grand Inconveniencies Accruing to their Sex from the Excessive Use of the Drying, Enfeebling Liquor.* London, pr. 1674. (H.U.)

NEWSPAPERS AND MAGAZINES (CONTAINING ARTICLES ON TEA AND COFFEE)

THE AUSTRALIAN, Sydney. v.6, no.652, June 11,1839.

DINGLERS POLYTECHNISCHES JOURNAL. 1820, 1838, 1847, 1856 (U.B.)

FAMILY HERALD. A domestic magazine of useful information and amusement. London. v.10, no. 497 week ending Nov.13, 1852.

GIORNALE DI MODE A DI ANEDDOTI. no.6, 20 Agosto,1805. (J.J.)

KATEKA (Kafee, Tee und Kakao Zeitung) Hamburg. no.25, 1914; no.36, 1925. (J.J.)

KUCHEN UND WIRTSCHAFTS ZEITUNG FUR DEUTSCHE HAUSFRAUEN UND IHRE TÖCHTER. no.3, Nov.1, 1845. (J.J.)

LEIGH HUNT'S LONDON JOURNAL to assist the enquiring, animate the struggling, and sympathize with all. no.14, July 2, 1834; no.15, July 9, 1834; no.16, July 16, 1834.

THE LEISURE HOUR: a Family Journal of Instruction and Recreation. ?London. no.307, Nov.12, 1857. no.308, Nov.19, 1857; no.309, Nov.26, 1857; no.355, Oct.14, 1858.

THE LONDON CHRONICLE. v.56, no.4367, October 26 to 28, 1784.

THE LONDON GAZETTE. no.2235, April 18 to 21, 1687

THE MIRROR OF LITERATURE, AMUSEMENT AND INSTRUCTION. London. (various issues 1823 - 1844)

THE PENNY MAGAZINE of the Society for the Diffusion of Useful Knowledge. London. (various issues 1832 - 1842)

THE SALISBURY AND WINCHESTER JOURNAL. v.46, no.2270, Dec.10, 1781.

SATURDAY MAGAZINE. London. Under the direction of the committee of general literature and education, appointed by the Society for Promoting Christian Knowledge. no.34, Jan.12, 1833.

THE STANDARD. London. no.2312, Oct. 8, 1834; no.2315, Oct.11, 1834

WHEELER'S MANCHESTER CHRONICLE. no.495, April 4, 1789.

SELECTED PATENTS

Inventor; Year of Patent; Number; Country of Registration
Referring to Number; Short Description; Nationality or
Country of Inventor.
Where the country of registration is different to the
country/nationality of the inventor, the latter is shown at the
end of the line. Many but not all the patents mentioned in the
book are listed.

Abram; 1923; 183543; U.K.; Cosy Teapot.

Absalom; 1932; 12555; U.K.; Automatic Teapot.

Aguirre-Batres, Sole, Murillo-Solis; 1965; 1429974; Germany;
Coffee Filter; Costa Rica.

Alloncius; 1866; 73641; France; Recirculating Pumping
Percolator.

Arduino; 1927; 293551; Germany; Espresso with Air Pump;
Italian.

Arduino; 1906; vol 60, 86408; Italy; First Victoria Arduino -
not Espresso.

Arduino; 1910; vol.79, 108873; Italy; Espresso Machine with
Screw.

Arduino; 1910; 114375; Italy; Group Control Tap.

Arduino; 1918; 126954; U.K.; Two Spout Handle for
Espresso; Italian.

Arduino; 1927; 293551; U.K.; Espresso Machine with Pumps;
Italian.

Baempfer & Patommel; 1957; 1094 950; Germany; Wigomat
Electric Filter Machine.

Bersten; 1991; PL2623; Australia; Two Stage Plunger.

Bersten; 1993; 5,185,171; USA; Roller Roaster; Australian.

Bezzera; 1901; vol 42, 61707; Italy; Espresso Machine.

Bezzera; 1902; vol 42, 62434; Italy; Espresso Machine with
Relief Valve (possibly by Pavoni).

Bezzera; 1912; vol 93, 126712; Italy; Espresso Machine.

Borchers; 1895; 245289; France; Filter Machine; German.

Bourdier & Houet; 1882; 146819; France; Compartment
Filter.

Bourgogne; 1849; 8188; France; Reversible Filter.

Brandl; 1944; 248441; Switzerland; Electric Filter Machine.

Brandl; 1954; 320,704 Switzerland; Electric Filter Machine.

Bremer; 1925; Drp 211214, 245,512; Germany; Bremer
Coffee Machine.

Burns; 1882; 22959; Germany; Roaster; American.

Caasen; 1926; 472391; Germany; Fluidised Bed Roaster.

Capette; 1837; 8078; France; *Myrosostique* Coffee Maker.

Capy; 1827; 3332; France; Pumping Percolator.

Carter; 1846; 4849; USA; Pull-Out Coffee Roaster.

Carton; 1927; 644457; France; Filter.

Caseneuve; 1824; 2334; France; Espresso Machine.

Charpentier; 1893; 225930; France; Recirculating Percolator.

Chevrier; 1880; 136 133; France; Balance.

Cordier; 1844; 15136; 1845; 1571; France; Long Espressos.

Coulaux; 1829; 4119, 4694; France; Coffee Grinder.

Coutant; 1855; 23396; France; Percolator with Tap Control.

Crookes; 1886; 5598; England; Teapot handle.

Dagand; 1855; 24312; France; Recirculating Percolators.

Dagand; 1870; 90779; France; Commercial Percolator.

Daussé; 1843; 14795; France; Filter.

Denobe, Henrion, Rouch; 1802; 186; France; Pharmo-
Chemical Brewer.

Gaggia; 1947; 432148; Italy; Boiler for Espresso.

Gaggia; 1947; 476178; Italy; Spring Lever Handle for
Espresso.

Galy-Cazalat; 1847; 6729; Balance Coffee Machine.

Gandais; 1827; 4317; France; Pumping Percolator.

Giarlotto; 1909; 222519; Germany; Hand Pump Espresso;
Italian.

Goyot; 1849; 8553; France; Espressos.

Grandin & Crepaux; 1832; 4946; France; Vacuum Pot.

Greutert & Flüe; 1971; 2132596; Germany; Interelectric Gold
Filter; Swiss.

Groetsch, Christian; 1927; 493,328; Germany; Turning
Karlsbader.

Gros & Perard; 1894; 240336; 1896; 254512; France; Plunger
(*La Française*).

Guppy; 1812; 3549; U.K; Teapot and Eggcooker.

Hadrot; 1806; 358; France; Filter.

Hertman; 1895; 250947; France; Automatic Clock Filter.

Hölterhoff; 1884; 20389; Germany; Adjustable Espresso.

Housiaux; 1869; 87775; France; Plunger with Agitator.

Jacquier-Jayet; 1856; 28036; France; Pumping Percolator.

Japy; 1846; 2815; France; Coffee Grinder.

Karageorges; 1955; 541673; Belgium; Cup Filter.

Kessel; 1878; 1823; Germany; Espresso Machine.

Kirmair; 1891; 216163; France; Pumping Percolator.

Laurens; 1819; 1471; France; Pumping Percolator.

Laureys; 1828; 5345; France; Pumping Percolator.

Lavigne; 1854; 18725; France; Compartment Plunger.

Lebrun; 1838; 8453; France; Espresso.

Lepeut; 1842; 13847; France; Automatic Vacuum Pot.

Leuschner & Schubert; 1971; 2023 596; Germany; Siemens
Electric Filter.

Levi; 1913; 279363; Germany; Automatic Espresso; Italian.

Lindo; 1884; 163191; France; Automatic Filter; English.

Loysel; 1854; 393; U.K.; Large Commercial Hydrostatic
Percolator.

Loysel; 1854; 2387; U.K.; Hydrostatic Percolator.

Mahler; 1885; 171289; France; Filter.

Mahler & Durietz; 1845; 861; France; Pumping Percolator.

Malaussena; 1922; 403283; Germany; Snider Electric
Espresso; French.

Malen; 1872; 94489; France; Recirculating Percolator.

Marzetti; 1910; 28480; U.K.; Electric Espresso; Italian.

Massot & Juquin; 1865; 66294; France; Recirculating
Percolator.

Mayer & Delforge; 1852; 13301; France; Plunger.

Melitta; 1932; 617100; Germany; Quickfilter.

Melitta; 1937; 652010; Germany; Quickfilter.

Meüdt; 1858; 36166; France; Revolving Dripolator.

Morel; 1898; 279397; France; Kafilta Single Filter.

Moriondo; 1885; 164427; 1886; 171837; France; Bulk
Espresso Machine; Italian.

Moriondo; 1910; 113332; Italy; Bulk With Single Cup Espresso.

Morize; 1819; 1001; France; Reversible Filter.

Neuhaus Neotec; 1984; 3116723; Germany; Rotating Fluid Bed Roaster.

Neuhaus Neotec; 1986; 3437432; Germany; Shop Roaster RFB.

Parker; 1833; 6362; U.K.; Espresso Machine.

Patry; 1869; 86576; France; Press Coffee Machine.

Pavoni; 1902; 17th May; 321492; France. Same as Bezzera 1902 Patent.

Pavoni; 1902; 19th September; 141433; Germany. Is the same patent.

Pavoni; 1905; 75150; Italy; Gas Control Valve.

Pavoni; 1911; vol 87,119093; Italy; Innovation to Relief Valve.

Penand; 1869; 84737; France; Balance.

Penant; 1851; 11915; France; Balance.

Penant; 1867; 75213; France; Balance.

Perlusz; 1935; 653 683; Germany; Electric Vacuum Pot; Hungarian.

Pique; 1865; 66686; France; 1875; 107147; Recirculating Percolator.

Platow & Vardy; 1839; 8201; U.K.; Vacuum Coffee Maker.

Pouzet & Zambrini; 1912; 439740; France; Automatic Roaster, Grinder, Espresso.

Prat; 1889; 201090; France; Large Shop Filter Machine.

Predari; 1872; 96969; France; Egg Cooker and Coffeemaker.

Preterre; 1849; 12766; U.K.; Roaster, Grinder, Balance, Veyron Pot; French.

Rabaut; 1822; 4686; U.K; Espresso Machine; French.

Raparlier; 1858; 33465; France; Vacuum Pot.

Richard; 1837; 8225; France; Recirculating Percolator by Mr. Van s. Loeff of Berlin.

Robertson; 1890; 18,413 U.K.; Napier Coffee Machine in Glass with Tap.

Rota; 1950; 876450; Germany; Espresso with Pump; Italian.

Rousselle & Danglos; 1856; 25924; France; Exploding Porcelain Balance mentioned.

Royle; 1886; 6327; U.K.; Pumping Teapot.

Saccani; 1955; 544 987; Italy; Water Circulation from Boiler to Heat Lever Group.

Salamon; 1889; 49493; 1890; 57520; 1892; 68811; Germany; Quick Coffee Roaster.

Scorza; 1936; 343230; Italy; Screw Lever for Espresso.

Schurmann; 1906; 183718; Germany; Commercial Filter Machine.

Séné; 1815; 997; France; Reversible Filter Pot.

Sivetz; 1976; 3,964,175 USA; Fluidised Bed Roaster.

Smit; 1962; 112978; Netherlands; Coffee Grinder.

Smit; 1968; 6808675; Netherlands; Electric Filter Machine.

Soden; 1900; 298743; France; Teapot.

Spaguolo; 1922; Italy; Horizontal Espresso Machine.

Tangermann; 1935; 660983; Germany; Cup Filter.

Tarallo; 1899; 294842; France; La Reine des Cafétieres.

Tiesset & Moupier-Pierre; 1841; 13070; France; Vacuum Pump Filter.

Tiesset; 1840; 11622; France; Vacuum Pump Pot.

Toselli; 1861; 51920; France; Locomotive Coffee Pot.

Turmel; 1853; 16873; France; Balance Coffeemaker.

Urtis; 1924; 440599; Germany; Espresso with Electric Pump; Italian.

Urtis; 1925; 433030; Germany; Espresso Machine with Electric Pump adding Cold Water.

Valente & Arosio; 1952; 1077404; Germany; Lever for Espresso Machine. Italian.

Valente; 1960; 1292325; Germany; Heat Exchanger and Group for the E61 Machine.

Valente; 1960; 1404816; Germany; Espresso Machine with Pump and Group (Faema).

Van Gülpen; 1884; 31281; Germany; Coffee Roaster.

Vassieux; 1842; 13013; France; Glass Vacuum Pot.

Vazquez Del Saz; 1912; 282677; Germany; Espresso Machine; Spanish.

Veyron; 1842; 14904; 14500; 1875; 104784; France; Veyron Filter.

Wagner; 1887; 183416; France; Roaster, Grinder, Brewer; German.

Wallin; 1969; 2017606; Germany; Tea Filterbag; Swedish.

Wigomat; 1967; 1679120; Germany; Electric Filter Machine.

ILLUSTRATION CREDITS

The majority of illustrated items in this book are from my personal collection of over 700 tea and coffee pots, grinders and roasters, plus early newspapers and books. The credit for the use of other illustrations belongs to the following individuals or organisations:

The Bakken Library and Museum of Electricity in Life, Minneapolis - b&w illus. pages 151,153,155
Ursula Becker (UB) - pages 90,98,127,127,156,158
Helen Bersten (HB) - pages 63,66,74
Guido Bezzera (GB) - pages 107(all),108
Paul Ciupka (PC) - page 64
The Folger Silver Collection, Cincinnati (FC) - page 69
Hamburgische Elektrizitäts-Werke AG, Museum der Elektrizität (HEM) - pages 202,232,233
Kristin Hardiman (KH) - pages 11,12(all),13(all),38,42,58,69,70,74,78,82,88,90,100,149,168
Houghton Library, Harvard University (HU) - pages 45,46,47
Johann Jacobs Museum, Zurich (JJ) - pages 34,56,64
NSW Department of Agriculture, Murwillumbah - page 254
Francesco Rossini (FR) - pages 106,111,128
Bernhard Rothfos (BR) - pages 242,230
Trabattoni Company, Lecco - Farina roasters and grinders pages 197,198,225
Unic Company, Nice - Mario Levi machine page 113
University of New South Wales Library - page 48
Charles White, *Three Years in Constantinople* (CW) - page 39

Special thanks to Ursula Becker of Cologne for locating written source material in Germany, Ambrogio Fumigalli of Milan for general assistance with locating items and written material, Johann Jacobs Museum for much source material, Vera Modiano of Milan for general information, the Peugeot Museum in France for brochures and catalogues and L'Institut National de la Propriété Industrielle, Compiègne, France for access to original patents.

I N D E X

Page numbers in bold type indicate illustrations.

1. Caffé et maniere de la préparer. 2. Cocos et son usage. 3. Palmiers, Maisons, Mats, Vaisseaux, etc. 4. Thé. 5. Inaja. 6. Tamarin. 7. Uricuri, Giosara, Aira, Iraiba, Miriti. 8. Thé phikken. 9. Banilles. 10. Boisson de Chocolat.

1. Caffy en bereyding. 2. Cocos en gebruyk. 3. Palmboomen en huyfen masten schepen etc. 4. Thee. 5. Inaja. 6. Tamar. 7. Uricuri Giosara Aira Iraiba Miriti. 8. Teephikken. 9. Banillias. 10. Chokolat drank.

THEE. CHA. en PALMITEN.

Plantes et arbres
des
Indes Orientales

a Leide, Che